1 CORINTHIANS

NCCS | New Covenant Commentary Series

The New Covenant Commentary Series (NCCS) is designed for ministers and students who require a commentary that interacts with the text and context of each New Testament book and pays specific attention to the impact of the text upon the faith and praxis of contemporary faith communities.

The NCCS has a number of distinguishing features. First, the contributors come from a diverse array of backgrounds in regards to their Christian denominations and countries of origin. Unlike many commentary series that tout themselves as international the NCCS can truly boast of a genuinely international cast of contributors with authors drawn from every continent of the world (except Antarctica) including countries such as the United States, Puerto Rico, Australia, the United Kingdom, Kenya, India, Singapore, and Korea. We intend the NCCS to engage in the task of biblical interpretation and theological reflection from the perspective of the global church. Second, the volumes in this series are not verse-by-verse commentaries, but they focus on larger units of text in order to explicate and interpret the story in the text as opposed to some often atomistic approaches. Third, a further aim of these volumes is to provide an occasion for authors to reflect on how the New Testament impacts the life, faith, ministry, and witness of the New Covenant Community today. This occurs periodically under the heading of "Fusing the Horizons and Forming the Community." Here authors provide windows into community formation (how the text shapes the mission and character of the believing community) and ministerial formation (how the text shapes the ministry of Christian leaders).

It is our hope that these volumes will represent serious engagements with the New Testament writings, done in the context of faith, in service of the church, and for the glorification of God.

Series Editors:
Michael F. Bird (Ridley College, Melbourne, Australia)
Craig Keener (Asbury Theological Seminary, Wilmore, KY, USA)

Titles in this series:
Romans Craig Keener
Ephesians Lynn Cohick
Colossians and Philemon Michael F. Bird
Revelation Gordon Fee
John Jey Kanagaraj
1 Timothy Aída Besançon Spencer
2 Timothy and Titus Aída Besançon Spencer
Mark Kim Huat Tan
2 Peter and Jude Andrew Mbuvi
1–2 Thessalonians Nijay Gupta
Luke Diane Chen

Forthcoming titles:
James Ruth Anne Reese
1–3 John Sam Ngewa
Matthew Jason Hood
1 Peter Eric Greaux
Philippians Linda Belleville
Hebrews Cynthia Westfall
Galatians Brian Vickers
2 Corinthians David deSilva
Galatians Jarvis Williams

1 CORINTHIANS
A New Covenant Commentary

B. J. Oropeza

CASCADE Books • Eugene, Oregon

1 CORINTHIANS
A New Covenant Commentary

New Covenant Commentary Series

Copyright © 2017 B. J. Oropeza. All rights reserved. Except for brief quotations in critical publications or reviews, no part of this book may be reproduced in any manner without prior written permission from the publisher. Write: Permissions, Wipf and Stock Publishers, 199 W. 8th Ave., Suite 3, Eugene, OR 97401.

Cascade Books
An Imprint of Wipf and Stock Publishers
199 W. 8th Ave., Suite 3
Eugene, OR 97401

www.wipfandstock.com

PAPERBACK ISBN: 978-1-61097-104-1
HARDCOVER ISBN: 978-1-4982-8768-5
EBOOK ISBN: 978-1-5326-3696-7

Cataloguing-in-Publication data:

Names: Oropeza, B. J.

Title: 1 Corinthians : A New Covenant Commentary / B. J. Oropeza.

Description: Eugene, OR: Cascade Books, 2017 | Series: New Covenant Commentary Series | Includes bibliographical references and indices.

Identifiers: ISBN 978-1-61097-104-1 (paperback) | ISBN 978-1-4982-8768-5 (hardcover) | ISBN 978-1-5326-3696-7 (ebook)

Subjects: LCSH: Bible. Corinthians, 1st—Commentaries.

Classification: LCC BS2675.53 O7 2017 (print) | LCC BS2675.53 (ebook)

Manufactured in the U.S.A.   10/25/17

The Bible translation used is the author's own. Unless otherwise stated, this translation uses and accepts the text of the Nestle-Aland 27th edition of the New Testament Greek text, the Stuttgart: Deutsche Bibelgesellschaft *Septuaginta* (1996), and the *Biblia Hebraica Stuttgarensia*, rev. ed. (1990).

Contents

Outline of 1 Corinthians vii

Preface xi

Abbreviations xiii

Introduction 1
   Corinth: Its People and Myths 1
   Paul and the Corinthian Church 7
   Occasion and Purpose of the Letter 9

Introduction (1:1–9) 11

Appeal to Be United and Avoid Discord:
Prothesis and Statement of Facts (1:10–17) 16

Wisdom and Leadership in Light of the Proclamation of the Cross:
First Supporting Proof (1:18—4:21) 23
   Excursus: Paul's Rhetoric against the Sophist Deliveries 33
   Excursus: Interpreting "What Is Written" in 4:6 55

Avoiding Sexual Defilement:
Second Supporting Proof (5:1—7:40) 65
   Fusing the Horizons: Mingling with Vice-Doers Today 72
   Fusing the Horizons: Christians, Same-Sex, and
     Loving Your Neighbor as Yourself 79
   Excursus: Unbelieving Spouses, Clean Children,
     and Pollution by Idols (7:14) 95

Idol Foods, Idolatry, and Relinquishing One's Right:
Third Supporting Proof (8:1—11:1) 107
   Fusing the Horizons: Ambiguity Related to Idol Foods Then and Now 138

Contents

Order and Solidarity When Assembling Together:
Fourth Supporting Proof (11:2—14:40) 140
  Fusing the Horizons: Custom and Modesty 150
  Fusing the Horizons: Women Speakers at Church 192

Solidarity in Belief of the Resurrection:
Fifth Supporting Proof (15:1–58) 196

Closing Matters (1 Cor 16:1–24) 224

Bibliography 235

Author Index 267

Subject Index 275

Biblical and Ancient Literature Index 281

Outline of 1 Corinthians

Introduction (1:1–9)

Letter Prescript (1:1–3)
Thanksgiving Period (1:4–9)

Appeal to Be United and Avoid Discord: Prothesis and Statement of Facts (1:10–17)

Appeal to Unity (1:10)
Divisive Alliances and Baptism (1:11–17)

Wisdom and Leadership in Light of the Proclamation of the Cross: First Supporting Proof (1:18—4:21)

Wisdom and Foolishness of the Cross (1:18–31)
God's Power Rather Than Rhetorical Wisdom (2:1–5)
Wisdom from God's Spirit Rather Than Wisdom of This Age (2:6–16)
Nurturing Babies in Christ (3:1–4)
On Planting and Building the Corinthian Congregation (3:5–17)
Exhortations against Boasting (3:18–23)
Paul the Administrator and Judgment Day (4:1–5)
Exhortations, Hardships, and Parental Instruction (4:6–21)

Avoiding Sexual Defilement: Second Supporting Proof (5:1—7:40)

The Fornicator's Expulsion (5:1–8)
The Limits of Mingling with Vice-Doers (5:9–13)
Court Litigations between Believers (6:1–11)
Sex with Prostitutes and the Corinthian Body (6:12–20)

Outline of 1 Corinthians

Advice for Married, Unmarried, and Widows (7:1–9)
Advice on Divorce and Being Married to an Unbeliever (7:10–16)
Remaining in One's Calling (7:17–24)
Advice Regarding Virgins and Widows (7:25–40)

Idol Foods, Idolatry, and Relinquishing One's Right: Third Supporting Proof (8:1—11:1)

Knowledge, Love, and One God and Lord (8:1–6)
Idol Foods and Weak Believers (8:7–13)
Paul's Release of Apostolic Rights (9:1–18)
All Things for the Gospel's Sake (9:19–23)
Competition and Self-Control (9:24–27)
Wilderness Episodes as Warnings against Idolatry and Vices (10:1–13)
Fleeing Idolatry and Demons (10:14–22)
Further Circumstances Regarding Idol Foods and a Recapitulation (10:23—11:1)

Order and Solidarity When Assembling Together: Fourth Supporting Proof (11:2—14:40)

Gender Distinction When Praying and Prophesying (11:2–16)
Divisions When Commemorating the Last Supper (11:17–34)
Gifts of the Spirit and Solidarity in the Body of Christ (12:1–31)
Love as the Superlative Way (13:1–13)
Prophecy as Greater than Tongues (14:1–19)
Tongues and Prophecy for Believers and Unbelievers (14:20–25)
Orderly Speech Gifts When Coming Together (14:26–40)

Solidarity in Belief of the Resurrection: Fifth Supporting Proof (15:1–58)

Proclamation of Christ's Resurrection (15:1–11)
Disadvantages of Denying the Resurrection and the Resurrection Forecast (15:12–28)

Exhortations and Supporting Arguments Related to Resurrection (15:29–34)

The Nature of Bodily Resurrection (15:35–49)

Transformation and the Defeat of Death (15:50–58)

CLOSING MATTERS (1 COR 16:1–24)

The Collection and Announcement of Visits (16:1–12)

Epistolary Close (16:13–24)

Preface

IT MIGHT SEEM STRANGE that this commentary arrives at the heels of another one I completed on 2 Corinthians for SBL Press last year (*Exploring Second Corinthians*; RRA 3; 2016), but my work on the Corinthian correspondence in reverse order actually enabled me to see things a bit differently than I would otherwise. For instance, I may not have fully appreciated the development of wisdom tendencies in the congregation without doing 2 Corinthians first and addressing relevant problems related to sophistry within that correspondence. My goal in this user-friendly commentary on 1 Corinthians is to provide the reader, whether student or minister or scholar (who can also benefit from this up-to-date interpretation and its many footnotes), with a fresh reading of the letter based on my studies and recent scholarship. In keeping with my intertextual interests, I have tried to concentrate at least on the clearer references Paul makes to Scripture and other sources, and from there hopefully provide helpful insights.

I would like to thank a number of people who, whether directly or indirectly, have helped with this project. Those deserving mention include Thomas Brodie and Linda L. Belleville, who at the annual Society of Biblical Literature conferences chaired the Theological Interweaving of Scripture in 1 Corinthians Seminar. As a steering committee member of this seminar, I was enabled to read and hear the most recent scholarly papers on 1 Corinthians. Thanks also goes to my Azusa Pacific University colleagues, including Robert Duke (dean of the School of Theology), Kenneth Waters (associate dean), Federico Roth (interim chair of Biblical and Religious Studies), Kay Higuera Smith (former chair), and Scott Daniels (former dean). They endorsed time off from my teaching load through our school's Teacher-Scholar award, and through the Center for Research on Ethics and Values (CREV) headed by Mark Eaton. Thanks also goes to Donald Isaak, executive director of the Office of Research and Grants, for heading the writer's retreat I attended in Malibu, California (2015–16).

I would also like to thank my beautiful wife Vonda, who assists me with some of the menial tasks that are part of writing and publishing. Finally, I would like to thank Michael Bird and Craig Keener for inviting me to contribute to the New Covenant Commentary Series several years ago, and who patiently waited as I cut the length of my manuscript by one-third to make it more compatible with other works in this series (and special thanks to Michael for editing the pre-published version and making helpful suggestions). As of this publication the reader can find some of the cut portions referenced in the footnotes and bibliography and posted on my Academia website: https://azusa.academia.edu/BjOropeza.

B. J. Oropeza

Abbreviations

AYB	Anchor Yale Bible
AYBRL	Anchor Yale Bible Reference Library
ABD	*Anchor Bible Dictionary*. Edited by David Noel Freedman. 6 vols. New York: Doubleday, 1992.
ABR	Australian Biblical Review
AcBib	Academia Biblica
ACCS	Ancient Christian Commentary on Scripture
ACNT	Augsburg Commentary on the New Testament
AGJU	Arbeiten zur Geschichte des Spätjudentums und Urchristentums
AJPS	*American Journal of Political Science*
AnBib	Analecta Biblica
ANTC	Abingdon New Testament Commentaries
ASCSA	American School of Classical Studies at Athens
ASNU	Acta Seminarii Neotestamentici Upsaliensis
ATJ	Ashland Theological Journal
ATRSupp	*Anglican Theological Review Supplement*
BA	*Biblical Archaeologist*
Bib	*Biblica*
BBR	*Bulletin for Biblical Research*
BDAG	Danker, Frederick W., Walter Bauer, William F. Arndt, and F. Wilbur Gingrich. *Greek-English Lexicon of the New Testament and Other Early Christian Literature*. 3rd ed. Chicago: University of Chicago Press, 2000.
BDB	Brown, Francis, S. R. Driver, and Charles A. Briggs. *A Hebrew and English Lexicon of the Old Testament*.
BDF	Blass, Friedrich, Albert Debrunner, and Robert W. Funk. *A Greek Grammar of the New Testament and Other Early Christian Literature*. Chicago: University of Chicago Press, 1961.
BECNT	Baker Exegetical Commentary on the New Testament

Abbreviations

BETL	Bibliotheca Ephemeridum Theologicarum Lovaniensium
BHT	Beitrage zur historischen Theologie
BIS	Biblical Interpretation Series
BJRL	*Bulletin of the John Rylands University Library of Manchester*
BNTC	Black's New Testament Commentaries
BR	Biblical Research
BSac	*Bibliotheca Sacra*
BT	*The Bible Translator*
BTB	*Biblical Theology Bulletin*
BZNW	Beihefte zur Zeitschrift fur die neutestamentliche Wissenschaft
CAL	Comprehensive Aramaic Lexicon (Logos software)
CBET	Contributions to Biblical and Exegetical Theology
CBNTS	Coniectanea Biblica New Testament Series
CBQ	*Catholic Biblical Quarterly*
CBR	*Currents in Biblical Research*
CCSS	Catholic Commentary on Sacred Scripture
CDCC	*Cambridge Dictionary of Classical Civilization* (2006).
CECNT	Critical and Exegetical Commentary on the New Testament
CIJ	*Corpus Inscriptionum Judaicarum*. 2 Vols. Rome, 1936–52.
CTXT	*Corinth in Context: Comparative Studies on Religion and Society.* NovTSup 134. Edited by Steven J. Friesen, Daniel N. Schowalter, and James C. Walters, James C., 231–56. Leiden: Brill, 2010.
CTST	*Corinth in Contrast: Studies in Inequality.* Edited by Steven J. Friesen, Sarah A. James, and Daniel N. Schowalter. NovTSup 155. Leiden: Brill, 2014.
CorBETL	*Corinthian Correspondence.* Edited by Reimund Bieringer. BETL 125. Leuven: Leuven University Press/ Uitgeverij Peeters, 1996.
CSEL	Corpus Scriptorum Ecclesiasticorum Latinorum.
CTJ	*Calvin Theological Journal*
CTQ	*Concordia Theological Quarterly*
CTR	*Criswell Theological Review*
CurTM	*Currents in Theology and Mission*

Abbreviations

DNTB	*Dictionary of New Testament Background*. Edited by Craig A. Evans and Stanley E. Porter. Downers Grove, IL: InterVarsity Press, 2000.
DPL	*Dictionary of Paul and His Letters*. Edited by Gerald F. Hawthorne, Ralph P. Martin, and Daniel Reid. Downers Grove, IL: InterVarsity Press, 1993.
ECL	Early Christianity and Its Literature
EDNT	*Exegetical Dictionary of the New Testament*. Edited by Horst Balz and Gerhard Schneider. ET. 3 vols. Grand Rapids: Eerdmans, 1990–1993.
EKKNT	Evangelisch-katholischer Kommentar zum Neuen Testament
ESEC	Emory Studies in Early Christianity
ESV	English Standard Version
ETL	*Ephemerides Theologicae Lovanienses*
ETR	*Etudes théologiques et religieuses*
EvQ	*Evangelical Quarterly*
EvTh	*Evangelische Theologie*
ExpTim	*Expository Times*
FRLANT	Forschungen zur Religion und Literatur des Alten und Neuen Testaments
HAR	*Hebrew Annual Review*
HNT	Handbuch zum Neuen Testament
HTA	Historisch Theologische Auslegung
HTR	*Harvard Theological Review*
HTS	Harvard Theological Studies
ICC	International Critical Commentary
Int	*Interpretation*
ISV	International Standard Version
JBL	*Journal of Biblical Literature*
JETS	*Journal of the Evangelical Theological Society*
JPT	*Journal of Pentecostal Theology*
JPTSS	Journal of Pentecostal Theology Supplement Series
JRASup	Journal of Roman Archaeology Supplementary series
JSNT	*Journal for the Study of the New Testament*
JSNTSS	Journal for the Study of the New Testament Supplement Series
JSOT	Journal for the Study of the Old Testament

Abbreviations

JTS	*Journal of Theological Studies*
KEK	Kritisch-exegetischer Kommentar uber das Neue Testament (Meyer-Kommentar)
KNT	Kommentar zum Neuen Testament
LCBI	Literary Currents in Biblical Interpretation
LCL	Loeb Classical Library
LEH	Lust, J., Eynikel, E., and Hauspie, K. *A Greek-English Lexicon of the Septuagint: Revised Edition*. Stuttgart: Deutsche Bibelgesellschaft, 2003.
LNTS	Library of New Testament Studies
LPS	Library of Pauline Studies
LSJ	Liddell, Henry George, Robert Scott, Henry Stuart Jones. *A Greek-English Lexicon*. 9th ed. with revised supplement. Oxford: Clarendon, 1996.
MNTC	Moffatt New Testament Commentary
NA27	Nestle-Aland, *Novum Testamentum Graece*, 27th ed.
NAC	New American Commentary
NASB	New American Standard Bible
NCB	New Century Bible
NCBC	New Cambridge Bible Commentary
Neot	*Neotestamentica*
NET	NET Bible Version
NETS	*A New English Translation of the Septuagint*. Edited by Albert Pietersma and Benjamin G. Wright. New York: Oxford University Press, 2007.
NICNT	New International Commentary on the New Testament
NICOT	New International Commentary on the Old Testament
NIDNTT	*New International Dictionary of New Testament Theology*. Edited by Colin Brown. 4 vols. Grand Rapids: Zondervan, 1975–1978.
NIGTC	New International Greek Testament Commentary
NIV	New International Version
NKJV	New King James Version
NovT	*Novum Testamentum*
NovTSup	Supplements to Novum Testamentum
NRSV	New Revised Standard Version
NTD	Das Neue Testament Deutsch

Abbreviations

NTL	New Testament Library
NTS	*New Testament Studies*
OCD	*The Oxford Classical Dictionary*. Edited by Simon Hornblower and Antony Spawforth. 3rd ed. Oxford: Oxford University Press, 1970.
OTKNT	Ökumenischer Taschenbuch-Kommentar zum Neuen Testament
OTP	*Old Testament Pseudepigrapha*. Edited by James H. Charlesworth. 2 vols. New York: Doubleday, 1983–1985.
PGRW	*Paul in the Greco-Roman World: A Handbook*. Edited by J. Paul Sampley. Harrisburg, PA: Trinity Press International, 2003.
PNTC	Pillar New Testament Commentary
PRSt	*Perspectives in Religious Studies*
PS	Pauline Studies
QD	Quaestiones Disputatae
RBL	*Review of Biblical Literature*
ResQ	*Restoration Quarterly*
RevExp	*Review and Expositor*
RIDA	*Revue internationale des doits de l'antiquité*
RRA	Rhetoric of Religious Antiquity
SBEC	Studies in Bible and Early Christianity
SBL	Society of Biblical Literature
SBLDS	Society of Biblical Literature Dissertation Series
SBLMS	Society of Biblical Literature Monograph Series
SBLSP	Society of Biblical Literature Seminar Papers
SBT	Society of Biblical Theology
SCJ	*Stone-Campbell Journal*
SEÅ	*Svensk exegetisk årsbok*
SIBL	Studies in Biblical Litarature
SNTSMS	Society of New Testament Studies Monograph Series
SNTW	Studies of the New Testament and Its World
SP	Sacra Pagina
SREC	Sociorhetorical Exploration Commentary
TDNT	*Theological Dictionary of the New Testament*. Edited by Gerhard Kittel and Gerhard Friedrich. Translated by Geoffrey W. Bromiley. 10 vols. Grand Rapids: Eerdmans, 1964–1976.

Abbreviations

TENTS	Texts and Editions for New Testament Studey
TGST	Tesi Gregoriana Serie Teologia
THKNT	Theologischer Handkommentar zum Neuen Testament
TR	Textus Receptus (Majority Text)
TrinJ	*Trinity Journal*
TynBul	*Tyndale Bulletin*
URRC	*Urban Religion in Corinth: Interdisciplinary Approaches.* Edited by Daniel N Schowalter and Steven J. Friesen. HTS 53. Cambridge, MA: Harvard University Press, 2005
WBC	Word Biblical Commentary
WGRWSup	Writings from the Greco-Roman World Supplement Series
WMANT	Wissenschaftliche Monographien zum Alten und Neuen Testament
WTJ	*Westminster Theological Journal*
WUNT	Wissenschaftliche Untersuchungen zum Neuen Testament
ZNW	*Zeitschrift für die neutestamentliche Wissenschaft*
ZTK	*Zeitschrift für Theologie und Kirche*

Ancient Sources

1 *Clem.*	1 Clement
1 *En.*	1 Enoch
1QM	War Scroll
1QpHab	Pesher Habakkuk
1QS	Rule of the Community
1QSb	Rule of the Blessings
2 *Bar.*	2 Baruch
3 *Bar.*	3 Baruch
4Q257	4Q Rule of the Community (4QpapSc)
4Q266	Damascus Documenta (4QDa)
A	Codex Alexandrinus
א	Codex Sinaiticus
ʿAbod. Zar.	ʿAbodah Zarah
Abr.	Philo, *De Abrahamo*
Ach.	Aristophanes, *Acharneneses*
Ad Mart.	Tertullian, *Ad Martyras*

Abbreviations

Aem.	Plutarch, *Aemilius Paullus*
Aen.	Virgil, *Aeneid*
Ag. Ap.	Josephus, *Against Apion*
Amat.	Plutarch, *Amatorius*
Ann.	Tacitus, *Annales*
Ant.	Josephus, *Jewish Antiquities*;
Ant. rom.	Dionysius of Halicarnassus, *Antiquitates romanae*
Apol.	Justin Martyr, *Apologia 1*
Apoc. Elij.	Apocalypse of Elijah
Apoc. Mos.	Apocalypse of Moses
Apoc. Zeph.	Apocalypse of Zephaniah
Argo.	Apollonius, *Argonautica*
Athen. pol.	Aristotle, *Constitution of Athens*
Ath. pol.	Aristotle, *Athenain politeia*
B	Codex Vaticanus
Bell.	Euripides, *Bellerophon*; Josephus, *Jewish Wars* (*Bellum judaicum*)
Bell. civ.	Appian, *Bella civilia*
Ben.	Seneca, *De beneficiis*
Bib. hist.	Diodorus Siculus, *Bibliotheca historica*
C	Codex Ephraemi
Calig.	Suetonius, *Caligula*
CD	Damascus Document
Cic.	Cicero
Comp. Dem. Cic.	*Comparatio Demosthenis et Ciceronis*
Claud.	Suetonius, *Divus Claudius*
Clem.	Seneca, *De Clementia*
Congr.	Philo, *De congress eruditionis gratia*
Conj. praec.	Plutarch, *Conjugalia praecepta*
Crat.	Plato, *Cratylus*
D	Codex Claromontanus; Codex Bezae
Deipn.	Athenaeus, *Deipnosophistae*
De esu	Plutarch, *De esu carnium*
De laude	Plutarch, *De laude ipsius*
De or.	Cicero, *De oratore*
Dem.	Isocrates, *Ad Demonicum* (*Or.* 1)

Abbreviations

Descr.	Pausanias, *Graeciae descriptio*
Det.	Philo, *Quod deterius potiori insidari soleat*
Dial.	Dialogue(s)
Dial. d.	Lucian, *Dialogi deorum*
Diatr.	Epictetus, *Diatribai* (*Dissertationes*)
Did.	Didache
Diss.	Epictetus, *Dissertationes*; Maximus of Tyre (same)
Eclog.	Virgil, *Eclogues*
Elect.	Sophocles, *Electra*
Eloc.	Demetrius, *De elocutione*
Ench.	Epictetus, *Enchridion*
Ep.	*Epistle(s)*; Seneca, *Ep.* (*Lucil.*)
Eum.	Aeschylus, *Eumenides*
Euthyd.	Plato, *Euthydemus*
Fals. leg.	Aeschines, *De falsa legatione*
Fam.	Cicero, *Epistulae ad familiares*
Fin.	Cicero, *De finibus*
Frag.	Fragment/*Fragmata*
Frat. amor.	Plutarch, *De fraterno amore*
Fug.	Lucian, *Fugitivi*
Garr.	Plutarch, *De garrulitate*
Germ.	Tacitus, *Germania*
Gen. an.	Aristotle, *De generatione Anamalium*
Gen. Rab.	Genesis Rabbah
Geogr.	Strabo, *Geography*
Georg.	Virgil, *Georgica*
Gig.	Philo, *Gigantibus*
Git.	Gittim
Gorg.	Plato, *Gorgias*
H.E.	Eusebius, *Historica ecclesiastica*
Her.	Philo, *Quis rerum divinarum heres sit*; Ovid, *Heroides*; Irenaeus, *Adversus haereses*
Hermot.	Lucian, *Hermotimus* (*De sectis*)
Hist.	*Historiae*; Thucydides, *History of the Peloponnesian War*
Hist. anim.	Aristotle, *Historia animalium*
Hist. rom.	Cassius Dio, *Historia romana*; Livy (same)

Abbreviations

Hom. 1 Cor.	John Chrysostom, *Homiliae in epistulam i ad Corinthios*
Hul.	Hullin
Il.	Homer, *Iliad*
Inst.	Quintilian, *Institutio oratoria*
Inv.	Cicero, *De inventione rhetorica*
Is. Os.	Plutarch, *De Iside et Osiride*
Jos.	Philo *On the Life of Joseph*
Jos.	Josephus
Jos. Asen.	Joseph and Aseneth
Jub.	Jubilees
Jul.	Suetonius, *Divus Julius*
Ketub.	Ketubbim
L.A.B	Liber antiquitatum biblicarum (Pseudo-Philo)
Lect.	Musonius Rufus, *Lectures*
Leg.	Plato, *Leges*; Cicero, *De Legibus*; Philo, *Legum allegoriae*
Legat.	Philo, *Legatio ad Gaium*
Leg. man.	Cicero, *Pro Lege manilia* (*De imperio Cn. Pompeii*)
Let. Aris.	Letter of Aristeas
Lev. Rab.	Leviticus Rabbah
Lex.	Lucian, *Lexiphanes*
Lib. ed.	Plutarch, *De liberis educandis*
Libr.	Apollodorus, Library
Lucil.	Seneca, *Ad Lucilium*
LXX	Septuagint (Greek Bible)
m.	Mishnah
Marc.	Tertullian, *Adversus Marcionem*
Med.	Euripides, *Medea*; Marcus Aurelius, *Meditations*
Mem.	Xenophon, *Memorabilia*
Met.	Ovid, *Metamorphoses*
Metam.	Apuleius, *Metamorphoses*
Migr.	Philo, *De Migratione Abrahami*
Mith.	Appian, *Mithridatic Wars*
Mor.	Plutarch, *Moralia*
Mos.	Philo, *On the Life of Moses*
mss.	Greek manuscripts (ancient and medieval)
MT	Masoretic Text (Hebrew Bible)

Abbreviations

Mut.	Philo, *De mutatione nominum*
Nat.	Pliny, *Naturalis historia*
Nat. puer.	Hippocrates, *De natura pueri*
N.E.	Aristotle, Nicomachean Ethics
Neaer.	Demosthenes, *In Neaeram*
Noct. att.	Aulus Gellius, *Noctes atticae*
Od.	Homer, *Odyssey*
Oec.	Aristotle, *Oeconomica*
Oed. Rex	Sophocles, *Oedipus Rex*
Off.	Cicero, *De officiis*
Ol.	Pindar, *Olympionikai*
Or.	Oration(s)
P.	papyri; abbreviations for individual papyri at http://library.duke.edu/rubenstein/scriptorium/papyrus/texts/clist_papyri.html
Pan.	Epiphanius *Panarion (Adversus haeresus)*
Part. or.	Cicero, *Partitiones oratoriae*
Phaedr.	Plato, *Phaedrus*
Phil.	Plutarch, *Philopoemen*
Pol.	Aristotle, *Politics*
Post.	Philo, *De posteritate Caini*
Praec. ger. rei publ.	Plutarch, *Praecepta gerendae rei publicae*
Prob.	Philo, *Quod omnis probus libert sit*
Prog.	*Progymnasmata*
Prof.	Sextus Empiricus, *Against the Professors (Mathematicians)*
Prot.	Plato, *Protagoras*
Prot. Jas.	*Protoevangelium of James*
Ps.-Phoc.	Pseudo-Phocylides
Pun.	Appian, *Punic Wars*
Pyth.	Pindar, *Pythionikai*
QG	Philo, *Questions and Answers on Genesis*
Quaest. rom.	Plutarch, *Quaestiones romanae et graecae*
Qidd.	Qiddušin
Rab. Perd.	Cicero, *Pro Rabirio Perduellionis Reo*
Rect. rat. aud.	Plutarch, *De recta ratione audiendi*
Reg. imp. apophth.	Plutarch, *Regum et imperatorum apophthegmata*

Abbreviations

Rep.	Plato, *Republic*
Rhet.	Aristotle, *Rhetorica*
Rhet. Alex.	Anaximenes, *Rhetorica ad Alexandrum* (*Ars rhetorica*)
Rhet. Her.	Rhetorica ad Herennium
Rom.	Plutarch, *Romulus*
Sacr.	Philo, *De sacrificus Abelis et Caini*
Sent.	Pseudo-Phocylides, *Sententiae*
Sib. Or.	Sibylline Oracles
Smyrn.	Ignatius, *To the Smyrneans*
Somn.	Philo, *De somniis*
Soph.	Isocrates, *In sophistas*
Spec.	Philo, *De specialibus legibus*
Stoic. abs.	Plutarch, *Stoicos absurdiora poetis dicere*
Suave viv.	Plutarch, *Non posse suaviter vivi secundum Epicurum*
Subl.	Longinus, *On the Sublime*
Suppl.	Euripides, *Supplices*
SVF	*Stoicorum Veterum Fragmenta*. Hans Friedrich August von Arnim. 4 vols. Leipzig: Teubne, 1903–1924.
Symp.	Plato, *Symposium*
Trall.	Ignatius, *Trallians*
T. Abr.	Testament of Abraham
T. Benj.	Testament of Benjamin
Tg.	Targum
T. Jac.	Testament of Jacob
T. Job	Testament of Job
T. Levi	Testament of Levi
t. Meg.	Tosefta Megillah
T. Mos.	Testament of Moses
T. Naph.	Testament of Naphtali
T. Reub.	Testament of Reuben
T. Sol.	Testament of Solomon
T. Zeb.	Testament of Zebulun
Theog.	Hesiod, *Theogony*
Thesm.	Aristophanes, *Thesmophoriazusae*
Tranq.	Seneca, *Tranquillitate animi*
Tu san.	Plutarch, *De tuenda sanitate praecepta*

Abbreviations

Verr.	Cicero, *In Verrum*
Vg	Latin Vulgate
Virg.	Tertullian, *De virginibus valandis*
Vir. ill.	Jerome, *De viris illustribus*
Virt.	Philo, *De virtutibus*
Vit.	*Vita/Vitae*
Vit. Beat.	Seneca, *De vita beata*
Vit. phil.	Diogenes Laertius, *Vitae philosophorum*
Vit. soph.	Philostratus, *Vitae sophistarum*
Vit. X orat.	Plutarch, *Vitae decem oratorum*

Introduction

Paul's transformation from a Pharisee and persecutor of Christ's followers took place only several years after Christ's crucifixion.[1] Once established in Antioch, he became an apostle to the Gentiles travelling to different cities proclaiming the gospel of Christ. It was during his so-called second missionary journey that he first evangelized Corinth, according to Acts 18:1–20.[2] If his stay in Corinth corresponds with Gallio's proconsulship of the region as portrayed in Acts, he was there somewhere between the years of 50–52 CE.[3] A few years later he stayed in Ephesus and there wrote 1 Corinthians (see 1 Cor 15:32; 16:8–9), having already sent them at least one previous letter now lost to us (5:9). The first canonical letter was written about 54 or 55 CE.[4] We will address issues surrounding Paul and the Corinthians, and the occasion and purpose for this letter, but first some information about ancient Corinth and its myths is in order.

Corinth: Its People and Myths

Corinth acquired the reputation of wealth and accessibility. It was situated strategically near the Isthmus of the Peloponnesus and had ports at Cenchreae and Lechaeum along with the *diolkos* road that enabled ships prior to Paul's day to pass from the Aegean to Ionian Sea. Among other things, the city was a center for commerce, high-quality bronze, and state-of-the-art ships.[5] The Corinthians demonstrated their military power when, together with Athenians and Spartans, they defended Greece against Persia (5th c. BCE). As a prime mover of the Peloponnesian War (431–404 BCE),

---

1. On Paul's early years, see Gal 1:11—2:15; Phil 3:4–6; 2 Cor 11:32–33; Acts 7:54—8:3; 9:1–30; 11:23–30; 13:1—15:25; 22:2–21; 26:4–23; Hengel 1997; Murphy-O'Connor 1996:1–101.

2. Although Acts has its own agenda, Keener 2014:3.2681–83, recently shows that its account of Paul in Corinth is generally reliable.

3. See inscription evidence in Fitzmyer 2008:40–42.

4. For the former date, see e.g., Schnabel 2006:38; for the latter, e.g., Schnelle 1998:57.

5. Thucydides *Hist.* 1.13.2–5; Strabo *Geogr.* 8.6.19, 20a, 23d; Dio Chrysostom *Or.* 37.36.

they stirred up alliances which eventually led to Athen's demise, and in the Corinthian War that followed they allied with other Greek cities against Sparta's expansions. They fought against Philip II of Macedon at Chaeronea, and later joined the Achaean League, which eventually led to their disaster when opposing Rome. The Roman general, Lucius Mummius, set the city aflame, put to death many of its men, and sold its women and children into slavery (146 BCE).[6]

Bravery, hardship, and heroism in the Corinthian battles were doubtless retold by its citizens, things that stand in tension with characterizations of Corinth as a place of leisure and sexual license. The Acrocorinth's alleged thousand sacred prostitutes devoted to Aphrodite, goddess of love (Strabo *Geogr.* 8.6.20c), at best seems exaggerated since sacred prostitution was not customarily a Greek practice.[7] Aphrodite's legendary origin from the foam of the sea, where the god Chronos had cut off the genitals of his father Ouranus (Hesiod *Theog.* 188–206), casts her in sensual light. But she also represented beauty, fruitfulness, safe seafaring, and protector of the Corinthians.[8] Perhaps in this last role the women of Corinth would climb the Acrocorinth; they begged for "a great and terrifying divine force to inspire their warriors to overwhelm the horrifying destructive power of war."[9] Nevertheless, Corinth did have a licentious reputation. Plutarch mentions an "army of harlots" in the Acrocorinth (*Amatorius* 21[767F]), Aristophanes uses the term *korinthiazesthai* to refer to practicing sexual immorality (*Frag.* 354), and Plato seems to equate Corinthian women with sexual promiscuity (*Rep.* 404D). Although these words come from outsiders and perhaps promote Athenian propaganda,[10] they are nonetheless complementary with what we find in 1 Corinthians. Here more than any of his other letters, Paul tries to correct the sexual misconduct of congregation members, including their affairs with prostitutes (1 Cor 5–7; cf. 10:8; 2 Cor 12:21).

---

6. See e.g., Pausanius *Descr.* 2.1.2; 7.7.1–16.10; Cassius Dio *Hist. Rom.* 21[9.31]; Strabo *Geogr.* 23a; Salmon 2006:235–37; Murphy-O'Connor 1983:42–43, 49, 63–64.

7. See Lanci 2005:205–20. Differently, Williams 1986:17–21; Schnabel 2006:22, suggest imported influence from Phoenician-Astarte. Pausanius connects Aphrodite's cult to Phoenicians (*Descr.* 1.14.7).

8. See e.g., Hamilton, 1969:32–33.

9. Lanci 2005:220.

10. So Conzelmann 1975:12; Murphy-O'Connor 1983:55–57, 105–6.

Introduction

Roman Corinth

After Mummius's conflagration of Corinth, some structures and a small population of primarily lower class Greeks remained.[11] Under Julius Caesar it was repopulated in 44 BCE as a Roman colony. Surviving Greek buildings were reused, such as the South Stoa, the theatre, the Peirene and Glauke fountains, and the Isthmian games were reinstated.[12] According to Benjamin Millis, the population included Greek freedman, provincials, and Roman freeborn; the amount of veterans was insignificant. The repopulated city was neither completely Greek nor Roman but a hybrid culture.[13] It was comprised of both colonist citizens and foreigners, and its governance, typical of Roman colonial cities, consisted of two magistrates (*duoviri*) who appointed councilors (*decuriones*). In addition, two *aediles* were in charge of edifices, street maintenance, and commercial affairs. The most honored position was the *agonothetes*, the president over the games.[14] Corinth prospered especially as a service city that provided cultural, educational, religious, and judicial activities.[15] Cicero called this large, thriving city the "light of all Greece" (*Leg. man.* 5) and Diodorus Siculus the "bright star of Hellas" (*Bib. hist.* 32.27.1).

Its civic reputation, along with many erections and inscriptions attesting to human pride, may warrant Corinth as "a city where public boasting and self-promotion had become an art form."[16] Although the *lingua franca* of the time was Greek, and Latin was the elite language of Rome, the majority of inscriptions in Corinth are written in Latin prior to the second century CE.[17] This doubtless suggests the influence of both Roman and high society in Corinth. While Roman ideology was surely pervasive in Corinth, legends attached to art and ancient structures provided its inhabitants with a sense of continuity with the older Greek city. Elite magistrates with Greek names uncovered in the city suggest not only that Greeks were becoming more like Romans, but that "Corinth was becoming more Greek."[18]

Unpoliced private cults flourished in the area enabling Greek and foreign religions to continue without harassment.[19] Some of the religious sites

---

11. See James 2014:17–36; Gebhard/Dickie 2003:261–78.
12. Walters 2005:403–4.
13. Millis 2010:13–36; Millis 2013:38–53.
14. Adams/Horrell 2004:3–7; Engels 1990:17–19; Harrison 2008:81–109.
15. Engels 1990:43–65, 121–30.
16. Witherington 1995:8.
17. See Kent 1966:19; Fitzmyer 2008:30; though the graffiti is Greek.
18. Walters 2005:409.
19. Rapid changes in Corinth's civic identity helped produce "a growing ambiguity

Introduction

in or near the city included those venerating Aphrodite, Poseidon, Apollo, Demeter and Kore, and Asclepius. The various deities associated with the twenty-six sacred locations in Corinth described by Pausanius complement Paul's words to the Corinthians that there are "gods many and lords many" (1 Cor 8:5).[20] The imperial cult was also strongly present with Julio-Claudian portraits on the east side of the forum, an altar to Divus (divine) Julius Caesar, and a statue of Divus Augustus Caesar in the middle of the forum.[21] Acts 18:4 also locates a Jewish synagogue in the city during Paul's visit. An inscription identifying the "Synagogue of the Hebrews" was excavated in the city (CIJ I§718). Certain scholars have dated it in a time frame compatible with Acts, but its origin may be much later.[22] Philo, in any case, confirms a Jewish community living in first-century Corinth (*Legat.* 281).

Corinthian Mythology

Although the Corinthians boasted of their origin in the hero Corinthus as the son of Zeus, other Greeks did not believe this familial tie.[23] Ephyra, daughter of the sea Titan, Oceanus, was said to dwell first in Corinth. Some prominent mythological stories about Corinthians are as follows.

The crafty king Sisyphus was one of Corinth's earliest rulers. Zeus punishes him for exposing one of Zeus's illicit affairs. He sends Thanatos (death) to take Sisyphus's life, but the king binds up this deity until Ares, god of war, frees Thanatos so that he could accomplish his mission. The dead Sisyphus then tricks Hades, god of the underworld, into letting him return to life temporarily so that he could arrange his own funeral proceedings. But he never returns to Hades and lives to a ripe old age. After he dies again, Sisyphus's punishment is to roll a boulder perpetually up a hill only to have it roll back down again once he gets near the top. A temple was built for him on the Acrocorinth.[24]

---

in the population's civic religious identity," which seems to have resulted in magistrates and *decurions* being reluctant to enforce laws on private associations (Walters 2005:410).

20. See Fee 1987:3 (though his identities for these terms may be too limiting).

21. See Bookidis 2005:156–64; Walbank 1996:201–14; Coutsoumpos 2008:175–76. For a convenient inscription list on the emperors that is keyed to Meritt 1931, and West 1931; see also Keener 2014:3.2691.

22. Contrast Deissmann 1965:16 (100 BCE–200 CE) with Adams/Horrell 2004:10 (5th c. CE).

23. Pausanius *Descr.* 2.1.1; Philostratus *Vit. soph.* 2.611.

24. Pausanius *Descr.* 2.5.1; cf. Apollodorus *Libr.* 1.9.3; Homer *Il.* 6.151–54; Sourvinou-Inwood 1996:1414.

Another myth centers on a boy named Melikertes whom Sisyphus finds; he was brought to shore by a dolphin, a scene minted on Corinthian *tessera* coins.[25] Sisyphus buries him on the Isthmus and in his honor establishes the Isthmian games (Pausanius *Descr.* 2.1.3). In one version of the story, Melikertes's mother Ino jumps into the sea with him to escape a deadly pursuit. She becomes the goddess Leukothea and he Palaimon, a marine god. At the games his funerary rites seem to be reenacted, and Roman colonists built a sanctuary for him.[26]

The hero Bellerophon, grandson of Sisyphus, tames the winged horse Pegasus after consulting a wise seer in Corinth who has him seek Athena at her temple for assistance. When he accidentally kills his brother, he stays in Argos with king Proetus and rejects queen Anteia's amorous advances. She then accuses him of attempted rape. The king sends him away with a sealed letter to king Iobates of Lycia requesting to kill him. This king refuses; he opens the letter after entertaining his guest and he fears such an act as a host would spark Zeus's wrath. Instead, he sends Bellerophon to do dangerous tasks, one of which is to kill Chimaera the monstrous lion-goat-serpent, which he succeeds in doing with Pegasus's help. In later years he becomes arrogant, attempting to ride Pegasus up to Olympus to live among the immortals, but Pegasus throws off his rider, and Bellerophon becomes hated by the gods.[27] The fountain-spring of Peirene in Corinth, enduring to Roman times, was considered sacred and commemorated the place where this hero tamed Pegasus.[28] Bellerophon's battle with Chimaera appears in Corinthian art,[29] and Corinthian coins with images of Pegasos connect the Greek myth in solidarity with the new Roman colony.[30]

Another popular myth centers on King Oedipus. Oedipus has been raised as the son of a royal couple in Corinth after his real parents, King Laius and Queen Jacosta of Thebes, fear an oracle that their infant son would eventually kill Laius. The king gives his servant the child to dispose of him, but the servant gives him to a Corinthian herdsman, who gives him to the Corinthian couple. When he grows up, Oedipus learns from the Oracle at Delphi that he would kill his father and marry his mother. Fate and tragedy take place as he leaves Corinth for Thebes to avoid fulfilling the prophecy.

25. See Bitner 2015a:177–78.
26. Gebhard 2005:165–203
27. Pindar *Ol.* 13.63–92; Homer *Il.* 6.152–202; Euripedes *Bell.*; Hamilton 1969:134–37.
28. Robinson 2005:116–27.
29. March 1996:237–38.
30. See Bitner 2015a:174–75, 179–80.

Introduction

On the way, he quarrels with a man on the road and kills him, not knowing it is his father Laius. After delivering the Thebans from the monstrous Sphynx, the people make Oedipus their king and marry him to the widowed Queen Jacosta, who is secretly his mother. The prophet Tiresias reveals Oedipus as the king's murderer and predicts calamity. Eventually, after the incestuous couple finds out the truth, Jacosta hangs herself and Oedipus blinds himself with his mother's brooches (Sophocles, *Oed. Rex*).[31]

A final myth we will mention is the tragedy of Medea. Being warned by prophecy against his nephew Jason, Pelias, the usurper of Iolcus, sends him with the Argonauts to retrieve a golden fleece in Colchis. Aphrodite and Cupid protect Jason by having Medea, daughter of King Aeetes of Colchis, fall in love with Jason. With the help of Medea's magic Jason accomplishes great feats and takes the fleece from Aeetes. The king chases them by ship, and Medea cuts up her brother, flinging occasional pieces into the sea to slow down Aeetes, who must give his son a proper burial. The couple escapes, and Jason delivers the fleece to Pelias but finds out that his uncle was responsible for his family's death. So Medea tricks Pelias's daughters into cutting up and boiling the pieces of their father in a cauldron, believing Medea's magic could bring him back younger than before. Of course, she doesn't do this and flees with Jason to Corinth.[32] In Corinth, Jason marries Glauke, King Kreon's daughter. This betrayal to Medea prompts her to give a "gift" of a crown and dress to Glauke. As Glauke puts these on, she burns up along with her father, and Medea kills her own children from Jason to get back at him as she escapes to Athens. The fountain of Glauke was reportedly where the princess jumped into the water in an attempt to save herself from Medea's deadly gift.[33] The fountain, like the Peirene, prompted Corinthians in the Roman age to remember its famed Greek past with these stories.[34]

Clearly, these myths center on conflict, tragedy, honor, love, and a preponderance with death, often brutal, along with the hope of immortality. Moreover, prophecy and fate are well-respected—predictions come to pass even when humans attempt to thwart them. Corinth's inhabitants would be daily reminded of these stories when seeing statues, paintings, sanctuaries, coins, and inscriptions that inundated their city. These myths prepare them to ponder on death and the afterlife (cf. 1 Cor 15), while at the same time prompt them to respect the words of wise orators and prophets (cf. chs. 1–4;

---

31. Mulroy 2012:73–75.
32. Apollodorus *Libr.* 1.9.27; Apollonius *Argo.*; Mulroy 2012:56–62.
33. Pausanius *Descr.* 2.3.6–11; Euripedes *Med.*; Epictetus *Diatr.* 2.17.19–22.
34. Robinson 2005:128–40.

12–14). If Paul was to proclaim his message successfully in this city, perhaps he prepared himself by learning about some of their religious traditions.[35]

PAUL AND THE CORINTHIAN CHURCH

The Corinth that Paul visits was one filled with sanctuaries, statues, shops, an agora, and a forum with tribunal that probably inspired his own depiction of Christ on the judgment seat (2 Cor 5:10). A number of small shop keepers, artisans, teachers, and secretaries were among the people of Corinth whom Appian considers poor (*Hist.* 8.136).[36] Alciphron speaks of the area having both immorally rich and miserably poor (*Ep.* 3.24[iii.60]). Dio Chrysostom, writing in the first century CE, describes the rabble at the Isthmian games: "One could hear crowds of wretched sophists around Poseidon's temple shouting and reviling one another, and their disciples . . . fighting with one another, many writers reading aloud their stupid works, many poets reciting their poems while others applauded them, many jugglers showing their tricks, many fortune-tellers interpreting fortunes, lawyers innumerable perverting judgment, and peddlers not a few peddling whatever they happened to have" (*Or.* 8.9).[37] Paul perhaps witnessed similar activities. The Corinthian population at this time was perhaps anywhere from 80,000 to 140,000.[38]

According to Acts 18 he teams up with Prisca and Aquila, fellow Jewish tentmakers recently expelled from Rome by Emperor Claudius,[39] and later on Timothy and Silas assist him there. His proclamation of the gospel turns out to be successful—"many" Corinthians believe and are baptized (18:8). The Lord speaks to him in a vision assuring his protection and encouraging him to preach, for "I have many people in this city," and so Paul remains there for eighteen months (18:9–10). We can assume that this church grew to be fairly large, probably over one hundred converts with their families. The houses of Titius Justus and Gaius became early gathering places (Acts 18:7; Rom 16:23).[40]

---

35. See Keener 2014:3.2695.

36. Murphy-O'Connor 1983:66–67, 113, associates freedmen among these workers. The city sites in Paul's day are conveniently described with maps in Murphy-O'Connor 1984:147–59.

37. Translation in Murphy-O'Connor 1983:94.

38. See various figures in Engels 1990:79–84; Keener 2014:3.2685.

39. On this edict of Claudius against the Jews, see Seutonius *Claud.* 25.4 (49 CE. Less likely is the date of 41 CE based on Cassio Dio *Hist. Rom.* 60.6.6). See Fitzmyer 2008:37–40.

40. Unless they are the same person, as McRay 2000:230, suggests.

Introduction

Of the names of seventeen members mentioned by Paul or Acts (1 Cor 1:1, 11, 14; 16:17, 19; Rom 16:1, 21–23; Acts 18:2, 7–8), nine are Greek (Achaicus, Chloe, Crispus, Sosthenes, Stephanas, Erastus, Jason, Phoebe, and Sosipater) and eight are Latin (Aquila, Prisca, Fortunatus, Gaius, Lucius, Quartus, Tertius, and Justus).[41] Among these, Crispus, Aquila, Prisca, and possibly Sosthenes, are Jews, but the church mostly consists of Gentiles when Paul writes this letter (1 Cor 8:7; 12:27; cf. Acts 18:6). The Latin names suggest that a number of congregants may be influenced by Roman culture with perhaps a few to several possibly belonging to the upper echelons of society, such as Gaius who houses a church. Among the Greek names, Phoebe, Stephanas, Crispus, and possibly Sosthenes and Erastus might have some prominent social standing.[42] Erastus served in a civic administrative capacity as *oikonomos* for the city (Rom 16:23; see 1 Cor 4:1). It is very questionable, however, that this is the same Erastus named from the famous Corinthian inscription who was an aedile in Corinth.[43] Regarding this congregation, Gerd Theissen's observation is still quite plausible from 1:26–29. When Paul writes that "not many" of the Corinthians were wise, powerful, and noble born, this implies that *some* of them were.[44] I regard this congregation as quite diverse and having many members from the lower classes, but a minority are well-to-do. This minority are those who can afford to purchase meat routinely at the *macellum* (10:25), be invited to dinners (10:27), and "have" better food at the Lord's Supper (11:17–34).[45] As a church they are better off financially than the Macedonian congregations, which in turn are better off than the poor in Jerusalem for whom they contribute money (16:1–4; 2 Cor 8:1–5).

41. McRay 2000:230.

42. See Theissen 1982:69–119; Meeks 1982:56–60, 215–17. Contrast Meggitt 1998:50–59 (cf. 2001:85–94), who argues the church was in abject poverty. Friesen 2005:351–70 (cf. 2004:323–61) has the Corinthian congregation at "level six," at or around bare subsistence level and one step away from the lowest poverty. See responses in Theissen 2001:65–84; Theissen 2003:371–91; Thiselton 2000:23–29; Martin 2001:51–64; Barclay 2004:363–66; Mihaila 2009:94–109. Recently, Sanders 2014:103–125, moderately suggests a "middling" population of 20 percent, half of which live several times above subsistence and the other half at or near subsistence. Horrell 2004:367, is similar.

43. On the inscription, see Kent 1966:99–100. Friesen 2010:231–256, argues that οἰκονόμος involves a slave's role and neither refers to the Latin *quaestor* nor the *aedile*. (Differently, Goodrich argues for the *quaestor* position: "the civic treasury magistrate": 2012:199; cf. 62–65). It is not clear that this inscription was made at the time of the biblical Erastus, and the full inscription may have possessed a different name prior to its fragmentation: [Ep]erastus. See also Meggitt 1996:218–23.

44. Theissen 1982:72.

45. Meat from the *popinae*, which the poor may afford, is not the same meat (see Theissen 2003:82–85).

Introduction

OCCASION AND PURPOSE OF THE LETTER

Paul learns through a report and letter that there are divisions among Corinthian congregation members over their self-identified allegiances with certain leaders—Paul and Apollos primarily—and the solidarity of members is being threatened by their assimilation with outsiders through sexual misconduct, idol meats, and other issues.[46] Other divisions and conflicts center on their spiritual activities, worship, the Lord's Supper, legal disputes, and disputes over the future resurrection. Paul's challenge is to respond to the plurality of these voices.[47] A number of factors may contribute to their factions, not the least of which is that the members are relatively new converts. Paul started the church only a few years earlier, and his departure left them without their founding leader, though others like Apollos temporarily stood in to fill that vacuum (cf. Acts 18:27—19:1). Their misperceptions about wisdom, speeches, freedom in Christ, use of spiritual gifts, and life after death are clearly evident (1 Cor 1:17; 6:12-13; 8:1-2, 8-9; 14:26; 15:12), and public speaking, human wisdom, and boasting stand over against the preaching of the cross, spiritual wisdom, and humility in this letter. This suggests that at least part of the conflict stems from external social and ideological influences on the congregation. I posit that members still esteem status symbols associated with social prestige and wise and eloquent speech.[48] The influences of sophism and Roman elitism affect the congregation (see esp. 1:17—2:12).[49]

Most scholars today hold that 1 Corinthians was originally one letter rather than a compilation of letters.[50] Margaret Mitchell's arrangement based on deliberative rhetoric convincingly supports the letter's integrity and rightly argues that the primary aim of this letter is to address factional behavior in the congregation and to encourage unity.[51] We notice that the central appeal (παρακαλῶ) for solidarity in 1:10 seems linked with an appeal for imitation in 4:16, which in turn connects with the charge for imitation in 11:1. Together these link up with other topics and correspondence questions

---

46. There is no evidence for itinerate opponents infiltrating the congregation at this time (see Oropeza 2012a:66–71).

47. Language adopted from Crocker 2004:118–19.

48. On ancient persona, see Aristotle *Rhet.* 1.5.5; Nguyen 2008a:146–47.

49. See Roman influence on Corinth and further sophist flaws in Winter 2001, esp. xi, 1–28; Winter 2002. I consider the term elitist not in a restricted sense of royalty, senatorial offices, and the super wealthy, but inclusive of the lower upper class: see Dutch 2005:45–46.

50. For compilation views, see recently, Welborn 2013:205–42; Jacon 2006; and discussions in Schnelle 1998:62–65, 73–74; Schnabel 2006:39–42.

51. Mitchell 1991. On rhetorical species and arrangements, see Kennedy 1984:15–25.

Introduction

to which Paul responds in 1:11; 5:1; 7:1; 8:1; 12:1; 15:12; 16:1; and 16:12. In terms of rhetorical arrangement, the supporting proofs of the *prothesis* in 1:10 include 1:18—4:21; 5:1—7:40; 8:1—11:1; 12:1—14:40; 15:1-58; and 16:1-12. The reader may wish to consult these sections for further understanding, and see the complete outline above. Paul, at any rate, is dealing with a unique set of problems in Corinth, and he must respond to specific issues. He is more concerned about the congregation's moral and spiritual state than orchestrating a one-tracked, perfect piece of rhetoric on bodily solidarity. Our apostle is foremost a minister of the gospel who, to be sure, attempts to persuade his recipients to accept and enact on his words, but at the same time he trusts ultimately in the Spirit of God for the power, wisdom, and guidance necessary to lead his recipients to that acceptance.

Introduction (1:1–9)

Paul's letters generally follow the opening conventions of ancient epistles, and this letter is no exception. Its prescript identifies the sender and recipients, and gives a greeting to those recipients (1:1–3). His thanksgiving in 1:4 begins the letter's proem, a rhetorical convention that includes introductory matters attempting to gain the auditors' goodwill, attention, and receptivity (1:1–9).[1] With this letter strategy intact, they might be receptive to the apostle's corollary teachings and exhortations.

Letter Prescript (1:1–3)

Paul introduces himself as one who is **called to be an apostle**. He is sent out as a travelling envoy and witness of the risen savior to proclaim this good news about him to Gentile nations. His calling to this vocation is dependable because it was not given through self-appointment but **through the will of God** (Gal 1:15—2:10; Acts 22:3–21). Paul stresses his apostleship in order to buttress his authority before the recipients.[2] He must gain their respect if he is to succeed in challenging them to abandon wrong behaviors and ideologies. At the same time his calling also displays power in weakness related to the cross (1 Cor 1:21; 4:9-13).[3] His authority is thus rooted in Christ-like service, suffering, and humility rather than in arrogance or attempts to rule over the congregation. **Sosthenes** is the co-sender and probable coauthor.[4] He may be the same synagogue leader who originally opposed Paul during his first visit to Corinth (Acts 18:17). But if so, it is strange that Acts fails to mention this synagogue leader's conversion. Sosthenes is not necessarily a unique name for that time, and so we cannot be sure this is the same person

---

1. See Aristotle *Rhet.* 3.14.1; Kennedy 1984:23–24.
2. e.g., 2 Cor 1:1; Gal 1:1; Weiss 1910:2.
3. See Thiselton 2000:66–67.
4. If Sosthenes is Paul's amanuensis, this would be unusual because secretaries are frequently anonymous and do not appear as coauthors (see Richards 2004:105). The secretary's mention in Rom 16:22 appears at the end (not beginning) of that letter.

Introduction (1:1–9)

from Acts.[5] What we do know is that he is a fellow believer in Christ—he is called a **brother** and is one of Paul's coworkers.

Paul identifies the Corinthian recipients as the **church** (ἐκκλησία), a term normally referring to political assemblies but here addressing the gathering of those who belong to God and Christ. Christ's earliest followers probably thought themselves to be the prophetic fulfillment of the last days community mentioned in Joel 2:16 (LXX).[6] They were experiencing the salvation and spiritual life anticipated in this prophetic discourse. Paul stresses this community's holiness as **sanctified** and **called to be saints**. Again, it seems that Joel 2:16 helped formulate early Christian self-references as saints, literally "holy ones." This verse shows that the end-time ἐκκλησία is to be holy. The apostles promoted the notion that Christ-followers are an end-time, holy assembly belonging to God.[7] To be sanctified or made holy has a cultic sense of being dedicated to the service of God and set apart from secular and profane things (Lev 19:1–8).[8] For Paul, ethical piety is also bound up with holiness (6:9–11; 2 Cor 7:1; 1 Thess 4:1–3). Relevant for the Corinthians is the implication that as saints their lifestyle should be consistent with their holy calling. They are an end-time assembly whom God has set apart to belong to God's people.

As with all churches in Christ this one consists of those who receive God's Spirit and **call on the name of the Lord** to be saved (Joel 2:28–32[3:1–5 LXX]; cf. Rom 10:9–13; Acts 2:17–22).[9] The apostles interpreted Joel's Lord to be Jesus Christ, and to call on his name imagines foremost an invocation at baptism in which the convert calls on Jesus for salvation, or confesses him as Lord, or both (Acts 9:14; 22:16). This identifies the person as belonging to and following Christ; it is what Acts seems to equate with being baptized in the name of Jesus (2:38; 10:48). To rely on this name, as Anthony Thiselton affirms, is *"to commit oneself in trust to the one whose nature and character have been disclosed as worthy of this trust."*[10] Christ's lordship, incidentally, may be compared with Caesar's. Those who confess Jesus as Lord become an alternative society in the world in contrast to the

---

5. So Schrage 1991:1.100.

6. See Oropeza 2016:53–55.

7. On saints as God's people in apocalyptic literature, see: Dan 7:21; 1 *En.* 62:8; 1QM 3.5; 1QSb 1.5; further, Schrage 1991:1.103–4. For non-apocalyptic references, see Lev 11:44–45; Exod 12:16LXX; Zeller 2010:73.

8. Cf. Fitzmyer 2008:122.

9. LXX uses κύριος ("Lord") for the Hebrew יהוה (YHWH). On Christ's deity in this regard, see Tilling 2012.

10. Thiselton 2000:79.

Introduction (1:1–9)

imperial society that dominates it.¹¹ This confession happens **in every place**, which may be alluding to a prophetic realization that the Lord God's name is worshipped by the Gentiles "in every place" (Mal 1:11).¹² The Corinthians are prompted to recognize a pan-Mediterranean horizon of Christ followers extending beyond their local church to churches in every nation.¹³ Their recognition of this may help deflate arrogance and self-centered ideas that they are not accountable to anyone (see 14:36).¹⁴

The letter's greeting is in the form of a benediction: **grace and peace to you**. This formula is uniquely Christian and possibly originates with Paul.¹⁵ He consistently uses it as an opening trademark in his letters (e.g., Rom 1:7; Gal 1:3; Phil 1:2). It goes beyond the letter conventions of typical Jewish and Hellenistic writers by invoking *shalom* and favor not only from the one Creator, God the Father, but also from the Lord Jesus Christ.

Thanksgiving Period (1:4–9)

After writing the prescript our apostle expresses gratitude by stating, **I thank my God always for you**. He typically includes a thanksgiving paragraph after his letter openings, though Galatians and 2 Corinthians are notable exceptions, and both these letters happen to be his most confrontational.¹⁶ Paul's thanksgivings feature five elements—the giving of thanks, mention of the person thanked (God), an adverbial "always," mention of the recipients, and reason for giving thanks, which is then unpacked.¹⁷ Paul is thankful that the congregation members have been **made rich in Christ, in all speech and all knowledge**. He possibly knew that the origin of the formulaic phrase "speech and knowledge" arose from clashes between philosophers and sophists.¹⁸ What Paul stresses here is that speech and knowledge is God

---

11. Cf. Horsley 1997:244–45.

12. Ciampa/Rosner 2010:57–58. Here again Paul interprets κύριος/*YHWH* as Jesus.

13. See further Hvalvik 2005:123–43.

14. Cf. Hays 1997:17.

15. See discussions in Doering 2012:407–15; Lieu 1985:168–69. I suggest that Paul originally adopted "greetings and peace" from the style of certain Jewish-Hellenistic letters (e.g., 2 Macc 1:1) but replaced "greetings" (χαίρειν) with "grace" (χάρις) since the latter reflected better the content of his messages.

16. Among disputed letters Titus also contains no introductory thanksgiving. In papyri letters the sender's thanks can be situational, motivated by good news of the recipients' welfare: cf. Arzt-Grabner 2010:149.

17. Fee 1987:36. We find similar thanksgivings to deities in other ancient letters (P. Mich. 8.473.29; 2 Macc 1:10–11), but their presence may be more the exception than rule if Van Voorst 2010:163–65 is correct.

18. See Betz 1986: 33; cf. 30–32. The combination of these words is likewise found

given, and doubtless the content of these terms includes prophecy, tongues, teachings, discernment, and revelations experienced by the Corinthians (cf. 12:8; 13:1–2; 14:26). His recipients are thus presented with a better way of perceiving the value of their spiritual gifts—these gifts come from God, and this should prompt them to praise their Divine Benefactor instead of human agents. The use of *all, any, always,* and *everything* in these verses highlights the total and abundant way they have been enriched by God who works favorably through them.

They have also received the benefit of salvation due to God calling Paul and sending him to proclaim the gospel, **the testimony concerning Christ** (cf. 1:18; 15:1–4). That message was **confirmed** as effectual among them by their acceptance of it, conversion, and spiritual gifts in which they now operate. They receive saving grace as a result of the accomplishments of Christ's death and resurrection, and they are being transformed through their continued fellowship in Christ. The designations of Son, Lord, Christ, Jesus, or "in him" appear in every verse of 1:1–10, which suggests for Dennis Stamps that "a christological premise is an essential part of Christian rhetoric, particularly as it is practiced by Paul."[19]

Their relationship in Christ will culminate with Christ confirming them to be **blameless** on **the day of the Lord**.[20] That day signifies a time in the prophetic calendar when God will deliver the faithful and judge the wicked (Isa 13:6–9; Amos 5:18; Joel 2:1, 31; Obad 15). It marks for Paul the second coming of Jesus and judgment day, when all humans must give account of their deeds (1:7b–8; 3:13; 4:4b–5; 5:5; cf. 2 Cor 5:10). The image envisioned here is one in which Jesus sits on the tribunal and declares the Corinthians innocent of anything worthy of eternal punishment. At that time the sanctification to which they had been called as saints finds its full realization.

Paul's thanksgiving ends by stressing that **God is faithful**, which recalls divine fidelity in relation to the covenant people (Deut 7:9; 32:4).[21] With this background in view the phrase implies praise and thanks to God who can be relied on to bless, protect, deliver, and maintain agreements with His own people. God **called** them **into fellowship with His son Jesus**

---

in wisdom traditions (Prov 22:21; Sir 21:18).

19. Stamps 2002:457

20. To be blameless (ἀνέγκλητος) here means to be without liability; it "belongs to the semantic domain of *accusation and declarative verdict*": Thiselton 2000:102. See similarly 1 Thess 3:13; 5:23; Col 1:22.

21. This declaration may function as a surrogate for Jewish "blessed be God" prayers (*beraka*), such as in the *Shemoneh 'Esreh* prayer. See Sanders 1962:358–59; Ciampa/Rosner 2010:67.

Introduction (1:1-9)

Christ, which not only reflects their being set apart as a holy people but also their becoming partners with Christ, the one who died for them and now shares a dynamic relationship with them. They can be assured that God is faithful to the saints and will bring to pass the anticipated second coming of Christ and final salvation pertaining to it.

Minus Paul's attempt to win the goodwill of his recipients in this section, I suspect the apostle would qualify more explicitly that the congregation's blamelessness on judgment day is contingent on its members persevering in faith (see Col 1:22–23). It will become clear in the remainder of this letter that the opening verses provide no guarantee that every individual who once had faith will necessarily receive final salvation, let alone be declared blameless, at the second coming if he or she abandons that faith or lives an unrepentant and immoral lifestyle that desecrates one's confession.[22] Final salvation will be the inevitable outcome for those who are "in Christ" (1:2, 4; cf. v. 9), that is, those who belong to and *remain* in the corporate body of Christ, maintaining spiritual fellowship with him. As we will notice in this letter, among the destructive vices threatening the Corinthians' new identity are divisions, idolatry, and fornication. They are also influenced by the ideology of Roman elitism and civic identity, which are set in opposition to the message of the cross.[23] It will turn out that Paul's commendation of God working through the Corinthians with regard to their knowledge, speech, charismatic gifts, and prospective final salvation sets him up to exhort and correct them on these very issues later on in the letter.

---

22. See Oropeza 2012a; 2012b:234–48.

23. On the problems of vices, see Oropeza 2007; 2012a; on ideology, Tucker 2011a; 2011b; Winter 2001.

Appeal to Be United and Avoid Discord: *Prothesis* and Statement of Facts (1:10–17)

After the letter's introduction Paul jumps straight into his primary concern and purpose for writing to the Corinthians—he appeals that members live in unity with one another and end their internal divisions (1:10). This is the letter's *prothesis*, which sets forth what the communicator intends to prove; it functions as the statement of purpose for the entire discourse (see also Introduction).[1] The appeal in 1:10 also suggests the letter body is deliberative in terms of rhetorical species.[2] Corporate unity and factions is language relevant to the political sphere, and our apostle primarily attempts to persuade the congregation to take a futuristic course of action in favor of solidarity.

The theme of bodily unity and discord is clearly prominent in various passages, but sometimes it is more implicit in others. After the *prothesis*, a brief statement of facts or *narratio* then follows in which Paul mentions that he learned of the factions from Chloe's people, and he addresses their divisions over apostolic leaders (1:11–17).[3] Repetition (*anaphora*) of the phrase "I am of . . . " followed by a string of ironic rhetorical questions elicit pathos. We find here a passionate apostle reasoning with this congregation against their divisive behavior. This section is followed up by supporting proofs of the *prothesis* starting in 1:18. The divisive allegiances named in 1:12 are repeated in chapter 3, providing a subtle structural message:

A Allegiances Divide the Body of Christ (1:10–17)

   B The Cross of Christ and Spiritual Wisdom Mend Divisions (1:18—2:17)

A^1 Allegiances Divide the Temple of God (3:1—4:5)

---

1. Aristotle distinguishes between the "statement of the case" (πρόθεσις) and the proof for it (*Rhet.* 3.13.1–2). The Latin *propositio* is the equivalent (Witherington 1995:94).

2. See Inkelaar 2011:77–80, 143; Mitchell 1991:198–99; cf. 20–64, 68–111.

3. On *narratio/diēgēsis*, see e.g., Quintilian *Inst.* 4.2.1–3, 31; Cicero *Inv.* 1.19.27–30; Kennedy 1984:24.

Prothesis and Statement of Facts (1:10–17)

Paul then discloses how he has presented himself as a paradigm to imitate in order to end these allegiances (4:6–21).

APPEAL TO UNITY (1:10)

The exhortative, **I appeal to you**, forms an *inclusio* with 4:16, which suggests that the first four chapters function as a unit with this same theme.[4] When the apostle makes strong urges he often addresses recipients as **brothers and sisters** (1:10; 16:15; Rom 12:1; 1 Thess 4:10; 5:14). This designation often identifies the beginning of a new topic or pericope in this letter (2:1; 3:1; 4:6; 10:1; 12:1; 14:6; 15:1). Such familial language exhibits Paul's solidarity with them so as to make what he insists on more attractive.[5] It likewise evokes pathos; the recipients get the impression that family members are to be affectionate with one another, and to live in agreement.[6] Although familial language is informal and compatible with private letters, Paul's appeal **by the name of our Lord Jesus Christ** gives the letter a formal ring found in public and official letters.[7] Paul speaks as Christ's representative, as though Christ himself were present and making the appeal.[8] The letter, then, portrays Paul with the blended imagery of a family member and political delegate, and his message is both affectionate yet authoritative.

He challenges them to strive for agreement by speaking **the same thing** regarding the issues he will address. They are to **be restored** to a condition they originally had when united in the **same mindset and opinion**.[9] His appeal invites them to recall their solidarity as one body in Christ after their conversion, a thought that naturally leads to a discussion about baptism in 1:13–17. At the same time, this exhortation aims to prohibit **schisms** from continuing among them. The idea of unity in the face of schism finds special relevance in the type of strife and quarreling typical of rhetorical students competing against one another (see on 1:17; 3:1–3). It is also found in po-

---

4. The appeal, παρακαλῶ, commonly appears in deliberative rhetoric, whether in oratory or epistolary form (e.g., Isocrates *Or.* 5.13.114; *Ep.* 1.5; Demosthenes *Ep.* 1.10; Mitchell 1991:44).

5. See Trebilco 2012:26.

6. Cf. Plutarch *Frat. amor.* 2.1[478D–479B]; Collins 1999:71.

7. Likewise, παρακαλῶ is found both in official (Schnabel 2006:85) and private letters (Arzt-Grabner et al. 2006:58).

8. Cf. Steyn 1996:484.

9. To be restored (κατηρτισμένοι; see LSJ 910) is variously rendered "be made complete" (NASB), "be perfectly joined together" (AV), "be refurbished" (Garland 2003:40). The idea of restoration, of fixing what is broken, dislocated, or torn (σχίσμα can refer to a rift or tear) best fits the idea of a fragmented corporate body.

litical debates.¹⁰ The oratory and political realms frequently overlapped one another, especially when sophists participated in city assemblies and could be sent on embassies before magistrates. Often, their success in political circles caused them to be puffed up and provoked caricatures of them as windbags.¹¹ Our apostle's language imagines a situation in which the strife in Corinth includes comparisons related to persona and quarrels over the oratory skills of their Christian leaders.¹²

DIVISIVE ALLIANCES AND BAPTISM (1:11–17)

The reason Paul exhorts them is because **it has been reported to me concerning you, my brothers and sisters, by those of Chloe, that there are discords among you.** Chloe is presumably a member of the Corinthian congregation who is an independent woman of high status, the *mater familias* or head of her own household. Those associated with her probably belong to her household, whether family members, slaves, or former slaves.¹³ They appear to be carriers of the Corinthians' letter to Paul (see 7:1).¹⁴ They either told him about divisions that were not mentioned in the letter, or more likely, he received this news from the letter (and perhaps their elaboration of it) that they read to him. In ancient papyri letters the passive reporting used here normally refers to written rather than oral information.¹⁵

In 1:11 the word for discord (ἔρις) Philo uses to describe sophist rivalries (*Mut.* 10; *Her.* 246).¹⁶ *Eris* is also the name of the goddess of discord. In Greek mythology she creates a golden apple with the inscription, "For the fairest," and presents it as a gift at a wedding feast. Hera, Athena, and Aphrodite, goddesses at the feast, quarrel over which one of them should have the apple. Zeus instructs them to ask the noble-bred Paris of Troy to decide which goddess is the fairest, and he chooses Aphrodite who had bribed him with the promise of giving him beautiful Helen, wife of Menelaus the My-

---

10. e.g., Polybius *Hist.* 5.104.1; Josephus *A.J.* 12.283; further, Malcolm 2013b:8–9; Welborn 1987b:85–107.

11. See Winter 2001:32, 38; Thiselton 2000:117.

12. See Introduction; Excursus at 2:1–5.

13. Other options include that they are business agents of Chloe (possibly a non-Christian from Ephesus: Fee 1987:54) or a woman's group opposed to hierarchical structures of the factional groups (Schottroff 2012:720–21).

14. On slaves as couriers, see Richards 2004:181. On Stephanas as the courier *back* to Corinth, see 16:17.

15. See ἐδηλώθη and examples in Arzt-Grabner et al. 2006:59–64.

16. See further, Winter 2001:38–39.

Prothesis and Statement of Facts (1:10–17)

cenaean.[17] When Paris abducts Helen, this ignites the entire tragedy of the Trojan War. As anyone in the ancient Mediterranean informed by this story would know, the potential damage that discord might initiate is virtually immeasurable! *Eris* now threatened the church in Corinth.[18]

Rivalry in this congregation centers on members claiming **I am of Paul**, and others, **I am of Apollos**, and still others, **I am of Cephas**.[19] Various attempts have been made to identify these groups.[20] Some important observations we suggest are as follows. First, except perhaps for the last claim, **I am of Christ**, these allegiances do not appear to be Paul's invention of Corinthian divisions.[21] He repeats the first two claims in 3:4 and the first three in 3:22. Had Paul invented these, his repetition would only serve to irritate the Corinthians who knew their own state of affairs better than Paul. They would doubtless contest his repeated claims of these alliances if they were not true. Second, there is no clear evidence that Paul, Apollos, or Cephas instigated or encouraged these allegiances. The Corinthians probably instigated this rivalry themselves, which stems from their lack of maturity as well as worldly influences. Third, this problem does not seem to involve well-established parties who have drawn their lines in the sand over distinctive theological positions.[22] The congregation members are being vocal about their preferences for one leader over the other, which as chapters 1–4 unfold, has more to do with prestige, persona, and oratory skills than the doctrines these leaders teach.

Why wouldn't Paul commend members who respected his apostolic authority when claiming, **I am of Paul**? Context reflects that they or their rivals or both expressed their loyalty with strife and derision against other members who did not share their sentiment. They may have quarreled with those who affirmed, **I am of Apollos**. The two groups apparently argued over who was the better minister (3:4–9; 4:1–6). If Acts 18:24—19:1 correctly portrays Apollos as an eloquent and forceful speaker, his supporters

---

17. Stasinus *Cypria*; Lucian *Dial.d.* 20; Mulroy 2012:80–82.

18. On ἔρις in vice lists, see 2 Cor 12:20; Gal 5:20; Rom 1:29; 13:13; 1 *Clem.* 35.5; 3 *Bar.* 8.5.

19. The genitive of relationship in Greek is used in 1:12: "I [am] of," or more freely, "I belong to" (3:22–23).

20. See surveys in Adams/Horrell 2004:13–26; Sumney 1999:34–78; Merklein 1992:1.134-52; Hurd 1965:75–142.

21. If the four slogans are caricatures of Corinthian allegiances (so Mitchell 1991:83–86), the first three seem real regardless of the precise words congregants might have used.

22. Rightly, Strüder 2003:431–55. Similarly, Clarke 1993:92–93.

Prothesis and Statement of Facts (1:10–17)

in Corinth likely argued that he was the better orator.[23] Paul does not appear to have any problem with Apollos' eloquent style; his problem is with Corinthian evaluations of that style in competition with other styles, such as his own. Comparisons of this sort provoke strife, arrogance, and encourage status seeking, as explicated in chapters 1–4. Paul challenges them instead with the radically different perspective that apostolic proclamations are centered on weakness and humility characterizing Christ's crucifixion, and they operate with Spirit-endowed wisdom (1:18—2:16).

Paul repeats the third claim **I am of Cephas** (Peter) again in 3:22,[24] which steers us away from accepting the allegiance as purely invention. If a faction relates to this leader it probably did not consist of many members; otherwise, we might expect Paul to discuss Peter as much as he does Apollos in later chapters (cf. 4:6). We can safely rule out the antiquated view that the apostles from Jerusalem or proselytizers in the name of Peter stirred up this contention in Corinth.[25] Earlier discords that Paul experienced in Jerusalem and Antioch with the circumcision party and Peter (Gal 2:1–15) are not problems in Corinth. If he were still in contention with Peter, we could surmise that Paul would not have mentioned him favorably in 9:5 and 15:5. A small minority of Corinthians may have regarded Peter's apostleship to be more authoritative than Paul's because Peter knew the pre-Easter Jesus personally and led the original witnesses (e.g., Acts 1–2). Perhaps he recently visited Corinth with his wife and left a positive impression (9:4–5).[26]

Unlike the other claims, **I am of Christ** is not repeated again. Is Paul referring to maverick members who reject all human leaders and listen only to Christ, whether by adhering only to Jesus's oral teachings or listening to his words allegedly through visions, prophecy, or some other charismatic experience? This is possible, but given that Paul ultimately supports this allegiance by affirming that the Corinthians belong to Christ (3:23; 6:15, 20), it may be better to suggest that this particular claim is Paul's own invention.[27] If so, this is an ironic twist that ends the string of claims by redirecting Corinthian thought to the perspective that all of them belong to Christ. This naturally

---

23. On Apollos's eloquence, see Pogoloff 1992:181–83; Winter 2002:178. More speculatively, Welborn 2011:403–10, suggests that Apollos accepted financial support in Corinth, and Gaius was his patron.

24. "Peter" (Greek *Petros*), the name Jesus gave Simon (Matt 16:17–18), is equivalent to the Aramaic *Kepha*' according to Fitzmyer 2008:143.

25. Revived recently by Goulder 2002. Against this view of the opponents in 2 Cor 3, see Oropeza 2016:232–38.

26. See Barrett 1982:28–39.

27. Prothro 2014:250–65, argues from the grammatical sequence "μέν ... δὲ ... δὲ ..." in 1:12 that a break in the fourth claim, "I am of Christ" cannot be ruled out.

leads to the rhetorical question **Is Christ divided?** The picture presented here invites the congregation to view its members in solidarity as one corporate body in Christ. Contrariwise their divisions evoke an image of Christ's body being dismembered. The feet no longer claim to be part of the same body with the hands. The ears no longer claim to be part of the same body with the eyes. Christ's limbs are being split apart.[28] The rhetorical force of this question thus prompts the response, "No, Christ is not split up!"

The subsequent questions and context of 1:13–17 recall the Corinthians' conversion (1:2) and present the ironic image of Paul being crucified for them and they being baptized into his name. These questions expect the reply, "No, it was Jesus, not Paul, who was crucified for us and we are baptized in Jesus's name!" Our apostle plays down the importance of his own role by claiming that **I baptized none of you except Crispus and Gaius** and **the household of Stephanas** (Acts 18:8; Rom 16:23; 1 Cor 16:17).[29] The households of Crispus and Gaius may be included though not mentioned.[30] Paul's trivialization may suggest that members thought themselves superior to others based on the prominence of the minister who had baptized them.[31] Perhaps in their new faith they still assumed from mystery religions that ceremonies of initiation created a special bond between the initiator and the one initiated.[32] Prior to their conversion some of them may have participated in such cults (cf. 12:2). The result in any case spelled tragedy—one of the very things that united unrelated Jews and Gentiles into one body as siblings in Christ had become a rallying point for divisions (1 Cor 12:13; Gal 3:27–28). This problem prompts Paul to make the unusual assertion that **Christ sent me not to baptize but to proclaim the gospel** about Christ crucified. Exactly who he baptizes is unimportant, for Paul is called to proclaim the gospel rather than perform baptisms (9:16; 15:1; Gal 1:15–16; Rom 15:20).[33] This sense of priorities is important for the Corinthians to know because they have a "tendency to magnify the messengers and miss the message."[34]

---

28. Conversely, see 12:14–17. The passive μερίζω in 1:13 suggests being "split up": see LSJ 1103.

29. Nash 2009:18, provides a convenient list of Corinthian members.

30. Cf. Acts 18:8; Pascuzzi 2009:823–24.

31. Another option is that the perpetrators of this division gave "special authority" to baptize only to certain leaders but not others: cf. Schottroff 2012:720–21.

32. See Chester 2003:290, 303.

33. "For" in 1:17 refers to 1:16b and explains "that is not my calling—nor my point" (Fee 1987:63).

34. Hays 1997:24.

Prothesis and Statement of Facts (1:10-17)

Even the very message of the gospel Paul must qualify so that it, too, does not become a pawn of these divisions through preferences over which minister proclaims it. The gospel he preaches is **not with clever wisdom of speech, lest the cross of Christ be** rendered ineffectual.[35] The "wisdom of speech" expressed in 1:17, when compared with 2:1-5 that also generally combines σοφία ("wisdom") with λόγος ("speech"), provides us with a strong clue that Paul is referring primarily to speeches associated with sophist rhetoricians. Though at times wisdom distinguishes philosophers from sophists (Plato, *Gorgias*; Plutarch, *De laude* 12 [543E-F]), it was also understood in relation to those possessing practical expertise, cleverness, and rhetorical skill.[36] Wisdom found special relevance in the rhetorical traditions of Greeks and Romans.[37] Eloquence and wisdom were in fact closely aligned as the rhetorical handbooks confirm; the former, for example, Cicero perceives as "nothing else but wisdom delivering copious utterance" (*Part. or.* 23.XXIII.79).[38] Paul speaks against a type of rhetoric similar to the sophists, which the Corinthians seem to hold in high esteem. Such speaking for Paul should never become the ground for disrupting fellowship, and it must not be permitted to eclipse the message of the cross that saves, transforms, and empowers lives.

---

35. In 1 Cor 1-3 the nuance of σοφία ("wisdom") varies depending on verse: cf. Mihaila 2009:92-93; Barrett 1968:67-68. Here the shade of cleverness/eloquence is apparent; at times philosophy may be more evident as Keener 2016:176, suggests. See options in Kammler 2003:28.

36. Cf. Pogoloff 1992:111-12; Litfin 1994:192; Vos 1996:93-94.

37. Cf. Litfin 189.

38. See also Quintilian *Inst.* 12.2.6; Cicero *Inv.* 1.1; cf. Dio Chrysostom *Or.* 47.1.

Wisdom and Leadership in Light of the Proclamation of the Cross: First Supporting Proof (1:18—4:21)

The first supporting proof of the appeal for unity centers on the proclamation of the cross among Jews and Gentiles (1:18-31).[1] Paul then applies the content of this message to his own persona and preaching in relation to spiritual wisdom (2:1-16), and subsequently to Apollos and himself as ministers (3:1—4:5). After this he makes another appeal, this time for his recipients to imitate him (4:6-16), and he warns them to be prepared for his upcoming visit (4:17-21). These passages reveal that apart from competitive allegiances, the congregation is plagued by quarreling, misperceptions about wisdom and speech, and boasting related to status.

WISDOM AND FOOLISHNESS OF THE CROSS (1:18-31)

The type of eloquence that our apostle discourages from becoming preeminent in the congregation does not prevent him from exhibiting his own stylistic features throughout the rest of this chapter, including rhetorical questions (1:20), chiasm (1:22-23), irony (1:21, 25, 27-28), anaphora or stressed repetition ("not many ... not many ... ": 1:26), and antitheses: perishing/being saved (1:18), foolishness/power (1:18), foolish/wise (1:21-25, 27), wisdom of God/wisdom of the world (1:20-21), weakness/strength (1:25, 27), noble/lowly (1:26, 28), and things that are/things that are not (1:28).[2]

The **message of the cross** refers to the apostolic proclamation about Christ crucified. This message elicits antithetical responses that interact with wisdom and prophetic-apocalyptic discourses. **Those who are being saved** believe in the message of the cross, and for them it provides a channel for God's power to save and transform their lives as well as endow them

---

1. See the Outline for other proofs. On their function (*pisits/probatio/confirmatio*), see Aristotle *Rhet.* 3.13.1-2; *Rhet. Her.* 1.3.4; 3.4.8; Quintilian *Inst* 3.9.1-6; Mitchell 1991:202-7.

2. Fitzmyer 2008:66-67, provides a convenient list of devices in this letter.

First Supporting Proof (1:18—4:21)

with true spiritual wisdom. **Those who are perishing** think the message of the cross is foolishness. They, too, have wisdom and power, but it is related to rhetorical eloquence and the authority of Caesar (2:4–5, 8).[3] They belong to the corrupted world and current age that found its inception through the fall of Adam and the old creation, which characterizes sin and death, belongs to Satan, and will ultimately meet its destruction in the age to come (1:20–21a; cf. 5:5; 15:21–28; Rom 5:12–20). The Christ event marks the inception of the new creation and salvific era invading the present world. Its participants will experience the full realization of this salvation in the age to come (Gal 1:4; 2 Cor 5:17; 6:2). The present tense of salvation and destruction in 1:18, then, implies that both are currently in the process of their respective states; their full realization does not take place until Christ returns. Before that day arrives, the present state of the perishing ones could be changed for the better if they start believing the message of the cross. Conversely, those who believe must continue believing if they are to experience final salvation on that day.

This antithetical pairing of destruction and salvific life perhaps imagines a triumphal procession similar to 2 Cor 2:14–16, where Paul classifies again two types of people using this similar terminology.[4] The Corinthians, highly influenced by Roman culture, no doubt had heard of such processions in Rome, and knew of these events via depictions in art, inscriptions, and literature.[5] A victory celebration of this sort for Romans included the victors of war entering and parading through their city on horses and chariots complete with an entourage of statues, paintings, gold, silver, and other booty, animals to be sacrificed, incense bearers, and of course, prisoners of war who were often executed at the end of the spectacle (cf. Plutarch *Aem.* 32.3–34.4).[6] In this light, Christ's death might be imagined in different ways depending on the viewer. For those who are perishing, he resembles a weak, Jewish rebel being crucified or, if in a triumphal procession is in view, bound as a prisoner of war at the feet of the Roman emblem, the *tropaion*.[7]

---

3. cf. Arzt-Grabner et al. 2006:85. Differently, Smit parallels Apollos' name (Ἀπολλῶς) with the concept of perishing (ἀπόλλυμι) to connect the perishing ones with Apollos's followers (2002:243–44). The Corinthian congregants, however, indiscriminately belong to those who are called, believe, and are being saved, and this doubtless includes the Apollos group—they all belong to Christ (3:22–23; cf. 1:2).

4. In this text, however, God does the triumphal leading "in Christ" and Christ may be imagined as the triumphant general.

5. For examples see Beard 2007; Perkins 2012:68.

6. For further, Livy *Hist. Rom.* 45.38–40; Josephus *Bell.* 7.5.4–6; Aus, 2005:3–4; Versnel 1970:56–57.

7. The *tropaion* originally marked the turning point of a war when the enemy was routed. It was placed at the location on the battlefield where this reversal of fortune

First Supporting Proof (1:18—4:21)

This symbol of triumph was made from wood, shaped like a cross, and bore the armor of the defeated foes. Whether through bearing his own cross or being tied to the *tropaion*, he is paraded through the city streets on his way to be executed. We could surmise that for Paul Christ's death represents the turning point of human history. Rome's displays of power eventually give way to the more powerful images of resurrection and the defeat of death. At the end of the metaphorical procession depicting the age of now and not yet, such worldly powers will be shamed and destroyed (1:19, 27–28; 2:6). And those deemed foolish by the world's standards, who identified with Christ and his cruciform sufferings, will be vindicated.[8] The cross in 1:18 will result in the triumph of resurrection in 15:57.

The apostle cites Isa 29:14 in anticipation of this victory—God will **destroy the wisdom of the wise and thwart the cleverness of the clever**.[9] In Isaiah, Israel's leaders are confronted for depending on human wisdom and Egyptian advisors instead of consulting God, the divine counselor (Isa 19:11–13; cf. 30:1–7; 31:1). Failing to seek their Lord, they become spiritually blind, and face impending judgment (29:1–12, 14), and a reverse ordering will occur in which the humble will be joyous and lifted up, but the proud will be humbled (29:18–19; cf. 27:1; 29:1–8).[10] Consequently, God will turn the counsel they receive into foolishness (19:3, 11–14). Paul's rhetorical questions in 1:20 continue to be informed by Isaiah: **Where is the wise?** recalls the elitist counselors of Isa 19:12. **Where is the clerical magistrate?** echoes 33:18b.[11] However, the third question, **Where is the**

---

took place and commemorated victory (see Mattingly 2006:912). For Romans it was displayed in processions and on military iconography that inundated Rome and its colonial cities. A procession relief with *tropaion* from the Roman Temple of Apollo Sosianus (1st c. BCE) can be seen in Maier 2013:41–42. See also the Gemma Augustea (101) and Dupondius coin at https://en.wikipedia.org/wiki/Tropaion. Special thanks to Brigitte Kahl for directing me here.

8. Malcolm 2013a:3–4, 156, 165, highlights this state in 1 Cor 1 and its outcome in 1 Cor 15.

9. In Isaiah the LXX and MT promote that God will *hide* (κρύπτω/סתר) the cleverness of the clever, whereas 1 Cor 1:19 uses *thwart* (ἀθετέω). Perhaps Paul replaced the term, being influenced by κενόω in 1:17 ("render ineffectual"). Otherwise, he might be combining Isaiah with Ps 33[32]:10, or his Greek version already rendered סתר based on its later sense of "to upset/tear down." See discussion in Stanley 1992:185–86. Paul's word strengthens rhetorically the citation's negative connotation (Barclay 2015:5).

10. Cf. Oropeza 2002a:104

11. The γραμματεύς, translated also as "scribe," could be understood as Jewish scholars of the Torah. In Isa 33:18 (cf. 29:11–12), however, it refers to the "one who counted" (cf. Wilk 2005:138), which seems to be clerical or a tribute collector. For Paul's audience, γραμματεύς might mean "civic leaders, instructors in the gymnasia and scholar/scribe": Dutch 2005:278–87 (287). In Acts 19:35 it refers to a magisterial

sophist debater of this age? finds no parallel in Isaiah.[12] Stephen Pogoloff is apropos that the last of the three questions "most naturally refers to the rhetorician skilled at declamation and extemporaneous courtroom displays. Increasingly, such persons were called sophists, and were sought by all status seekers as prizes."[13] Paul apparently wants to make sure that his auditors do not miss the point that this question pertains to the way they esteem oratory performances. All the same, three inquiries begin with "where" and are probably informed by the threefold pattern in Isa 33:18. The questions prompt the response that clever and prominent speakers are nowhere to be found at the time of the Lord's visitation. Paul's fourth question, **Has not God made foolish the wisdom of this world?** may come from Isa 44:25 where the Lord again turns the advice of wise counselors into foolishness.[14] "Yes" is the answer Paul expects from Corinthians.

Our apostle recontextualizes Isaiah's discourse in order to associate human counsel void of divine direction with the wisdom of this age characterized by sophists and royal elitists (cf. 1 Cor 2:4–8). Through Isaiah the relevant message for the Corinthians is that divine wisdom stands over against worldly wisdom; the latter incurs divine judgment, and there is an anticipation in which the absence of true wisdom will be remedied.[15] Whereas the concept of foolishness turns out to be antithetical to this wisdom, Paul presents a reverse ordering in which proclamation of the crucified Messiah, perceived by the wise in this world as foolishness, has become the means by which divine wisdom is revealed. This wisdom, incidentally, is not measured by the entertainment value of the speaker's performance, nor by the weight of eloquent words used, but by the divine mind's penetrating and disclosing insights communicated through God's Spirit by his messengers (cf. 2:6–16). Such wisdom is not recognized by worldly wisdom; the latter is foolish in comparison.

Both Jews and Gentiles can accept or reject the message of the cross (1:22–24). Unbelieving **Jews ask for signs** which seem related to miraculous proofs verifying Jesus as Messiah (Mark 8:11; 15:29–32; John 6:30). This request, as Ciampa and Rosner affirm, does not reflect an "open-minded plea, but an obstinate insistence on powerful confirmation of God's deliverance

---

position in Ephesus (where Paul happens to be as he writes 1 Cor). This meaning seems more appropriate for 1:20.

12. On συζητητής as a sophist, see Meyer 1877:1.38–39.

13. Pogoloff 1992:160.

14. Wilk 2005:139, shows that active forms of the verb μωραίνω ("to make foolish") connect these texts.

15. These themes are also prevalent in other Jewish literature, as Williams 2001:61–81 demonstrates.

that renders faith unnecessary."[16] The sign given them is an unexpected king—Jesus became a cursed criminal who hung on a tree (Deut 21:22–23), which is how Jewish interpreters understood crucifixion.[17] As such, the prophetic cornerstone of Zion from Isa 28:16, which Paul interprets as Jesus, became their **stumbling block** obstructing their way to faith and deliverance (Rom 9:33; cf. 1 Cor 3:10–11).[18]

Unbelieving **Greeks seek wisdom**.[19] The wisdom in this phrase appears to be very broad; it most likely includes philosophy and not merely rhetoric. Those who pride themselves in this pursuit might be expected to respond to the cross with mockery, akin with how the Epicurean and Stoic philosophers respond to the message of resurrection in Acts 17:31–32. The many allusions to thoughts similar to Stoicism in this letter may suggest that some Corinthians were influenced by this philosophy.[20] Together with other Gentiles they interpret a crucified Jew who claims to be savior as **foolishness**. Crucifixion is for criminals and communicates weakness, defeat, humility, shame, and low status.[21] Seneca, for example, mentions crucifixion as a way to depict humiliation related to his own situation (*Vit. Beat.* 19.3), and Cicero considers crucifixion to be a shameful thing that should not be seen or heard (*Rab. Perd.* 5.16).[22] This was a punishment for slaves (*Verr.* 5.169–70).[23] Foolishness of this sort does not convey merely intellectual nonsense but social worthlessness. The fool is typically imagined as an ugly, despised, subhuman of low status; the butt of jokes and object of ridicule.[24] And this particular crucified man made claims of sovereignty as Messiah. Hence, to follow and confess him as Lord risks an affront to Caesar that invites persecution.[25]

A third group, however, views crucifixion in a different light (1:24–25). These are Jews and Gentiles who are **called** by God to be a holy people in fellowship with Christ (1:2, 9); they are the ones who believe they are saved

16. Ciampa/Rosner 2010:99.

17. See e.g., Gal 3:13; 11QTemple 64.6-13; 4QNah 3+4 i 4-9; cf. Josephus *Bell.* 1.4.6[97].

18. See further Williams 2001:51–54; Schnabel 2006:128–29.

19. On the Greek pursuit of wisdom, see e.g., Herodotus *Hist* 4.77.1; Aristides 1.330; Aristotle *N.E.* 6.7.2; Fitzmyer 2008:159.

20. See Paige 2004:207–18.

21. See examples in Adams 2008:112–21; Elliott/Reasoner 2011:102–7; Cook 2014.

22. Cf. Dodson 2012:1–2.

23. See further Hengel 1977:51–63.

24. See examples of such characters related to theatre mimes in Welborn 2005, and now Barclay 2015:7–9.

25. Similarly, see Schottroff 2012:722.

First Supporting Proof (1:18—4:21)

(1:18b, 21b). They consider **Christ** to be both **the power of God and the wisdom of God**. These designations do not appear to identify Christ as distinctive attributes, emanations, or personifications of God. Rather, as the context suggests, "Christ" in 1:24 stands for the message of Jesus Christ being crucified, and this message effectually works in the believers divine power to live a transformed life and receive disclosed wisdom. This perception of the cross is expressed further with the ironic declaration that God's folly and weakness is wiser and stronger than human wisdom and strength (1:25; cf. 3:18). The cross of Christ exposes as worthless and utterly mistaken the entire human system of values, epitomized by Roman society, which considered crucifixion a "symbol and enactment of abject worthlessness."[26]

In 1:26–29 the Corinthian auditors are to review their **calling** not merely in terms of divine initiative and invitation for them to respond favorably to becoming God's people through Paul's preaching, but in terms of their social status at conversion, a status they currently maintain (cf. 7:17–24). **Not many** of them are **wise according to the flesh, not many powerful, not many noble-born**. Although "not many" does not mean "none," most did not belong to the upper classes of Roman Corinth.[27] They are what the apostle describes as **the foolish things of the world**. The weak, ignoble, despised nobodies according to the world's perspective often are the ones God chooses; they accept the message of the cross in contrast to those of high social standing who often reject it.[28] Among the church's members are slaves, widows, and poor (7:21–23, 39–40; 11:2–16, 22). This calling and election involves divine favor on the humble for the express purpose of shaming **the wise** and **mighty** along with prideful boasters (1:27, 29).[29] It is similar to the divine pattern one finds in early Jewish traditions (Deut 4:37–38; 7:6–7; Bar 3:26–27; Jdt 9:11–14).[30] Conversely, Pliny the Elder captures Roman sentiment when writing about a funerary oration in which Metellus the senior is praised for achieving ten of the greatest things for wise men to pursue. Among the ten are to become a top warrior, supreme orator, enjoy highest honor, possess complete wisdom, be a most distinguished senator, and acquire a large fortune (*Nat.* 7.45). Similarly, Aristotle's components of human

---

26. Barclay 2015:10.

27. See Introduction.

28. In 1:26 the tripartite use of the wise, powerful, and noble seem informed by Jer 9:22–23 (see 1:30 below).

29. Hence, this election involves social status rather than individual predestination to final salvation. The latter conflicts with believers being in danger of apostasy (e.g., 3:16–17; 8:5–13; 10:1–12).

30. See further sources in Inkelaar 2011:211.

happiness includes, "noble birth . . . wealth . . . health, beauty, strength, stature . . . glory (reputation), honor, good luck, virtue" (*Rhet.* 1.5.4).[31]

To Paul's frustration, high regard for status and sophistry seems to reflect some of the Corinthians' own sentiments *despite* many of them originating from the lower class. They seem to desire pandering to the wise, eloquent, and elite of the world. They mirror behavior more appropriate for outsiders and adopt its ideology of prestige. Paul undermines this way of thinking by insisting that not only does God frequently bypass those whom society deems honorable but God utterly confounds their entire honor and status-based ranking system.[32] They are put **to shame**, not merely in a psychological sense but eschatological.[33] These words may echo prophetic traditions that declare God's judgment against those who place all their trust in human wisdom (Isa 30:3, 5; Jer 8:9; 9:22–23).[34]

In their pursuit of status-seeking the Corinthians perhaps bragged about their respective leaders and themselves in relation to those leaders (1:12; 3:3–4, 21).[35] Paul subverts this boasting by maintaining that all believers receive a new status in Christ. Their **boasts** should not be centered on pride and self-achievements but **in the Lord** (1:29, 31). The apostle paraphrases Jeremiah where the Lord declares that the wise should not boast in their own wisdom, the strong should not boast in their strength, and the wealthy should not boast in their wealth. They rather should all boast in knowing the Lord who is merciful, just, and righteous (Jer 9:22–24).[36] Because Israel and its leaders had turned away from divine reliance and trusted in their own wisdom, strength, and wealth, they faced impending judgment and their wise men would be put to shame (Jer 8:8–11; 9:12; 10:7; cf. 5:26–29; 17:5, 11; 23:10).[37] In this situation, Jeremiah tries to bring them back to God as the true source of wisdom. Paul, informed by this prophetic-wisdom discourse, redirects his audience to focus on God as the source of all benefits. They should boast in the Lord instead of taking pride in human

---

31. See further sources in Welborn 1987b:96–97; Winter 2002:193–94.

32. Similarly, Barclay 2015:5.

33. Cf. Garland 2003:76–77. On shame as judgment, see Mark 8:38; Matt 10:38–42; Luke 9:26; 1 John 2:28.

34. Inkelaar 2011:212, perceptively adds that those with renewed worship and faith in the foundation stone, which Paul interprets as Christ, will not be put to shame (Isa 29:16–23 cf. Rom 9:33; 10:11).

35. This was nothing new in a city whose people were famous for making empty boasts of their founder as the son of Zeus: see Introduction.

36. See also 1 Sam[Kgdms]2:10, though Inkelaar 2011:220–22, shows that Jeremiah's text reflects Paul better.

37. See Lim 2009:165.

wisdom, power, and persona.[38] There is no room for boasting in human achievements when **in the presence of God**.

From the divine presence flows salvific benefits through their union **in Christ**, which includes spiritual **wisdom** (2:6–16), a **right standing** before God (2 Cor 5:21), **sanctification** (1 Cor 1:2; 3:16–17), and **redemption** from sin and death (Rom 3:24). These benefits, which are both present and futuristic, are imparted to them from God through Christ. The believers become righteous at conversion (1 Cor 6:11) and yet receive final justification on judgment day (4:4). They become holy saints at conversion (1:2) and yet complete sanctification is experienced at the second coming (1 Thess 5:23). They are presently redeemed from sin (1 Cor 6:20; 7:23; Rom 3:24) and yet look forward to the redemption of their mortal bodies via resurrection (Rom 8:23). The now and not yet component of these benefits are complementary to what it means to be currently in the process of being saved (1 Cor 1:18).

GOD'S POWER RATHER THAN RHETORICAL WISDOM (2:1–5)

Paul continues in wisdom discourse to present himself as a role model of weakness and humility related to the cruciform life in the passage. Through use of antithetical statements and anaphora ("and I in ... and in ... and in ... " 2:3) he contrasts worldly wisdom with the message of the cross and power of God's Spirit. The Corinthians are reminded about the first time Paul visited them (cf. Acts 18:1–18): he did not come to them **with superiority of eloquence or of wisdom**. A comparison of 2:1, 4, and 1:17 makes clear that Paul is referring to an excess of rhetorical eloquence when speaking. In these verses "speech" (λόγος) and "wisdom" (σοφία) are combined, proclamation is the subject, and Paul disavows the form of speaking described.[39] His thought in 2:1 comes close to Eunapius's description of Maximus the Neoplatonist—this sophist being puffed up with pride and "superabundant eloquence" despised logical proof (*Vit.* 475 cf. 470).[40]

The **persuasive words of wisdom** in 2:4 adds the thought of persuasion that captures the central aim of rhetorical discourses (Aristotle *Rhet.* 1.1.14; Longinus, *Subl.* 44.1; Philostratus *Vit. soph.* 1.498).[41] Paul's message

---

38. Christ is normally Lord, but in 1:31 God may be meant or God as revealed through Christ (cf. 2 Cor 5:19).

39. Cf. Litfin 1994:205. See also 2:13 though here teaching is the subject.

40. i.e., "λόγων ὑπεροχήν." On ὑπεροχή as social prestige related to wisdom and eloquence, see Diodorus Siculus 34/35.5.5; Eunapius *Vit.* 466; Pogoloff 1992:132–33.

41. NA27 has "πειθοῖ[ς] σοφίας [λόγοις]" (2:4). On Greek manuscript variations, see Ebojo 2009:10–21; Metzger/United Bible Societies 1994:481; BDAG 791.

instead disclosed **the mystery of God** (2:1).[42] This refers to the divine plan of salvation,[43] and for Paul that plan finds its center in the message of the cross. When he first preached to them he **decided to know nothing** among them; that is, he regarded nothing to be of primary importance in his gospel **except Jesus Christ and him crucified** (2:2).[44] His coming to their city and preaching in this manner contrasts sophists entering a town and expecting to be greeted by enthusiastic crowds, invited to declaim in their midst, and followed by young men desiring to become their students (Dio Chrysostom *Or.* 47.22; Aristides *Or.* 51.29–34; Philostratus *Vit. soph.* 2.571–72).[45]

Paul's presence among the Corinthians exemplified **weakness ... fear and much trembling**.[46] This description conflicts with that of sophists who are typically characterized by confidence, courage, good looks, great rhetorical skills, and a commanding presence (see Excursus). Paul's weakness, fear, and trembling characterize instead the type of stage fright experienced by nervous orators (cf. Cicero *De or.* 1.xxvi.120; xxvii.123). Speakers might show signs of being intimidated by their audiences by blushing, perspiring, stuttering, or trembling (Seneca *Lucil.* 11; Pliny *Ep.* 7.17).[47] A prime example of this is when Demosthenes, whose reputation of masterful eloquence was renowned, speaks in the presence of Philip of Macedon. Instead of exuberating great confidence, the famous orator was frightened out of his wits and even collapsed before the monarch, failing to continue his speech (Aeschines *Fals. leg.* 21–22, 34–35). It is quite plausible to suggest that Paul showed bodily signs of weakness or nervousness when speaking; in later correspondence some Corinthians consider his bodily presence to be weak and his speeches detestable (cf. 2 Cor 10:10; 11:6). His weakness would seem to indicate a person of lowly status, the way Plutarch describes poor speakers who are ugly, servile, needy, dishonored, and unlearned, unlike wise sages who are eloquent, handsome, wealthy, and learned (*Frat. amor.*

---

42. Some Greek manuscripts have μαρτύριον ("testimony" cf. 1:6) instead of μυστήριον ("mystery"). My tentative choice of the latter prepares for 2:7 (see Metzger, 480).

43. Cf. Dan 2:28; 2 *Bar.* 81.4; 1QpHab 7.4–8; Perkins 2012:59.

44. This resolve was not a new decision but Paul's normal practice (Gal 3:1; Fee 1987:92).

45. Winter 2002:144–47; Russell 1983:76–80.

46. Possibly, "fear and trembling" is lifted from Isa 19:16, or alternatively, what prophets experience when confronted with divine revelation or mysteries (Dan 7:15; 10:7–9; 1 *En.* 14.14; Selby 1997:368–70).

47. In Acts 19:12 Paul's sweat cloths might reflect his perspiration when speaking, but then again the sweat might be from his labor as a tent-maker.

485D; cf. 485A; Seneca *Lucil.* 11).⁴⁸ But if Paul was perceived negatively, his weakness extends beyond preaching and persona to include also what he personally experienced as a *result* of his preaching.⁴⁹ In Corinth Paul apparently feared external opposition to his messages (Acts 18:9–13). Likewise, personal inadequacies both on and off stage may have plagued him due to this city's size, reputation, Roman influence, and potpourri of intimidating people (cf. 1 Cor 16:10).

Raymond Pickett rightly affirms that our apostle takes on the posture of someone who "deliberately failed to measure up to the standards of rhetorical excellence."⁵⁰ His self-deprecation in 2:1–4a has the aim of subverting Corinthian adoration of human wisdom in 2:4b–5 branded by orators whose method of operation centered on forceful rhetorical demonstrations.⁵¹ Differently, Paul's proclamation involved **demonstration of the powerful Spirit**.⁵² His preaching connoted "proof consisting in possession of the Holy Spirit and miracle-working power."⁵³ The Corinthians are to recall such phenomena so that their **faith may not rest in clever human wisdom, but in the power of God**.⁵⁴ It is through the apostle's weakness that spiritual power is greatly manifest. Power in weakness reflects Christ's own crucifixion, which gave way to resurrection and becomes the catalyst unleashing God's Spirit on Christ's followers to convict, transform, and work miracles among them. Paul's messages possess such power, which become tokens of the divine authenticity of his ministry and apostleship (1 Thess 1:5; 2:13; Gal 3:5; Rom 15:18–19; cf. 1 Cor 4:20–21).⁵⁵ These words promote a different kind of wisdom in which miracle and prophetic discourse are

---

48. See Martin 1995:51.

49. In 2:3, γίνομαι in "I was with you . . . " describes his state of being rather than speaking.

50. Pickett 1997:74–75.

51. On δύναμις as the power of persuading, e.g., Aristotle *Rhet.* 1.6.14; Quintilian *Inst.* 2.15.3–4; for ἀπόδειξις as rhetorical demonstration, e.g., Aristotle *Rhet.* 1.1.11; Quintilian *Inst.* 5.10.7; Weiss 1910:50.

52. "Spirit and power" is a hendiadys ("powerful Spirit"): Lindemann 2000:56; Schnabel 2006:156.

53. BDAG 109.

54. This demonstration informs the meaning of "faith" (πίστις) in 2:5. In rhetorical discourses πίστις was often understood as "proof" (πίστις): cf. Isocates *Or.* 3.8; Aristotle *Rhet.* 1.1.14–2.2; Acts 17:31; LSJ 1408. And here a double entendre is in view (Winter 2002:161, 163)

55. Gräbe 2008:61–66, rightly includes this charismatic emphasis. That Acts 18:1–18 records no miracle of Paul in Corinth (Riddlebarger 2013:55–56) is no evidence that Paul is not including signs and wonders here, especially when elsewhere he claims he *did* perform miracles when with them (2 Cor 12:12).

blended. If Zech 4:6–10 is being alluded to here, Paul's renovated meaning through this text is that the building up of the Corinthians as the temple of God is accomplished not by human might nor by rhetorical power but by God's powerful Spirit.[56] Hence, the Corinthians should not measure a leader's worth based on status or rhetorical skill but on the value of spiritual preaching and power manifest through weakness.[57]

Excursus: Paul's Rhetoric against the Sophist Deliveries

Scholars frequently notice an apparent tension with Paul's use of rhetoric to criticize Corinthian attraction to rhetoric. Among the various ways this issue is addressed, it makes good sense to suggest that Paul rejects only certain aspects of rhetoric.[58] More particularly, he disdains rhetoric when coupled with certain sociocultural values such as status seeking, and especially manifest in the form of a speaker's delivery. Our apostle comes against a type of rhetoric that characterizes the sophists in Plato's *Gorgias*. Their speeches stressed form, superficiality, and showmanship over philosophical content. Paul, however, stresses spiritual knowledge about Christ as the proper content of his messages (2 Cor 11:6; cf. 1 Cor 2). It will turn out that certain Corinthians show contempt for the apostle's speeches and physical presence (2 Cor 10:10). This way of scrutinizing preachers already seems to be a problem in 1 Cor 1–4, perhaps prominently by the faction loyal to Apollos (see 1:12), and that is why Paul promotes a different way of perceiving wisdom and proclamation.

Doubtless the Corinthians learned how to criticize oratory performances by listening to many sophists and philosophers who preached publicly in their city. This may have conditioned them to place too much value on the actual appearance and performance of orators, known in rhetorical handbooks as *delivery* (one of the five components of rhetoric).[59] In *Lives of the Ten Orators*, when asked what is most important in rhetoric, Demosthenes responded, "delivery." When asked the second and third most important things, he replied, "delivery," and again, "delivery" (Ps.-Plutarch, *Vit.*

---

56. Cf. Williams 2001:133–56; Schnabel 2006:158.

57. Similarly, see Mihaila 2009:6, 148–49, 219.

58. See survey of viewpoints in Mihaila, 135–46; Winter 2002:143–44. On Paul's knowledge of rhetoric, see Oropeza 2016:18–32.

59. See *Rhet. Her.* 1.ii.3; Aristotle *Rhet.* 3.1[1403b]; Kennedy 1984:13–14; LSJ 1886 (ὑπόκρισις).

Excursus: Paul's Rhetoric against the Sophist Deliveries

845D; Theon, *Prog.* 3.[5]104).⁶⁰ To impress audiences, orators had to command an appealing appearance and dress and perform well when speaking. The sophists excelled in theatrical qualities.⁶¹ Thucydides has the Athenian warrior Cleon bemoaning Athenian susceptibility to eloquent speeches, being persuaded by their eyes and ears instead of facts. He calls them dupes and "worshippers of every new extravagance" left at the mercy of their own ears "like spectators attending a performance of sophists" (*Hist.* 3.38.2–7). A confident look, pleasant tone of voice, a radiant smile, animated gestures such as striking one's thigh or stomping one's foot at climactic moments in one's speech are some descriptors of delivery (Philostratus *Vit. soph.* 1.519–20; 537).⁶² The sophist Herodes Atticus is described as having grace, beauty, urbane wit, pleasing diction, a smooth tone, and eloquence "like gold dust shining beneath the waters of a silvery eddying river" (2.564). Even philosophers might be admired for having similar qualities. Given the stoic allusions in the letter (e.g., 1 Cor 6:12–13), the wisdom Paul comes against may extend beyond sophists. Pliny the Younger lauds the Stoic Euphrates who marshals respect and speaks with well-chosen words and "special charm which can captivate and so convince the most reluctant listener. He is moreover tall and distinguished to look at, with long hair and a flowing white beard. . . . His dress is always neat, and his serious manner makes no show of austerity, so that your first reaction on meeting him would be admiration rather than repulsion" (*Ep.* 1.10).

A combination of pleasant appearance and eloquence also marked out orators to be educated and of prominent status, like elitists or even deities. Alexander the sophist reportedly possessed a "godlike appearance," curly hair, large eyes, a stately nose, white teeth, and long slender fingers "well fitted to hold the reins of eloquence" (Philostratus *Vit. soph.* 2.570). More relevant for first-century Corinthians was Favorinus who possessed smooth skin, spoke with charm, beautiful eloquence, fascinating tones and rhythms in his speech that enthralled even Romans unfamiliar with Greek (Philostratus *Vit. soph.* 1.489, 491). The Corinthians, enamored by this sophist, built a statue in his honor before he fell into disfavor (Dio Chrysostom, *Or.* 37). Sophists, normally coming from high ranking backgrounds, were also associated with wealth and social eminence (Philo, *Det* 33–35; Aristides,

---

60. Kennedy 2003:22.

61. Or "scenic effects": cf. σκηνή in Philostratus (tr. Wright 1998:120–21, 574).

62. See further *Rhet. Her.* 3.19–27; Isocrates *Antidosis* 253–57; Quintilian *Inst.*11.3.4–103; 12.5.1–5; Philostratus *Vit. soph.* 1.519; Oropeza 2016:573–77, 602–6.

First Supporting Proof (1:18—4:21)

Or. 33.19),[63] and charged lucrative sums of money to speak (Isocrates, *Soph.* 13.3–5; Themistius *Or.* 23.288-89).[64] They also encouraged strife, disputes, and contests with other speakers (Dio Chrysostom, *Or.* 8.9; Philostratus, *Vit. Soph.* 2.576, 579–580, 586–88; Isocrates *Soph.* 14[*Or.* 13]; Plato, *Protag.* 335A). It is precisely this type of competitive nature, boasting in rhetorical deliveries, and pandering to social prestige that Paul comes against. The congregation seems to reflect the wisdom of this world in this regard, and ironically resemble Epictetus's description of a stunning Corinthian student of the sophists whose primary concern centered on his outward appearance instead of moral virtues (*Diatr.* 3.1). Such mores influenced congregation members to evaluate Christian speakers amiss, and this ultimately caused strife and thinking one person superior to another. Pogoloff aptly explains Paul's response in this situation: "In Paul's narrative world, the normal cultural narratives of eloquence and status are radically reversed. What persuades is speech about what is ordinarily unfit for contemplation: not a life which is cultured, wise, and powerful, but one marked by the worst shame and the lowest possible status. Paul's rhetoric of the cross thus opposes the cultural values surrounding eloquence."[65]

WISDOM FROM GOD'S SPIRIT RATHER THAN WISDOM OF THIS AGE (2:6–16)

Paul speaks of a **wisdom** that is not of this age nor of the rulers of this age. This is **God's wisdom**—it belongs to and comes from God—and in this text it functions prominently in the mode of teaching revelatory discourse. The passage takes on a "quasi-logical" form that strings together the explanatory conjunction "for" five times (2:8, 10, 11, 14, 16).[66] This suggests Paul argues from the artistic proof of *logos* (invented persuasion based on probable

---

63. Winter 2002:34–35, 103–4, 253–54; cf. Bowersock 1969:21–23; Bowie 1982:29–59.

64. Further, Plato *Protag.* 313C-D; Dio Chrysostom *Or.* 32.10; Philo *Post.* 150; Winter 2002:164–69.

65. Pogoloff 1992:119–20.

66. In agreement with Collins 1999:123, 127.

First Supporting Proof (1:18—4:21)

argument), and his scripture citation in 2:9 functions as inartistic proof (non-invented persuasion based on law, witnesses, oracles, contracts, etc.).[67]

Several points are noteworthy in 2:6-8 and together they highlight wisdom in the form of pedagogical and prophetic-apocalyptic discourses. First, our apostle now takes on the role of a teacher. His verb **we speak** (λαλοῦμεν) replaces preaching (καταγγέλλω) to suggest a pedagogical emphasis (2:6, 13).[68] Aristotle and other ancient educators spoke in the first-person plural, as did teachers of practical exercises on rhetoric. Theon's "we" in the prelude of his *progymnasmata* refers to himself before the personal pronoun includes his students subsequently.[69] Similarly, Paul may be using "we" in 2:6-7a inclusive of himself and perhaps his colleagues as teachers, and then he seems to include his many students who have received God's Spirit in 2:7b, 12. Given a time in which orators were hired by wealthy parents who sought to have their sons trained in rhetorical skills for future public careers,[70] it follows that Paul might discuss an alternative form of education in wisdom.

Second, Paul teaches wisdom **among those who are mature**. Are these his Corinthian recipients? Yes, because they have received the prerequisite of God's Spirit needed to discern this wisdom (6:11, 19; 12:13)—and no, because they still behave immaturely (3:1-3). They still need to realize the implications of who they are as Christ's followers.[71] Maturity here imagines advanced or adult learners who understand and live up to standards of teachings disclosed to them. A state of being mature or τέλειος may suggest completeness in training (cf. 14:19-20; cf. Col 1:28; Eph 4:11-13).[72] This term is used also of skilled sophists and philosophers (Isocrates *Antidosis* 199-200; Plato *Phaedr.* 269E; *Crat.* 403E; Philo *Det.* 32-49, 65-68, 132-33).[73] Perhaps certain Corinthians used it to identify skillful orators. When Paul denies speaking with **words taught by human wisdom** (2:13), as Pogoloff discerns, "the most natural teachers would be the rhetorical

---

67. On the proofs, see e.g., Aristotle *Rhet.* 1.2.2-7; 1.15.1-33.

68. Cf. λαλέω + διδακτός (2:13) with λαλέω + διδασκαλία (Tit 2:1). Notice also "instruct" (συμβιβάζω) in 1 Cor 2:16. He also emphasizes knowing verbs: οἶδα in 2:11-12 and γιγνώσκω in 2:8[2 x], 11, 14, 16. The latter may relate to "greater insight into things spiritual, the product of education and culture" (Welborn 1987b:105).

69. See Kennedy 2003:3 fn. 8.

70. Cf. Quintilian *Inst.* 2.1.1-2; 2.8.1-8; Winter 2001:33, 35, 43. On cognitive development related to elite education, see Dutch 2005:260-61.

71. See Grindheim 2002:708.

72. On this meaning in other sources, see LSJ 1769§3.

73. See Horsley 2008:32; Pogoloff 1992:142-43.

schools ... the Hellenistic reader would find the meaning unmistakable."[74] If so, Paul gives maturity in education a new meaning. Maturity in Christ is not measured by rhetorical skills but teaching that unveils God's wisdom through the Spirit. This type of learning is neither competitive nor gained by money but comes as a gift from God. Unlike rhetorical education that was reserved for upper classes, divine wisdom is granted to anyone willing to receive it—whether slave, free, man, woman, educated, or uneducated—as long as the person has God's Spirit.[75] This wisdom comes fully to those who regard the wisdom of this age to be insufficient.

Third, Paul identifies **the rulers of this age** among those who adhere to the wisdom of this age and **are passing away** (2:6–8).[76] These are elitists who from the arena of politics think themselves wise in deliberating rhetoric. Their effectiveness depends on "their own or their cohorts' power to persuade," and this reliance blinds them from perceiving the power behind the "supposed weak wisdom" of God in Christ.[77] If they had truly known this wisdom **they would not have crucified** Christ. More specifically, then, they are represented by Pilate, the Roman prefect, who in collaboration with the chief priests, scribes, and perhaps Herod Antipas, sentenced Jesus to death. An oral tradition of this sort was probably known by Paul before written in the Gospels.[78] Equally, Paul may be informed by Ps 2:1–2 in which the kings of the earth and rulers (οἱ ἄρχοντες) come against the anointed one, which in early Christian tradition is interpreted as those who put Jesus to death according to God's predetermined plan (Acts 4:25–28). If Satan and his minions are meant by the ἄρχοντες and "spirit of the world," they play an indirect role inadvertently influencing Jesus's eventual crucifixion (Luke 22:3–4; John 13:26–27; 14:30), but Paul's argument here seems to foreground human rulers. God's wisdom confronts Roman ideology and elitists by disrupting their order through the power-in-weakness of the cross.[79] What at first seemed to be the execution of just another pretender to the throne and opponent of Caesar unleashed divine power both mightier and wiser than anything the Greco-Roman world had to offer.

---

74. Pogoloff 1992:140.

75. See similarly the Lord giving wisdom and the Spirit in Wis. 9:6, 17; Keener 2016:177.

76. Doubtless, these rulers are part of the same macro-society as those who are *perishing* and adhere to the wisdom of this *world* (1:18–21).

77. Pogoloff 1992:142.

78. E.g., Matt 26–27; Mark 14–15; Luke 22–23; cf. 3:2; John 18:13–14; Acts 4:27.

79. On Paul's challenge to Roman authority here, see Lestang 2015:16–17; Elliott 1997:181.

Fourth, Paul calls the crucified Christ **the Lord of glory**. Perhaps he derives this title from prophetic-apocalyptic traditions; "the glory of the Lord" in Isa 40:5 may be his primary source.[80] The Isaianic context is cited more explicitly in 1 Cor 2:16, and perhaps informs some of Paul's other thoughts, too. The Isaianic glory is associated with salvation and divine presence for both God's people and the Gentiles (40:5b; 66:18–19), and this presence guides the restored people through a new exodus and wilderness journey to Zion as though in a triumphal procession (40:3; cf. 43:2–17; 48:20–21).[81] This anticipated era is characterized by God's Spirit being poured out on God's people and making the wilderness fertile ground (32:6–20; 44:3; 59:21; cf. 42:1; 58:4–7; 59:4, 15; 61:1–4). The glory of the Lord also stands over against the "glory of man" representing what is beautiful and prestigious in the eyes of the world. Human glory passes away, but God's word abides forever (40:6–8). Paul interprets these prophetic words as fulfilled in his day with the crucified and resurrected Christ imparting his glorious salvation and presence through the Spirit that teaches and guides faithful people during their travels in the metaphoric new exodus-wilderness to final salvation (cf. 1 Cor 10:1–11). Such teaching is God's "word," divine wisdom that confounds transient human prestige.

Fifth, this wisdom is **spoken in a mystery, the hidden wisdom which God preordained before the ages.** Two implied reasons rulers cannot grasp this wisdom is because it has been hidden and originated before the present age to which they belong. Paul might be presupposing wisdom personified in precreation discourse (Prov 8:22–31; Sir 1:1–10). This idea, however, seems developed from the disclosure of salvation in Isa 40 again, and Paul adds from his quote in 2:9 the idea of preordination—God has prepared beforehand amazing things for those who love God (2:9 cf. Rom 16:25–26). As well, prophetic traditions that anticipated Christ's crucifixion, especially by the hand of rulers, he probably interprets as predestined by God (Ps 2; cf. Acts 4:25–28). Namely, God determined ages ago that this salvation through the Christ event would take place, and God revealed it to the prophets, though in a hidden manner prior to Christ's advent. It remains a hidden mystery to those who do not have God's Spirit, but God is now disclosing that plan to Christ's followers in a progressive way. This wisdom is **for our glory**, that is, for the purpose of bringing salvation to those who love God and follow the Lord (cf. Rom 8:18, 28–30).

---

80. The "glory of the Lord" is a genitive of source: the glory that finds its origin in the Lord. The "Lord of glory" is a genitive of (characteristic) quality: "the Lord to whom glory belongs" (Edwards 1897:54; cf. Eph 1:17; Acts 7:2).

81. Goldingay 2005:18, suggests from Isa 40:3 the idea of "processional routes used for religious festivals and triumphal royal processions in Babylon."

First Supporting Proof (1:18—4:21)

Scripture allusions in 2:6–8 are interwoven with his artistic argument, but now in 2:9 he presents an inartistic proof in the form of an oracle or testimony of the ancients, by using an explicit citation formula, **just as it is written.** The citation in 2:9 may be loosely referencing a string of scriptures emphasizing divine revelation: **what eye has not seen and ear has not heard** (Isa 64:3[4]), **nor has entered into the heart of humans** (65:17) **what God has prepared for those who love him** (Sir 1:10). Another possibility is that he cites from a text no longer extant. Pseudo-Philo *L.A.B.* 26.13 and 1 Clem. 34.8 may be two independent sources that cite from such a text.[82] If the Isaiah texts are primarily in view, their context and thematic parallels may imply that in the anticipated era of restoration and new creation, God's people who were spiritually blind will once again see and hear, along with Gentiles, and be saved (33:17–22; 40:5; 52:10, 15; 66:18–19).[83] For Paul, in any case, now that the Christ event has taken place, the anticipated era is currently being fulfilled. Christ's followers can now "see" and "hear" (i.e., understand) the profound revelation of God's salvific plan and spiritual benefits pertaining to it.

His citation is followed up by an analogy between God's Spirit and the human spirit along with three guiding antitheses contrasting worldly and spiritual-revelatory wisdom—the spirit of the world/the Spirit which comes from God, human teaching/spiritual teaching, and the natural (soulish) person/extra-natural (spiritual) person (2:10–15). He advances a rhetorical question that prompts the response that **no one knows the things of a human** (i.e., one's inner thoughts, plans, and intentions) **except the spirit** of that human. This is not referring to the Holy Spirit but the "I" or inner self of humans that engages the mind though not equated with it (14:14; 16:18; Rom 8:16; 2 Cor 12:2–3).[84] Then from lesser to greater Paul argues that the things of God no one could know, except the **Spirit of God** who searches God's thoughts, plans, and intentions, **the depths of God**.[85] And such plans and thoughts are disclosed to those who are in Christ.

The first antithesis affirms that **we have not received the spirit of the world but the Spirit who is from God.** In Pauline cosmology this phrase

---

82. Cf. Clivaz/Schulthess 2015:192, 199. Origen and Ambrosiaster believed Paul was referencing the *Apocalypse of Elijah* (Bray 1999:23). For further parallels, see Williams 2001:175–99; Berger 1978:270–83.

83. Contrast God's people previously being blind and deaf (Isa 6:10; 29:9–14; 30:9–11; 42:18–20).

84. This "I" or self, whether immaterial or of airy material (as some ancients taught: Martin 1995:6–15), also survives death (2 Cor 5:6–8), and may flow through, link with, seat, or be the "stuff" of the human mind/intellect.

85. Cf. Rom 11:33–34; Jdt 8:14; *T.Job* 37.6; Fitzmyer 2008:180.

might convey satanic power over the world (cf. 1 Cor 5:5; 2 Cor 4:4),[86] but in this context it stresses the ideology of the present age epitomized by elitism that values human power, high status, and clever speech. At conversion the confessors received God's Spirit, not this ideology (12:13; Rom 8:9). There is an implicit exhortation from this that since the Corinthians value this ideology, they lack the spiritual maturity needed to fully appreciate divine wisdom. The Spirit enables believers to **know the gifts granted us by God**. This phrase points back to 2:9.[87] Those who have God's Spirit can understand and receive all kinds of salvific blessings, not the least of which are wisdom from and fellowship with God. Not only does God's Spirit reveal wisdom but it also takes an active role as its teacher.[88] The Spirit, it seems, prompts and works with the mode of communication Christian teachers like Paul employ as they connect with others. The Spirit helps supply the teachers' words, which then become a powerful tool for persuasion. Such teaching is effective not because of the teachers' rhetorical talents but because they are Spirit-led and committed to the task of **interpreting spiritual things to those who possess the Spirit**.[89] Spirit-inspired words, then, contrast words taught by clever human wisdom, and this identifies a second antithesis. In 2:13 λόγος (speech/word) and σοφία (wisdom) are again combined as in 1:17, 2:1, 4, this time to contrast rhetorical education with the Spirit's wise and transformative teaching disclosures.

A third antithesis compares **the natural (soulish) person** (ψυχικός), with **the extra-natural (spiritual) person** (πνευματικός). The former is natural in the sense of being created human with the life principle, like Adam (Gen 2:7; cf. 1 Cor 15:44–46), but without revelatory abilities coming from God's Spirit.[90] The point is that the in-breaking of God's Spirit in the present age has brought about a new condition in which the natural person's thoughts are rendered insufficient for spiritual purposes. It is only with the aid of God's Spirit that spiritual things (e.g., divine truths, insights, gifts, and revelation) can be discerned. The natural person does not accept these things; **they are foolishness to him**, just like the message of the cross. This person cannot understand **because spiritual things are examined and understood spiritually**.[91] On the other hand, the spiritual person (i.e., the

86. See Vos 1996:110; Meyer 1877:1.69.

87. Fee 1987:113, rightly compares neuter plurals in both verses.

88. See Frestadius 2011:66–67. On God as teacher see Isa 54:13.

89. For various renditions of "πνευματικοῖς πνευματικὰ συγκρίνοντες," see BDAG 953.

90. See Fitzmyer 2008:182–84.

91. In 2:14 the singular verb ἀνακρίνεται takes on a neuter plural subject (cf. Wallace 1996:399–400), and what is discerned are the things of God's Spirit, not the natural

First Supporting Proof (1:18—4:21)

one who operates by God's Spirit) **examines and understands all things**. Because this person has God's Spirit, who investigates all things pertaining to God's own hidden thoughts and salvific plan (2:10), this individual realizes and receives all the benefits God has for him or her (cf. 3:21–22).

Conversely, the spiritual person **is examined and understood by no one** who is not spiritual. In other words, the natural person is not in a position to discern and judge the spiritual person. What does Paul have in mind? There are three prominent possibilities. The first imagines persecution. Paul may be aware of an oral tradition that assured the persecuted believer of being endowed with wise speech originating from God's Spirit that the rulers, judges, and leaders they stand before will not be able to gainsay (Matt 10:19–20; Luke 12:11–12; 21:12–15). Perhaps, too, Paul implies that the rulers of this age were in no spiritual position to sentence Jesus to death (cf. 2:8). A second option functions as a prelude to passages such as 4:1–5 and 9:3 where Paul, who spiritually has the mind of Christ, discourages the Corinthians from criticizing him.[92] Their behavior shows that they evaluate things by worldly standards of this age, and so they are not in a position to examine his abilities—the Lord will be his judge instead. A third possibility anticipates the content of 6:1–8. Paul anticipates correcting the Corinthian assumption that magistrates void of God's Spirit should be judging cases between congregation members who do have God's Spirit. Possibly a combination of these options is meant.

The apostle concludes this passage by quoting Isaiah with the inquiry, **Who has known the mind of the Lord that he will instruct him?** (cf. Isa 40:13).[93] The context in Isaiah highlights the knowledge and power of God as creator over the nations (40:12–15). What is stressed is that if no one is able to measure God's creation, how much less could anyone hope to know or measure the mind of God?[94] This question expects the answer "no one" but receives instead the outlandish claim that the Spirit-led are able to receive divine thoughts (cf. 1 Cor 2:10–11). Paul plays on the title "Lord" from Isa 40:13, which originally refers to God, but as usual he gives this title to Christ: **we have the mind of Christ**.[95] This grand image of Paul's, of the Lord

---

person (Lambrecht 2013:367–70, responding to Dingeldein 2013:31–44). Incidentally, ἀνακρίνω appears three times in 2:14–15 with Paul playing on its meaning that ranges from "discern" to "judge." Perhaps the most consistent sense is "examine and understand" (Ellingworth/Hatton 1995:62).

92. Fee 1987:118–19.

93. In this verse the MT has "spirit (רוח) of Yahweh," whereas the LXX has "mind (νοῦς) of the Lord." The latter adds after Lord, "and who has become his counsellor . . ."

94. Inkelaar 2011:258, is similar.

95. Capes 1992:140, notices Isa 40:13 in Rom 11:34 has the Lord as God, but in 1 Cor 2:16 the Lord is Christ.

being both God and Christ, or perhaps God-in-Christ, seems to present the mind of God and the mind of Christ almost interchangeably. To be sure, the word "mind" indirectly exhorts the Corinthians to be of the same "mind" in unity with the mind of Christ (1:10, 13), but Paul is stressing a revelatory understanding of this mind based on Isaiah.[96] This notion of Spirit-filled believers in Christ knowing divine thoughts sounds like boasting, and in one sense it is—they are rightly boasting "in the Lord" who grants them salvation and spiritual gifts (1:30-31). If having the mind of Christ seems to promote a privileged status, we should remember that Paul's Christ was crucified, and as such this knowledge serves to criticize all privilege related to boasting, quarrelling, arrogance, and self-directed elitist wisdom.[97]

Nurturing Babies in Christ (3:1-4)

Paul continues in the same mode of discourse but now directly addresses the Corinthians' shortcoming related to spiritual wisdom: **And I, brothers and sisters, could not speak to you as spiritual but as fleshly people, as babies in Christ**. Such language elicits pathos; emotions are aroused by the use of familial language and shame with the aim of dissuading the auditors from divisive behavior. This is reinforced by rhetorical questions in 3:3-4 that prompt them to admit their fleshly behavior. The Corinthians are still babies rather than mature adults who can digest divine wisdom. They need to be fed **milk, not solid food**. This metaphoric consumption relates to learning elementary teachings (cf. Epictetus *Diatr.* 2.16.26-37; Philo *Congr.* 18-19; Heb 5:12-14).[98] Paul has to take on the role of a nurse and feed them again the basics of spiritual training.[99] This does not mean, however, that they should move on from the message of the cross to more "mature" teachings.[100] Their problem is more ethical than intellectual. They do not properly comprehend what Christ crucified means for their *behavior*. The message of Christ crucified must always remain their foundation (3:11), and any further wisdom and ethics they might learn should be in conformity to that message. But instead of emulating humility and power in weakness,

---

96. Rightly, Lambrecht 2007:440. Differently, the moral-exhortative sense is stressed by Strüder 2005; Petersen 2013:77-79.

97. Hays 1997:47; Schrage 1991:1.267.

98. Cf. Dutch 2005:251; Gaventa 1996:104-5.

99. On ancient men in this role, see Bradley 1991:37-75; Dutch 2005:250.

100. If God's wisdom is in Christ (1:30), there is little distinction here between milk and "meat" (Hooker 1966:21).

First Supporting Proof (1:18—4:21)

they have been feeding off the metaphoric staples of self-emulation, status seeking, and competitive oratory evaluations.

Their current state and behavior are described as **fleshly**,[101] and this predicament evokes the Corinthians to see themselves in similar light with the natural person who being void of God's Spirit finds divine wisdom incomprehensible (2:13).[102] To be fleshly in this regard is to **walk in a human way**, that is, they regularly conduct themselves in accordance with the people of this age who are subject to vices and ideologies contrary to the new creation in Christ. If we tease out this line of inference, the implicit way they should be walking is in the Spirit, as being in conformity with the Spirit's guidance and exercising moral virtues such as love, peace, kindness, and meekness (cf. Gal 5:16–25).

Their behavior exhibits **envy and discord**.[103] Both appear in Paul's vice lists, and their practice results in eternal consequences (Gal 5:19–21; 2 Cor 12:20; Rom 13:13). The latter vice (ἔρις) we explored in relation to the congregation's divisive allegiances (1:11–12), though here only the main rivalry between **I am of Paul** and **I am of Apollos** is stressed. The former vice (ζῆλος) connotes a type of zeal or envy which harms rather than helps others, being concerned primarily about one's own advancement.[104] It also may arise when a person feels left behind by another's upward mobility (Cicero, *De or.* 2.52.209) and connote competition that benefits one's group while leading to dishonor others (Jas 3:13–16). Clement, writing to the Corinthians a generation after Paul, provides examples of envy from Israel's scriptures, each having harmful consequences including Cain's envy over Abel, Jacob's sons over Joseph, and Saul over David (*1 Clem.* 3.1–6.4 cf. Gen 4, 37; 1 Sam 18). More contemporary with Paul's time, Caligula became envious of Seneca's eloquence and contemplated ordering his death (Cassius Dio 59.19.6–8; cf. Suetonius *Calig.* 53.2). What Paul perhaps fears is a congregational scene similar to one witnessed in Corinth's vicinity by Dio Chrysostom in which quarreling among sophist students devolved into a shouting and abusive match (*Or.* 8.9). As Bruce Winter points out, "the conduct of the

---

101. Thiselton 2000:288–89, rightly distinguishes the two "fleshly" terms here as follows: "σάρκινος [3:1] means moved by entirely human drives, while σαρκικός [3:3] means *moved by self-interest.*" Garland 2003:109, adds, "The -ινος suffix connotes 'made of' (cf. 2 Cor. 3:3), while the -ικός suffix connotes 'characterized by' (cf. 9:11)."

102. One distinction, however, is that God's Spirit dwells in and among the Corinthians, and they belong to the Lord—they are babes *in Christ*.

103. Some manuscripts of 3:3 add "dissensions" (διχοστασίαι), but its absence in others is hard to explain unless it was not in the original text (Metzger 1994:482–83).

104. Stumpff 1964:2.881–82. In a political sense, see Welborn 1987b:87, and more generally, Malina 2001:108–33.

disciples of the sophists and the Christian disciples was identical. There were the same assertions of loyalty to one's teachers, the same pride ('puffed up') with the same strife resulting as they denigrated other teachers while at the same time singing the praises of their own."[105] Envy and discord manifested among congregants as they claimed loyalty to their mentors.

ON PLANTING AND BUILDING THE CORINTHIAN CONGREGATION (3:5–17)

This passage depicts Paul and Apollos in the metaphors of field workers and builders with the Corinthians as the field of God they cultivate (3:5–9b) and temple of God they erect (3:9c–17). Through the first image Paul teaches against discord several ways.[106] First, with the rhetorical questions, **What, then, is Apollos? And what is Paul?**, the apostle sets up an answer that deflates status seeking and competition—Paul and Apollos are lowly **servants** through whom the Corinthians believed the gospel.[107] The congregation must envision their leaders being no better than slaves and day-laborers, the very people despised by elitists and sophists who pride themselves in not working with their hands.[108] Second, **the Lord has given** Paul and Apollos their assigned roles; both of them are **God's coworkers** under divine authority and belonging to God (3:5c; 3:9a).[109] Their unique gifts are given by God who increases their produce, and if God is doing the work through them and granting it success, this leaves no room for boasting in human talent. Third, Paul and Apollos **are one**; they are unified in laboring for the Corinthians' spiritual growth (3:5, 8a). Paul **planted** by first evangelizing the Corinthians (Acts 18), and **Apollos watered** afterward by nurturing them (Acts 19:1). Auditors can draw the inference that Paul, not Apollos, is founder of their congregation, and yet they are equal despite different roles.[110] Fourth, the one who evaluates Paul and Apollos's work should not be the Corinthians, but God. These workers, who get paid at the end of the "day," will receive their **own reward** from God for their **own labor**, which

---

105. Winter 2001:41.

106. On teaching with agricultural language, see Plutarch *Mor.* 1.2B–C; Philo *Spec. Leg.* 2.29; Quintilian *Inst.* 2.4.8–9; Dutch 2005:255–60. For possible OT allusions here, see Williams 2001:237–55; Lang 1994:50; Ciampa/Rosner 2010:151, though none seem essential for Paul's interpretation.

107. Schnabel 2006:191, rightly stresses the contextual nuance for διάκονοι as servants/slaves rather than ministers or deacons.

108. Cf. Philo *Det.* 34; Winter 2001:39.

109. Cf. Hays 1997:52–53.

110. Rightly, Mihaila 2009:198.

presumably will take place when Christ returns; each person is accountable for what they do (cf. 3:13; 4:1–5).

As Paul turns to the building metaphor, he also switches to an exhortation with the imperative to **be careful** (3:10). He elicits pathos by warning them through a blend of priestly and apocalyptic images related to a holy temple and end-time judgment. Believers in Christ must pay close attention to their respective places related to this building. Asyndeton, the omission of conjunctions ("and"), helps highlight the materials of the project (3:12), and fiery purification and destruction related to the end of the age, along with a rhetorical question affirming the auditors as this building, which is a holy temple of God, contribute to the fear Paul wishes to provoke. He presents himself as a **wise master builder** who **laid the foundation** of this building by proclaiming the message of Christ crucified (cf. 2:2).[111] Our apostle perhaps assumes an early tradition that Christ is the foundation of God's assembly, which is viewed as an edifice (Matt 16:16–18; Rom 9:32–33; cf. Isa 28:16; Ps 118:22).[112] Paul is the supervisor of contractors involved in Corinthian temple construction. Such an edifice needed to pass an inspection that imposed penalties on those who failed to build it according to agreed specifications.[113] Similar to the field workers this position leaves no ground for boasting since Paul laid the foundation **by the grace of God granted to** him; credit goes not to the proclaimer but the one proclaimed, who is Christ.[114]

Some interpreters suggest that in 3:10 the singular pronoun **another** is a covert allusion to Apollos as the one who builds on Paul's foundation, and the warning of impending judgment in this passage hints at a problem Paul has with this minister.[115] However, the similar designation in this verse, **each one**, doubtless includes all Christian teachers and laborers who are *each individually responsible* to pay attention to the way they build up the community in Christ. Paul often uses nameless third-person singulars in this letter when warning multiple persons (e.g. 3:17; 10:12; 11:29; 14:38; 16:22).[116]

---

111. Williams 2001:258–60, associates Isa 3:3 (σοφὸν ἀρχιτέκτονα) with 1 Cor 3:10, but Isaiah declares that God will take away such a person from Judea in divine judgment, which is not how Paul presents himself.

112. See Inkelaar 2011:284–85.

113. Shanor 1988:461–71; Watson, 1992:35. Bitner 2015b:212–24 relates this building to construction politics.

114. See Schrage 1991:1.298; Garland 2003:115.

115. E.g., Ker 2000:89; Smit 2002:242. Bitner 2015b:265–71, combining indefinite pronouns in this text, suggests this is Crispus, Apollos's alleged advocate. Barrett 1968:91, believes Cephas's party is in view.

116. See further, Oropeza 2012a:100.

First Supporting Proof (1:18—4:21)

The activity of building here seems to be ongoing, and since Apollos had already left Corinth (16:12), it is difficult to maintain that Paul is only or primarily referring to him as someone who builds improperly.[117] *Anyone* who leads, teaches, or presently influences the congregation members is being exhorted, and this includes some of the letter's recipients since a number teach the congregation and exercise spiritual gifts that are supposed to edify members (4:15; 12:7-10, 25-30; 14:3-5, 12, 17, 26-31).

The materials used for the building are listed in two groups. The more valuable and less combustible **gold, silver, and precious stones** are first mentioned, then the less valuable and more combustible **wood, hay, and straw**. The valuable materials recall those Israel used to build its tabernacle and temple (Exod 25:3-7; 35:31-33; 1 Chr 22:14-16; 29:2).[118] And the less valuables were used on houses of poor quality that could rapidly burn (Diodorus Siculus 20.65.1; cf. 5.21.5; Seneca *Ep.* 90.9-10).[119] The sequence of materials leads up to a climax—they go through the process of **fire**.[120] Elements such as gold and silver are refined though this process, whereas wood and straw are destroyed. Alexander Kirk persuasively advances in 3:11-15 that the building materials represent human persons and the **work** should be understood as the "product" or "undertaken work" rather than "deed" or "action." That product is the Corinthian congregation.[121] This is supported by explicit affirmations in 3:9 that the Corinthians are God's field and **God's building** (i.e., God's temple, 3:16).[122] As well, this congregation is viewed as Paul's "work" in the Lord (9:1), and temple imagery for earliest Christians describes believers themselves rather than their deeds (Eph 2:19-22; 1 Pet 2:4-8).[123] We can add to this that Paul returns with another structural metaphor of building up and tearing down that refers to the Corinthians in 2 Cor 10:8, 12:19, and 13:10 (cf. Jer 1:10). The word for **build** (ἐποικοδομέω), which appears four times in 3:10-15, connotes the activity of erecting God's temple that is comprised of those who are in Christ.

This labor is rewarded and requires workers to preach, baptize, train, encourage, or in some other way help establish the faith of new converts who represent the material of this temple. The end product, then, which

---

117. See Mihaila 2009:201.
118. Cf. Kuck 1992:177.
119. See further Arzt-Grabner et al. 2006:151.
120. Bullinger 1898:141.
121. Kirk 2012:549, 552.
122. On another community as both plantation and holy place, see Qumran (1QS 8.5-8); Frayer-Griggs 2013b:522; cf. Hogeterp 2006:330-31.
123. Kirk 2012:554, 556-57.

consists of Corinthian believers, will be revealed for what it is truly worth on the appointed **day** in which it will be tried **by fire**. Our text resembles an apocalyptic scene in which the day of the Lord brings about fiery judgment (Isa 66:15–19, 22, 24; Mal 3:2–3, 18–19; Zeph 1:18; 2 *Bar.* 48.39).[124] Often fire is associated with the destruction of the wicked,[125] and perhaps Paul assumes the essence of divine presence ignites the flames (2 Thess 1:8; cf. Heb 12:27–29), but ultimately this fire is symbolic of judgment, punishment, and purification. The day when this will be revealed happens at Christ's return (1:8; 4:3–5; 5:5; Rom 2:16; cf. 2 Cor 5:10).

Paul's narrative depicts a fire that tests the materials (i.e., human persons) of God's temple. The workers whose materials survive the fire receive payment in the form of a **reward**; other workers are not rewarded since their materials are **burned up**.[126] The workers themselves, however, are **saved through the fire**. This scene is not about bad saints losing their eschatological reward as opposed to losing their salvation.[127] A careful distinction must be made between the workers and their work. If the materials represent various persons who comprise the congregation, it is *these people* who are destroyed by the fire—they fail to persevere in Christ or are otherwise unfit for final salvation on judgment day. The workers lose their disciples in the fire; their many hours of laboring to convert and nurture them turn out to be a costly waste of time. The workers themselves, however, remain saved.[128] This loss imagines the realization of what Paul means when he fears that his own work among his converts will turn out to be in vain if they commit apostasy (Gal 4:11; 1 Thess 2:1; 3:5; Phil 2:16).[129] The Corinthian believers are susceptible to such judgment if they persist in discord, vices, and assimilation to worldly ideologies.[130] Their destruction would take away from the

---

124. Terms such as "temple," "day," burning, and associating the righteous with precious materials and wicked with flammable products, make Malachi a possible informant to Paul's words. cf. Proctor 1993:11–13; Frayer-Griggs 2013b:523–24; Williams 2001:264–65, 269–72.

125. E.g., 1 *En.* 91.9–11; *T. Zeb.* 10.3; 4 Macc 12:12; Matt 3:12; Mark 9:48; 2 Pet 3:7.

126. In 3:15 ζημιόω can refer to punishment or suffering loss. Given the reward in 3:14, the latter is preferred (Yinger 1999:218–19).

127. Contrast Oberholtzer 1988:326. See further, Oropeza 8/2016.

128. In this apocalyptic context, σῴζω does not merely mean *escape*, as though fleeing from a burning house. The person is *saved* from divine wrath and final condemnation (1:18; 5:5; 9:22; 15:2; 2 Cor 2:15; Rom 5:9).

129. On Paul's concept "in vain," see Oropeza 2009:148.

130. Philo similarly mentions Jews who assimilate and abandon their religious traditions to gain social prominence in foreign lands (*Jos.* 254); his nephew Tiberius Julius Alexander exemplifies such apostasy (Josephus *Ant.* 20.100).

joy, honor, and other rewards Paul and his team of workers might otherwise receive on the day of the Lord (cf. 2 Cor 1:14; Phil 2:16; 1 Thess 2:19-20).[131]

Rewards in the afterlife are not unknown,[132] but in our text any boon beyond blissful experiences is left unspecified and may be variegated depending on the worker's labor (3:8, 14).[133] Paul's warning to be careful how one builds pertains to all workers in Christ—they must make sure their messages and teachings are Christ-centered and promote the cruciform way. Everyone, including all workers, will have to go through the fire of eschatological judgment and in this manner be purified.[134] Hence, the popular image of this worker escaping the burning house's fire by the "skin of his teeth" is not accurate. He goes through the fire rather than escapes it.[135] Both worker and work are engulfed in the flames, and only those of quality material survive the ordeal.

Do you not know? With this question Paul urges auditors to ponder on their present behavior (3:16; cf. 5:6; 6:2-3, 9, 15-16, 19; 9:13, 24). The question might assume they already know from previous teachings what Paul will now tell them.[136] More pointedly, however, it may be expressed ironically in light of their boastful knowledge as something they *ought to* know and do something about. Belief that the Spirit dwells in God's temple was not a new concept for Jews,[137] but Paul speaks metaphorically of his Gentile audience as this sanctuary: **You** Corinthians **are God's temple!** His aim, as John Lanci affirms, is not to replace Jerusalem's temple, "but to provide powerful imagery that will engage the emotions of the audience and kindle in the imagination a different way of looking at community."[138] As such, Paul implies that this community in Christ is to be **holy**; the very **Spirit of God dwells** in their midst.

---

131. On eschatological loss of honor, see 1 *En*. 50.1-5; Herms 2006:187-210.

132. E.g., Isa 40:10; *L.A.B.* 64.7; Plato *Rep.* 10.613B; Plutarch *Mor* 943C-D; Kuck 1992:143-44, 233-34; cf. 169.

133. Wendland 1946:23; Yinger 1999:213.

134. Although this purification is sometimes understood as purgatory (see Gregory the Great, *Dial.* 4.39; Montague 2011:76), it refers to an event taking place at Christ's return, not a postmortem state between heaven and hell (Frayer-Griggs 2013b:526).

135. "By fire" ("ἐν πυρί" 3:13) and "as through fire" ("ὡς διὰ πυρός" 3:15) should probably be understood in an instrumental sense. Notice BDAG 1103, regarding "as" (ὡς): "marking the manner in which someth. Proceeds ... corresponding to οὕτως='so, in such a way' ... *as* (one, in an attempt to save oneself, must go) *through fire* (and therefore suffer fr. burns)."

136. So Liu 2013:121.

137. E.g., Wis 9:1-18; Josephus *Ant.* 8.108-114; Hogeterp 2006:327-29.

138. Lanci 1997:134.

In Jewish tradition a person who desecrated God's temple or holy objects may be put to death (e.g., 2 Sam 6:6–7), and an inscription at Herod's temple warned Gentiles of this same fate if they entered the balustrade of the sanctuary (Jos. *Bell.* 6.2.4).[139] It is in this sense of holiness that Paul's warning becomes lucid. Any Corinthian among them who damages or **destroys God's temple**—that is, anyone whose divisive and immoral behavior causes fellow members to stumble in their faith—**God will destroy** that person. The indefinite **anyone** (τις) in 3:17 recalls the same pronoun in 3:12, 14–15, all of which refer to believers. Those who are susceptible to destruction are not outsiders, but insiders, the Corinthian believers. The congregation's problem involves members harming other members (e.g., 8:7–13). The idea of reciprocating destruction recalls the *lex talionis* principle of ruin for ruin,[140] and is akin with the common adage, "whoever does x will receive x."[141] The notion of recompense is clear, and since Paul is referring to divine judgment, what may be foremost elicited is that on judgment day when Christ returns, everyone will receive as their works deserve, whether good or bad (2 Cor 5:10; Rom 2:6, 16; 14:12; Col 3:25; cf. Jer 32:19; Job 34:11; 1 *En.* 100.7). Consequently, this punishment is more than merely physical death.[142] It refers to eschatological destruction on judgment day.[143] It follows that the one who damages the temple where the life-giving Spirit dwells will be severed from the Spirit and that life which the Spirit gives.[144]

Exhortations against Boasting (3:18–23)

With further imperatives Paul discourages his auditors from self-deception and boasting. With **let no one deceive himself**, one of the main causes of potential damage to the temple's holiness is evident—some of its members have been misled to follow and emulate an ideology that exemplifies the **wise in this age** and **wisdom of this world**, which as we already explored (1:18–21; 2:6–8), helps instigate factions. The apostle now challenges the Corinthians to abandon this influence—if any among them want to be wise,

139. See Deissmann, 1965:79–81.

140. Yinger 1999:225.

141. See on the former point, Yinger 1999:225, and the latter, Keener 2005:43 (cf. Prov 26:27; Sir 27:25–27).

142. Rightly, Konradt 2003:278.

143. See "destroy" (φθείρω) in end-time judgment in Jude 10; 2 Pet 2:12. The term can alternatively mean "to corrupt" in a moral sense (Liu 2013:122–23), and so there is a possible play on the word φθείρω: "if anyone *corrupts* God's temple, God will *destroy* that person."

144. Cf. Thiselton 2000:318.

First Supporting Proof (1:18—4:21)

let him become foolish so that he may become wise.[145] This inverted way of thinking recapitulates earlier thoughts in which weakness related to the crucified Christ marks truly divine wisdom and power, and what is wise in this world is **foolishness in God's sight** (e.g., 1:18–25).

Two quotes from Israel's scriptures reinforce the idea. The first seems to be a loose reference to Job 5:13 in which God is **the one who catches the wise in their own craftiness.**[146] Paul may have been attracted to the wisdom in Job 5 because, complementary with what he argues, God graciously *waters* earth (Job 5:11/1 Cor 3:7), and there is an anticipated *day* in which darkness will come upon the wise (Job 5:14/1 Cor 3:13) as well as a request that clever ones be *destroyed* (Job 5:15/1 Cor 3:17). For Paul, the catching of the clever ones means more than simply making their wisdom look foolish, as Job's context and Paul's similar language in 1:18-19 make clear. The second scripture comes from Ps 94[93]:11—**the Lord knows the thoughts of the wise; that they are useless.**[147] Hook words relevant for Paul, such as *wise, fools,* and the idea of cultivation with the God who *plants* (94[93]:8-9), may have drawn him to this psalm after being informed by Job. Likewise in this text, the Lord judges with recompense the proud and boastful (94[93]:1-3), similar to how Paul connects the advocates of worldly wisdom with arrogance and boasting (3:21; cf. 1:31; 4:6-7, 18-19). Together these quotes confirm that human cleverness is folly before God, and divine judgment awaits those who are deceived by it.

The final imperative in this passage exhorts the Corinthians to **let no one boast in humans.** This seems to reference their divisive claims of allegiances to **Paul, Apollos,** and **Cephas** (cf. 1:12) and advances a compelling resolution. These allegiances are turned upside down by Paul's assertion that he and other leaders belong to *them*—they are committed to serving the Corinthians and being in solidarity with this congregation. Moreover, he affirms to them that **all things are yours**! This affirmation may be adopted from the Stoic maxim, "all things belong to the wise person;" that is, sages

---

145. In 3:18 γενέσθω may be imperative or ingressive aorist indicating the start of the act (Thistelton 2000:321).

146. Paul refers to God as ὁ δρασσόμενος ("the one who catches"), but Job 5:13 uses ὁ καταλαμβάνων, which is similar in meaning. His version may reflect a Hebraizing of the LXX or a different Greek variant (see Stanley 1992:189–92). In any case δράσσομαι (more than καταλαμβάνω) reflects the ease of this activity (Inkelaar 2011:288). Job 5:13(LXX) uses "cleverness" (φρόνησις) instead of "craftiness" (πανουργία). Paul's πανουργία may be influenced by Job 5:12, which states that God changes the counsel of "the crafty ones" (πανούργων).

147. Ps 93:11(LXX) has the thoughts "of men" (ἀνθρώπων) rather than thoughts "of the wise" (σοφῶν). Perhaps Paul changed the wording by connecting the term "wise" from 93:8 with 93:11 so as to stress wisdom in his own quote.

First Supporting Proof (1:18—4:21)

are lords over whatever circumstances might come their way (Seneca, *Ben.* 7.2.5; Cicero *Fin.* 3.22.75; Diogenes Laertius *Vit.* 6.37).[148] But if so, our apostle reconfigures its meaning to suggest to the Corinthians that they are gifted with every salvific benefit that comes from God. They are receiving the future inheritance of the new creation, eternal **life**, victory over **death**, and conquest of the present world through the cross and resurrection, not because of any power or cleverness of their own, but because they **belong to** and have an ultimate allegiance with **Christ**, and **Christ belongs to God**. The eight correlative conjunctions of **whether ... or ...** (εἴτε ... εἴτε ...) in these verses lead up to and stress this sense of belonging along with its salvific benefits.[149] If they have all sufficiency in Christ, then it follows that their only ground for boasting is in the Lord. Such privilege subverts any need to compete their leaders against one another or seek status recognition based on this world's standards.

PAUL THE ADMINISTRATOR AND JUDGMENT DAY (4:1–5)

Paul continues his discourse on wisdom and apocalyptic images related to judgment day. Some add that this section is an apology, a self-defense of Paul's character and ministry.[150] His explanation in 4:6, however, along with further instructions, exhortations, and a call to imitate his behavior (4:1, 5, 14, 16–17), suggest that his *primary* goal remains a deliberative attempt to change Corinthian discordant behavior.

His opening exhortation, **thus let a person consider**, begins a string of words related to judgment in 4:1–5. In correction of the way he and Apollos have been placed on pedestals to compete with one another, Paul challenges the congregation to regard them as mere **assistants and administrative stewards** of Christ.[151] The term *assistants* (ὑπηρέτης) originally referred to under-rowers in a ship and suggested helpers to someone else as instruments of that person's will.[152] In a religious sense the word describes Cynics as Zeus's assistants (Epictetus, *Diatr.* 3.22.82, 95), and Moses as God's faithful servant (Josephus *Ant.* 4.49). In our present context it may designate someone in an official capacity as subordinate to a higher authority.[153] The

---

148. Lindemann 2000:93; Fitzmyer 2008:208.

149. Bullinger 1898:238, recognizes this type of literary repetition as *paradiastole*.

150. See Schrage 1991:1.318–19; Dahl 1967:313–35.

151. Though mentioned in 3:18–23, allegiances to Cephas appear to be quite minor in comparison (cf. 4:6).

152. See sources in Rengstorf 1964:8.539.

153. See papyri sources in Arzt-Grabner et al. 2006:162.

apostles are depicted having an administrative position in God's domain as delegated servants doing the bidding of their Lord, Jesus Christ. The second term, *administrative steward* (οἰκονόμος), portrays a similar image in which the apostles are commercial managers.[154] John Goodrich's study of this position distinguishes between different types of administrators and concludes that Paul resembles most the private administrator. These "were almost always slaves during the Roman period, normally serving a κύριος/ *dominus* [lord] as business managers."[155] Paul and Apollos are portrayed metaphorically as God's competent servant-treasurers entrusted with **the mysteries of God** (the wealth of God's wisdom related to the plan of salvation). This position would be known and relevant for congregation members who knew Erastus, a fellow church member who served as οἰκονόμος for their city (Rom 16:23). Though unlike Paul's nuance, Erastus seems to be a civic rather than private administrator and probably not a slave. As a fellow believer and Paul's colleague, Erastus appears to have the time, money, and freedom to do missionary travelling, which would hardly be possible for slaves (cf. Acts 19:22; 2 Tim 4:20).[156]

As God's administrative steward, Paul must **be found faithful**, a virtue that has implications for the Corinthians who must learn that faithfulness rather than clever words is the proper criteria for evaluation.[157] Since Paul considers them incompetent as spiritual judges (cf. 2:11–15), he thinks it **a very small matter** that his ministerial and speaking performance should be evaluated and criticized by them in comparison with other leaders like Apollos. He mentions three incompetent tribunals—the Corinthians, the human court system, and Paul's self-awareness: **I do not even judge myself**. Although he is **not conscious** of doing anything wrong, he is **not acquitted** on that basis, for there is one to whom Paul is accountable and that person can reveal things Paul may have neglected and forgotten about, whether good or bad. He implies here that if he cannot fully determine his own innocence and secret motives, how much less the Corinthians? The only competent judge is **the Lord** who will preside on judgment day. This takes place at the second coming of Christ and day of the Lord (cf. 3:13), which stands in contrast to any **human day** in which a human court is appointed to decide a case.[158] Both Christ (2 Cor 5:10) and God seem to be active as the end-

---

154. Cf. Goodrich 2012:106–7.
155. Ibid. 200; cf. 25–116.
156. *Pace* Friesen 2010:231–56.
157. See Litfin 1994:226.
158. In 4:3 ἀνθρώπινος ἡμέρα is often translated as "human court" (NRSV), but it literally means "human day."

First Supporting Proof (1:18—4:21)

time judge (Rom 14:10; 1 Thess 3:13). Perhaps Paul imagines a judgment in which God works in and through Christ who is the visible representative of the divine presence on that day (cf. Rom 2:16). Hence, "Lord" in this context may refer to God in Christ. This apocalyptic scene partially resembles Dan 7:9–15, which depicts both the Ancient of Days in a courtroom as judge and also the Son of Man.

Paul mentions three things that will take place at this judgment. First, the Lord **will bring to light what is hidden in the darkness**. Here, darkness is not necessarily metaphorical for what is evil or immoral but what is unseen and secretive (cf. Ps 139:1–12; Dan 2:22; Matt 10:27). Second, the Lord **will reveal the motives of the hearts**. Paul's assumption is that the Lord knows all things including human inner thoughts (Prov 15:11; 1 Cor 14:25; Rom 8:27; Heb 4:12–13).[159] Third, **each person will receive praise from God** on that day. Our apostle's words betray an optimism about that day probably because he thinks of Apollos and himself foremost as those being examined. As far as he can determine, he is free of any personal wrongdoing and is confident that faithful servants will be honored by God after the examination (4:4a; cf. 3:8, 14; 2 Cor 1:14; Phil 2:16; 1 Thess 2:19). Hidden motives are something the Corinthians cannot know; hence, unless given divine revelation they cannot properly criticize Paul.

Exhortations, Hardships, and Parental Instruction (4:6–21)

Paul's appeal (παρακαλῶ) for the Corinthians to imitate him in 4:16 forms a subtle *inclusio* with 1:10 that signals the close of this entire letter section and first supporting proof against congregational divisions. A number of stylistic devices fill this pericope including ellipsis (4:6), rhetorical questions (4:7), anabasis (the gradual ascent of successive words) (4:8), irony (4:8a, 10), sarcasm (4:8b), antitheses (4:10, 12–13), hyperbole (4:8, 13b, 15), polysyndeton (multiple conjunctions) (4:9, 11–12a), asyndeton (no conjunctions) (4:12b–13), and epanalepsis (repetition after a break: "until this present hour," "until now") (4:11, 13).[160] The text ends with an aphorism (4:20) and an ultimatum posed as a question (4:21). Paul provokes pathos by attempting to stir Corinthian emotions through strong exclamations (4:8), pity (4:9–13), shame (4:14), fear (4:18–20), familial affection (4:6a, 15, 17), parental instruction, exhortation, and admonition (4:6b, 14–17, 21). All this is aimed at deflating their arrogant and discordant attitude (4:6c–7, 18–19).

---

159. See further, Konradt 2003:290.
160. Bullinger 1898:206.

First Supporting Proof (1:18—4:21)

In 4:6 **these things** probably refers to the content of what Paul has written since 3:5. More particularly, it points to the different metaphors that describe Paul and Apollos as day laborers in a field, builders of a temple, and assistants and administrative stewards under the Lord's authority. With these various occupational roles, Paul says, **I have figuratively transformed into myself and Apollos for your sake.**[161] The apostle is not literally a farmer, building contractor, etc., but has in a figurative sense taken on these positions for the two-fold purpose of teaching his auditors not to go beyond proper boundaries they have been taught, and not to be arrogant.

If we unpack the latter purpose, no one among the Corinthians are to **be puffed up in favor of the one against the other**. This attitude by extension condemns all such dissensions in the congregation, but most immediately the "one" can refers to Paul and the "other" Apollos. This notion of over-estimation of oneself resurfaces elsewhere in the letter and may be understood as conceit and arrogance (φυσιόω: 4:18–19; 5:2; 8:1; 13:4; cf. φυσίωσις: 2 Cor 12:20). Peter Marshall asserts that the word is further explicated in 4:7–8, which convey thoughts of self-superiority and boasting, and are further associated with the similar vice of *hubris*, a type of insolence that, among other things, characterizes the behavior of those with power who intend to dishonor others.[162] The sophists are thus described with conceit and thinking themselves better than others (Dio Chrysostom *Or.* 6.21). Welborn appropriately adds regarding Corinthian arrogance:

> It is all too familiar to the student of political history as the caricature of the political windbag, the orator inflated at his success (Ps.-Plato *Alcibiades* 2 145e; Plutarch *Cicero* 887b; Epictetus *Diss.* 2.16.10), the young aristocrat, the aspiring tyrant, filled with a sense of his own power (Alcibiades and Critias in Xenophon *Mem.* 1.2.25; Gaius in Philo *Legat.* 86.154; Pausanias in Demosthenes 59.97; see also Thucydides 1.132.1–3; Dio Chrysostom 30.19; 58.5), the supercilious officeholder (Demosthenes 19.314; Philo *Legat.* 69.255).[163]

---

161. Among the many ways translators have rendered the aorist verb μετεσχημάτισα (which I render "figuratively transformed") Paul probably uses it in the normal sense of changing the form of something (cf. Phil 3:20). For a survey of interpretations, see Mihaila 2009:202–12; Bitner 2015b:290–94. A prominent view is that this is a veiled argument or "covert allusion" used to censure or correct someone indirectly (Fiore 1985:89, 92–93). But Paul is not indirect in 3:1–5, 9, 16–23, and the rhetorical term σχηματίζω is not μετασχηματίζω (cf. Mahaila 2009:204).

162. Marshall 1987:204–6; cf. 182–90 (ὕβρις).

163. Welborn 1987b:88.

Excursus: Interpreting "What is Written" in 4:6

With forceful riposte, then, the figures of Paul and Apollos's service and servanthood challenges Corinthian arrogance.¹⁶⁴ Divisive members should not deem themselves better than others by virtue of their leaders, status, or spiritual gifts.

The former purpose for Paul taking on figurative positions is that the Corinthians might learn **the (saying) "not beyond what is written."** This may reflect a saying familiar to the Corinthians or one or more of Paul's earlier Scripture citations. I suggest a merging of the two ideas in the form of double entendre as a viable alternative (see Excursus).

Excursus: Interpreting "What is Written" in 4:6

The Corinthians are to learn "the 'not beyond what is written'" (τὸ μὴ ὑπὲρ ἃ γέγραπται). The position of the neuter article τό ("the") suggests Paul is introducing a quote, and the quote's content is perhaps a popular one the Corinthians would recognize.¹⁶⁵ Among many interpretations of this phrase, the most prominent are these: 1) some words fell out of the original text that our extant copies did not preserve, or conversely, a gloss was written into the extant copies; 2) Paul refers to what he has just written in this letter; 3) Paul refers generally to Scripture, the Old Testament canon; 4) Paul refers to a non-scriptural maxim; and 5) Paul refers to one or more of his previous scriptural citations in 1:19, 31; 2:6, 16; 3:19, 20.¹⁶⁶

Option 1 is a formidable possibility, but there is no evidence in early manuscripts that directly supports it (and if we stopped here, it would take away the fun of speculating about other possibilities!). Option 2 is unlikely because we would expect the grammatical inflections Paul normally uses when referring to his own writing, such as the present tense "I write" (γ'Αάφω: 4:14) or the aorist "I wrote" (ἔγραψα: 5:9) rather than the perfect passive, "is written" (γέγραπται).¹⁶⁷ Option 3 is also unlikely given the more specific and contextually based option 5. Moreover, if Paul meant to say the canon of Israel's Scripture, it is odd that he himself cites sources for moral

---

164. Rightly, Finney 2012:107.

165. On τό introducing a quote, see Gal 5:14; Rom 13:9; Tyler 1998:97; cf. Welborn 1987a:328, 345 on maxim sources.

166. See elaborate surveys in Thiselton 2000:352–56; Hanges 1998:275–85; Fitzmyer 2008:215–16.

167. Further on γράφω: 1 Cor 14:37; Gal 1:20; on ἔγραψα: 1 Cor 5:11; Rom 15:15; 2 Cor 2:4, 9; 7:12; Phlm 21.

Excursus: Interpreting "What is Written" in 4:6

instruction "beyond what is written" in these Scriptures (e.g., 15:33), and in any case, the entire corpus of these scriptures does not center on the prevention of being puffed up (4:6c).[168]

With option 4 there is no consensus regarding the content of this saying. Some arguments are that it refers to written cultic by-laws in the Corinthian congregation, political formulae promoting reconciliation, or the politics of building construction in which building contractors direct workers not to violate contract stipulations.[169] If option 4 is correct, I tend to agree with John Fitzgerald and others that the saying is pedagogical.[170] This passage is filled with pedagogical words including the necessity to learn (4:6), tutors (4:15), parental guidance (4:15), imitation (4:16), remembrance (4:17), and teaching (4:17). We already know that the Corinthians are immature and still have to be taught the basic A, B, C's of faith because they do not understand spiritual wisdom (2:6–3:4). Hence, Paul instructs them about the cross (1:18–31) and teaches them figurative roles so that they might learn not to pit their leaders against each other (3:5—4:6). They must now *learn* the saying at hand. This setting evokes a depiction of Paul as teacher of the Corinthian students. Paul's term for learning (μανθάνω), *inter alia* was used for those learning how to write.[171] Reading and writing were among essential disciplines to be learned from the age of seven, and beginners learned to identify, pronounce, and write the Greek alphabet, often following models from their teacher.[172] Teachers trained children how to write the alphabet and basic words by having them trace the letters over the teacher's own lines (cf. Plato, *Protag.* 326D; Seneca *Lucil.* 94.51). Quintilian explains the procedure: "As soon as the child has begun to know the shapes of the various letters, it will be no bad thing to have them cut as accurately as possible upon a board, so that the pen may be guided along the grooves. Thus, mistakes such as occur with wax tablets will be rendered impossible; for the pen will be confined between the edges of the letters and will be prevented from going astray" (*Inst.* 1.1.27).[173] In this light, Paul is quoting to the Corinthians a saying for children learning how to follow their

---

168. The word φυσιόω is not even found in the LXX.

169. See respectively, Hanges 1998:275–98; Welborn 1987a:320–46; Bitner 2015b:294–300.

170. Fitzgerald 1988:122–28; Tyler 1998:97–103.

171. See Josephus *Ap.* 1.10; papyri examples in Arzt-Grabner et al. 2006:171.

172. See Hock 2003:200; cf. 220; Cribiore 1996:139–152.

173. Tyler 1998:102.

Excursus: Interpreting "What is Written" in 4:6

teacher's instructions and not to write "over the lines."[174] The importance of elegant handwriting is quite evident in papyri, based on school text comments criticizing poor styles.[175]

Unfortunately, like the other possibilities in option 4, the exact phrase in 4:6 is not found in relevant ancient sources that would confirm this viewpoint. Nevertheless, if the quote was not normally written down but understood orally in that culture, evidence for it may be rather difficult to uncover. Robert Dutch suggests that elitist children may be in view since poor children would not be afforded the opportunity to write, and if so, the idea of elitists being puffed up is relevant for the context: "To indicate that the educated elite need to behave like one learning to write is a put-down. They would be proud of their education that separated them socially from the non-elite in the church."[176] But if so, who among the number of lower class congregation members, many who might not have received even an elementary education, would know the saying? Is Paul targeting here congregants from the upper or at least in-between classes who might understand him? An affirmative answer to this second question cannot be ruled out, especially when his auditors are expected to be familiar with the role of tutors (see 4:15).

Option 5 has its setbacks, too. First, γέγραπται does not introduce a quotation as it does in Paul's other citations of Scripture; it is *part* of the quotation. Thus, the "not beyond what *is written*" seems to be a saying rather than Scripture citation. Second, none of the passages Paul cites earlier mentions being puffed up (φυσιόω). Even so, this notion of being puffed up is similar to and sometimes used in tandem with boasting, and the latter term appears in 4:7.[177] In Paul's most immediate citation in 3:20 (Ps 93[94]:11), the term for boasting, καῖΟάομαι, appears in Ps 93[94]:3, as well as in Paul's negative imperative after the reference (3:21). ΚαῖΟάομαι is likewise found in the citation of 1:31 (Jer 9:22–23). Although "these things" in 4:6 is more concerned with the content of 3:5—4:5, verse 3:21 may be built on the earlier boasting in 1:31.[178] In 4:6, then, is γέγραπται

---

174. Fitzgerald 1988:127.

175. See Morgan 1998:41, who references P.*Oxy* III.469; XLII.3004; P.*Harr.* 1.59; P.*Amh.* II.21.

176. Dutch 2005:294–95; cf. 292.

177. E.g., Philo *Cong.* 107, 127; Plutarch *Comp. Dem. Cic.* 2.1–3; Mitchell 1991:95; Weiss 1910:104.

178. Cf. Zeller 2011:181.

referring to 3:19–21 despite Paul's convoluted grammar, and would his Gentile audience be informed enough to connect the dots between being puffed up and boasting with Paul's citation? Perhaps a minority would.

Since both options 4 and 5 seem to target at least a minority of the congregants, another relevant question to ask is this: would Paul make these connections, whether by maxim or citation, regardless of whether most of his auditors would have understood them? I think the answer would be yes. As any learned communicator knows, past or present, certain quotes and words of theirs will not be understood by everyone. Sometimes the words are understood only by few, and yet that does not prevent communicators from saying them anyway. Film makers are experts at this—for example, in a children's film, the majority of their youthful audiences do not understand every part of the film, especially humorous double entendres that are targeted at their parents! Double entendre (ἀμφιβολία), in fact, was an admirable quality for communicators in the ancient world; use of this device characterized the speeches of Hermocrates of Phocaea (Philostratus *Vit. soph.* 2.609).[179] Might Paul being doing something similar here? Perhaps he deliberatively framed his words in a way that would enable some of his auditors to think back on the Scripture he just cited, while others would recognize a popular saying recalling children learning how to write.

Three rhetorical questions now challenge the Corinthians in 4:7:[180] **Who regards you to be superior (to others)?** expects the answer "no one" (cf. Acts 15:9). **And what do you have which you did not receive?** expects the answer "nothing." **And, why do you boast as though not the receiver?** anticipates the response, "I should not be boasting; all that I am and everything I receive is a gift from God." Seneca admonishes his elite readers that wealth and possessions are meant to share and give away, but instead of being mere stewards of these things, their wealth has caused them to swell with pride and exalt themselves over others (*Ben.* 6.3.1–4; cf. 2.18.1; 4.6.3). Paul's words similarly aim to admonish the Corinthians who instead of wealth receive knowledge, salvific benefits, spiritual gifts, and leaders like Paul and Apollos. What they receive should not inflate them with arrogance against others but prompt them with the realization that *nothing* is theirs as

---

179. See further examples in LSJ 90; Wright 1998:567.

180. Paul's switch to second person singulars in 4:7 is motivated by "one against the other" in 4:6c. He is not singling out one congregation member (cf. Schnabel 2006:244).

a result of their own achievements. Every good thing they have is a gift from God (cf. Ps 85[84]:12; Jas 1:17; Philo *Post.* 80)

These questions are followed by three grandiose exclamations: **Already you have been satiated! Already you have become rich! Already you have become kings without us!** Paul's irony criticizes the Corinthians' puffed up attitude by imagining them as smug, wealthy rulers of this world whose high and lofty position contrasts lowly lives like Paul and other apostles.[181] These words may reflect sophist boastings (Philo *Det.* 33–35) or perceptions that characterize *hubris* among the arrogant (Aristotle *Rhet.* 2.2.5–6; Herodotus *Hist.* 3.80).[182] Another possibility is that the Corinthians are influenced by Stoic notions of wise persons as wealthy kings.[183] Paul may have conversed with similar philosophers (e.g., Acts 17:18, 34), and if so, he knows that such things are said of them.[184] He thus uses this language of wisdom effectively to deflate the arrogant Corinthians. We should stress, in any case, that Paul's overstatements make the Corinthians' status to be something "other than it really is."[185]

With their new make-believe status intact, the Corinthians are now prompted to envision the end of a triumphal procession or an arena spectacle or both (4:9–10).[186] The apostles are apparent captives of war in which **God has exhibited** them **last**, as the final public **spectacle**. If a procession is imagined,[187] the very end of the celebration is in view when execution is determined for the captives at the Roman temple, *Jupiter Capitolinus*. The apostles are **as those condemned to death**.[188] The captives may be slain or sacrificed on the spot,[189] or they might be condemned to die at a later point in the arena. Henry Nguyen makes a case for the spectacle portraying arena

---

181. On Apollos as an apostle, see Wilson 2013:325–35

182. See respectively, Winter 2002:198; Marshall 1987:205–6.

183. Cf. Diogenes Laertius *Vit. phil.* 7.122; Lucian, *Hermot.* 16; Plutarch *Stoic. Abs.* 1058B–C; Paige 2004:211–14; Pogoloff 1992:115–17. Unlike Thiselton 1978:510–26 and my earlier Oropeza 2002a:88–90; 2007:180–82, I now think it less likely that realized eschatology is in view.

184. E.g., Plato *Rep.* 5.473C–D; Epictetus *Diatr.* 3.22.49; Musonius Rufus *Lect.* 8.

185. Planck 1987:39 cf. 48, defines this type of irony as dissimulation.

186. Josephus *Bell.* 7.131, portrays Vespasian's procession through Roman theatres to make it widely visible.

187. As BDAG 108 claims of ἀποδείκνυμι, though if captives are last in the sense of *parading order*, this is not typical of Roman triumphs (cf. Plutarch *Aemil. Paul.* 32.2—34.4; Appian *Pun.* 9.66; *Mith.* 17.116–17).

188. The sentence of death, ἐπιθανατίους, is rare; e.g., in the Septuagint it appears only once in reference to those thrown to the lions (Bel 31). This term weakens the idea that the fool of mime theatre is in view (cf. Adams 2008:111–30, *pace* Welborn 2005).

189. See Versnel 1970:58–63, 83–87; Hafemann 2000:105.

First Supporting Proof (1:18—4:21)

games (cf. Seutonius *Claud.* 21; Apuleius, *Metam.* 4.13).[190] In these games the *noxii*, or condemned criminals, frequently were captives of war, though other unwilling participants may include local criminals, deserters, and rebel slaves.[191] Their death became a source of entertainment that might include being thrown to beasts, burned with fire, crucified, or made to play "fatal charades" in which they were forced to play popular roles that included their actual death.[192] Likewise, an unskilled gladiator normally died in the arena.[193]

Paul's spectacle is presented not only to Romans but also **to the world and to angels and humans**, with God as the *editor*, the benefactor who supports the event financially.[194] Both heaven and earth, then, witness the apostle's suffering, which has the effect of prompting Corinthian pathos due to the magnitude of ignominy endured by Paul in conformity to his calling that recalls the cruciform Christ. Paul's audience is indirectly prompted to choose between its desire for elitist wisdom, power, and eminence, or the apostolic plight viewed by the world as **foolish, weak,** and **disreputable** scum whose lives do not matter. A reality check for the Corinthians might remind them that they, too, resemble the apostle (cf. 1:26–27).[195] But in Paul's ironic scene they are imagined instead as royal, rich, and satisfied elitists. They are the ones who take the best seats in this arena as they watch the bloody spectacle. Paul's call for them to be his imitators, then, might compel them to get out of their privileged seats as spectators and jump into the arena with the apostle.[196]

The catalogue of hardships Paul experiences is composed of triadic sets (4:11–13). Although "we" is used, Paul thinks foremost of his own experiences and secondarily of any colleagues who happen to be with him to share them.[197] The first set is **hunger, thirst, poorly clothed** (cf. 2 Cor 11:27; Phil 4:12). These are bodily setbacks the apostle experiences during his missionary travels, which may indirectly apply to the conditions of captives of

---

190. Nguyen 2007:495–98. Corinth also had death spectacles (Nguyen 2007:492; Walters 2005:405–6), but the sources reflect a time later than Paul's.

191. Cf. Kyle 1998:79, 91–93, 119–20, 268. For captives of war as spectacle, see e.g., Josephus *Bell.* 6.418; 7.23–24, 37–40; Cassius Dio *Hist.* 67.8.2.

192. Kyle 1998:53–55.

193. On the gladiator game view, see Concannon 2014:207–13 (pro); Nguyen 2007:495–98 (con).

194. Cf. Tertullian *Ad Mart.* 3; Pucci 2000:114.

195. See Lambrecht 1996:327.

196. Cf. Nguyen 2008b:43–44.

197. For similar catalogues, see 2 Cor 4:7–12; 6:4–10; 11:23–33; Rom 8:35; Fitzgerald 1988; Hodgson 1983:59–80.

First Supporting Proof (1:18—4:21)

war. The next set depicts more missionary experiences, including violent opposition by being **brutally treated**, perpetual travelling and thus being **homeless**, and Paul toiling as a tentmaker by **laboring with** his **own hands** to support himself (cf. 2 Cor 4:9; 6:4–5; 11:23–25; Acts 18:3). The next triad reflects apostolic responses to experiencing injustices. When Paul and his team are **verbally abused**, they **bless** the revilers in return; when they are **persecuted**, they **endure** whatever affliction takes place as a result; and when they are **slandered**, they attempt to **conciliate** in a friendly manner (cf. 2 Cor 6:6–8). These responses resemble the voice of Jesus who urges his followers to do good to those who hate them, bless those who curse them, and pray for those who mistreat them (cf. Luke 6:27–28).[198]

The list ends in hyperbolic language with the apostles having **become the refuse of the world and off-scouring of all things**. These words might describe the waste and filth that is scrapped away from whatever is cleansed from a utensil. But given that 4:9 forms an *inclusio* with 4:13 with the parallel phrase, "we have become . . . to/of the world," the grisly remains of the earlier captives of war, this time after the spectacle is over, may be foremost in view. Paul's audience might envision the remains of the apostle's dead body after being mauled by beasts, burned, crucified, slaughtered, or otherwise mutilated.[199] These remains are thrown out as refuse to be left exposed on the street or at the dumpsite where they rot away and are eaten by vermin instead of given proper burial. Paul's words nonetheless may reflect a double entendre—the nearly synonymous "refuse" (περικάθαρμα) and "off-scouring" (περίψημα) sometimes have cultic meaning in which they become the means of purification by virtue of their removal (e.g., Prov 21:8; Tob 5:19).[200] Paul's bodily remains may be thus perceived both as a dead and mangled stench of flesh and, similar to Christ, as a sacrificial offering that purifies those who come to faith. His imagery alternates from utter defeat through the world's eyes to ultimate victory through heaven's eyes. Among the many afflicted sages in Hellenistic tradition and righteous and prophetic sufferers in Jewish tradition, Paul patterns his own suffering most pointedly after Jesus Christ. As Christ sacrificed his life by suffering on the cross so that others might be cleansed from sin, Paul daily sacrifices his life, suffering as a missionary in order to proclaim the message of the cross.

Although our apostle expresses **these things** not wanting **to shame** the Corinthians (4:14), this is what his language nevertheless does. His primary goal at any rate is to admonish and **correct** them as his **beloved children**, and

---

198. See Neirynck 1996:157.
199. See Nguyen 2007:500; cf. Kyle 1998:162–68.
200. See BDAG 801, 808; Weiss 1910:113–14.

First Supporting Proof (1:18—4:21)

so his exhibition of apostolic hardships is for an exhortational purpose that combines familial and pedagogical discourse. An exaggerated **ten thousand tutors** (παιδαγωγούς) mark the congregation's teachers and visiting ministers who guide, protect, and provide them with moral education.[201] Paul on the other hand claims to be their **father**—it was **through the gospel** he proclaimed that they came to faith in Christ (Acts 18).[202] As their spiritual parent he should be honored by them; parental honor may be assumed second only to honoring God and perhaps country (Cicero *Off.* 1.160; *Ps.-Phoc.* 8; cf. Sir 3:8–11; Eph 6:1–2).[203] A father like Paul is to be respected, imitated, and should receive affection in reciprocity.[204] This assertion prompts discordant Corinthians to submit and be unified under the one household in Christ in which Paul functions as their father.[205] Moreover, fathers are considered teachers of their children (Aristotle *N.E.* 8.12.5; Philostratus *Vit. soph.* 1.490),[206] as Benjamin Fiore affirms, "The teaching in the school is considered an extension of, or at least analogous to, the parent in the home."[207] Part of that teaching role was for children to imitate their parents by way of example, which is how Paul exhorts the Corinthians: **Be imitators of me**. They are to follow the apostle's servant-like and cruciform conduct in 3:5—4:13.

Rhetorical and philosophical training encouraged students by way of imitation as well (Philostratus *Vit. soph.* 2.586-88; Theon, *Prog.* 2.70–71; Isocrates *Soph.* 13.17–18; Xenophon *Mem.* 1.2.3).[208] The example our apostle promotes is subversive to the status-seeking ideology wed with imitating sophist rhetoricians. Ben Witherington rightly notes that "Paul distinguishes himself both from the sort of father figure the emperor might be and from the sort other teachers, especially Sophists, might be, especially by means of his hardship catalog."[209] To imitate Paul is to imitate what is contrary to the standards of the present age and its rulers—it embraces humility, suffering, and strength in weakness in Christ (4:10–13, 17). Paul, however, has the

---

201. On the role of the παιδαγωγός see e.g., Philo *Legat.* 53; Diogenes Laertius *Vit. phil.* 3.92; Gal 3:24–25.

202. In 4:14, "not many fathers" may be an ironic understatement about Paul as their one father in faith, or Paul concedes that God also used a few other missionaries to convert them (e.g., 3:5).

203. Cf. Burke 2003:100–101.

204. E.g., Seneca *Ben.* 3.37:1–3; Isocrates, *Dem.* 4.11; Aristotle *N.E.* 8.12.2; Burke 100–104.

205. See Barton 1986:239; Burke 2003:107.

206. Cf. Watson, 2000a:309, 311; Burke 104–5.

207. Fiore 2003:234; cf. 251.

208. Cf. Winter 2001:33–34.

209. Witherington 1995:145.

First Supporting Proof (1:18—4:21)

problem of being an absent father, and so he must send **Timothy** to Corinth for proxy parental duties (cf. 16:10–11).[210] Timothy, one of Paul's converts, reflects a prime example of this sort of parent-child imitation; he will help reinforce Corinthian imitation of Paul's moral standards and patterns of conduct in Christ.[211] Such values are taught by Paul **in every church**, and the Corinthians should not think themselves an exception.

Paul concludes this section by promising his own follow-up visit to Corinth (4:18–21; cf. 16:3–7). That **some** members **have become arrogant as though I were not coming to you** recalls Corinthian attitudes in 4:6-7. They are like children who are left alone and suppose that they will get away with their misbehavior because the parent is not present. Those who are critical of Paul, presumably those who do not regard him as their spiritual parent, may not have thought he was coming back at all.[212] Paul mentions his coming as a way to deflate their arrogance—he will set things right, that is, **if the Lord permits** him to visit. These inflated individuals will encounter the Spirit's power that works mightily through the apostle (2:4-5), and a similar power had better work through them because their bombastic talking will get them nowhere on that day! The aphorism in 4:20 is not exhaustive in definition but expresses an important feature relevant to this context:[213] **the kingdom of God** that is being revealed to them is not characterized by clever words but the Spirit's **power** that works miracles and transforms lives.

In prospect of Paul's return, the Corinthians must now decide how to behave; the result of their choice will determine Paul's actions when he arrives. If they follow his exhortations, he will visit them with the parental affections of **love and an attitude of gentleness**. If they persist in arrogance, he will discipline them with a metaphoric **rod** of correction. Fathers in patriarchal homes were expected to physically discipline their children, even with a stick (Prov 22:15; 2 Sam 7:14; Philo, *Spec. Leg.* 2.231–32). In wisdom discourse this was not considered abusive but reflected instead God's love as a disciplining Father (Prov 3:11–12; Sir 30:1–2).[214] In like manner, teachers and tutors punished students in order to improve their learning.[215] Both father and teacher roles enable Paul's metaphor of the disciplining rod, but the former has more authority here. What type of punishment might Paul

---

210. So Wanamaker 2006:348.
211. See Schrage 1991:1.360.
212. Cf. Fee 1987:190.
213. Conzelmann 1975:93; cf. Rom 14:17.
214. Cf. Myrick 1996:165.
215. E.g., Philo *Migr. Abr.* 116; further, Elliott/Reasoner 2011:71–72; Dutch 2005:263, 278; Young 1987:162–64.

First Supporting Proof (1:18—4:21)

be referring to with this rod? Richard Hays relates this to the showdown between Elijah and the prophets of Baal (1 Kgs 18:20–40), and Roy Harrisville, with Moses and Pharaoh's magicians (Exod 7–9).[216] Perhaps a more relevant parallel describes Paul being filled with the Spirit's power and temporarily blinding a false prophet who attempts to obstruct his ministry (Acts 13:6–11). Similar discipline might be enforced when Paul warns the Corinthians that he will not "spare" them in an upcoming visit (2 Cor 13:1–2). This power represents the apostle's God-given and effectual authority to impose a discipline appropriate to the offense, such as when he expels the fornicator in the next chapter.

---

216. Hays 1997:75; Harrisville 1987:78.

Avoiding Sexual Defilement: Second Supporting Proof (5:1—7:40)

The second proof for congregational unity focuses on membership solidarity as a corporate body in Christ, a cohesion that is being threatened primarily by sexual affiliations with outsiders (5:1–7:40). This section begins with further reporting, probably again through Chloe's household (cf. 1:11), that one of the congregants is guilty of gross sexual misconduct. The problem requires swift judgment (5:1–13), which then leads to a discussion on intra-member court litigations (6:1–11) before returning to another matter related to sexual misconduct (6:12–20). Together these units form a small chiasm with the center reflecting on what might be called a "rhetorical interlude."[1]

   A Sexual Misconduct Related to Incest (5:1–13)

      B Unrighteous Court Litigations (6:1–11)

   A¹ Sexual Misconduct Related to Prostitution (6:12–20)

Other sexual and domestic matters are then addressed, prompted by questions from the Corinthian letter being read to Paul (7:1–40).

THE FORNICATOR'S EXPULSION (5:1–8)

Paul uses irony and shame to incite pathos and stir the congregation regarding their sexual misconduct before participating in the expulsion of the culprit (5:1–5). After this he explains through Passover tradition how the expulsion will benefit membership purity (5:6–8). The passage opens by conveying a sense of astonishment—**it is actually reported that there is fornication among you.**[2] One of the members is having a sexual affair with **his father's wife** (the stepmother), an action that Paul condemns based on Mosaic sex codes (Lev 18:7–8; Deut 22:30[23:1LXX]; 27:20; *m. Sanh.*

---

   1. Malcolm 2013b:65, 121.

   2. Though here incest, fornication (πορνεία) is an umbrella term in Scripture for different types of sexual deviances: see Oropeza 2006:27–63.

7:4B).³ Since no judgment is mentioned in relation to this woman, she probably was not part of the congregation. Paul is generally correct when saying that this kind of relationship was not practiced **even among the Gentiles**.⁴ Among Greeks and Corinthians, Sophocles' tragedy, *Oedipus Rex*, stigmatized incest with King Oedipus blinding himself after discovering he married his mother.⁵ Roman law condemned incestuous unions—a rule from *The Digest* punishes extramarital incest with severity (48.39).⁶ Winter suggests that the incestuous man's father was still alive, and so the man's offense combined incest and adultery, which would constitute a policy of no leniency in Roman law.⁷

The Corinthians **are puffed up** instead of mourning about this situation, which possibly means that they are boasting in liberties inclusive of sexual freedom (cf. 6:12), or boasting in the man's upper class status as their patron, or boasting in a recent victory this man won in the courtroom against other church members wanting to have him punished by law.⁸ Another possibility is that Paul, having addressed Corinthian arrogance already (4:6, 18), now presents this case as a way of bursting their bubble. They are not boasting because of the incest but despite it.⁹ A paraphrase of Paul's words highlights this irony: "Are you so inflated that you don't even mind that there is incest in your congregation? Are you going to boast about that, too, or be ashamed and confront this person?" If they had **mourned** over the situation, they would recognize that this person's affair is appalling, and they would oppose him despite any influence or social-economic prominence he might have.

Paul claims that although he is **absent in body** from them, he is **present in spirit** and has already determined to expel the wrongdoer. In what sense might his spirit be present in Corinth when his body remains in Ephesus? This peculiar notion might be explained as a letter topos in which the

---

3. Although Paul teaches a circumcision-free gospel to Gentiles, he still upholds Mosaic Law regarding the condemnation of incest and fornication perhaps based on the apostolic decision in Jerusalem (Acts 15:1–20).

4. There are exceptions, however (see Paschke 2007:169–92), for example with certain emperors (Suetonius *Calig.* 24.1; *Claud.* 39.2). But at least some of these relations might confirm the general sentiment *against* incest. Paul, at any rate, may be presenting the general sentiment of his time as universal, or he uses a little bit of hyperbole.

5. See Introduction.

6. 18 BCE (Winter 2001:46). See also the *Institutes* of the jurist Gaius (1.63 [c. 161 CE]; Collins 1999:206, 209–10).

7. Winter 2001:49.

8. See respectively, Collins 1980:253; Clarke 1993:73–88 (cf. McNamara 2010:307–26; Chow 1992:130–40), Deming 1996:294. See various options in Dawson, 2012:1.

9. Cf. Konradt 2003:300–308.

Avoiding Sexual Defilement: Second Supporting Proof (5:1—7:40)

apostle is with them through the words of his letter (Col 2:5; cf. Seneca *Lucil.* 40:1–4; Demetrius *Eloc.* 227).[10] The reader who performs this letter before the Corinthians represents Paul's "spirit" (i.e., Paul's authoritative and Spirit-led thoughts, intentions, and decisions in relation to this matter). In keeping with ancient spiritual cosmology, however, it is perhaps more likely that Paul believes he will in some sense actually be present with them by the power of God's Spirit that dwells among them all (6:17; 12:12, 27). This is not astral projection but similar to clairvoyance in the sense of "seeing" something at a different location take place without being there in physical body. This divine gift, which seems prophetic in nature, is akin with Jesus seeing Nathanael under the fig tree without being physically present, or Elisha's "heart" being present to witness Gehazi's deed when his protégé was not physically with him (John 1:47–48; 2 Kgs 5:26). Perhaps Paul believes that God's Spirit will prompt him at the right moment to "see" or otherwise sense when the congregation will be confronting the fornicator. At that moment, even though he will not be physically present with them, he will be able to intercede, praying to God for them as they pronounce judgment against the offender. The apostle being "present" adds authority to the event as a witness and judge against the man (cf. 2 Cor 13:1–2/ Deut. 17:6–7; 19:15).

The verdict against the offender is expulsion.[11] He is officially cut off from belonging to the community in Christ. Paul makes this judgment **in the name of our Lord Jesus**, suggesting a formulaic reversal of the man's entrance ritual of baptism "in the name of Jesus" that enabled him to participate in the corporate body of Christ (6:11; 12:12–13, 27; cf. 1:14; Acts 2:38).[12] Such punishment apparently functions as an exit ritual from the community in Christ.[13] As a bona fide apostle of the Lord, Paul can use the name (i.e., authority) of Jesus with confidence that his words and actions are divinely endorsed.

This expulsion bears some similarities to ancient curse formulae in which victims and offenders are handed over to deities so that calamities might befall them.[14] The incestuous man is handed over **to Satan for the destruction of the flesh**. Unlike pagan curses, however, the purpose of this calamity is remedial, in hope of the offender's ultimate salvation: **so that the**

---

10. Cf. Klauck 1984:42; 2006:191, 321.

11. See Oropeza 2012a:78–79; Callow 1992:205–6; Forkman 1972.

12. The placement of this phrase with the right contextual verb or verbs is notoriously difficult (see Allo 1956:121, for options). When combined with the parallel "power of our Lord Jesus" (5:4b), this suggests that Paul, not the offender, is doing the action related to Jesus's name.

13. See Neyrey 1990:87–92.

14. See further, Smith 2008a; Fotopoulos 2014:296; Deissmann 1965:301–3.

spirit might be saved in the day of the Lord.[15] The "flesh" and "spirit" here refer respectively to the man's physical body (6:16; 15:39; 2 Cor 4:11) and inner person (2:11; 7:34; 14:14).[16] The parallel Pauline punishment in 1 Tim 1:19-20 is also in hope of remedial benefit for the culprit, complementary with this interpretation.

Since the offender is expelled from the church, he must fend for himself as an outsider associated with the fallen world that is destined to perish and where anti-god powers such as Satan rule (2:6; Gal 1:4; 2 Cor 4:4; cf. Eph 2:2). With this apocalyptic imagery Paul seems to combine notions of purity and protection informed by the Passover discourse.[17] In Exod 12 "the Destroyer" (ὁ ὀλεθρεύων: 12:23LXX) refers to an angel who brought death to those who did not have their homes protected by the blood of the Passover lamb.[18] Paul's related term for destruction here, ὄλεθρος, may suggest a recontextualization of this Passover event. The messenger of death is now Satan who brings destruction on those who are not covered by the blood, the sacrificial death of the crucified Christ who redeems the faithful (5:7; cf. 1:30; 6:20). One of two possibilities account for the incestuous man's destruction: 1) he no longer has any spiritual protection, and so his physical death is expected to happen, perhaps supernaturally;[19] or 2) Paul anticipates the man's arrest by civil authorities who will beat and/or execute him for the crime of incest.[20] Paul may imagine the rulers of this age—judges and magistrates—to be inadvertently part of Satan's realm (2:6-8).[21] Either way, as the man faces a potential death sentence, Paul hopes he will repent. At least this way even if his earthly flesh is destroyed in death, he will be saved and his spirit will be with the Lord (2 Cor 5:6-8; Phil 1:20-24); and in the coming age he will be raised bodily from the dead (15:20-56).

Paul's verdict is swift and uncompromising, unlike the repetitive attempts to restore offenders before banishing them as taught in Matthew

---

15. Rightly, Moses 2013:176; Konradt 2003:315-17.

16. For other interpretations, see Pascuzzi 1997:114-17. The "spirit" of the church or Holy Spirit is not meant; Paul always speaks of being saved in reference to *humans* (cf. 1:18; 3:15; 9:22; 10:33; 15:2). And if "flesh" meant sinful nature here, it makes no sense that Satan would destroy it (see further Oropeza 2012a:78-82).

17. Cf. Moses 2013:186.

18. See also 1 Cor 10:10; Heb 11:28; Philo *Leg. All.* 2.34; BDAG 703.

19. Cf. 11:30; Acts 5:3-10; Allo 1956:123; Robertson/Plummer 1925:99.

20. See Derrett 1979:11-30. If this view is correct, however, Paul does not appear to be advocating congregants to physically hand this man over to be arrested but believes that without divine protection his arrest is inevitable.

21. Paul's own apparent persecution by authorities is explained as Satan's attack in 1 Thess 2:18.

Avoiding Sexual Defilement: Second Supporting Proof (5:1—7:40)

18:15–17. This decision may reflect a sense of urgency on his part, perhaps because of this man's influence on the congregation and the spiritual harm he might cause, and because, if outsiders hear of this illegal affair, the entire church risks being discredited.

If the Corinthians in their indifference toward this sin have tolerated it, they have nothing to boast about. They are too smug in their thinking, and their **boasting is not good**.[22] The offender and his vice, if not removed, will affect other congregation members, which leads to the metaphorical maxim, **a little leaven puffs up the whole batch of dough**.[23] The entire batch represents the congregation, and the old leaven represents **wickedness and evil** that seems to include the man's sexual misconduct along with inflated Corinthian arrogance that turns a blind eye to it. Such vices are currently present and will spread throughout the congregation if unchecked. The man must therefore be purged from among the congregants so that they might become a new batch of dough, one that is unleavened (purified), which is in fact what they truly are in Christ. With the notion of **unleavened** bread, Paul reminisces again on the Passover **feast** that includes slaying and eating the lamb and the removal of all leaven from one's house (Exod 12:3–20; cf. Deut 16:1–8).[24] In Paul's meal, however, Jesus functions as the **Passover lamb**. In celebrating the Lord's Supper (11:23–25), the congregation appears to be familiar with their sacred meal originating from the Passover feast in which Jesus broke unleavened bread and claimed it represented his body.[25] Hence, when Paul mentions the Passover and unleavened bread here, the Corinthians may have automatically heard the Lord's Supper as the subtext, and commemoration related to the meal conjured up images of Christ's sacrificial death on the cross that eventually brought about their redemption and purification from sin (cf. 1 Pet 1:18–19; John 1:29).[26] In this pristine state they are holy like unleavened bread.[27] But now the heinous sexual acts of this man, along with other vices, jeopardize the moral purity of the congregation. As Margaret Mitchell affirms, "Like the orators who describe factionalism as a disease which attacks one member and then spreads like an inflammation throughout the body, Paul draws upon the traditional im-

---

22. Fitzmyer 2008:240.
23. This is introduced by "Do you not know?" (see 3:16).
24. On the possibility of Christians celebrating Passover, see Works 2014:147–49; Eusebius *H.E.* 5.24.16.
25. Mark 14:12–25; Luke 22:17–23; Matt 26:17–28; Oropeza 2004:49–54.
26. On Passover lamb as an expiation, see Num 28:22; Ezek 45:22; Fitzmyer 2008:242. The feast of Unleavened Bread and Passover were linked together as were sacrifice and purity (Ezek 45:21–25; Jos. *Ant.* 2.311–13; Works 2014:139–42).
27. See Merklein 2000:2.46.

age of the lump of dough and the leaven to warn of the consequences of such behavior for the whole community."[28]

THE LIMITS OF MINGLING WITH VICE-DOERS (5:9–13)

If the congregation is to expel the incestuous man, how are the members to relate to others who commit similar vices? Paul seems to anticipate an inquiry of this sort as he uses *reductio ad absurdum* and employs vice lists, rhetorical questions, and scripture quotation in 5:9–13.

With the words, **I wrote to you in my letter**, Paul wants the Corinthians to recall an earlier epistle he wrote to them that we no longer have.[29] In it he urged them **not to mingle with fornicators**. The lists of vice-doers to be shunned in 5:10–11, showcasing **fornicators**, **greedy persons**, **idolaters**, **drunkards**, **swindlers**, and **revilers**, are merely representative of innumerable others (see 6:9–10). The first four vices clearly reflect the congregation's current practices, and the last two probably do also if we consider how members are financially defrauded and speak against one another's allegiances (6:8; 1:10—4:21). Paul selects these vices as a way of prompting Corinthian recollection of their present and past behaviors.[30] At any rate, he did not mean in his previous letter that the Corinthians should have no interactions with *any* vice-doers. Such prohibition would involve a *reductio ad absurdum*, as Paul explains—**otherwise, you would have to escape the world** itself when trying to avoid vice-doers! He meant that believers should not mingle with anyone who **calls himself a brother** (a fellow believer in Christ) and yet is in the habit of committing the above-mentioned vices.[31] They are not to associate in a close way or mix indiscriminately with such persons.[32] Thiselton rightly favors that Paul discourages a *qualified* mixing

---

28. Mitchell 1991:329.

29. "I wrote" (ἔγραψα) is likely not epistolary in 5:9 and 11: cf. Conzelmann 1975:102, who adds that "now" (νῦν) in 5:11 "is logical.... Paul is explaining what he really wrote, i.e., meant." BDAG 681, translates νῦν δέ as "but, as a matter of fact ..." NASB has this sense, *contra* NRSV.

30. Both Rosner 1994: 68–70 and Hays 1997:87–88, suggest Paul is guided by the vices in Deuteronomy (13:1–5; 17:2–7; 19:16–19; 22:18–22, 30; 24:7). But if so, Deuteronomy does not mention the greedy person (πλεονέκτης), and Paul seems more concerned about relevant vices for his auditors than including a stock list.

31. See May 2004:74–75. Gundry Volf 1990:124–25, interprets ὀνομαζόμενος as a "so-called" brother to argue that this offender is a false believer. The *current* spiritual state of this hypothetical person may be questionable, but this says nothing about whether his earlier state and conversion were inauthentic.

32. Cf. συναναμίγνυμι in Hos 7:8; Ezek 20:18; 2 Thess 3:14; *Let.Arist.* 142; Thiselton 2000:409.

Avoiding Sexual Defilement: Second Supporting Proof (5:1—7:40)

with such persons because this meaning "fits the context better than either *have nothing to do with* (are they to cut them dead in the street?) or *not to associate with* (should they check what meetings or functions they attend?).... Paul calls for *discrimination* about boundary markers, corporate identity, and the recognition of the Christian community as a corporate witness to overt beliefs, values, and lifestyles."[33] Vice-doers who claim to be fellow believers should be made well aware of the congregation's position about their behavior, and outsiders should not get confused into thinking that such vices are approved by the church.[34] It is one thing if the church imposes its values on the world; quite another when the world imposes its values on the church and the church passively accepts that imposition.

Paul charges the Corinthians **not to eat** with this type of person.[35] Jonathan Schwiebert has problems with versions of 5:11 that translate the prohibition μηδέ as "not even" to eat with such a person (e.g., ESV, NRSV, NIV). This makes the exclusion drastic and "the *substance* of the exclusion into an insulting metaphorical gesture."[36] He suggests instead the rendition: "As it is, I wrote to you not to associate—if someone (nom.) who is called a brother should be a *pornos* (nom.) [etc.] ... —nor to eat with such a person."[37] The ramification of this translation is that the congregation's disassociation with the vice-doer in 5:9 is more closely linked with its refraining from table fellowship with this person in 5:11. Are the congregants being discouraged from eating with other believers in idolatrous settings (8:9–13)? Are they to treat drunken members at the Lord's Supper this way (11:21)? If corporate shunning is being emphasized, then the vice-doers of 5:10–11 seem to be shunned foremost from eating at the Lord's Supper and other church meals. Kenneth Bailey appropriately writes, "Paul is saying that mixing with sinners in the pagan world is not the same as mixing with them in the body of Christ and at the Eucharist. The very identity of the church is at stake in the latter."[38] The importance of table fellowship for emergent Christians should not be underestimated, since it is among the most forceful expressions of

---

33. Thiselton 2000:409.

34. See Garland 2003:185. Schwiebert 2008:163, raises corporate examples of συναναμίγνυμι to this effect (cf. Philo, *Mos.* 1.278; Plutarch *Phil.* 21; Josephus *Vita* 242).

35. See similarly, Seneca *Lucil.* 19.10; Irenaeus *Her.* 3.4; Ps 101:5(LXX); Newton 1985:94–95.

36. Schwiebert 2008:164.

37. Ibid. 162. The syntax of "μή ... μηδέ connected with the requisite infinitive mood is better translated as 'not ... nor' (cf. Rom 6:12–13; Mark 13:15; John 14:27; Heb 12:5)."

38. Bailey 2011:169.

bonding together socially.³⁹ The significance of corporate shunning in this regard preserves the purity and identity of the community. This judgment is perhaps similar to the punishment against unruly and idle congregants in 2 Thess 3:14–15. Likewise, violators in the Qumran community were excluded from the community's meal (1QS 6.24; 7.25; 8.16–18). But whereas Qumran brings out a shared punishment for anyone who sympathizes with an ostracized member (4Q266 11.14–15), Paul does not threaten individuals who, apart from church fellowship, might continue communicating with the offender.⁴⁰

FUSING THE HORIZONS: MINGLING WITH VICE-DOERS TODAY

What is our responsibility when it comes to associating with those whose lifestyles contradict basic moral principles? On the one hand, Paul discourages the Corinthians from associating with those who commit sexual immorality and other vices; on the other, Jesus ate and drank with "sinners," and was criticized by his opponents because of it (Matt 9:9–13; 11:19; Mark 2:15–17; Luke 5:30–32; 15:1–2; 19:10). This alleged tension is specious, however, when we hear Joseph Fitzmyer's explanation: "Jesus' reason is explained: 'I came not to summon the righteous, but sinner' i.e., those who could be converted to his cause. Paul's principle, however, is different: it concerns the purity of the Christian community, tainted unfortunately by the moral failure of one who is already a convert."⁴¹ Kenneth Bailey expresses this sentiment on a practical level: "When I mix with people in the office or shop who have no faith, the identity of my Christian community is not threatened. But 'mixing up together' as the body of Christ, for Paul, was a very different matter."⁴² The main distinction, then, centers on Paul shunning vice-doers who already claim to be fellow believers, not unbelievers who make no such claim. And compatible with Jesus, Paul permits Christ-followers to dine with unbelievers, as long as such eating does not include idolatry (1 Cor 10:19–21, 27–33).

If fellowship with insiders who commit vice is at stake in 1 Cor 5, how should a congregation today respond to such a parishioner? In an attempt to follow the procedures of Matt 18:15–20 many churches include

39. Cf. Ciampa/Rosner 2010:218.
40. See Hägerland 2008:51.
41. Fitzmyer 2008:244.
42. Bailey 2011:169.

attempts by the church's ministers to communicate privately with the offending member in an effort to foster reconciliation. If such attempts are unsuccessful, and the member remains recalcitrant, the ministers will need to determine whether the offense is jeopardizing the physical, emotional, and/or spiritual safety of other congregation members, and whether central beliefs, practices, reputation, or integrity of the respective church might be tarnished by the offense. Offenders will normally be asked to step down from any leadership position in the congregation, and in some cases they might be asked to leave the church.[43] If such discipline seems distasteful, it might be because we have misconstrued Christian love as unqualified acceptance, and tolerance has perhaps become a euphemism for indifference and deficient moral courage.[44] In highly regulated communities reminiscent of the earlier eras, societal pressures frequently gained the upper hand when persuading an offender to conform to societal standards both on corporate and individual levels.[45] The shunning of offenders in tight-knit cultures, as well as in many ancient communities in Paul's world, might succeed in prompting offenders to reconsider their ways. Such communities, however, are not normally what we find in contemporary Western societies where independence and individual liberties are often valued far above church discipline. The remedial aim of corporate and individual shunning of such an offender would seem to be less successful for those who have few family connections at church, and can easily join another community and attend another church denomination.

If the decision against the offender in Corinth was a corporate affair involving the entire congregation, what does that mean on an individual level? In private and non-church settings, should we still follow Paul's mandate to not eat with such vice-doers? There are no easy answers. Mingling of this sort is perhaps best discerned on a case-by-case basis. Each person must prayerfully ask him- or herself questions such as these: What do I plan to accomplish by maintaining this connection? What might biblically based love, mercy, justice, prudence, and discipline have to say in reference to my relationship with this person? Would my connection with this person compromise or threaten my own faith and values? Would my connection with this person threaten another person's faith and values? Could my or another person's physical and emotional well-being be jeopardized by this mingling?

43. On ex-communication, see recently, Long 2014:205–28.
44. See Fisk 2000:30; Hays 1997:89.
45. See, e.g., Ossom-Batsa 2011:293–310; Vander Broek 1994:5–13.

Avoiding Sexual Defilement: Second Supporting Proof (5:1—7:40)

If the offender is a relative, what boundaries, if any, might I need to implement if the offender visits for the holidays or comes to a special family event? These and similar questions are worth probing as we determine the best course of action to take.

The rhetorical questions in 5:12 are essentially answered in 5:13. **God judges outsiders** who commit vice, and Paul and Christ's community are permitted to **judge insiders** who commit vice. Obviously, Paul distinguishes such judgment from the Corinthians judging *him* (4:3–5). The distinction is that they judge according to the worldly standards of this age, and he, a spiritual man, judges with the mind of Christ (2:15–16). The apostle's decision on vice-doers who profess to be Christ's followers, of which the incestuous man exemplifies and is foregrounded here, integrates a repetitive phrase from Deuteronomy on expulsion—**drive out the wicked person from among you** (Deut 17:7; 19:19; 21:21; 22:21, 24; 24:27).[46] If we must narrow down these verses, Deut 22:21–24 perhaps best fits Paul's aim because it uses the phrase in relation to fornication. Moreover, its proximity to Deut 23:1 (22:30 MT) contextually links the vice with the prohibition against sexual relations with one's step mother. In Deuteronomy, covenant transgressors are cut off from Israel's community often by execution. In Paul's reconfiguration, however, Satan is involved in the potential execution of the man expelled from Christ's community. Paul adopts the Deuteronomic phrase for his Gentile audience with the assumption that they are included among God's people and have inherited their own covenant privileges as well as obligations that include sanctions against covenant disloyalty.[47] This pattern he adopts for believers whose founder at the Last Supper established a new covenant (11:25).

Court Litigations between Believers (6:1–11)

Judgment against the fornicator with the use of Deuteronomic legal texts and insider/outsider language prompt our apostle to continue along the topic of judgment.[48] His emotions are still running high from the previous

---

46. All these verses correspond verbally with our text, and a variation of the phrase is found in Deut 13:6 (Waters 2013:2). Paul does not use a citation formula with his quote, which has the rhetorical effect of heightening pathos in this emotionally charged passage (Ciampa/Rosner 2010:220).

47. See Heil 2005:89–90; Waters 2013:1, 4–5.

48. McDonough 2005:99–102, goes further to suggest judgment in Deut 17:2–7

Avoiding Sexual Defilement: Second Supporting Proof (5:1—7:40)

chapter as he expresses indignation with the opening question, **Dare any of you?**[49] To elicit pathos Paul employs shame and kinship (6:1, 5–6, 8). He presents himself in the imagery of a prudent head of the family attempting to reconcile divisions in the form of sibling rivalry within the household of faith. Ten questions are posed in the first nine verses.[50] Among these, **Do you not know?** is ironic (6:2, 3, 9)—the congregation *ought* to know differently than how it presently knows and acts. Paul presents further irony in 6:4–5 and uses "lesser to greater" (*qal wahomer*) argumentation (6:2–3), reduplication (6:7), antitheses (6:1, 6), and multiplicity of conjunctions (polysyndeton) (6:9–11).

The issue at hand in 6:1–8 is a **legal dispute** among congregation members, which is brought before the unbelieving Roman courts instead of kept inside the church. The **least significant court cases** ("κριτηρίων ἐλαχίστων") and **daily life matters** (βιωτικός) contrast the astounding commission of the saints to judge the world and angels. Paul urges unity by stressing "how insignificant are the matters about which the various sides contend."[51] Such trifling, according to Dio Chrysostom, is compared to "an ass's shadow" (*Or.* 34.48). Paul's stress on triviality suggests that civil disputes rather than weighty legal matters, such as murder and uprisings, are at issue in the congregation. Everyday matters include, among other things, money, property disputes, and matters of inheritance.[52] Although we are not privy to the Corinthian litigations at stake, fraud and wrongdoing may suggest issues involving money (6:7–8; cf. Phlm 18–19; Jas 5:4).[53]

Roman lawsuits are generally conducted between social equals; charges could not be filed by those of lowly status against elitists.[54] The wealthy, however, could take someone of lower status to court.[55] As Winter affirms, the powerful "exercised a number of unfair advantages in the judicial system. . . . These included financial qualifications for jury service, influence over honorary magistrates and judges, and the importance given to social status in weighing judgment."[56] Dio Chrysostom specifically describes Co-

---

reflects 1 Cor 5, and more difficult judgments in Deut 17:8–13 reflect 1 Cor 6.

49. Cf. Konradt 2003:331.

50. If 6:6 is posed as a question and independent of 6:5 (e.g., NET) this would make eleven.

51. Mitchell 1991:117. See Isocrates *Or.* 4.11, 171; Philo *Post.* 119.

52. See respectively, Carter 2010:151–52; Perkins 2012:89; Pepperd 2014:179–92.

53. See further, Lev 6:2–5; Philo *Spec. Leg.* 4.34; Welborn 2011:56–58. The plurals in 6:7–8 suggest more than one case (Horrell 1996:110).

54. Winter 2001:59–60; cf. Garnsey 1970.

55. Cf. Mitchell 1993:562–86.

56. Winter 2001:62; cf. 63–64.

Avoiding Sexual Defilement: Second Supporting Proof (5:1—7:40)

rinthian lawyers as "perverting justice" (*Or.* 8.9).⁵⁷ Hence, Paul's designation of court personnel as **the unrighteous** may not merely be synonymous for "unbeliever" but implies the general injustice and corruption of judges, lawyers, and court systems of the time. This view invites a contrast with Jewish discourses in which judges are to show no partiality, especially when judging those who are poor and disenfranchised (Lev 19:15–18; Deut 1:16–17; 16:18–20; 27:19; Prov 24:23).⁵⁸ Such conduct might be expected all the more among family members,⁵⁹ and Paul emphasizes Christ's community as believing **brothers and sisters** (6:1, 6–8).

Along with familial solidarity Paul reminds them that they are an assembly of **saints**, holy ones set apart by God for righteous conduct (cf. 1:2). In this regard, they are destined to **judge the world** and **angels** (6:2-3). The former idea populates Jewish apocalyptic and wisdom texts (1 *En.* 95.3; Sir 4:15; 1QpHab 5.4; *Jub.* 32.19; Wis 4:16). In Wis 3:1–8 deceased souls of the righteous will judge nations during the time of God's visitation. Paul's assumptions may be that the saints take on a similar role as the righteous at the second coming. But if so, he does not reconcile how God in Christ will be the judge if the saints are also judges (Rom 2:16; 2 Cor 5:10). One possibility is that the righteousness of the saints, inclusive of Jews and Gentiles, might be revealed as some sort of standard by which the unrighteous are judged, similar to how the Queen of Sheba will "condemn" the wicked generation whom Jesus rebukes (Matt 12:42).⁶⁰ Perhaps more likely, Paul believes the saints are directly involved as the jury, witnesses, or in a shared authoritative role with Christ at the eschaton (Dan 7:12–14, 22; cf. Matt 19:28; Luke 22:29–30; *T.Ben.* 10.10). Paul also believes that fallen angels are likewise judged (cf. 2 Pet 2:4; Jude 6; 1 *En.* 15; 41.8–9; *T.Abr.* 13.6).⁶¹ The saints' participation in this task may be relative to Christ's own dominion and judgment over all things (15:24–28; cf. Dan 7:22, 27; Rev 2:26–27; 20:4).⁶² Paul's main point is that if the Corinthian saints inherit God's kingdom and will judge all creation, they are surely fit to judge between their own members' petty litigations.

Apart from Paul emphasizing their saintly identity as a means to discourage litigation, a couple of other solutions to their problem are as

---

57. Ibid. 64; cf. 61–62, 69.
58. See Robertson 2007:597–99; Zeller 2010:215–16.
59. Cf. e.g., Cicero, *Fam.* 9.25.3; Winter 2001:71.
60. Similarly, Thiselton 2000:426.
61. See further Hoskins 2001:294.
62. Rosner 1994:112, grounds a similar hypothesis on Ps 8:4–6, which is referenced in 1 Cor 15:27. See also Ciampa/Rosner 2010:228; Godet 1893:1.288.

Avoiding Sexual Defilement: Second Supporting Proof (5:1—7:40)

follows. First, Paul affirms through irony that they could arbitrate such matters for themselves. Since they are disputing over lesser matters, he poses a somewhat facetious question to the effect that they could appoint as arbitrators **those who are of least importance in the church**, since even these individuals would be competent enough to handle trivial cases. He then poses another question with the expectation that they should select a **wise** member among them **who will be able to judge between** fellow believers. Given their propensity to boast about wisdom, we detect a hint of sarcasm. They consider the wise to be someone schooled in declamation, the practice of rhetorical speeches (see chs. 1–2). A prominent type of declaiming included *contraversiae* (legal case studies), which often centered on fraternal disputes.[63] It is as though Paul were saying, "You who are so prone to eloquent and clever words, how is it that you cannot find anyone among yourselves with enough declamation skills to judge such matters?" This he says to **shame** them regarding how they are currently handling the matter. Second, Paul advises them to endure being **wronged** and **defrauded** rather than have their reputation tarnished before unbelievers.[64] This solution may be somewhat reminiscent of Jesus who taught that if someone takes you to court and takes away your tunic, give them your cloak also (Matt 5:40). In essence doing wrongly is worse than suffering wrongly (cf. Plato *Gorg.* 509C; Philo *Jos.* 4.20).[65]

Paul also anticipates negative outcomes in this situation. Regardless of how the litigations might transpire in court, the result is an **utter defeat** for them all (6:7). They lose solidarity as a congregation and, among outsiders, they lose reputation by failing to exemplify Christian love and righteous conduct (cf. 10:31–32; 1 Thess 4:9–12; Rom 2:24).[66]

To deter the congregation from wrongful and fraudulent conduct in this regard, Paul poses a question in which they ought to know that **the unjust will not inherit the kingdom of God**. The Corinthians are warned, **do not be deceived** into thinking there are no consequences for unjust conduct in these court cases: vice-doers will have no part in God's kingdom but will perish along with all the unrighteous of this present age (cf. 2:6, 8; 3:17). Congregation members are faced with the possibility that exclusion

---

63. See Peppard 2014:190; Winter 2002:24, 30–33, 118–21. Paul may also be hinting that the genuinely "wise" do *not* go to court for wrong reasons (cf. Musonius Rufus *Lect.* 10; Cicero *Off.* 3.6.28; Robertson 2007:593–94).

64. Since these matters are trivial, Paul could advise this way. Today, if an alleged "Christian" raped or murdered someone, such things are *not* trivial and that person should be brought to justice!

65. Cf. Fitzmyer 2008:254.

66. See Edsall 2013:35–36.

Avoiding Sexual Defilement: Second Supporting Proof (5:1—7:40)

from God's kingdom might happen to *them* (10:1-12; cf. Gal 5:19-20). In 6:9-10 exclusion from the kingdom forms an *inclusio* with ten vices in between, possibly hinting at the Ten Commandments, though not duplicating them.[67] Although vice lists are common in both Jewish and Greco-Roman moral traditions,[68] the former reflect Paul's list better since destruction and exclusion from God result from vice-doing (1QS 4.9-14; 4Q257 V.7-13; Philo *Virt*. 182; *T.Jac*. 7.19-20; cf. Rev 21:8; 22:15). Early Jesus sayings add more specifically that exclusion is from God's kingdom (Matt 5:20; 7:21-23; 8:11-12; 13:41-42; 25:34-46; John 3:3-5).

Paul's list includes vices the Corinthians commit. These include the practices of **fornicators** (5:1; 6:18; 10:8), **idolaters** (10:7, 16-22; cf. Col 3:5), **greedy persons** (6:1-8; 2 Cor 9:5; cf. Eph 5:5), **drunkards** (11:21; cf. Gal 5:21), **swindlers** (5:10-11; cf. Luke 18:11), and **revilers** (5:11; cf. Sir 23:8). Vices on this list reflect pre-converted behaviors, and Paul expects better things of his converts. **Adultery** is relevant to the Corinthian situation if one surmises that some of the congregants having sex with prostitutes in 6:12-20 are married.[69] But it is not necessary for us to connect every vice on this list with a *current* problem in their church; these vice-doers represent what the congregants *used to be* prior to conversion (6:11). Some once were idolaters, adulterers, swindlers, revilers, **thieves** (1 Pet 4:15; John 10:10), and **passive** and **dominant** same-sex erotic partners.[70]

But such vices were **washed** away when the Corinthians accepted the gospel, confessed Christ at baptism (Acts 22:16; Rom 10:9-10), and were **consecrated** as saints (cf. 1:2) and **justified** by faith. They were set in right standing with God by the authority of the **Lord Jesus Christ** and by **the Spirit of our God** who filled them at their conversion-initiation and continues to transform them (Gal 2:16; Rom 3:24, 26; cf. 1 Cor 12:13). The Holy Spirit dwells in and among them, sanctifying and empowering them to resist these vices and produce virtuous characteristics instead (cf. Gal 5:22-23; Rom 8:1-16). This review of their conversion reinforces the Corinthians to identify themselves not with the way they formerly lived when practicing unrighteousness, but as they are supposed to be currently living—as a righteous and holy community in Christ.

---

67. Cf. Bailey 2011:176, 178. For other Pauline vice lists, see Oropeza 1998b:9-10; Lopez 2011:301-16.

68. For the former, see e.g., Ps 15; Hos 4:12; Wis 14:22-31; CD[A] 8.1-9; Philo *Sacr*. 32; *T.Reub*. 3-6; for the latter, Seneca *Ben*. 1.10.2-5; Aristotle *Rhet*. 1.10.3-6; Quintilian *Inst*. 2.4.22; Crates *Ep*. 7.

69. Both married and unmarried men are the targeted audience of moral exhortations against being with prostitutes (see Loader 2013:112-13).

70. Μαλακός and ἀρσενοκοίτης, respectively (see Fusing the Horizons).

Fusing the Horizons: Christians, Same-Sex, and Loving Your Neighbor as Yourself

Paul and his disciples generally consider homoerotic sexual acts to be a vice (Rom 1:26–27; 1 Tim 1:10).[71] And some of the Corinthians engaged in this sexual behavior prior to their conversion—"and such were some of you" (1 Cor 6:11). The first relevant term in 6:9, μαλακός, technically means a "soft" person, but its immediate context places it in the midst of sexual vices and thus implies it as another sexual vice. Its meaning in this passage probably should not be restricted to a "male prostitute" or an "effeminate call boy."[72] Paul's sense is probably closer to that of Philo, a near contemporary and Hellenistic Jew. Philo uses μαλακότης for males undergoing a feminizing process implemented by sexual intercourse with another male (*Abr.* 135–37).[73] This person's role in this sexual union is passive, pointing to the male whose orifice is penetrated by another male's penis. This may be how Paul understands μαλακός in relation with ἀρσενοκοίτης. In this union it is unlikely that he refers only to pederasty or sex between a slave and his master or exploiter.[74] Otherwise, Paul would be excluding children and those who are essentially raped by their masters from God's kingdom! Such are victims, not vice-doers. If anything, Paul comforts rather than condemns slaves when their masters abuse them (see notes on 7:21–23).

The second term in 6:9, ἀρσενοκοίτης, may be coined by Paul from ἄρσεν ("man") and κοίτης ("bed") and is probably derived from the prohibitions against same-sex in Lev 18:22 and 20:13(LXX).[75] These verses come from the same code that informs Paul's condemnation of incest in 5:1–5 (see *ad. loc.*). Even though he rejects the works of Mosaic Law as a

---

71. See e.g., Gagnon 2001:229–303. Rom 1:26–27 also includes lesbianism (Brooten 1996). For Jewish examples, see e.g., Philo, *Spec. Leg.* 2.50; 3.37–42; Josephus *Ag. Ap.* 2.25.199, 273; *Sib. Or.* 2.73–74; 3.185, 764; Ps-Phoc. *Sent.* 3, 192; *T.Naph.* 3.4–5; *Let. Aris.* 152; Jude 7.

72. *Pace* NRSV and Skroggs 1983:108, respectively. Martin 2006:47, uses "effeminate," but this obscures why it would be considered vice. Boswell 1980:107, 338–39, presents numerous translations and suggests it means a masturbator (see also Countryman 1988:202), but he adopts this meaning from much later Christian sources.

73. See Gagnon 2001:306–12 (309).

74. *Contra* Regele 2014:167–68.

75. Or alternatively he adopted it from early rabbinic use: *mishkav (b)zakur* ("lying of/with a male": Skroggs 1983:83, 108), which is nonetheless derived from Mosaic sex codes.

correct paradigm for his Gentile converts (Gal 2–3; 2 Cor 3), it appears that he and other emergent Christians still affirmed that the Levitical sex code must be kept by Gentiles, the "aliens" who live among Israelites. In Acts 15:19–29, where this connection is established, fornication (πορνεία) may be an umbrella term for various illicit sex acts in Leviticus 18:6–30.[76] This may be one reason why Paul rejects same-sex unions.[77] For Paul, then, it seems that μαλακός refers to the penetrated male and ἀρσενοκοίτης identifies the "bedding male" or the dominant partner who penetrates.[78] The terms in 6:9 identify both passive and dominant consenting partners of same-sex eroticism.

In recent decades many attempts have been made to qualify Paul's words so that they do not suggest a denunciation of marital and committed same-sex relationships. Such attempts have been unsuccessful partly because Paul does not make any distinctions that would preclude same-sex marriage. As a first-century Jew informed by traditional sexual values, it is doubtful that, hypothetically speaking, Paul would have made such qualifications if pressed on the issue.[79] If our apostle promptly rejects a monogamous incestuous relationship involving a church member in 5:1–5, one suspects he would have also rejected a monogamous homosexual relationship. The conclusion of William Loader's extensive research on sex in ancient Jewish and Christian worlds is sobering: "Nothing . . . indicates that he is exempting some same-sex intercourse as acceptable. It is all an abomination for Paul."[80] Our contemporary discussions about sexual orientation, then, would probably ring foreign to Paul. He believes that God's Spirit transforms those who come to Christ and is thus able to change anyone's sexual behavior (6:11), which is a point frequently ignored in current discussions. He probably would perceive one's tendency in this regard no differently than the converted fornicator or alcoholic whose desires beckon them on to resume their former urges. For Paul, such inclinations are to be resisted and, with the Spirit's power and Christ-community's proactive assistance, successful resistance could be achieved. We can speculate further

76. See Hays 1996:382–83.

77. He gives other reasons in Rom 1:26–27: such acts are unnatural and characterize human rebellion against God that venerate creature over Creator.

78. See Loader 2013:138; Via/Gagnon 2003:82–90; Soards 1999:126.

79. Commitment among same-sex partners was not unheard of in Paul's world: see sources in Gagnon 2001:384–85; Brooten 1996:140–41, 172, 242–43, 360–61. Nero would soon have two same-sex marriages (cf. Cassius Dio 62.28, Tacitus *Ann.* 15.37).

80. Loader 2013:137; cf. Loader 2012.

Fusing the Horizons: Christians, Homoeroticism, and Loving Your Neighbor

that Paul might encourage believers whose orientation remained a perpetual struggle to stay single and celibate like himself. As a new creation believer, the ways of the old creation are passing away, and as such, he suggests that celibacy is better than marriage (see 1 Cor 7). A life of celibacy is, in fact, how certain Christians today with same-sex attraction claim to honor God and remain faithful to Christian morals and Scripture.[81]

It must also be stressed that same-sex eroticism is just one of many vices on Paul's list. Regarding a church's internal affairs, then, the churchgoer with this struggle should not be stigmatized as somehow "worse" than a churchgoer who struggles with greed, or fornication, or drinks too much, and so on. Virtually everyone in the church has a story of brokenness, imperfection, and sin. We are all works in progress. Regarding a church's external affairs, Paul expects believers to do good to outsiders (10:31–33; Gal 6:10). Unfortunately in recent years, some who claim to be Christian and hold up signs that express God's alleged hatred toward certain groups have received excessive media coverage. This gives the false impression that these angry extremists represent what the typical Christian believes or ought to believe. On the contrary, *love your neighbor as yourself* is what Paul holds to be central to Christian values (8:1; 14:1; 16:14; Gal 5:14; Rom 13:8–10), and one's neighbor includes people from the LGBT community. Nevertheless, and contrary to what media, politics, and the world might say, to show love to another person does *not* mean that we must endorse or agree with that person's beliefs and lifestyle. (Indeed, something is terribly wrong when the church conforms to the world's standards!) Instead, love means that a Christian should accept and value as a fellow human being who is worthy of open dialogue, respect, care, and friendship the person he or she disagrees with, and will treat that person the same way the Christian would want to be treated. Such love is reminiscent of Jesus who dined, taught, and conversed with those whose status and lifestyles were despised by others. We also can surmise that Paul must have known, conversed with, and shown God's love to same-sex people in Corinth so that some of them accepted his message and were transformed through the power of Christ and the Spirit (6:11).

---

81. E.g., Shaw 2015.

Avoiding Sexual Defilement: Second Supporting Proof (5:1—7:40)

SEX WITH PROSTITUTES AND THE CORINTHIAN BODY (6:12-20)

The previous vice list includes fornicators, which now becomes the focus of 6:12-20. The problem in Corinth centers on congregation members having sex with prostitutes.[82] In a city like Corinth, apart from the brothels, men could meet prostitutes almost anywhere, whether in the market place, near a temple, or next to a government building (e.g., Dio Chrysostom *Or* 7.133-34).[83] Relevant for congregation members who were invited by unbelievers to dinners (10:27), banquets and symposiums were characterized by gluttony, drunkenness, and promiscuity with prostitutes called *heterai* (Plutarch *Tu. san.* 4[123E-F]; *De esu* II.2[997B-C]; Athenaeus *Deipn.* 13. 573C-574E).[84] Paul makes an appeal to advantage in which the audience is persuaded to take a course of action in their best interest for future benefit.[85] A diatribe pattern appears in this text that includes an interlocutor who debates against the communicator (Paul).[86] Elements that stand out include a Corinthian voice of worldly wisdom that contests Paul (6:12-13), to which our apostle provides wise responses. Other stylistic features include anaphora (6:12) and the repetitive interrogative phrase, "Do you not know?" (6:15, 16, 19), which attempts to dissuade through reason (logos). The first and last appearances of this question help create a chiasm with the central point highlighting a scriptural quote:[87]

  A Do you not know that your bodies are members of Christ? (6:15a)

    B Implicit sin against Christ (6:15b)

      C Joining one body with a prostitute (6:16a)

        D Scripture citation of two becoming one flesh (6:16b)

      C¹ Joining one Spirit with the Lord (6:16a, 17)

    B¹ Explicit sin against one's body (6:18)

  A¹ Do you not know that your body is the temple of the Holy Spirit . . . ? (6:19)

---

82. On πορνεία as harlotry, see e.g., Num 25:1(LXX); Sir 41:17; *T.Jos.* 3:8; Jos. *Ant.* 5.7. Ford 1993:128-35.

83. See Mackie 2013:320; Kirchhoff 1994:37-68. Unlikely at this time was cultic prostitution (see Introduction).

84. See further, Fotopoulos 2003:169-74; Winter 2001:81-93.

85. Mitchell 1991:25-39.

86. With Fitzmyer 2008:67.

87. See Bailey 2011:183.

Avoiding Sexual Defilement: Second Supporting Proof (5:1—7:40)

The way Paul argues suggests the Corinthians are not convinced they are doing anything wrong. They already heard Paul's warnings about sexual misconduct in a previous letter (5:9), and yet they continue in fornication. Paul must first dismantle their ideology through Scripture and reason before giving them new commands in 6:18–20 encouraging bodily purity.

Paul may have derived the interlocutor's justification, **all things are permissible for me**, either from a popular maxim or the congregation's own slogan, possibly in response to Paul's previous letter (6:12a, c).[88] Both views are not incompatible if we assume the congregants adopted the saying as their own from what was "in the air" at the time. Elitists are described by Dio Chrysostom as those to whom "all things are permitted" but needing self-control (*Or.* 62.3; cf. 3.10).[89] He relates the notion of permissibility to kings and wise persons (*Or.* 14.13–17), an idea aligned with Stoics who consider the wise as lords over their circumstances and free to do as they please (Plutarch *Stoic. abs.* 1058B–C; Epictetus *Diatr.* 2.1.23; Diogenes Laertius *Vit. phil.* 7.121).[90] Through this saying the Corinthian interlocutor works with philosophical wisdom to claim it is permissible to indulge in sexual urges; to relieve these impulses is as natural as satisfying one's appetite: **foods are for the belly, and belly is for foods** (6:13a). The belly (κοιλία) suggests the entire cavity of the body inclusive of the stomach and organs such as intestines and womb.[91] The word sometimes refers to sexual organs, which move beyond mere appetites of the stomach (2Sam [2Kgdms] 7:12; 16:11; Ps 132[131]:11).[92] Indulgence of both food and sexual activities characterize certain dinner symposiums, as noted earlier. The interlocutor adds, however, that **God will do away with both one and the other** (6:13b). This assumes that indulgent behavior is morally irrelevant.[93] The Corinthian claim may be paraphrased as follows: "We should gratify our appetites for food and sex; that's what the center of our bodies is designed to do. God will eventually get rid of these things when we die anyway, so let's enjoy them while we still can!" (cf. 15:32).

Paul uses his own wisdom to respond. First, what they consider permissible may **not** be **beneficial** for them (6:12b). What is permitted should be conducive to what is righteous, virtuous, and advantageous for the

---

88. For the maxim view, see Garland 2003:226–231; for the slogan, Murphy-O'Connor 1978:391–96.
89. Cf. Winter 2001:86–93.
90. See further, Paige 2004:216; Horsley 2008:103–4.
91. LSJ 699.
92. Garland 2003:230.
93. See Sandnes 2002:196.

believer's own body as well as their community. Second, some things have a way of bringing individuals **under the power** and enslavement of the thing permitted (6:12d). This is what vices and addictive habits do and should therefore be avoided. Third, against moral irrelevance, Paul argues that the believer's **body is not for the purpose of fornication** but **for** (i.e., belongs to) **the Lord, and the Lord** gave himself **for the body** of the believer on the cross (6:13c; cf. 6:20a). The full redemption of the believer's body that was first implemented by Christ's sacrificial death will become fully evident when **God,** who **raised the Lord . . . will raise us up by His power**. As such, the believer's body is sacred; it belongs to the Lord, not prostitutes, and awaits its own resurrection. Regardless of what might happen to the belly at death, the body will not be done away with but transformed by divine power, similar to Christ's resurrection (cf. 15:20–56).

Our apostle now presents three more perspectives guided by the rhetorical question, **Do you not know** (6:15, 16, 19), which insinuates they ought to know better, and so they should change their current way of thinking. The first question informs the Corinthians that their individual **bodies are members** or body parts of the corporate body **of Christ** (cf. 12:12–27). This body is not simply a metaphorical construct for the church but a communal entity that actually connects the resurrected body of Christ with the individual bodies of believers through God's Spirit who dwells in and joins them all together in solidarity.[94] With this understanding intact, a further question is posed: **Shall I take away parts of (the body of) Christ and make them parts of (the body of) a prostitute?** Paul answers using the diatribe negation, **may it never be!**[95] The conjoining of Christ's body parts with a prostitute via his followers intends to shock the auditors.[96] This is a picture of mutilating the body and distorting the image of Christ.[97] The body parts probably should not be thought of as generic; Paul just mentioned the κοιλία inclusive of sexual organs. The scene elicits sexual organs being attached to the vagina or womb of the prostitute, which implies a surrendering of one's bodily and sexual powers to her. If the members are metaphorically removed from Christ's body, another implication is that their identity

---

94. The Spirit metaphorically functions as though the blood or arteries of this body. Alternatively, if "spirit" is perceived materially, then "those in Christ are literally of the same stuff. All share the very same pneuma—Christ's" (Stowers 2008:360).

95. Cf. Malherbe 1980:231–40.

96. Martin 1995:176–78, imagines Christ's body penetrating or being penetrated by the prostitute, but the verb αἴρω, does not mean "take" from Christ's body (NRSV) but "take away" from it (NASB), which may depict removing the body parts and then joining them to a prostitute (see Robertson/Plummer 1925:125).

97. See Liu 2013:165–94.

in Christ is at stake; as fornicators they are in danger of perishing with the fornicators of this world (6:9–10).

The second thing the Corinthians should know is that the man **who joins himself with a prostitute is one body with her**, sharing solidarity with her. This perspective is reminiscent of the way sexual unions with outsiders defiled God's people both individually and as a group (*Jub.* 30.7–17; Jos. *Ant.* 4.126–158; Num 25). The prostitute represents the fallen world and age that passes away at Christ's return. This unholy union joins both physical bodies along with all their spiritual connections.[98] The saints thus join themselves to the realm that opposes Christ, and another identity is formed through the sexual union.[99] This unification apes the story of the original man and woman as Paul cites from Genesis: **the two shall be one flesh** (cf. Gen 2:24).[100] What originally described a sacred union that constitutes marriage is now contaminated by Corinthian fornication with outsiders. The union in Genesis is properly analogous to the union between the Corinthians and Jesus, who are **one Spirit** with him.[101] Paul deploys an argument from lesser to greater—if a man joined to a wife is not to be in union with a prostitute, how much more believers who are joined to Christ through one Spirit?[102] Paul works with the assumption of family imagery in which Christ is the husband of believers (2 Cor 11:2–3; Rom 7:4; cf. Eph 5:21–23; Isa 54:5), and as such, the believer's body belongs to its rightful spouse (6:13c, 19; 7:4).

The third thing the Corinthians should know is that each Corinthian **body is a temple of the Holy Spirit**. Epictetus the Stoic philosopher has a similar view:

> When you are in conjunction with a woman ... know you not that you are nourishing a god, that you are exercising a god? Wretch, you are carrying about a god with you, and you know it not. Do you think that I mean some God of silver or of gold, and external? You carry him within yourself, and you perceive not that you are polluting him by impure thoughts and dirty deeds. And if an image of God were present, you would not dare to do any of the things which you are doing: but when God himself is present within and sees all and hears all, you are not ashamed of thinking such things and doing such things,

---

98. Cf. Garland 2003:233.

99. See Schnabel 2006:341; Merklein 2000:2.76.

100. The ambiguous φησίν "it says" or "he says" introduces the quote. If the latter, perhaps Jesus is meant (Matt 19:5).

101. See Heil 2005:116.

102. Cf. Ciampa/Rosner 2010:260.

ignorant as you are of your own nature and subject to the anger of God" (*Diatr.* 2.8.11–14).

Although Paul does not assume that God or Zeus is part of the human being, he does affirm that God's Spirit dwells in humans. The Spirit dwells within both the temple of the corporate body of the congregation (3:16) as well as in the temple of the body of each believer (6:19; cf. v.14, 17; 2 Cor 1:22; Rom 8:11; Gal 4:6).[103] As such, both the community in Christ and the believer's own body are holy, set apart from outsiders, and must not be defiled with the vice of fornication.

Two moral imperatives are advanced to ensure sexual purity of the community (6:18, 20). The first command is a prohibition. The Corinthians must **flee fornication**. A parallel thought is found in Theon who writes that Sophocles was asked how he fared in relation to sex with women, to which the poet responds, "Hush, man. I have escaped these things most gladly, like a slave running away from a mad and savage master" (*Prog.* 2[66]). More generally, Horace writes, "To flee vice is the beginning of virtue, and to have got rid of folly is the beginning of wisdom" (*Ep.* 1.1.41; cf. Crates *Ep.* 15). Similarly, Jewish wisdom warns readers against the temptress who ruins lives (Prov 5:1–11; 7:4–27; Sir 41:17–22), and the patriarch Joseph must flee from Potipher's wife who attempts to have sex with him (Gen 39:7–13; T.Reub. 4.6–11). Such texts establish that escape from sexual sin was a well-worn theme for Paul to adapt without immediate dependence on only one source. For the Corinthians any location where prostitutes might tempt them becomes the place from which to flee.

The notion that **every sin a person commits is outside the body** might employ again a Corinthian interlocutor who justifies fornication.[104] It perhaps reflects Stoic thinking in which there is nothing good or evil outside of intention or moral purpose (Epictetus, *Diatr.* 3.10.18; cf. 2.10.25; Marcus Aurelius *Med.* 6.32), and in later writers this idea seems to have extended to indifference toward sexual activities.[105] The apostle makes the qualification, **but the one who commits fornication sins against his own body**. This, too, resembles Stoic thinking. Musonius Rufus claims that those who commit adultery and are joined with a courtesan prostitute (ἑταίρα) do wrong (ἁμαρτάνει) and ruin themselves, making themselves dishonorable

---

103. In 6:19 "the body" (τὸ σῶμα) is singular with a distributive genitive plural "of you," (ὑμῶν) as in 2 Cor 4:10; Rom 8:23; Phil 3:21: (Gupta 2010:522–23): "'the body of *each of* you' is *a* temple . . .'"

104. See Murphy-O'Connor 1978:391–96, and interpretative options in Allo 1956:148–50.

105. See Smith 2008b:69–74.

Avoiding Sexual Defilement: Second Supporting Proof (5:1—7:40)

and worse men (*Lect.* 12). Similarly, our earlier quote from Epictetus claims that the one who has impure thoughts and dirty deeds defiles the deity in himself. It is possible that Paul is fighting fire with fire by countering Stoic influence with Stoic ethics.[106] A stronger option (or at least in addition to this Stoic stream) is that Paul is informed by Sir 19:1–4, which claims that a man who joins with a prostitute brings destruction on himself.[107] To be sure, other sins affect one's body also, such as drunkenness, but sexual sins uniquely join bodies together and thus confuse identity as well as defile.[108] Paul perhaps assumes here that no other type of vice physically joins together bodies as one.

Paul's second command advances positive engagement—he directs the Corinthians, **glorify God in your body**.[109] They are to remain sexually pure, knowing that they must honor and acknowledge God everywhere, whether at home, at work, in the marketplace, or in another's house as a guest. A double entendre is possible in which the congregation also glorifies God as a collective body through worship, fellowship, and service. The reason they are to honor God is because their bodies are not their own; they have been **bought with a price** by Christ. Given that slaves and freedmen comprised a large portion of Corinth's population, these words may have special relevance to certain congregants due to purchases and manumission related to their own bodies (cf. 7:23).[110] Some suggest here a transference from one owner to another is imagined; the new owner is the Lord of the universe. The slave gains unprecedented high status by virtue of his/her new master, and the expectation is that this fortunate slave glorifies his master because of this.[111] Slavery, however, functions as a theological metaphor here related to Israel being redeemed by God to become God's covenant people rather than mere property (e.g., Exod 6:6–9).[112] The Corinthians have been delivered by the redemptive price of the blood of the crucified Christ; they are set free from slavery to sin and the fallen world governed by Satan (1:30; 11:25; Rom 3:24–25; 5:9; Col 1:20; cf. Eph 1:7; 2:13). At the same time, Paul's words may evoke the hire of both a prostitute and slave. What he portrays parallels Hosea's purchase of a prostitute named Gomer from the slave block as a picture of God's redemptive love for his people. Hosea makes the purchase so

---

106. Ibid. 76.
107. See Fisk 1998:555–56; cf. 545–55.
108. Ibid. 556–58.
109. See Barton 1998:366–79.
110. See Nasrallah 2013:54–73.
111. See Martin 1990:63; Mackie 2013:323–24.
112. See Schrage 1994:2.35–36.

Avoiding Sexual Defilement: Second Supporting Proof (5:1—7:40)

that she can be freed from slavery and become his wife instead (Hos 3:1–3).[113] This imagines the slave no longer a mere slave even though purchased and belonging to another; she is given a bride's status, and so are those whom Christ redeems.

Advice for Married, Unmarried, and Widows (7:1–9)

The apostle now addresses various domestic issues including married couples (7:2–7, 10–11), unmarried and widows (7:8–9, 39–40), those married to unbelievers (7:12–16), circumcised and uncircumcised (7:17–19), slaves and free persons (7:20–24), and virgins and betrothed (7:25–38). We could imagine quarrels, disagreements, and status differentiation when such members collided together in the congregation. This likely contributed to the discord thematically addressed in this letter.[114] If family households are to mimic the house of God, then Homer's words are fitting: "nothing is greater or better than this, when man and wife dwell in a home in one accord" (*Od.* 6.182–84). Domestic matters prompt practical wisdom, which here is informed by discourses that engage bodily purity, two-age apocalypse, and divine calling. The structure of this chapter follows an A, B, A pattern:

A Advice for the Married and Unmarried (7:1–16)

   B Remaining in One's Calling (7:17–24)

A¹ Advice for Virgins about Marriage (7:25–38)

Level B formulates the basis upon which Paul's advice rests. The concept of remaining in one's calling (7:20, 24; cf. 7:8, 11, 40) looks forward to the end of the present age and full establishment of the new era (7:29–31). If believers are undistracted by present-age institutes, they could use such opportunities to concentrate on what best honors the Lord. If they do not have such opportunities, they must honor the Lord the best they can in their respective states until either the Lord returns or their circumstances change.

The first topic concerns marriage, and a small chiasm is noticeable in terms of abstinence from sex (A: 7:1, 7), sex in marriage to avoid fornication (B: 7:2, 5b–6), sex in marriage as mutual obligation (C: 7:3, 5a), and the ground for this sexual union—one's body belongs to one's spouse (D: 7:4). Paul responds to questions in the Corinthian letter he received, presumably from Chloe's people (1:11), with the opening phrase, **now**

---

113. See Klein 1989:373–75; Ciampa/Rosner 2010:265.
114. Cf. Mitchell 1991:235.

Avoiding Sexual Defilement: Second Supporting Proof (5:1—7:40)

concerning the things you wrote. The introductory "now concerning" (περί δέ) introduces new topics and perhaps Corinthian questions as well (7:25; 8:1; 12:1; 16:1, 12).[115]

With the statement, **it is good for a man not to touch a woman**, the word "touch" (ἅπτω) is a euphemism for taking a woman for sexual gratification (e.g., Plato *Leg.* 8.840A; Aristotle *Pol.* 7.14.12 [1335b]; Prov 6:29; Josephus *Ant.* 1.163–64).[116] Paul promotes celibacy here. It is far from clear, however, that the statement reiterates a Corinthian slogan or reflects a sexually ascetic faction.[117] Such a view is not implied anywhere in the Corinthian correspondence, unless here. Not only does this view run counter to the church's excessive sexual promiscuity (chs. 5–6; 10:8; 2 Cor 12:21), but the tone of this entire chapter suggests that Paul is addressing recipients who *want* to have sex (7:4–5, 8–11, 25–39).[118] Moreover, Paul refers to celibacy demurely, as though the Corinthians would not be sympathetic with the idea (7:5b–9). If we assume that both single and married men in the congregation are having sex with prostitutes (6:12–20), one man is committing incest (5:1), and possibly certain wealthier members who could afford slaves are having sex with them, these words appear to be against *all* sexual intercourse outside of marriage (cf. 7:2).[119] Paul seems to be responding to their questions about fornication and sexual purity, and these inquiries are probably motivated by what he had previously instructed them in an earlier letter (cf. 5:9). Some of their questions may have been similar to these: "If we are to be sexually pure as you instruct, Paul, what does that mean for married couples in our congregation?" "And should our unmarried members avoid marriage to stay sexually pure?" "Should members who have unbelieving spouses get divorced?" Paul now responds to their questions starting with a thematic statement in 7:1 that guides this entire chapter: celibacy is best (7:7–8, 26, 38), and sex in marriage is second best.

Paul, not the Corinthians, employs the word **good** (καλόν) in 7:1, just as he does in 7:8, 26, and 38.[120] It reflects his reluctance to give commands in

---

115. More reservedly, Mitchell 1991:235, claims that περί δέ only introduces a new topic or argument (cf. 1 Thess 4:9; 5:1). On περί + γράφω as a response to previous correspondence, see Arzt-Grabner et al. 2006:243–44.

116. See Ciampa 2009:336–37. For Ciampa, ἅπτω may suggest sexual exploitation but not necessarily rejection of all sex.

117. Pace, e.g., Deming 1995:5–49; Valentine 2013:520.

118. See May 2004:144–204; Ciampa/Rosner 2010:268–69.

119. As 7:2 clarifies, sex *within* marriage is excluded from this abstinence. Although ἄνθρωπος in 7:1 can refer to "husband," and γυνή could mean "wife," the more generic "man" and "woman," are preferred, respectively (*contra* NIV).

120. See also 5:6; 9:15; Rom 14:21; Gal 4:18; *pace* Garland 2003:249.

Avoiding Sexual Defilement: Second Supporting Proof (5:1—7:40)

this passage; his advice is a matter of what is good, beneficial, and permissible for the Corinthians (7:6; cf. 12, 25, 35). At the same time, this word may echo the context of Gen 2:18—the Lord God said that "it is not good (καλόν) that the man (Adam) be alone," so he proceeded to create woman (Eve), which resulted in the first couple. Paul may be recontextualizing these thoughts so that, unlike the original couple, what is good now pertains to the new creation in Christ (cf. 2 Cor 5:17; Gal 6:15). The old world order, and its creation with Adam and Eve, is now passing away along with its rulers, institutes, Satan, and fornication (7:31). In the new creation, when it fully arrives, even marriage as an institute will be completely transformed to represent purely the union between believers and Christ (cf. 6:13c–17, 20). The apostle seems to agree with a saying attributed to Jesus that in the coming age, humans neither marry nor are given in marriage (Mark 12:25; Luke 20:34–35; Matt 22:30). This new creation discourse attaches goodness to celibacy, which for Paul is even better than human marriage (7:1, 8). For emergent Christians, then, the primary paradigm for bodily union is not the prevailing norm of their day, nor the old creation model of marriage in Genesis, but the new creation model in Christ, the sphere in which all believers are joined to the Lord Jesus.[121] Contrary to what our culture today might assume, Paul's model shows that our longing for and finding a lifetime partner is not the ultimate goal of human existence. Union with Christ fills that role.

Nevertheless, Paul is well aware that the new creation has not fully arrived. Various present age tensions in Adam, such as fornication, sexual passions, and a lack of self-control agitated by Satan are still prominent influences. With this recognition he concedes to the second best alternative in 7:2, and together 7:1–2 seems to enact the commands from 6:18 and 20.[122] The plural **fornications** refer to multiple types of sexual relations outside the realm of marriage, which can be avoided by letting **each man have his own wife, and each woman have her own husband**. There is no compelling reason why we must decide between Paul telling single men to get married and have sex, or his telling married men to have more sex in their already existing marriages.[123] Both can be meant.[124] Likewise, since Paul is responding to Corinthian inquiries rather than giving them a comprehensive tome about Christian marital sex, we should not read too much into his silence on

---

121. On prevailing expectations of marriage in Roman and Jewish culture, see Crocker 2004:150–52.

122. See von Thaden 2012:263–64.

123. On the former, see Caragounis 1996:547–48; 2006:196–98; the latter, Fee 1987:278–79; 2003:209–211.

124. The present imperative "have" (ἐχέτω) can refer to sexual intercourse (cf. Deut 28:30; Isa 13:16) or to marry/be in a married state (7:29; Tob 3:8BA; John 4:17–18).

Avoiding Sexual Defilement: Second Supporting Proof (5:1—7:40)

sex for the purpose of procreation.[125] His concern here is for sexual purity and that marital sex be **mutual**, selfless, and frequent.[126]

At least three streams of thought can inform Paul's sense of mutuality. First, if the believer's body belongs to Jesus (cf. 6:12-20), this sets up a comparison in which the married sex partner **does not have rights over** his/her **own body**; it belongs to the spouse.[127] This results in tending to the sexual needs of the other spouse before one's own needs. It also helps prevent the husband from doing as he pleases sexually with household slaves, courtesans, or anyone else—authority over his body belongs to his wife rather than himself, and she disapproves of these relationships.[128] Second, since males and females are on equal ground in Christ (Gal 3:28), their sexual needs should be equally met. Third, Scripture may inform Paul, especially on the point of **conjugal duty**—the husband must **not deprive** his spouse of her basic necessities, clothing, and conjugal rights that include sexual intercourse (Exod 21:10-11). Also, mutual possession of one's lover, such as expressed in the erotic poem wherein the woman's lover "is mine and I am his" (Cant 2:16; 6:3), might inform Paul. Spouses can withdraw from sexual activities only with the consent of their partner for a time of separation **in order to devote yourselves to prayer**.[129] The reason may be to avoid distractions on account of the urgency of the petition. The couple must then resume sex again right after that time is over so that **Satan may not tempt you because of your lack of self-control**.[130] God's nemesis lures believers to fornication, presumably by sending attractive but unscrupulous individuals their way.

In 7:6, Paul appears to qualify his earlier statements. It is **by way of concession, not as a command**, that he advises sex in marriage. He prefers that believers be unmarried and celibate **like I am**. It is not clear whether he had been single his whole life, was a widower, or was abandoned by his wife after he started following Christ. The latter gains support if Paul's "us" in

---

125. On sex for procreation, see Josephus *Ag. Ap.* 2.199; Musonius Rufus *Lect* 13A. Differently, Philo (like Paul) can affirm marital sex is pleasurable: *QG* 3.20-21; *Abr.* 245-46; Loader 2013:117.

126. How frequent? Opinions range from daily to 6 months in Plutarch *Solon* 20.3; *m.* Ketub. 5.6; Ciampa/Rosner 2010:280.

127. On similar mutuality, see Musonius Rufus *Lect.* 13A; Plutarch *Conj. praec.* 9-10[139C]; and for conjugal rights/obligations in Hellenistic and Rabbinic sources, see respectively, Grant 2001:127; Garland 2003:258.

128. Cf. Ciampa/Rosner 268, 281. Notice Musonius Rufus *Lect* 12.

129. See similarly, *T. Naph.* 8.8. Weaker manuscript support includes "fasting" (cf. KJV).

130. On Beliar luring through sexual enticement, see CD[A]4.15-20; *T.Reub.* 6.1-4; cf. Tob 6:16-22 (VT).

7:15 includes himself among those who have been abandoned. Being single and celibate must be by way of concession as well since not everyone has such a **gift from God**. God grants to some "the power to be continent in sexual matters."[131] This idea of giftedness as a single person seems related more to spiritual virtues, such as self-control (Gal 5:23), than to spiritual gifts such as in 12:4–12.

Paul briefly addresses **the unmarried and widows**; the latter he returns to in 7:39–40, and the former seem to be distinguished from virgins in 7:25–38. The unmarried probably includes those of both sexes who were divorced prior to their conversion, widowers (if any), and those who had never been married but are not virgins, such as former fornicators (6:9–11) and manumitted slaves who were once the unfortunate sex objects of their masters. People in this group should remain celibate like Paul, **but if they cannot control themselves they should marry, for it is better to marry than to burn** with passionate sexual desire and thus be vulnerable to fornication. When this thought is combined with 7:1–2, it becomes quite evident that Paul considers any sex outside of marriage to be fornication, including premarital sex as assumed here and again in 7:25–38. His advice about burning desires would not sound too strange for Roman Corinthians who might be prompted to imagine from their traditions Queen Dido, whose burning but deprived lust for Aeneas ends in her self-destruction (Virgil *Aen.* 4.96–102, 642–705; Ovid *Fasti* 3.544–49). It was sometimes thought inappropriate to show lust for one's own wife, whereas it might be permissible, especially among elitists, that a husband's passions could be vented through extra-marital sex (Demosthenes *Or.* [*Neaer.*]59.122; Plutarch *Conj. praec.* 16[140B]). Against this, Paul's advocacy for passion in *marital* sex stands out.[132] This reason for getting married, however, may sound deficient by today's standards, but Paul is writing in an age when marriages were typically arranged rather than singles freely dating a number of prospects before falling in love with the "right" person. Paul makes this statement attempting to curb sexual promiscuity in Corinth; it is doubtful that he meant to say that burning sexual passion is the only, let alone best, motivation for marriage.[133]

---

131. BDAG 1081. Paul's gift of celibacy along with his condemnation of homoeroticism (6:9–11) and valuing slaves as people, not tools (7:21–23), undermines Marchal 2011:749–70, who thinks Paul had sex with the slave Onesimus.

132. See further Oropeza 2006:31–32; contrast Martin 1995:209–17 (critiqued by Ellis 2007:147–59). Similarly, Jewish sources also consider marital sex a preventative against illicit sex (Prov 5:15–18; Tob 4:12; *T.Lev.* 9.9–10).

133. See further, Brenk 2012:87–111.

Avoiding Sexual Defilement: Second Supporting Proof (5:1—7:40)

ADVICE ON DIVORCE AND BEING MARRIED TO AN UNBELIEVER (7:10–16)

Regarding divorce, Paul's words become more a command than advice by appealing to an oral tradition from Jesus in which **not I but the Lord** orders these things. A saying of Jesus recorded later on in the Gospels claims that if a person divorces and remarries, he or she commits adultery (Mark 10:2–12; Matt 5:31–32; 19:3–12; Luke 16:18). Given the complexity of marital relationships, Paul recognizes that the charge, **let not wife be separated from husband**,[134] must be quickly followed up with the qualification that if she does happen to get separated, **let her remain unmarried or be reconciled to her husband**. Likewise, **the husband must not divorce his wife**.[135] Paul apparently adds the point about reconciliation; with Jesus he discourages both divorce and remarriage to another. In Matt 19:9 remarriage is permitted if one's spouse were sexually unfaithful, but Paul does not mention this. Perhaps he was unaware of this exception,[136] or if he did know it, he omits it perhaps because it would have been counter-productive to disclose it to members bent on divorcing their spouses. Some husbands were in fact sexually unfaithful; they were having sex with prostitutes! He only affirms in 7:10–11 that in emergent Christian marriages the initiator of the marriage's breakup does not have the option of getting remarried.

When Paul addresses **the rest** of the congregation members, he targets those who are married to **unbelieving** spouses (7:12–16). Although he does not approve of single believers marrying unbelievers (cf. 7:39),[137] in the Corinthian situation some of the spouses of those who converted to Christ remained unbelievers. And unlike the ethos of Paul's patriarchal world, the believing husbands did not force their unbelieving wives to convert. They apparently held that each spouse, whether man or woman, must willingly believe. What then should be done about a marriage in which one's spouse refuses to accept Christ?

---

134. The passive aorist infinitive χωρισθῆναι ("to be separated") may reflect Jewish audiences in which women found it difficult to initiate divorce (Josephus *Ant.* 15.259; m. *Yebamot* 14.1; Fitzmyer 2008:289–90), unlike Romanized women (7:13, 15). Contrast synoptic parallels with Mark 10:12; further, Neirynck 1996:166–76.

135. The distinction between "I separate/leave" (χωρίζω) and "I divorce" (ἀφίημι) should not be understood in the modern sense. See 7:15 below.

136. E.g., the exception clause might originate with Matthew's community (c. 80 CE) rather than Jesus (c. 30 CE).

137. Similarly, Israelites are not to marry foreigners, often with assumption that foreigners worship idols (Ezra 9:1–2; Tob 4:12–13; *T.Lev.* 9.10; *Jos Asen.* 8.5–7; *T.Sol.* 26; cf. *P.Mur.* 19).

Avoiding Sexual Defilement: Second Supporting Proof (5:1—7:40)

The apostle imparts no saying from Jesus here but gives his own perspective on the matter. First, the believer, whether husband or wife, should **not divorce** the unbelieving spouse if the unbeliever still **consents to live** with them. The unbeliever in this circumstance obviously tolerates the spouse's new religion and ethical conduct, which includes the worship of only one God. Second, in such relationship the unbeliever does not contaminate the believer but is **sanctified**, made holy, in the presence of the believing spouse. Related to this, the couple's **children** are not **unclean** but **holy**. Holiness here is probably best understood against the background of believers and their children being potentially contaminated by the unbelieving spouses' idolatry (see Excursus). Third, **if the unbelieving spouse gets separated** from (i.e., leaves) the believer, the believer **is not under bondage in such cases**. The spouse who was abandoned is no longer enslaved to the abandoner and is thus freed from that marriage. In the Greco-Roman world, if a person leaves a marriage, this constitutes "divorce by separation."[138] Although Paul would doubtless recommend celibacy for a believer who is divorced by an unbeliever, the option to remarry is permissible in keeping with the language of being "bound" or "free" from divorce contracts (*m. Git.* 9.3; *P. Mur.* 19; cf. 1 Cor 7:39; Rom 7:2).[139] Fourth, the general principle in all this is that **God has called us to peace**.[140] This reflects the end of strife in a marriage that has conflicting values, beliefs, and deities; peace is now possible because the unbeliever has departed. As well, the believer could have peace of mind about the broken relationship and move on with his or her life. Abusive marriages, incidentally, would also be contrary to such peace even though Paul does not explicitly mention domestic violence.[141]

Paul permits divorce and remarriage here based on a unique situation that is not found in Gospels. This perhaps lends credibility to the idea that the Gospels do not record all potential circumstances related to divorce and remarriage. They provide boundaries upon which later Christian leaders might build and discern the most prudent course of action to take relative to counseling their own married parishioners. Paul ends this subject by

---

138. Instone-Brewer 2002:190; Ciampa/Rosner 2010:292, 305–6; Treggiari 1991a:31–46. Similarly, in Jewish thinking (Exod 21:10–11), the wife is free to leave the marriage if her spouse neglects to provide her with material necessities and fulfill his marital duties, such as have sex with her. On the danger of broadening or restricting Paul's words in relation to this thought, see Ciampa/Rosner 2010:293–94 (fn. 115).

139. See Keener 2005:65; Loader 2013:90.

140. ἡμᾶς ("us") has stronger manuscript witnesses than ὑμᾶς ("you"): see Fee 1987:297.

141. Household peace would seem to mandate direct intervention and/or separation from the abusive spouse.

leaving open the question of whether a member's unbelieving spouse will ultimately believe. **For how do you know ... whether you will save** your unbelieving spouse? The question is posed to both husbands and wives and could be interpreted optimistically or pessimistically. If optimistically, the unbeliever might come to faith, and so it is a good idea to stay with that person (cf. 1 Pet 3:1). If pessimistically, the implication is that the abandoned spouse does not need to attempt reconciliation—there is no way of knowing whether the unbeliever will come to faith and be saved. The negative sense is more contextually present, but "how do you know?" (τί οἶδας) is often posed in a positive sense.[142] Perhaps Paul left the question deliberately ambiguous.

Excursus: Unbelieving Spouses, Clean Children, and Pollution by Idols (7:14)

In what sense is an unbelieving spouse made holy by the believing spouse? The typical unbeliever in Corinth is not a secularist in the modern sense of the word. He or she believes in other deities rather than the one God of Jews and Christians. This person likely found it annoying or even sacrilegious that the Christian spouse no longer venerated other gods and household spirits.[143] Paul assumes a conflict over religious beliefs and practices at stake in such homes. Their children, who are perhaps assumed to be young, unbaptized, dependents,[144] were expected to follow the customs of their parents, but in this case which parent? With regular religious conflicts of this sort at home, we could surmise that some believing fathers may have asked Paul if they could end their marriages. On the other hand, believing mothers may not have wished the dissolution of their marriages if J. D. Gordon is correct in suggesting that in patriarchal societies, children legally belonged to the father.[145] That would mean the unbelieving father would be able to take the children if the marriage ended, and believing mothers might fear their "clean" children would become "unclean" at their unbelieving father's home. In addition, believers of both sexes probably asked whether they and their children might become polluted via the unbelieving spouse's idolatry if they all continue to live under one roof. If children were to respect their

---

142. See Garland 2003:294, for references.
143. Hodge 2010:1–25, does a good job of showing how in ancient mixed marriages, the Christian's view of deity comes into conflict with the unbeliever's view.
144. Cf. Macdonald/Vaage 2011:537.
145. Gordon 1997:124.

Excursus: Unbelieving Spouses, Clean Children, and Pollution by Idols (7:14)

parents, they were probably taught by the unbelieving parent to pray to and venerate other gods. The believing spouse also ate the same food at the dinner table with the unbelieving spouse, food which might have been dedicated to idols. This issue would be especially relevant for believers with "weak" consciences (see 8:7–13). Since the Corinthians are taught that an unbeliever's body belongs to the fallen present age and realm of Satan (5:5; 6:12–20), might they infer from this that having sex with their unbelieving spouses could pollute or otherwise jeopardize their own spiritual safety?

Paul's answer to these believers would seem to be very comforting. Due to the believing spouses' presence in the home, the unbelieving spouses are sanctified, which here probably means that they do not become a pollutant through idols and the demons idols might attract (8:4–7; 10:20–21).[146] Such powers are prevented from doing harm to believing spouses and their children because they belong to Christ. God's Spirit, who is more powerful than other forces, will continue to be present in and favor such households, and their prayers to God will not be hindered. The believer's holiness either becomes a contagion, or the unbeliever's impurity is neutralized in the "powerfield" of God's Spirit that protects their household.[147] Paul, of course, does not mean that unbelieving spouses are automatically saved or filled with God's Spirit; rather, these spouses are prevented from being pollutants in their own households despite not being saved. Since the believer's children are holy, not polluted by idols or demons via the unbelieving spouse, they could participate as members of the Christ community.[148] It follows from this that they are permitted to eat at church meals that commemorate the Lord's Supper.

---

146. This consecration happens regardless of whether or not the unbelieving spouses behave like Christians (*pace*, Murphy-O'Connor 2009:43–57). The perfect passive ἡγίασται ("sanctified") and locative ἐν ("in the presence of") suggest a state rather than praxis. Similarly, though considering ἐν as instrumental, are Schrage 1994:2.105; Fee 1987:300.

147. On the former, see Hays 2002:251; on latter, Schnabel 2006:376. On transference of holiness in the LXX, see Ciampa/Rosner 2010:299. Differently, Gillihan 2002:711–44, considers Paul to be saying that such marriages are holy by virtue of being licit marriages (cf. *m. Qidd.* 2:1–3.12).

148. See Gillihan 2002:730.

Avoiding Sexual Defilement: Second Supporting Proof (5:1—7:40)

Remaining in One's Calling (7:17-24)

The opening **nevertheless** (εἰ μή) points back to the "call to peace" in 7:15 in relation to the dissolution of a believer's marriage; *nevertheless,* this circumstantial "change is not to be the rule" for congregation members.[149] The rule is normally that **as God has called each one,** so let that person walk and remain in that same calling. This idea is repeated in different words three times in chiastic form:

- A. Let each believer walk in their God-given assignment and calling (7:17)

  - B. Instructions on being called into circumcision and uncircumcision (7:18-19)

    - C. Let each believer remain in the calling in which they were called (7:20)

  - B^1. Instructions on being called into slavery and freedom (7:21-23)

- A^1. Let each believer remain with God in whatever calling they were called (7:24)

This repetitive pattern highlights the verbs **walk** and **remain** with reference to one's **calling** as important principles not only for Corinthian perception but for **all the churches** of Paul's mission (4:17; 11:16; 14:33). The metaphor of walking seems derived from Jewish *halakah,* the notion of "following a moral pattern for conducting one's life."[150] In Paul's other letters, the believer's walk is to be holy, pleasing to God, and guided by the Spirit (1 Thess 4:1-3; Gal 5:16, 25; Rom 8:4). Doubtless such conduct is expected regardless of the family, vocation, location, education, and circumstances of life one finds oneself in when following Christ. We misinterpret Paul, however, if we make him say that people should never change their respective circumstances, especially in relation to their behavior after conversion. This would be counterproductive to the radical transformation he promotes in 6:9-11. The drunkard should be free from his addiction, the swindler should make an honest living, and the idol maker should alter his career. Paul is also not prohibiting a change of status.[151] He essentially means, "Do not let the set of conditions into which you were converted become a source of hindrance to your relationship and service to the Lord" (cf. 7:32a, 35). The believer is

---

149. Fee 1987:309; cf. Ramasaran 2003:446, 454-55.
150. Oropeza 2012a:49.
151. Cf. Braxton 2000:53; Garland 2003:300.

thus challenged to be obedient to Christ and not let family, work, habits, circumstances, or anything else get in the way of that. As Thiselton puts it, "A Christian does not have to seek 'the right situation' in order to enjoy Christian freedom or to serve God's call effectively."[152]

In diatribe fashion Paul poses the questions, **Was anyone called being circumcised? ... Has anyone been called in uncircumcision?**, and then answers with exhortations for both not to attempt changing their present condition.[153] Since Jews and Gentile proselytes in the church were already circumcised,[154] they are charged to not do an *epispasm*, the pulling of their foreskin back over their penis.[155] Some of these members possibly desired status upgrades through uncircumcision (circumcision would be generally ridiculed by their Gentile compatriots). There is no good reason, however, why Paul would need to discourage uncircumcised Gentiles from getting circumcised.[156] The Corinthian congregation is not legalistic regarding Mosaic Law; they already accept Paul's circumcision-free gospel.[157] Paul's exhortation, then, may not reflect an actual conflict in this congregation; he may simply be teaching this precept because he does so in all his churches, some of which do struggle with Mosaic Law (7:17d; cf. Gal 5:6; 6:15).[158]

Both **circumcision and uncircumcision amount to nothing** for Paul; **what matters is keeping the commands of God**. This saying is contrary to Mosaic Law, since circumcision is prescribed and assumed in the Torah and constituted by God (Lev 12:3; Gen 17:9–14).[159] For Israel, keeping God's commands *includes* circumcision. Which commands does Paul refer to if he discourages his Gentile converts from keeping circumcision and the works of the Law, and believes the Ten Commandments are being set aside in Christ (2 Cor 3:3–16; Gal 2:16; 3:10–25; Rom 3:20; cf. 1 Cor 15:56)? Fee suggests that he must be assuming ethical "imperatives" of "Christian

---

152. Thiselton 2000:545.

153. See the diatribe pattern of inquiries and responses in Seneca *Tranq.* 4.3–4; Epictetus *Ench.* 15; Deming 1995:159–64.

154. Acts 18:1–8 complements this view.

155. See 1 Macc 1:14–15; Josephus *Ant.* 12.241; *T.Mos.* 8.3.

156. Ciampa/Rosner 2010:311, suggest a Jew-Gentile marriage in the congregation, but this is quite questionable.

157. There is no evidence of Torah-abiding opponents in the Corinthian church (see Oropeza 2016:232–38).

158. Notice also Paul's change from generic third person singulars in 7:18–19, which fit well with his maxims in 7:17, 20, 22, 24, to his more personalized second person singulars and plurals when addressing slaves in 7:21, 23.

159. Cf. Tucker 2011b:77.

Avoiding Sexual Defilement: Second Supporting Proof (5:1—7:40)

faith."[160] But what are those imperatives given that Paul sometimes uses a commanding voice even when giving his own opinion about matters, as in this chapter? It seems that some of his own imperatives may be regarded as God's when they are given by the Lord's authority (7:10; 14:37; similarly, Acts 15:22–29). Also, God's commands may be considered synonymous with precepts taught as "the law of Christ" (9:21; Gal 6:2). These are Jesus's teachings, some of which are Torah teachings *as interpreted by and fulfilled through Jesus* (Matt 7:12; 22:33–37; Mark 12:28–34; Luke 10:25–28). Paul acknowledges such commands—e.g., loving the one true God (8:1–6) and loving one's neighbor as oneself (Gal 5:14; Rom 13:7–10; cf. 1 Cor 13).

Paul then addresses those in the congregation who were **called being a slave** and charges them, **do not let it trouble you** (7:21). Such words would be comforting to enslaved auditors who might have feared that involuntary sex with their masters somehow displeased God as though the fault were their own. Paul seems to recognize that slaves are responsible only for actions in which they have control.[161] Apart from concerns about their masters who might abuse, beat, or otherwise hurt them, Paul affirms that they should not feel unworthy before fellow believers on account of their status—they, too, are loved and important to God and can contribute to the life of the congregation. But if they **are able to become free**, they should **make use all the more** (μᾶλλον χρῆσαι). The latter statement is not self-evident regarding what the slaves are to make use of—should they take advantage of their slavery or their freedom from slavery?[162] If Paul were encouraging slaves to remain slaves and take advantage of this status, this seems to conflict with his charge to the free congregants *not* to sell themselves into slavery (7:23). Since freedom is better than slavery for those who are free, it also would seem to be for those who are enslaved. We could surmise that Paul thought it preferable for a slave to gain his freedom than remain a slave. If freed, he would be able to care for the things of the Lord rather than the things of the world and how to please his master. A manumitted slave would be in a far better position than a bound slave for tasks such as Christian service, discipleship, evangelism, giving to the poor, and missionary work. Paul also would be quite aware of slaves' aspirations for freedom. Both slaves and freed persons in the congregation probably knew that Corinth was partly founded on manumitted slaves, and many of its current residents enjoyed that status.[163] With the majority of scholars, then, we support that Paul is

---

160. Fee 1987:313.
161. Cf. Ciampa/Rosner 2010:319.
162. On the history of the debate, see Harrill 1998:74–108.
163. See Nasralla 2013:60–62; Byron 2008:91–107.

Avoiding Sexual Defilement: Second Supporting Proof (5:1—7:40)

encouraging slaves to take advantage of any opportunities they might have to become free.[164]

A metaphorical status reversal occurs for slaves and free persons who are converted to Christ. **The one who was called as a slave is the Lord's freed person**, a manumitted slave for Christ; whereas **the one who was called as a free person is Christ's slave**.[165] This distinction is not so drastic when we realize that manumitted slaves had obligations that involved honoring their former masters as patrons.[166] In Christ, converted slaves who are spiritually set free are still obligated to honor and serve Christ as their metaphorical patron and spouse (see 6:20). In return, Christ bestows them with great spiritual and salvific benefits. Likewise, free members who have become metaphoric slaves in Christ must serve Christ faithfully, and they will be rewarded by him. The conversion of both slave and freeperson has delivered them from enslavement to sin; the Lord purchased their bodies from this bondage with the price of his death on the cross (7:22–23; cf. 6:11, 20; Rom 6:6, 15–23). The price of this redemption would be especially moving to those who knew how costly their own manumission from slavery was.[167] Christ did not redeem their bodies so that they might sell them again into slavery; hence, Paul commands them, **do not become slaves of humans**.[168]

For Paul, slavery is an institute of the Roman Empire, which is passing away in Christ. But when master or slave or both converted to Christ, issues surrounding their status in the congregation might have become rather complex for him.[169] Paul, at any rate, views slaves differently than certain ideologies that regarded them merely as tools and property.[170] He considers believers among them to be equal partners in Christ and members of the body of Christ (12:13; cf. Gal 3:28), and non-believing slaves he sees as po-

---

164. E.g., Harrill 1998:108–22, 126–27; Garland 2003:108–14; Merklein 2000:2.131–34; Horrell 1996:162–66; contrast Huttunen 2009:29; Conzelmann 1975:160–61. For mediating views, see Bartchy 1973:155–59; Thiselton 2000:544. For Braxton 2000:220–33, Paul is ambiguous.

165. See Martin 1990:63–68.

166. See Garland 2003:314–15. On types of manumission, see Harrill 2003:580–81; 1996:54–55, 169–72.

167. See Nasralla 2013:72–73.

168. On selling oneself to slavery, see Bartchy 1973:47; Glancy 2002:82.

169. Barclay 1994:175–84 and Byron 2004:130–36 have good discussions along these lines.

170. E.g., Aristotle *N.E.* 8.11; *Pol.* 1.1–7, though this reflects Athens rather than Rome centuries later. Seneca *Ep.* 47.1, 10–13, 17, is more contemporary with the NT, and he considers a shared human existence for both slaves and free; slaves unfortunately have had misfortune (Harrill 2003:576).

Avoiding Sexual Defilement: Second Supporting Proof (5:1—7:40)

tential converts to this new spiritual status.[171] His compassion for the latter is evident with Onesimus, whom he brings to faith and charges his master Philemon to accept Onesimus "no longer as a slave, but better than a slave, as a beloved brother" (Phlm 10 cf. 16). He also calls slaves in the Corinthian congregation "brothers and sisters" (7:24), reversing the social order of his day by including them in the household of God not as slaves but as *persons* and fellow siblings in Christ. These Paul considers the socially weaker and less-honored members of the congregation, which are thus considered more honorable in Christ (12:22–24). As fellow siblings in Christ, they along with others are not to be wronged or defrauded by congregation members (6:8), ruined by a stronger person's liberties (8:12), not to be despised (Rom 14:10), not to be caused to stumble by what another believer does (Rom 14:21), and not to be exploited in matters of sex (1 Thess 4:6).[172]

ADVICE REGARDING VIRGINS AND WIDOWS (7:25–40)

The phrase **now concerning virgins** begins Paul's response to another question the Corinthians wrote to him about (see 7:1), or, alternatively, it simply starts another topic related to domestic relationships. Since Paul assumes that sex apart from marriage is fornication (7:1-2, 9), he considers virginity as the norm before marriage, which is typical of Jewish communities (Deut 22:13–21; Tob 3:14–15; Sir 26:10–12; *Sib. Or.* 2.279–81).[173] As in 7:12 our apostle instructs by virtue of his own **opinion, as one shown mercy by the Lord to be trustworthy.**[174] His advice is a matter of practical wisdom,

---

171. Glancy 2002:34–38 argues that Paul does not hold his vision in Gal 3:28 consistently because he reinscribes divisions between slave and free in Gal 4. But her view misses the rhetorical impact Paul's words in Gal 4:7 would make on slave auditors. Such liberating words are characteristic of what would attract slaves to become devote believers in the first place.

172. This perspective undermines Glancy 1998:496; 2002:59–65; 2015:227–28, who insinuates that Paul advocates Christian masters to have sex with their slaves. If such sex were to provide a second sexual outlet for believers, then Paul's repeated point that marital sex is the only alternative to unfulfilled passion could hardly make any sense (7:1–2, 5, 9, 37–38). When we add to this Paul's points that believers should not take a woman for sexual gratification (7:1), the husband's body is owned by his wife (7:4b), Paul's preference for celibacy (7:7), and his positive view of slaves as persons, such ideas almost certainly negate that Paul would allow, let alone encourage, masters to have sex with their slaves. His lack of discussing the matter more explicitly need not be interpreted as indifference but probably agreement with moralists like Musonius Rufus: "What need is there to say that it is an act of licentiousness and nothing less for a master to have relations with a slave? Everyone knows that" (*Lect* 12).

173. See further examples in Loader 2013:45–46; Harper 2012:363–83.

174. This, then, is an argument from ethos (Collins 1999:289).

though he does attempt to persuade by questions with exhortory answers (7:27; cf. 7:18, 21), five repetitive expressions (anaphora) that use multiple conjunctions (polysyndeton) (7:29–31), and the use of same sounding words (paranomasia) (7:32–35).[175]

Paul addresses both male and female virgins, a group distinct from unmarried non-virgins (see 7:8).[176] The language of being **bound** and **released** is legal, suggesting the ratifying or breaking of a marriage contract, respectively (7:27, 39; cf. 7:15).[177] But since virgins are being addressed, these words identify someone who is engaged to be married. Betrothal can be viewed as a binding contract (cf. Aulus Gellius *Noct. att.* 4.4; Philo *Spec. Leg.* 3.12.72).[178] Paul advises that a betrothed believer does not need to end the relationship, but if that person has recently ended one, such should not seek another betrothal. If the latter decides to get betrothed again and marry anyway, he or she **has not done wrong** by refusing to take Paul's advice. Paul is concerned, though, that new marriages will have **trouble in the flesh**. These words suggest there are unique challenges of daily responsibilities married couples face in relation to pleasing each other and also earning enough money so as to feed, nurture, and protect their children. Virgin believers only need to fend for themselves, and given the way things are presently shaping themselves in Paul's world, fewer responsibilities are better. This trouble aside, Paul says regarding those who get married, **I spare you**. In other words, "I desist from claiming that you must remain virgins, and I will not consider you to be doing wrong for not following my advice" (cf. 7:28a, 35–36).

Paul provides two major reasons why he encourages virgins to remain in their present state. The first centers on the **present distress** (7:26). Winter posits that this relates to a grain and food shortage that affected Corinth roughly around the 40s and 50s CE.[179] If so, perhaps Paul interprets this calamity through an apocalyptic lens. In the Jesus traditions famine belongs to the beginning of "birth pangs" signaling the beginning of the end

---

175. I.e., ἀμέριμνος/"free from care"; μεριμνάω/"to care for"; μεμέρισται/"he is divided" (ibid.).

176. On male virgins, see e.g., *JosAsen* 4.7, 8.1; Rev 14:4.

177. See Zeller 2010:260–61; Arzt-Grabner et al. 2006:292–93.

178. Cf. Schrage 1994:2.158.

179. Winter 2001:215–25; cf. e.g., Suetonius *Claud* 18.2; Tacitus *Ann.* 12.43.1; Inscription to Dinippus. Carter 2010:161–65, questions whether scarcity in such sources caused "major social unrest" (even though he later supports Winter's shortage for interpreting 11:21–22 [172–73]). His alternative is that ἐνεστῶσαν ἀνάγκην in 7:26 reflects ἀνάγκη in 7:37 and is paraphrased, "the ever-present threat of sexual immorality" rather than "current distress." I question whether the Corinthians would have first heard it this way without prior conditioning from 7:37.

Avoiding Sexual Defilement: Second Supporting Proof (5:1—7:40)

times (Matt 24:7; Mark 13:8; Luke 21:11; cf. 4 *Ezra* 16.18; Rev 6:8; 18:8). One the other hand, we may not be privy to the nature of the distress. For Paul, in any case, Christ's first advent is itself a sign of the prophetic turn of ages. Since then, the **time** of the old creation **has been drawn in together** with the time of the new creation so that these eras collide and overlap, with the latter supplanting the former completely at Christ's second advent (7:29; cf. 10:11).[180] Time in the present age, then, is limited; it cannot continue indefinitely.[181] If the institutes of the old creation, including marriage, will eventually pass away, then to hold on too tightly to such things is inadvisable. Moreover, Paul perhaps agrees with apocalyptic discourses that discourage marriages due to end time calamities (4 *Ezra* 16.33-34; 2 *Bar.* 10.13-14; Rev 18:23; cf. Joel 2:16; Jer 16:1-4).[182] In light of Paul's "now and not yet" perspective of the ages, the antithetical statements in 7:29-32, guided by the phrase **as though not**, are to pervade the believers' way of thinking about marriage, weeping, rejoicing, purchasing, and anything else that might **make use of this world** in the present era. His inclusion of rejoicing and weeping on this list, which are valued human emotions in their own right, probably views them relative to purchasing worldly goods (cf. Ezek 7:12).[183] The present way of life with its preoccupations and socioeconomic order will come to an end.[184]

The second reason Paul wants virgins to remain as they are centers on his desire for them **to be free of concern** so that they might be **constantly in service to the Lord without distraction** (7:32, 35). Jesus similarly encourages his disciples not to be concerned about daily necessities. He warns them against becoming unfruitful due to the cares of this world (Matt 6:25-28; 13:22; Mark 4:19). Certain Stoics and Cynics who speculated on marriage affirmed that, at least for some in the pursuit of wisdom, marriage can be a distraction (e.g., Epictetus *Diatr.* 3.22.69-72; Diogenes *Ep.* 47; Diogenes Laertius *Vit. phil.* 6.2.54).[185] Although a philosophically unperturbed state in which one is detached from distracting things might resonate with Paul, Thiselton rightly distinguishes the apostle's nuance: "*Trust in God relativizes all other concerns; it does not 'detach' the Christian believer from them.*"[186]

---

180. Though often translated as time "shortened" (e.g., NASB) συστέλλω can mean to "draw together" (LSJ 1735).

181. See Tucker 2011b:209.

182. Cf. Deming 1995:188; cf. 179f.

183. See sources in Deming 1995:178-79.

184. Cf. May 2004:247; see further Luke 17:26-37; 4 *Ezra* 16.40-50; *Apoc. Elij.* 2.31; *Sib. Or.* 2.327-9.

185. Cf. Huttunen 2009:82-83; Balch 1983:429-39.

186. Thiselton 2000:587.

Avoiding Sexual Defilement: Second Supporting Proof (5:1—7:40)

Believers who get married are at a disadvantage because their time, interest, and concentration will be **divided** between the Lord and pleasing their spouse, not to mention caring for their children that will come later on in life. Virgin believers, on the other hand, can spend more time being devoted and of service to the Lord, and unmarried females also focus on being **holy in body** (i.e., keeping chaste) **and in spirit** (i.e., having purity of thoughts, emotions, and volition; cf. 2 Cor 7:1; 1 Thess 5:23).

Paul then addresses the betrothed male (7:36–37) and father of the virgin daughter (7:38). The betrothed risks behaving **indecently toward his virgin** (7:36b);[187] he behaves in a manner sexually inappropriate.[188] Some examples of indecency include the way Philip of Macedonia sits with his tunic pulled up and exposed before his subjects (Plutarch, [*Reg. imp. apophth.*] 178D), a courtesan disallowing her lover to behave indecently under a portrait of the chaste Xenocrates (Plutarch *Fragmata* 85), and the utterance of licentious phrases (Dio Chrysostom, *Or.* 40.29). Winter stresses sexual respectability was the Roman norm for engaged couples.[189] And certainly, Jewish sentiment promotes guarding virginity well (Sir 42:9–14; Ps.-Phoc. *Sent* 215–17).[190] The extent to which intimacy might be a part of courtship at this time is elusive. A period of "warming" is assumed by Ovid in which kissing seems permissible (*Her.* 21.195–96),[191] but romantic literature of this sort might be more the exception than rule. For Paul, the male's indecency could be anything from fondling his fiancée inappropriately (if he were even allowed to embrace her) to gazing at her and getting aroused because of it. We simply do not know Paul's thoughts on courtship boundaries.[192] Since Paul wants virgins to remain virgins until marriage, he suggests that if the male betrothed cannot keep his sexual urges in check he could go ahead and get married. If he could remain self-controlled, however, he does well by keeping his betrothed a virgin and not marry her. The multiple conditions in which the betrothed **stands firm in his heart, not having necessity but has power over his own will, and has decided this in his own heart**, are to assure that he is absolutely sure about his decision to end the engagement.

---

187. ἀσχημονέω means "to behave disgracefully, dishonorably, indecently" (BDAG 147; cf. εὐσχήμων: 7:35: "proper"/"noble"/"appropriate").

188. Winter 2001:243–46, shows that ἀσχημονέω and its cognates frequently have sexual nuances. Differently, in papyri material the term conveys non-sexual innuendos (see Arzt-Grabner et al. 2006:310–11).

189. Winter 2001:245.

190. See Malcolm 2013b:84.

191. See Treggiari 1991b:159–60.

192. For contemporary Christian singles, I discuss such boundaries in Oropeza 2006:27–63.

Avoiding Sexual Defilement: Second Supporting Proof (5:1—7:40)

Roman engagements could be ended by letter or person, and dowry or gifts might be returned if already given.[193] Normally, the father was the one who could break up the couple, but Julius Caesar at sixteen broke off his own relationship with Cossutia (Suetonius *Jul.* 1.1). Joseph is also portrayed attempting to end his own engagement to Mary (Matt 1:18–19).

A turn of subjects takes place from the betrothed in 7:37 to the father in 7:38: **he** (the father) **who gives her** (the daughter) **in marriage does well, but he who does not give her in marriage does better**. This change of subjects is not as abrupt as it first might appear.[194] The father or patriarch of the household normally gives the bride in marriage, and Paul is well aware of this custom (2 Cor 11:2–3). In arranged marriages parents have a voice in the relationship.[195] Without the father giving away the bride here, we run into an unrealistic portrait of first-century weddings in which parents play no major role in the decision of their virgin daughter. With these concluding words that sound like a maxim, Paul remains consistent with his view of celibacy by confirming that it is good for couples to marry, but it is even better if they stay single.

As is typical in patriarchal societies, the male figure initiates the marriage, and the virgin female, perhaps as young as 14 years old, has no voice, unlike older women such as widows, whom Paul addresses in 7:39–40.[196] Perhaps Paul returns to this subject from 7:8 because he now wants to specify that believers who become widows *after* their conversion could enjoy the same freedom as widows who were *already* widows when they were converted. She is bound by marriage to her believing husband as long as he lives, **but if her husband has fallen asleep in death, she is free to be married to whom she wishes**. Paul uses the metaphor of falling asleep as representing death only in reference to believers (11:30; 15:6, 18, 20; 1 Thess 4:13–15). There is no reason to suppose, however, that the same privilege would not apply if her deceased husband were not a believer. Likewise, we assume that a husband whose wife dies is permitted remarriage under the same circumstances. Perhaps for brevity's sake Paul does not include wid-

---

193. Cf. Treggiari 1991b:156–57.

194. The active imperative of γαμέω, "let them marry" (7:36c), is something the betrothed or couple does (cf. 7:28), whereas γαμίζω (7:38) normally means giving (a woman) in marriage (Matt 24:38; Mark 12:25), which is something the father does. Although the verbal ending–ίζω does not need to be causative and could mean "make a marriage" (Lietzmann/Kümmel 1949:35–36), Fitzmyer 2008:327, notices that no one has documented a case in which γαμίζω is non-causative, unless here. NKJV is a commendable translation of 7:36–38.

195. On parental roles in arranged marriages, see Loader 2013:40–43; Arzt-Grabner et al. 2006:313.

196. See Perkins 2012:113.

Avoiding Sexual Defilement: Second Supporting Proof (5:1—7:40)

owers, or more likely certain women in the congregation found themselves in this predicament and were the ones asking the relevant question. Along with a spouse's abandonment by divorce, then, a spouse's death is another condition given by Paul that allows for remarriage. The believing widow can remarry, but **only in the Lord**—she could marry only a fellow believer in Christ.[197] Our apostle, however, gives his opinion that the widow would be happier remaining a widow than getting remarried. The reasons would seem to be the same as he has already given. The present distress in their world along with distraction from single-minded service to the Lord warrant that it is better to be single than married.

The final sentence in this section, **and I think I also have God's Spirit**, is probably not a sarcastic jab at an overtly spiritual faction in the congregation but Paul's modest self-confidence. He is not just giving his personal advice anymore but may be guided by God's Spirit. Namely, Paul may be writing under spiritual inspiration as he states that widows are better off remaining single, and if they do marry, they should marry only another believer.[198]

---

197. This would be in keeping with endogamous Jewish marriages: see Garland 2003:343–44.

198. We find in Ephesus a very different situation that warranted Timothy's encouragement of younger widows to get remarried (1 Tim 5:14; Oropeza 2012a:272–78). This suggests that Paul's advice against the widow's remarriage in 1 Cor is relative to the Corinthian situation. Nowhere among NT believers, however, do we find encouragement to marry unbelievers (see also 2 Cor 6:14).

Idol Foods, Idolatry, and Relinquishing One's Right: Third Supporting Proof (8:1—11:1)

In 8:1 **now concerning** introduces the next topic and possible inquiry from the Corinthian letter received by Paul (cf. 7:1). This verse also functions as the beginning of a third deliberative proof related to the letter's central appeal for solidarity and against divisions (1:10). Apparently, some in the congregation have knowledge that idols are harmless and the deities they represent are not real. These members, identified by scholars as the strong or *gnosis* (knowing), justify their consumption of food sacrificed to idols.[1] Other members who have a weak conscience can be harmed by their act.[2] The unity Paul deliberates here reconstructs knowledge and wisdom in a way that caters to solidarity via strong members sharing love and consideration for the weak. At the same time, he warns these members against idolatry and partnering with demons. This threat is one in which insiders risk spiritual pollution by becoming one with outsiders. The most basic contours of 8:1—11:1 are as follows:

A Idol Foods and the Weak Believer (8:1–13)

B Relinquishing One's Right (9:1–27)

A¹ Idolatry and Idol Foods (10:1—11:1)

Although a change in subject takes place at point B, the unity of these chapters will be made evident.

Knowledge, Love, and One God and Lord (8:1–6)

Paul addresses the issue of **things sacrificed to idols** (εἰδωλοθύτων), more specifically in this context meat has been offered (8:13; 10:25), though what he says can pertain to other idol foods also (8:4, 8; 10:31).[3] The statements,

---

1. Paul, however, does not use the word "strong" here except in 10:22. See also 4:10; Rom 15:1.

2. On the history of interpretation in 1 Cor 8–10, see Willis 2007:103–12; Phua 2005:1–28; Fotopoulos 2003:1–47; Cheung 1999:306–22; Gooch 1993:135–55.

3. The term may be coined either by Jews (Arzt-Grabner et al. 2006:328) or early

Third Supporting Proof (8:1—11:1)

we know that we all have knowledge (8:1b), and, **we know that an idol is nothing in the world and that there is no God but one** (8:4), are perhaps his paraphrased versions of the strong members' sayings.[4] Paul will correct their views.

To their first saying he responds that such **knowledge puffs up**; it could inflate members to think too highly of themselves and better than others, which would only engender more congregational divisions. Paul advances instead the idea that **love builds up**; it edifies rather than alienates members. This antithesis between knowledge and love is explicated further in 8:2-3. In a passive-active word play, he deflates conceited members by asserting that they do not know as they ought to know. What they ought to know is that they are to **love God** and desire to **be known by Him**. The assumption is that God knows and has fellowship with those who obey God and Christ's teachings. To be known by God is to belong to God.[5] Paul's stress on love echoes the Jewish *Shema*: "Hear O Israel, the Lord our God is one Lord. And you shall love the Lord your God with all your heart, and with all your soul, and with all your strength" (Deut 6:4-5). Perhaps Jesus's words are also remembered here since he taught his followers to love God and their neighbors as themselves (Mark 12:28-34; Lev 19:18). Paul's auditors are to ponder on the idea that those who know the one true God are characterized by their love, and they should recognize that weaker members in Christ are their neighbors.

In response to their second saying, Paul again alludes to the *Shema*. Both he and the strong members believe that there is only **one God** to the exclusion of all other deities (Isa 41:4; 43:10). That there are many **so-called** gods among the nations suggests these deities are not real to Paul. The idols that represent them are dumb and lifeless (12:2; cf. Isa 40:18-21; Jer 10:3-11; Deut 32:21). If there is one God, there are no other gods (Deut 6:4-5; cf. 32:12, 31, 39; Isa 41:4; 43:10). The congregation's city included numerous temples and statues of deities, including Poseidon, Athena, and Aphrodite (Pausanius, *Descr.* 2.1-5), and its inhabitants devoted themselves to gods such as Asclepius, Isis, Demeter, Kore, and Dionysus.[6] Corinth's inhabitants, along with the weaker congregation members, believe that **many gods and many lords** do exist, though this does not reflect Paul's

---

Christians (Gardner 1994:15-16; Newton 1998:179-83). On the definition, see Still 2002:231.

4. Another Corinthian saying is possible in 8:8 (see Murphy-O'Connor 2009:76-86).

5. This idea reflects divine election as Schnabel 2006:442-43, affirms.

6. See e.g., Fotopoulos 2003:49-157; Coutsoumpos 2008:171-77; Bookidis 2005:41-64.

Third Supporting Proof (8:1—11:1)

own belief.[7] Although Paul will mention that demons can be present with idols (10:20-21), he never claims they are actual gods. And while Satan and the lawless man whom Satan influences are called *god* (2 Cor 4:4; 2 Thess 2:3-4), this designation for them is in the singular, relative to the fallen world, and hence, shown to be a false and temporal claim that opposes the only true God by nature (2 Thess 2:8; Rom 16:20; cf. Gal 4:8-9).[8]

Along with the many gods worshipped in Corinth, congregation members would be aware of the imperial cult and its veneration of Augustus among **many lords** and divinities (8:5).[9] As well, the lords Paul mentions might include apotheosized heroes such as Hercules and Asclepius; and the term also was related to divinities among Egyptians, Syrians, and Thracians.[10] Even so, Paul may be informed by Deut 10:17 where God is "God of gods and Lord of lords." In this light his language reflects rhetorical motivation—the *many* gods and lords in the cosmos highlight the contrast between these powers and Paul's *one* deity and lord who created the cosmos: **But for us there is one God, the Father from whom are all things, and we to Him, and one Lord Jesus Christ through whom are all things, and we through him**. In this reconfiguration of the *Shema*, it appears as though Paul (or an earlier Christian tradition he recites) has split "the Lord your God is one Lord" from Deut 6:4 (LXX) and attributed "God" to the Father and God's name as "Lord" to Jesus Christ.[11] The one God, as it were, becomes both the one Father and one Lord Jesus Christ.[12] God is the Father and creator of all things in heaven and earth which derived their existence *from* (ἐκ) Him, and it was *through* (διά) the agency of the preexistent Lord Jesus Christ that this was accomplished (cf. Col 1:15-18). The created order also progresses *to* (εἰς) God *through* the Lord Jesus, which anticipates the new creation as the old creation's goal (2 Cor 5:17).[13] This terminus implies

---

7. See Waaler 2008:379-80; Cheung 1999:123-24.

8. Although it can be argued that, given the similar terminology of the "rulers of this age" (2:6, 8) and "rulers and authorities" (Col 2:15; cf. 2:20; Eph 6:12), the demons might refer to the "many lords" mentioned by Paul, Paul never actually uses "lord" (κύριος) to designate demons or Satan, unless here. Contrast Shen 2010:143, 146, 200.

9. The phrase "*many* lords" does not resemble well merely the Caesars because only several had reigned by Paul's time. Although Winter 2001:272-74, 282, gives evidence that members of the imperial family were also venerated, more than simply the imperial household is meant given the vast number of deities and lords known to Paul and the Corinthians.

10. Cf. Fitzmyer 2008:341; Zeller 2010:289.

11. See Tilling 2012: 91; Koperski 1996:390. See also 1:2.

12. See Waaler 2008:434-35.

13. See implications in Zeller 2010:292-93.

Third Supporting Proof (8:1—11:1)

the ultimate salvation of "we," that is, those who believe in the Lord Jesus.[14] It is *through* the Lord that reconciliation, righteousness, salvation, and the triumph of resurrection takes place (15:21, 57; 2 Cor 5:18–19; Rom 5:18–21; 1 Thess 5:9).[15] Paul affirms that everything created will inevitably be put in its proper order under God's headship and dominion through the Lord Jesus Christ (see 11:3; 15:27-28).

The *Shema* for the new creation is not merely a theological excursion but also has ethical implications. The solidarity between God and the Lord Jesus is an exemplary model for the Corinthians to imitate in terms of their own solidarity as believers. Moreover, to know God is to love God and have fellowship with God and Christ, which should result in knowing, loving, and having fellowship with one's neighbor.

Idol Foods and Weak Believers (8:7-13)

Even though Paul concedes with the strong members that there is no God but one, he states that **this knowledge is not in all** believers, particularly some who were formerly idolaters. Such members **are accustomed to the idol until now**, that is, they have been in the habit of believing that the deity representing the idol really exists. They **eat idol food as though (truly) to an idol**, with the implication that by doing so, they become aware of performing a religious act to another god. Such believers are susceptible to spiritual disaster. They have a **weak conscience** (ἀσθενής συνείδησις),[16] which can be defiled, wounded, emboldened, and, most prominently, prompt them to commit apostasy (8:7, 10, 12). Superstition may have characterized these weak congregants,[17] and so fear of the gods and how they might curse or hold them accountable may be their anxiety and concern. A popular saying of the time was that nothing escapes notice of the gods (Theon *Prog.* 3[5]97). Pausanius provides a relevant example of how Corinthians believed they could never escape the oaths that were made at the temple of Palaemon (*Descr.* 2.2.1). If Garland is correct that conscience is the "moral compass . . . [that] comprises the depository of an individual's

---

14. Waaler 2008:413; cf. Giblin 1975:535.

15. Cf. Zeller 2010:293.

16. The precision of συνείδησις is evasive and perhaps best appreciated in light of its respective context than our word choice. See discussion in Thiselton 2000:640–44. Other renderings include "consciousness" or "self-awareness." This conscience cannot be reduced to having strong scruples against idol foods; otherwise, the weak should be appalled rather than emboldened to participate with the strong in 8:10 (cf. Dawes 1998:90).

17. Calvin 1996:176.

moral beliefs and principles that makes judgments about what is right and wrong," then someone with a *weak* conscience is prone to make poor moral judgments and base them on defective criteria.[18]

Along with internal conflicts, the weak members likely face external pressure from unbelieving compatriots and family members who would like nothing more than for their relative, friend, or neighbor to return to eating idol meals just like before. And now these believers potentially find fellow congregation members also participating in these meals! What concerns Paul the most is that if these weak members consume food dedicated to other deities, they will interpret the act as idolatry since they believe these deities are real. As a result, they may lock into their minds their failure and unfaithfulness to Paul's deity, and they would then resume their obligations and devotion to former deities as they abandon faith in God and Christ.[19]

It is clear that Paul does not fault them for being weak; their weakness is not associated with sin or evil. But beyond the maxim-like statement in 8:8, why doesn't he do more to correct their misperception about deities? They probably are recent converts who never had the privilege of Paul's tutelage. If so, they may still need to grow in some of the basics of their faith in order to become mature enough to fully appreciate apostolic teachings. Stanley Stowers astutely writes that the goal of living in Christ with which Paul identifies is not "to relieve the weak of every irrational belief by means of arguments over arguments . . . such a narrow view is counterproductive in achieving an inclusive and mutually enhancing community."[20] If we add to this their former lifestyle of serving other deities has already been woven into the very fabric of their being for many years, such convincing to the contrary by Paul might require many face-to-face conversations with them, something he could not presently do given his missionary schedule. We could only imagine the difficulty teachers in the church might have attempting to change the beliefs of a convert who, during her pre-converted years, had prayed to the god Asclepius for healing and that healing took place. Despite anything they might claim about this deity not existing, this believer would think otherwise, and even be tempted to pray to Asclepius again, especially if the Christian God did not seem to be answering her prayers.[21] Paul introduces a better plan for the congregation, at least until he

---

18. Garland 2003:383.

19. Alternatively, they might syncretize worship of the Christian God with other deities (Borgen 1995:51).

20. Stowers 1990:284.

21. Interestingly, Fotopolous 2003:63–70, makes a case for the dining area of the Asklepion being functional at this time, a likely place to eat idol food.

Third Supporting Proof (8:1—11:1)

could revisit them. He teaches the strong members to relinquish their right to eat idol foods out of love and concern for the weak.

Paul claims that idol foods have no intrinsic properties of good or evil. **Food does not bring us to God**, whether into His favor or judgment. There is no spiritual advantage or disadvantage with regard to what a believer eats (8:8).[22] If this is a saying of the strong, Paul seems to agree with it because elsewhere he promotes indifference toward food (Rom 14:14; cf. 1 Cor 9:4; 10:30–31). His view on the matter is rather progressive given Jewish food laws and disdain for idol meats (cf. 4 Macc 5:2; *Jos.Asen.* 10:12-13; 21:13-14; *Sib. Or.* 2.95). He cannot be indifferent, however, given the current circumstance, and so he warns the strong to **beware that this right of yours does not somehow become a stumbling-block to weak believers**. This "right" (ἐξουσία) has undertones of freedom and authority and is perhaps the strong's own terminology for justifying their eating; Paul now uses it in conversation with them. The word *stumbling-block* (πρόσκομμα: cf. Rom 14:13) is virtually synonymous with the verb σκανδαλίζω that Paul uses in reference to causing a fellow believer to stumble/fall down (8:13). In the LXX both terms are used in relation to committing idolatry.[23] Since this stumbling results in the believer's destruction (8:11), it does not merely connote sin or giving offense but falling away from faith (cf. 2 Cor 11:29; Matt 24:10; Mark 4:17; Luke 17:2; John 16:1).

The way the strong members' eating might become a stumbling-block is explicated in the form of a question expecting an affirmative answer—if any among the weak **sees you who has knowledge reclining in an idol's temple, will not his conscience be emboldened to eat things sacrificed to idols?** Paul does not seem to disallow the strong from eating in these temples, probably because he is aware that not every meal in a temple setting involves idol worship. Such facilities also serve community and private clubs and have dining areas that seem to be used for many different purposes.[24] Idol foods might also be served at events as diverse as funerals, weddings, birthdays, holy days, and other occasions, whether in private homes or temples.[25] Since Paul speaks hypothetically here, we cannot determine for certain that the strong are actually eating in such temples. But given the extended warning in 10:1-22, the imperatives against idolatry in

22. Cf. Konradt 2003:358.

23. Exod 23:33; 34:12; Sir 17:25; 34:16 (πρόσκομμα); Josh 23:13; Judg 2:3; Ps 106[105]:36; Wis 14:11 (σκάνδαλον [noun form]).

24. See Newton 1998:298–300. For discussions on which dining facilities might be open during Paul's years, see Bookidis 2005:157-59; Fotopoulos 2003:251-60; Murphy-O'Connor 1983:161-67.

25. See Arzt-Grabner et al. 2006:321-27; Gooch 1993:31-37, 45-46.

10:7 and 14, the reality of weak believers falling away (2 Cor 11:29), and Paul's repeated use of idolatry in his vice lists relevant to the Corinthian situation (5:9–10; 6:9–10; cf. 2 Cor 6:16), the reality of this activity is more likely than not.[26]

Paul's words suggest that the dining area in the temple precinct is visible to those passing by, and the weak passer-by happens to see the strong there. If portions of food were set on a table before a given deity, and the deity's statue stood near the recliners, it might be easily believed that the deity was present at the dinner and sharing in the meal.[27] But it is questionable whether the food eaten by recliners ever touched the table,[28] and for the strong who do not believe in deities, it would not matter even if it did. The weak believer, however, draws religious conclusions about the recliners and is thus encouraged to eat idol food after perceiving that the strong believer has done so. The strong eats based on knowledge that no other gods exist except the one true God, but the weak does not have this knowledge, and so he commits idolatry when eating and is tragically **destroyed . . . the brother for whose sake Christ died**. This person's faith is ruined as he abandons the one true God to worship idol deities again, and this eventually results in his condemnation on judgment day.[29] In this situation Christ's costly and redemptive death for him turns out to be in vain.

By causing the weak to commit apostasy, the strong members wrong these believers and **sin against Christ** who died for the weak brothers and sisters. Paul's unspoken premise here may be that Christ and the weak believers are united.[30] This suggests solidarity as one body and may be similar in thought to Christ's own words when he first appeared to Paul on the road to Damascus—when Paul persecutes the church, he is persecuting Christ (Acts 26:14–15). The thought also comes close to warnings against those who neglect the least of Christ's "brothers and sisters" (Matt 25:40, 45) and those who ruin the faith of "little ones" that belong to him (Mark 9:42–49; Luke 17:2; Matt 18:6–9).[31] Paul exhorts the strong members and encourages them to follow his example—**If food causes my brother to fall, I will never eat meat again so that I will not cause my brother's downfall**. The strong should be more concerned about the spiritual welfare of their weak broth-

---

26. *Pace* Sandelin 2003:116–19.
27. See Fotopoulos 2003:175.
28. Newton 1998:366–67.
29. On destruction (ἀπόλλυμι) in this sense, see 10:9–12; Rom 14:15; Mark 8:35; Matt 10:28.
30. See Eriksson 1998:164.
31. On the former, see Weiss 1910:231; on the latter, Oropeza 2012a:95–96.

Third Supporting Proof (8:1—11:1)

ers and sisters in Christ than their right to eat idol meats. Cicero's unity for the political body is relevant for the body of Christ: "if the individual appropriates to selfish ends what should be devoted to the common good, all human fellowship will be destroyed" (*Off.* 3.6.26).

Paul's Release of Apostolic Rights (9:1-18)

Prompted by the charge he just made for strong members to relinquish their rights for the weak members' sake, Paul now expands on what it means for an apostle like himself who has freedom and entitlements to relinquish his rights for the sake of the gospel. Although he includes forensic words of self-defense (9:3), he primarily continues using deliberative rhetoric by providing proof by example.[32] Four introductory questions in 9:1 and three more in 9:4-6 all expect the answer "yes." Then three analogical questions in 9:7 expect the answer "no one." Six more questions follow that relate to a citation from Scripture and maxim (9:8-12a). Paul's answer formulates a chiastic pattern with pathos (9:12b-18). This collage of rhetorical questions makes Paul's arguments persuasive by eliciting his auditors to agree with his statements, anticipate objections, and summarily dismiss them.[33] Persuasion by argument (logos) and credible self-presentation (ethos) aim to get the strong members to imitate him.

The initial questions our apostle poses may reflect diatribe that assume hypothetical interlocutors who ask Paul regarding 8:13, "What argumentative proofs could you show us that we should follow your example of refraining from idol food for the sake of others?" To which he responds, **Am I not free? Am I not an apostle?** These questions function thematically for this chapter. The first converges with Paul's apostolic rights, in particular his freedom to eat what he pleases (9:4). Rhetorically, he first establishes what is acceptable with his auditors before altering their perception of permissibility. The second question should be self-evident to the Corinthians; they know that Paul was divinely sent to proclaim the gospel since his message led to their transformation. His apostolic calling is confirmed by his next two questions, **Have I not seen Jesus our Lord? Are you not my work in the Lord?** The first assumes that being an eyewitness of the risen Lord is relevant criterion for being an apostle (cf. 15:5-8).[34] Although Paul was not an original disciple who had seen and heard Jesus before the crucifixion, he considers his Damascus encounter with Jesus to be a valid substitute for this

---

32. Mitchell 1991:47-50, 130.
33. See Watson 1989:312-14; Witherington 1995:204-6.
34. Further criteria are given by Thiselton 2000:669.

witness (Acts 9; Gal 1:11–12). The importance of seeing the Lord reflects prophetic authority (Isa 6:1–10; Jer 1:4–10).

When Paul claims that he is **not an apostle to others**, the "others" probably refer to members of congregations in which he is not the founder.[35] Most churches seem to be tightly knit with their founding apostles (2 Cor 10:13–16). This does not necessarily mean that these other churches reject his apostleship; rather, Paul's mention of them underscores that he, not some other apostle, has been sent to the Corinthians.[36] They are his metaphorical **seal**, a visible token that certifies and validates his apostolic office as divinely commissioned.[37] Thanks to Paul the Corinthians now live **in the Lord**,[38] and since God used him to reach them, they cannot deny his apostleship any more than they could deny their own conversion to Christ (see 2 Cor 3:2–3).

Paul then presents a defense against examiners who question his right to do what he does as an apostle.[39] Three times he repeats the question, **Do we not have a right to . . . ?** expecting affirmative answers.[40] The "we" identifies Paul and other apostolic missionaries. They have the right to **eat and drink** when doing the work of the Lord. Perhaps some auditors might have interpreted these words as Paul's own entitlement to eat idol foods as a guest in an unbeliever's home (cf. 8:8; 9:21; 10:27). He probably agrees in principle with the saying of Jesus that his disciples could eat whatever is set before them when evangelizing (cf. Luke 10:7–8).[41] All the same, he does not stress here his right to eat whatever he wants but his right to eat at the expense of others when on the mission field. Paul and his colleagues also have a right to bring on their trips **a sister, a wife even as the rest of the apostles**. This sister is a fellow believer in Christ (i.e., a believing wife) and may suggest that women were also itinerant apostles and prophets on the mission field.[42] John Granger Cook explains that these women "became well trained in apostolic teaching and, if they so chose, could have taught other people in the workplaces, 'women's quarters', or other settings in the Medi-

---

35. Garland 2003:405.
36. Collins 1999:335.
37. See 2 Cor 1:22; Rom 4:11; Barrett 1968:201.
38. In 9:1–2 "in the Lord" belongs to ὑμεῖς: "You, as being in the Lord" (Edwards 1897:227).
39. These are either his Corinthian critics (4:3) or more likely the hypothetical interlocutors assumed from 9:1.
40. See Gardner 1994:77–78.
41. Albeit, Luke may portray more generally foods that might be defiled according to the Law (Tucker 2011b:96).
42. Cf. Schottroff 2012:730.

Third Supporting Proof (8:1—11:1)

terranean world."[43] The wives of **Cephas** (Peter) and **the brothers of the Lord** (James and other brothers of Jesus: cf. 15:7; Gal 1:19; Mark 6:3) apparently accompanied them on their missions.[44] Missionary couples working with Paul include Prisca and Aquila (Rom 16:3–5; Acts 18:2, 26) and Junia and Andronicus (Rom 16:7).

Paul and Barnabas may be somewhat unique with their "pay our own way" policy on missionary trips. The Corinthians knew Barnabas even though in Acts 18 he is not mentioned with Paul when the latter went to Corinth.[45] Perhaps Barnabas visited them afterward, whether sometime during Paul's year and a half stay or afterward. Paul asks ironically, **or only I and Barnabas do not have a right to refrain from working?** Whenever possible Paul raised his own support money as a tentmaker (Acts 18:3; cf. 1 Cor 4:12; 2 Cor 11:27; 1 Thess 2:9).[46] Despite Paul's practice, no apostle is required to do other work when proclaiming the gospel. His claim is supported by three analogical questions expecting "no one" as the answer (9:7). First, no soldier goes to war and has to provide his own food and provisions; second, no farmer refrains from eating fruit from the vineyard he plants; and third, no shepherd refrains from consuming the milk of his flock. The point in agreement with apostolic ministry is that those who work at their roles are able to eat from their own labor.[47]

To support this further Paul cites Scripture: **For it is written in the Law of Moses, "You shall not muzzle an ox while it treads grain"** (9:9; cf. Deut 25:4).[48] The context in Deuteronomy supports the notion of promoting justice economically.[49] Poor workers, for example, should not be deprived of a prompt return for their labor (24:13–14), and both laborers and marginalized people are entitled to eat.[50] In Paul's recontextualization

---

43. Cook 2008:367–68.

44. These brothers (ἀδελφοί) may be Joseph's sons from a previous marriage (*Prot. Jas.* 9.1–2), Jesus's non-sibling relatives (Montague 2011:153; but ἀνεψιός, not ἀδελφοί, is used in Col 4:10), or more likely in my opinion, the actual siblings of Jesus (and normal meaning of ἀδελφός). See Matt 12:46–50; 13:54–55; Luke 8:19–21; John 2:12; 7:3–5; Acts 1:14.

45. On Barnabas see further, Thiselton 2000:679

46. See further Hock 1978; 2008.

47. Rightly, Heil 2005:138.

48. On the term "Law of Moses" as Scripture, see Luke 24:44; Acts 13:39; Collins 1999:339. The Greek word φιμόω (to "muzzle" LXX), has stronger manuscript witnesses than the variant κημόω (cf. 1 Tim 5:18).

49. Verbruggen 2006:699–711; Hays 1997:151.

50. See Ciampa/Rosner 2010:405.

Third Supporting Proof (8:1—11:1)

of this passage, God's primary concern is not for oxen but **for our sake**.[51] His argument is from lesser to greater (*qal wahomer*)—if oxen are permitted to eat of their labor, how much more should humans?[52] He continues in 9:10 to reinforce the previous citation in the form of a maxim-like statement: **Yes indeed, for our sake it was written** (i.e., the content of the quote from 9:9), **because the one who plows ought to plow in hope, and the one who threshes (to thresh) in hope of sharing (the harvest)**.[53] The quote and its explanation Paul makes relevant to his auditors by two follow-up questions. If apostolic laborers like Paul and Barnabas **have sown spiritual benefits** to the Corinthians, is it such an extraordinary thing that they be entitled to **reap fleshly** (material) **benefits** for this labor? The expected answer is "no" and sets up an implied affirmation for the second question. **Others** had apparently visited them, such as Peter, and exercised their right to be supported. If they, then how much more are apostles like Paul and Barnabas, who are specially commissioned to Gentiles like the Corinthians (Gal 2:7–9), deserving of this right?

The adversative **but** in 9:12b signals a strong turning point in the argument. *Despite* their apostolic entitlement Paul and Barnabas **have not exercised this right**. Instead, they endure all adverse circumstances—the menial labor of tent making included (for Paul)—so that they **may not cause a hindrance to the gospel of Christ**. Sometimes it is necessary to compromise one's freedom for the greater good (cf. Dio Chrysostom *Or.* 40.34; Philo *Abr.* 216).[54] In what sense might the gospel be hindered if Paul were to imitate apostles who do exercise their right? A combination of five answers are probable. First, he might hinder certain "weak" persons from being saved if he did not conform to becoming "weak" himself (9:22), and this means among other things that he willingly associates with their

---

51. For Pauline communities, Scripture inclusive of Moses's Law is authoritative and instructive in so far as it is interpreted in light of the Christ event and new era it has ushered in (10:6, 11; Rom 15:4; Gal 3:19–26).

52. Cf. Instone-Brewer 1992:554; Ciampa/Rosner 2010:404.

53. Paul is not citing a second scripture in 9:10, *pace* Stanley 1992:196–97; Heil 2005:125–26, and others; none are able to provide a convincing verse being cited. In 9:10 γάρ means "Yes indeed" (BDAG 190) and ὅτι ("because"/"that") does not introduce another quote but gives further explication of the quote already given (Smit 2000b:246–49). There is no reason Paul should change to the aorist "it was written" (ἐγράφη) in 9:10, unless he is pointing back to the content of the perfect "it is written" (γέγραπται) from 9:9. He sometimes uses ἐγράφη to elaborate on the Scriptures he referenced earlier, e.g., in 1 Cor 10:11 of 10:7–10, in Rom 4:23–24 of 4:22, and Rom 15:4 of 15:3.

54. Cf. Mitchell 1991:130–33.

socioeconomic status by doing manual labor (cf. 1:26–29; 4:10).[55] Second, he probably thinks that too much dependence on others' finances could slow down his missionary agenda. He would have to spend added time requesting, collecting, and relying on money from congregations before advancing to new territory. If some were unable to pay up after committing to do so, this would cause further delays. Third, Paul's policy spares poorer members from being burdened by supporting him financially (1 Thess 2:9; 2 Thess 3:8; 2 Cor 11:9; 12:13–16).[56] Fourth, this congregation is simply too immature to handle sponsoring Paul without it affecting them negatively. They would likely boast about it or feel that Paul now "owes" them. Finally, Paul may want to differentiate his ministry from sophists whom the Corinthians are so prone to admire and who speak for exorbitant fees (see 1 Cor 2 Excursus). Paul's manual labor was not fitting for these orators who normally despise such work (Philostratus, *Vit. soph.* 2.615; Philo *Det.* 34).

Our apostle's insistence on refusing material support forms a combined chiasm:[57]

A. Paul does not take advantage of his right for support (9:12b)

  B. Temple workers live off of temple offerings (9:13)

  B^1. The Lord arranged that workers live off of the gospel (9:14)

A^1. Paul does not take advantage of his right for support (9:15a)

  B^2. Boasting of the non-use of this right (9:15b)

    C. Compulsion to proclaim the gospel (9:16–17)

  B^3. Reward for the non-use of this right (9:18a)

A^2. Paul does not take advantage of this right for support (9:18b)

Point A repeats Paul's policy of rejecting support from the Corinthians.[58] This is central to the passage as is his compulsion to proclaim the gospel in point C.

The question in 9:13, **Do you not know?** implies, "you ought to know" (see 3:16). Paul argues for apostolic rights using an analogy. As ministers in Jerusalem partake of food from **the temple** and **alter** (Num 18:8–19; Deut

---

55. See Goodrich 2012:171.

56. Ibid.

57. Bailey 2011:249, is similar though "commission" dubiously guides his point at 9:17.

58. Notice "for" (γάρ) appears five times in 9:15–17, underscoring Paul's refusal to use his right.

Third Supporting Proof (8:1—11:1)

18:1-8),[59] so apostles may eat from their own missionary efforts. Paul seems to know an oral tradition affirming that when **the Lord** Jesus sent out his disciples to evangelize, he **instructed** them that **those who proclaim the gospel get their living from the gospel** (cf. Matt 10:10; Luke 10:7; 1 Tim 5:17-18). Paul reinterprets this instruction as a right he could give up rather than a command that he must keep.[60] Although he risks the impression of distancing himself from authorized practice,[61] he doubtless believes that expediting the gospel at no charge so that more lives might be saved would be endorsed by Jesus.

His determination to continue in this practice is emphasized by using pathos (9:15-18). Paul has not used these rights and does not want to use them now; in fact; **it is good for me rather to die than . . . no one will empty my boasting!**[62] Our apostle cuts off his sentence (known as *aposiopesis*), which prevents us from knowing how the original sentence would finish. Garland reasonably suggests the completion as, "it is better for me rather to die than to live off the gospel."[63] This hyperbole stresses firm conviction against receiving financial support (cf. 2 Cor 11:10). His boasting here is not in self-adulation but in what his free gospel accomplishes for the cause of Christ. As such, it anticipates a reward for his preaching that is paradoxically to be paid by the Lord and yet involuntary.[64] Regarding the latter, Paul perceives his calling as prophetic (Gal 1:15-16; cf. Jer 1:4-10; Isa 42:1-10), and his **compulsion** to preach echoes a commission in which the prophet encounters divine constraint to fulfill the task at hand regardless of personal shortcomings (Jer 1:4-10; 20:7-10; Isa 8:11; Amos 3:7-8; Exod 3-4).[65] Paul's expression, **woe to me if I proclaim not the gospel** reflects prophetic formulae anticipating great lament or divine judgment if he fails to fulfill his vocation (cf. Isa 5:8-22; 6:5; Jer 15:10; Hos 7:13; Amos 6:1; Luke 22:22).[66] Persuaded by his own encounter with the Lord (9:1), he is thus compelled to fulfill his calling, which for him precludes any other choice but to align himself with the divine purpose for his life. For all practical purposes, then,

---

59. Hübner 1997:260-61.

60. See Collins 1999:342. On διατάσσω as to "instruct" rather than "command" in 9:14, cf. Matt 11:1. Even if the word meant "command" here, the "command is not given *to* the missionaries, but *for* their benefit" (Fee 1987:413).

61. So Butarbutar 2007:150.

62. Ellingworth/Hatton 1993:204, translate this correctly.

63. Garland 2003:422.

64. See Goodrich 2012:173-89.

65. See Aernie 2012:82.

66. Paul anticipates divine judgment rather than distress (see Aernie 2012:83-84).

his call to preach is involuntary; he could only disregard it at the cost of his own spiritual detriment.

In terms of **reward**, however, his proclamation of the gospel anticipates compensation from the Lord, though with diminishing returns if he undermines his own policy to proclaim it free of charge. Paul's role of being entrusted as a steward administrator over the Lord's territory (cf. 4:1), even if performed involuntarily as a slave, still involves remuneration.[67] His labor will eventually result in a reward during the coming age (cf. 3:8, 14). Even so, Paul is more concerned here about reward in the *present*. Since his gospel is expedited through self-support, he is able to travel more frequently and thus win more converts than he would if contingent on the slower process of depending on others to support him (see 9:12 above). Hence, his boast and reward foremost refer to the enjoyment of seeing a surplus of saved lives on account of his preaching free of charge. This boon prevents him from taking complete advantage of his right to live off of the gospel.[68]

ALL THINGS FOR THE GOSPEL'S SAKE (9:19–23)

Despite being **free from all people** Paul voluntarily makes himself **a slave to all** in order to win as many as possible to salvation through the gospel.[69] Paul's accommodation, however, has limits. He denies being disingenuous or flattering (1 Thess 2:5; Gal 1:10; Rom 16:17–20). And he is motivated not by the hope of upward social mobility but proclaiming the gospel, which is the higher good to which freedom should submit, and salvation becomes the supreme good.[70] As such, Paul works with the language of divine "condescension," a "coming down to the level of" those he attempts to reach (Philo *Somn*. 1.147; 1.232–33).[71] More importantly, as Troels Engberg-Pedersen affirms, he follows "Christ's own practice in the Christ event. It is

---

67. See e.g. Matt 25:14–15; Goodrich 2012:182–84.

68. Καταχράομαι ("to make *full* use of" 9:18) intensifies χράομαι ("to make use of" 9:15). Is there admittance that he sometimes uses this right? Perhaps this qualification admits what the Corinthians might already know—Paul accepts money from other churches (cf. 2 Cor 11:7–11; Garland 2003:427). Congregational maturity is one reason why he could receive money from the Philippians (Phil 1:7; 4:10–19) but refuse it from the Corinthians (see Oropeza 2016:606–13; Briones 2013:128–30, 219–24).

69. "That I might gain . . . " is repeated five times in 9:19–22, stressing this idea. In 9:19 "all" (πάντων) can refer to "all things" (Lindemann 2000:209–11) or "all people" (Coppins 2011:279). The latter makes better contextual sense.

70. See Galloway 2010:23 for the former idea; Sandnes 2013:129, for the latter.

71. Cf. Mitchell 2001:205; cf. Glad 2003:35; Vollenweider 1989:217–20; Richardson/Gooch 1978:91–93. Nanos 2012:106–40 argues for "rhetorical adaptability," which I find attractive, but (unlike Nanos) not to the point of exclusivity.

Third Supporting Proof (8:1—11:1)

a matter of love in the sense of giving up one's own preferences," as in the Christ hymn of becoming a servant and dying on the cross for humankind's sake (Phil 2:5–11).[72] Paul wants to imitate Christ who, motivated by love, selflessly gave up his own privileges for the sake of saving others, a pattern Paul aspires the Corinthian strong to mimic regarding idol foods and their indifference toward weaker believers.

Paul accommodates four groups. He says of the first group, **To the Jews I became as a Jew so that I might gain Jews**. These words are problematic since Paul, a Jew, claims, "I *became as* a Jew" (ἐγενόμην ... ὡς Ἰουδαῖος), and this might suggest that he distances himself from Jewish identity.[73] But elsewhere he takes pride in being Jewish (Rom 9:1–4; 11:1). Perhaps he distinguishes between formative Judaism as a religion shaped by Mosaic Law and having its cultic center in Jerusalem, and his ethnic heritage as a Jew (Gal 1:13–14; Phil 3:4–9). He does not appear to be Torah-abiding when relativizing circumcision (7:18–19; cf. Gal 5:1–4) and food laws (8:8; cf. Rom 14:14).[74] Nevertheless, beyond observing the Law, we wonder whether Paul considers his identity in Christ to be transcending cultural and ethnic identities so that, for him, to belong to the new creation is to start setting aside one's old creation ties (1 Cor 10:32; 12:13; Gal 3:28; 6:16; 2 Cor 5:17; Col 3:11).[75] In any case, for Paul to be "as a Jew" suggests his adaptation of religious, cultic, and cultural language and certain practices when with other Jews who are not in Christ. Similarly in Acts, his attending synagogues and circumcising Timothy are for the sake of evangelism (e.g., Acts 13:14; 14:1; 16:1–3).[76]

A second group identifies **those who are under the Law** of Moses, which seem to be distinguished from the Jews just mentioned. This group probably does not refer to Christian Jews, such as James and Peter, since he would consider them already saved (15:1–7), and those he considers "false brethren" he does not attempt to accommodate (Gal 2:3–5). Nor does he seem to refer to those who hold to a stricter form of the Law, such as the Pharisees.[77] More likely, Paul refers to non-Christian Gentile proselytes to Judaism and "god fearers," similar to the type Acts portrays him encountering on his missions (e.g., Acts 13:42–48).

---

72. Engberg-Pedersen 2013:100. See similarly, Horrell 2005:168–82.

73. See Sechrest 2009:154–56; Bird 2016.

74. If he held to such observances this would seem to disrupt his fellowship with Gentiles: see Schnabel 2013:109–11 in response to Rudolph 2011:190.

75. See Ciampa/Rosner 2010:425.

76. See Sandnes 2013:136–40.

77. *Pace* Rudolph 2011:153–59. Paul could have simply said, "To the Pharisees, I have become as a Pharisee."

Third Supporting Proof (8:1—11:1)

The third group, **those who are without the Law**, are doubtless the majority of other Gentiles. They do not follow Mosaic Law and are typically considered idolaters. With this group Paul does not follow Torah observances as he might when with the other two groups. To qualify that he does not mean he engages in immoral activities typical of Gentiles, he must say that he is **not without the Law of God**, which he explicates as **the law of Christ**. This refers to a set of commands inclusive of living by faith, walking in God's Spirit, loving God and one's neighbor, and similar precepts whether taught by or resembling the ways of Jesus (cf. 7:19; 8:1–6; Gal 5:13–16; 6:2; Rom 3:27; 8:2). That Paul could follow the "law of Christ" and still be "without the Law" makes proper sense if the former is distinguishable from Mosaic Law. The law of Christ would seem to be Paul's own default behavioral code to follow independent of any group he attempts to evangelize.

The fourth group Paul accommodates is **the weak**. This is probably not referring to believers who are weak in conscience; their salvation must be kept rather than gained (8:7–13). He means non-believers who must be persuaded to believe the gospel and then be saved. Perhaps social rather than psychological weakness is emphasized here, and if so, this identifies people of lower status such as slaves, the poor, and marginalized (cf. 1:26–29). Paul could readily identify with them as a foreigner on the mission field. He himself experiences frailty through sufferings and hard labor as a tentmaker (4:9–13). He omits "as" (ὡς) only with this group. Is this an ellipsis in which ὡς is already assumed, or did he rhetorically wish to identify most with this group? The second option is more likely not only because Paul wished to honor the socially weak above others (cf. 12:22–24), but also because the money he makes by hard labor is precisely why his proclamations can remain free of charge. Similar to Greek political leaders such as Agathocles and Cleon, who turned from the upper class to win favor with the lower class,[78] our apostle gladly identifies and mingles with those whom society deems lowly.

Paul says he accommodates all people so **that I might by all means save some**. He is motivated for **the gospel's sake** so that he may be **a partner of it** (9:23). Does partnership here connote participation in the *work* of the gospel or the *salvific benefits* of the gospel? To be sure, if Paul were to turn away from his calling, this would seem to disqualify his partnership in salvific blessings (cf. 9:16, 27). But this interpretation would seem to be anticlimactic—with it, we might surmise that Paul is not so selfless after all,

---

78. Diodorus Siculus *Bib. hist.* 20.63.1; Plutarch *Praec. ger. rei publ.* 13.1[806F–807A]; further, Marshall 1987:313.

Third Supporting Proof (8:1—11:1)

since he is motivated to preach in order to save himself.[79] Hence, partnership here probably means, or at least includes, the work of proclaiming the gospel. Paul modestly suggests to being a fellow partner, presumably with God and Christ, in advancing the good news (cf. 2 Cor 5:19-20).

COMPETITION AND SELF-CONTROL (9:24–27)

Although Paul's calling is still the subject of this chapter's ending, 9:24–27 looks both ways, sharing virtually as much with the previous text as with the subsequent.[80] All three pericopae are concerned about gaining salvation and exercising self-control to get there, whether by abandonment of rights (ch. 9) or abandonment of vices (ch. 10). In this transitory text Paul presents athletic imagery through the language of contest (known as *agon* discourse) in which one must exert self-control to win, whether in a footrace or boxing match.[81] The scene is perhaps colored by Paul witnessing the famous Isthmian games near Corinth (51 CE), which took place every two years and rivaled Olympic and other panhellenic games.[82] Paul may have produced tents to shelter visiting athletes, though his own familiarity with sports games probably goes back to his boyhood in Tarsus.[83]

The opening question, **Do you not know that those who run in a stadium race all run but one receives the prize?** assumes an affirmative answer. This prompts the following imperative, **so run that you may obtain it!** This metaphor of running a footrace has an apocalyptic goal in which Corinthians of this present age win the prize of final salvation in the coming age. The race is also relevant for Paul whose calling is bound up with final salvation (9:16, 27; cf. Phil 3:11-14),[84] and it includes all believers, both men and women.[85] That only one person wins the prize is consistent with

---

79. Hooker 1996:85; Garland 2003:436.

80. Emphasizing its relation with ch. 9 is Carter 2010:156–58; with ch. 10 is Sumney 2000:329–33.

81. Alternatively for the latter, *pankration*, a sport that combined boxing and wrestling, may be imagined.

82. See Brändl 2006:186–244. Paul's agonistic discourse likewise may be influenced by Jewish traditions (e.g., Wis 4:2; 10:10–12; Sir 4:28; Brändl 2006:76–137, 412).

83. See Metzner 2000:566–75; Zeller 2010:321; Strobel 1989:157–58. On Diaspora Jews attending sports games, see Philo *Prob.* 26; Harrison 2008:90.

84. See Pfitzner 1967:85. On Paul's prophetic call and running, see Oropeza 2009:141–48.

85. On female athletes, see Poplutz 2004:86–95, 269; Papathomas 1997:235–36; and for potential relevance to Corinthian women, Barnes 2009:49–60.

Third Supporting Proof (8:1—11:1)

panhellenic games.[86] But Paul could hardly mean that only one believer will win the game of salvation![87] The notion of *one* might invite the Corinthians as a unified congregation to win;[88] however, the contrast between *all* and *one* in this verse has a rhetorical aim that is particularly relevant to the strong members. In order to shake up their overconfidence regarding idol foods Paul's words suggest a number of them might fail in this race, similar to *all* Israel entering the starting line of the wilderness but the *majority* dying by divine judgment before getting to the finishing line of the promised land (10:1-5). Paul's point is that final salvation is not a foregone conclusion for them; it requires the participants in the present to endure and **exercise self-control in all respects**. Ancient competitive training was very rigorous. About a month before the games competitors swear by oath that they had been preparing for ten months, and judges then test the fitness of the athletes.[89] A competitor's self-renunciation includes the same things Paul has been discussing with the Corinthians—diet and sexual abstinence.[90]

Since ancient boxing matches did not have weight divisions, a large boxer had an advantage over smaller opponents, but skill, speed, strength, stamina, strategy, and courage were all necessary for either opponent to finally win. And knockouts, injuries, and disfigured faces were all too common in a day when matches were without any rounds or breaks.[91] The boxer's training is described by Seneca as torture—as athletes punish their bodies to win a garland, so one should do the same to gain virtue, peace, and steadfastness of soul (*Lucil.* 78.16; cf. 80.3; *Tranq.* 3.1). Epictetus compares becoming a philosopher with becoming a winner in the Olympics. The latter requires special dieting, hours of exercise, and endurance during the contest (*Diatr.* 3.15.2-12). Even though Paul and stoic philosophers both describe virtuous practice with agonistic metaphors, Paul has a different goal in mind. Athletes discipline their bodies for a **perishable wreath**, but believers do so for a better prize, an **imperishable** wreath.[92] Our apostle

---

86. See Popovic 2014:23; Brändl 2006:225.

87. Such a view misunderstands allegory for analogy according to Thiselton 2000:711.

88. Cf. Poplutz 2004:269-70; Popovic 2014:24.

89. See Brändl 2006:216-17; Popovic 2014:28.

90. On sexual abstinence, see Plato, *Leg.* 8.839E-840C; Philostratus *Gymn.* 52; Mitchell 1991:249. On athletic dieting see, Philo *Somn.* 2[II].2.9; Epictetus *Diatr.* 3.15.2-3, 9-11; Ciampa/Rosner 2010:438-39.

91. See examples in Dutch 2005:226-30; Hullinger 2004:354-55. For depictions of ancient boxers with injuries like puffed eyes, cauliflower ears, broken nose, see Harrison 2008:98-100. On boxing to death, see Brändl 2006:227.

92. Wreaths in the Isthmian games were comprised of celery, though in some eras

Third Supporting Proof (8:1—11:1)

argues this point perhaps in the face of inscriptions of his day that allegedly conferred the rhetoric of immortality to champion athletes and their benefactors.[93] The coveted wreath was emblematic of great honor and status for champions.[94] For Paul, greater honor and glory await winners of the race for salvific life, and the imperishable wreath intimates the immortal, resurrected body that becomes the believers' legacy when Christ returns (15:20–24).

Paul presents himself as an exemplar for the Corinthians. He does **not run aimlessly**, but with purpose and resolution he determines to finish the race and obtain the salvific prize (cf. Phil 3:14). He does not fight as a boxer **who beats the air** but strikes with precision to make every blow count in order to defeat the opponent.[95] To win, Paul must train by punishing his **body with blows**[96] of self-imposed discipline in order to **subjugate it** into obedience that it might be fit for the contest. In essence, he enslaves his own body so that his bodily appetites and sinful nature do not enslave him.[97] This metaphoric training also may recall his bodily hardships experienced as a missionary, including labors, beatings, and lack of food and sleep whether from travelling, moonlighting as a minister, or prayer and fasting vigils (2 Cor 11:23–27).[98] Such experiences have a way of building one's faith and self-discipline.

It may be significant that Paul uses κηρύσσω rather than εὐαγγελίζω as his word for **proclaiming** (9:27). The former relates κῆρυξ, which refers to the herald of athletic games. This individual declared competitive rules, called athletes to the track, and proclaimed the good news of victory to the winners.[99] Although Paul's apostolic ministry fits well with this description, unlike the herald, he also participates in the contest and must prepare well so that he himself will **not be disqualified** (i.e., excluded from the competition).[100] Given that the prize is final salvation, disqualification

---

pine was used (Broneer 1962:16–17).

93. See examples in Harrison 2008:106–7.

94. Dutch 2005:236–37; further, Papathomas 1997:225–33.

95. Beating the air does not refer to shadow boxing but to the inexperienced boxer who fails to land punches against an agile opponent (Popovic 2014:33; Metzner 2000:575).

96. BDAG 1043: ὑπωπιάζω is to "strike under the eye, give a black eye to."

97. Building on bodily enslavement, Concannon 2014:202–9, adds gladiator games to the scene.

98. On sports competition analogous to hardships, compare Dio Chrysostom *Or.* 8.11–19.

99. Cf. Harrison 2008:102; Popovic 2004:38–39.

100. For examples of game disqualification, see Hullinger 2004:356–59; Harrison 2008:101.

Third Supporting Proof (8:1—11:1)

here can only refer to salvific forfeiture. Even Paul has the potential to become apostate.[101] The apostle's confidence of his position in Christ, however, makes it doubtful that he lost any sleep over this possibility. His point has the rhetorical aim of unsettling the presumptuous security of the strong members. If even an apostle can ultimately fail so as to be excluded from futuristic benefits in Christ, where does that leave them? They must be diligent to ensure that their consumption of idol meats does not result in idolatry and divine judgment (cf. 10:1-22). Moreover, since they insist on rather than limit their right to eat such food, Paul's example functions as an incentive for them to control themselves and relinquish their rights for the sake of weak believers.[102]

WILDERNESS EPISODES AS WARNINGS AGAINST IDOLATRY AND VICES (10:1-13)

The opening **for** (γάρ) connects this passage with 9:24-27 and continues the themes of self-control, endurance, and movement toward a goal, this time through the wilderness of Sinai rather than a footrace, and the implied prize is the promised land rather than a wreath. Both metaphoric treks point to receiving salvific reward at the culmination of the ages.[103] The adjectival "all" appears five times in 10:1-4 and highlights the people's solidarity and shared experiences of grace in the wilderness. This is offset by the adversative "but" in 10:5, which ensues with "the majority of them" being killed in the wilderness; "some of them" appears four times in relation to four vices that entail different punishments (10:7-10). This pattern evokes pathos related to fear and helps emphasize the climactic warning in 10:12. Comparison between the wilderness generation and Corinthians is stressed by way of chiasm:

    A. "Now these things as types . . . " (10:6)

        B. "Do not . . . as some of them . . . " (10:7)

            C. "Let us not . . . as some of them . . . " (10:8)

            C.¹ "Let us not . . . as some of them . . . " (10:9)

        B.¹ "Do not . . . as some of them . . . " (10:10)

---

101. See Oropeza 2012a:96-97.
102. See Ellington 2011:310.
103. The most thorough examination of this passage in recent years is Oropeza 2007:67-222. Also see update in Baron/Oropeza 2016:63-80.

Third Supporting Proof (8:1—11:1)

A.[1] "Now these things by way of type . . ." (10:11)

Paul opens with the formulaic, **I do not want you to be ignorant, brothers and sisters**, which has a hint of irony since he is addressing members who are prideful of their knowledge.[104] This congregation already knew the basic exodus-wilderness episode (5:5-7), but what they may not have known is how this episode pertains to them in relation to divine judgment. Paul seems to be creating a new storyline by stringing together references from several sources through catch words.[105] Paul uses familial language to invite his predominantly Gentile audience to review Israel's wilderness generation as **our fathers**.[106] The language assumes his converts have joined God's elect people and benefit from their promises (Gal 3:6-9, 27-29; Rom 11:17-26). All the wilderness people **underwent baptism into Moses in the cloud** of divine presence **and in the** Red sea (see Exod 13:21-22; 14:21-24; Ps 78:13-14).[107] Paul's insertion of baptism into Moses prompts the congregation to recall their own conversion. As Israel's deliverance transpired through Moses in the cloud and sea, so the Corinthians' salvation took place in the name of Jesus and through baptism in the Spirit and water (1:13-17; 12:13; Rom 6:3). Paul's connection between God's Spirit and the cloud of divine presence is informed by traditions such as Num 11:16-30, where the cloud Presence delegates the Spirit to Moses and among the elders who begin to prophesy.[108]

The **spiritual food** and **drink** all the Israelites consume in the wilderness recalls foremost their wilderness experience of eating manna and drinking water from the rock (Exod 16:1-17:7; Num 20:1-13; 21:16-18). To these elements Paul attaches the multifaceted word "spiritual" to convey the miraculous and that which has, transmits, or originates from the divine presence. The rhetorical effect of this word intimates foremost the Corinthians' unified participation in the Lord's Supper (see 10:16-17). If they experience spiritual benefits and communion with God and Christ via this food, their predecessors likewise experienced similar things. Moreover, if the Corinthians claim to belong to Christ, they should consider that their forefathers in the wilderness **were drinking from the spiritual rock that**

---

104. See also 12:1; Starling 2014:275.

105. On the midrash devises and *gezerah shavah* used in this passage, see Baron/Oropeza 2016:65-71.

106. "Our fathers" is adopted from wilderness traditions (Num 20:15; cf. Ps 78:3-5; Neh 9:9-34).

107. I prefer Greek manuscripts that use the middle voice ἐβαπτίσαντο ("they underwent baptism"/"let themselves be baptized") over the passive ἐβαπτίσθησαν ("they were baptized"); the former is the harder reading and emphasizes Israel's choice (Oropeza 2007:77-78).

108. See also Isa 63:7-14; Ps 106[105]:32-33; Luzarraga 1973:234-39.

Third Supporting Proof (8:1—11:1)

followed them, and the rock was Christ. Christ's preexistence is assumed; he was present with the wilderness generation, nurturing and feeding them. Paul associates Christ with the Lord in Jewish Scripture (8:6; 10:9), whose presence stood at the rock of Horeb, from which water flowed at the beginning of Israel's travels (Exod 17:5-6) and the rock of Kadesh from which water flowed toward the end of their travels (Num 20:7-11). Ancient Jewish interpreters like Paul drew the inference that the rock in both passages was the same rock, and it must have followed them throughout their journeys giving them water during their forty years of travelling.[109]

If the wilderness generation all experienced these gracious blessings from God, this did not prevent **the majority of them** from being massacred, **strewn out in the wilderness**.[110] This reflects divine judgment at Kadesh against the wilderness generation which murmured against God and Moses and wanted to return to Egypt (Num 14:16). God punishes them by having them wander for forty years in the wilderness; the older generation would die in the desert as a result (14:29-33). If God's pleasure suggests favor and calling (Gal 1:15; cf. Exod 4:22; Deut 1:11), the notion that **God was not pleased** with that generation may constitute a reversal of such things (Heb 10:38; Hab 2:4 LXX).[111] Paul's vivid portrayal of divine rejection helps drive home an important comparison in 10:6 and 11. The forefathers' initial deliverance, miraculous preservation, and subsequent rejection in the wilderness **happened as types** of us.[112] These *types* refer to more than the events of the wilderness generation being mere examples for the Corinthians to learn from. Christ's followers are connected with and sharers of God's elect people in the Scriptures. As such, the events seem to be advance presentations in which "the way God worked with Israel prefigures the way God works through the Corinthian congregation."[113] The wilderness events, then, may be understood both as actual (10:1-4) and hypothetical prerepresentations (10:5-10); the latter are given to warn the Corinthians *against* fulfilling what their forefathers did and similarly incur divine punishment.[114]

The wilderness episodes are presented **so that we might not crave evil things as they also craved**. These words recall the people craving foods

---

109. See e.g., Ps.-Philo, *L.A.B.* 10.7; Enns 1996:30-31; Baron/Oropeza 2016:73-75.

110. On καταστρώννυμι as massive devastation of life, see Jdt 7:4; 2 Macc 11:11; Oropeza 2007:126-27.

111. See Willis 1985:143; Schrage 1994:2.396.

112. Alternatively, DiMattei 2008:59-93, argues for "model" against "types."

113. Oropeza 2007:131-32; cf. Davidson 1981:223, 251-69.

114. See Bandstra 1971:15-16.

from Egypt and despising manna (Num 11:4-9, 34).[115] The Corinthians are thus implicitly warned not to crave idol foods, which is confirmed by Paul's following exhortation that they should **not become idolaters as some of them** (the wilderness generation) **did**. He cites Exod 32:6 regarding their cultic festivities related to worshipping the golden calf: **The people sat down to eat and drink and rose up to play**. This mimics activities related to the establishment of their covenant with God, as Jerry Hwang affirms: "The God who provided Israel with food and drink in the wilderness, and with whom the leaders were just worshiping and dining in Exodus 24, has now been rejected using these very same ritual actions."[116] Israel's consumption while sitting down before the golden calf doubtless implicates the Corinthians reclining in an idol's temple to eat food (8:10), and suggests they, too, are in danger of committing idolatry and apostasy. The notion of "play" suggests sexual behavior and cultic dancing (Gen 26:8; Judg 21:21; Philo *Mos.* 1.302; 2.162), which builds a sturdy bridge to the next exhortation: **And let us not commit fornication as some of them**. Paul alludes to the Israelites committing fornication with Moabite women, and 24,000 died as a result (Num 25:1-18).[117] Again both idolatry and cultic eating are involved. The Israelites "ate of their sacrifices and bowed down in worship to their idols" (Num 25:2; cf. Ps 106[105]28-31). Paul's selection of this Scripture possibly implies for the Corinthian situation a banquet or symposium setting. The primary task in this verse, however, is more obvious—congregation members must flee from fornication wherever they might be tempted to commit it (6:9-20).

The next warning, **let us not test Christ**,[118] places Christ once again in the wilderness. As in 10:4, Paul interprets the Lord God with the Lord Jesus Christ, and as such, when the wilderness generation tempts or speaks against the Lord, they tempt Christ (e.g., Exod 17:2, 7; Deut 6:16). Their speaking against the Lord in Num 21:4-9, alluded to in Ps 78[77]:18-19 as testing God, is echoed here—many of them **were destroyed by serpents**. In that episode they complained about manna, having no food and water, and

115. In 10:5-13 several source texts are noteworthy including Num 11 (Collier 1994:55-75); Exod 32 (Meeks 1982:64-78); Ps 106[105] (Oropeza 2007:136-37); Deut 32 (Oropeza 1998a:57-68).

116. Hwang 2011:580.

117. Paul's 23,000 may be memory lapse, perhaps with Num 26:62. Or he knew and/or confused it with another text variant, perhaps of Exod 32:28 (having 23,000 rather than 3,000). Or he blended numbers from Exod 32:28 and Num 25:9. See options in Mody 2007:61-79; Schnabel 2006:537-38.

118. Some manuscripts have "Lord" rather than "Christ" in this verse. The latter is the more difficult reading and is thus more likely the original. See further Osburn 1981:201-12; Oropeza 2007:153-55.

that they were taken out of Egypt to be killed in the wilderness. Again the rebellion centers on food, which anticipates Paul's accusation of the strong members provoking the Lord to jealousy by their presumptuous freedom to eat idol meats (10:22–23). Testing the Lord, if unchecked, leads to provoking him.[119] The next warning, **do not grumble**, becomes the occasion for the wilderness generation being **destroyed by the destroyer**. This is presumably an angelic being (Exod 12:12–23; Ps 78[77]:49; 1 Chr 21:12–15). Perhaps Paul, influenced by Wis 18:20–25 or a similar early interpretation of Korah's rebellion, associated the destroying angel with Korah's death, a prime exemplar of grumbling and rebellion (Num 16:1–50; cf. vv. 11, 41).[120] Paul may be anticipating congregants grumbling over his present warnings against idol foods, or he may recall their earlier criticisms against him in relation to their factions (4:3–5). Judgment by destruction is significant for Paul because he believes that wrongdoers will be destroyed at the end of the age (1:18; 2 Cor 2:15; Rom 14:15; 2 Thess 2:10). In the Corinthian situation, the weak might be destroyed via idolatry due to the strong members' liberties (8:11), and here in our current passage the strong learn that they, too, are susceptible to destruction.

These hypothetical prerepresentations, Paul claims, are **for our admonition upon whom the ends of the ages have come**. The plural "ends" or "events" ("τὰ τέλη") of the ages seem to come in opposite directions to meet (see 7:29).[121] The events of the past and future have now intersected or overlapped in the present time.[122] Paul works with apocalyptic imagery that evokes the presence of the new era and eventual judgment it brings when Christ returns. This leads to his final warning in this passage that essentially sums up (**so then**) the point of the Scripture references in 10:1–11 and draws attention especially to the strong members—**the one who thinks he stands in salvation should take heed, lest he fall**. This fall (πίπτω) does not merely refer to falling into sin; from Paul's perspective a number of Corinthians are already sinning (cf. 1 Cor 6:12–20; 15:34). It refers to apostasy, a falling away from the grace and salvation adumbrated in 10:1–4 and thus incurring divine judgment akin with the wilderness generation in 10:5–10. That generation died in the desert never to experience the place of rest promised to them, and the Corinthian who falls away experiences divine rejection and

119. Rightly, Phua 2005:159.

120. See rabbinic sources in Perrot 1983:440.

121. See Fitzmyer 2008:388; Héring 1949:80–81. Differently, Court 1982:62–63 criticizes the notion of "back end"/"front end." On τέλος as "event," see LSJ 1773.

122. Alternatively, the plural τέλη may reflect apocalyptic traditions that depict several eras (Dan 2, 7, 8; 1 *En.* 93; *T.Lev.* 10.2; *T.Abr.* 19.7), and perhaps Paul collides the past eras with some future eras (cf. 15:20, 23–24).

exclusion from God's kingdom, the same fate as vice-doers (6:9–11; 9:27; cf. Gal 5:1–4, 19–21; Rom 11:22; Heb 4:11).[123] Like Stoic sages who were thought to be unconquerable, the strong members in Corinth seem to think themselves unable to fall from their wise status.[124] Through their puffed up knowledge that an idol is nothing, they deem themselves immune to idolatry. A smug sense of spiritual security has led them to the brink of divine displeasure, and Paul exposes this attitude as deceptive and dangerous.

The intensity of this text is partially relieved in 10:13. Paul rhetorically offsets his auditors' potential to be overwhelmed by counter-balancing the warnings with a word of encouragement.[125] **No temptation has overtaken you except what is common to all humanity.**[126] Not only do other people face similar struggles, but the humanness of the temptation suggests its inability to overpower one's capacity to endure it.[127] Temptation to commit vice can be successfully overcome. For those who genuinely desire to do what is right in this situation, **God is faithful** (cf. Deut 32:4).[128] God can be relied on not only to prevent the temptation from going beyond what the believer is able to endure, but at the same time of the temptation **He will provide the result that you may be able to bear up under it.**[129] God will certainly help the one who is tempted *if* that person really wants help.[130] This involves more than merely a passive waiting on God but active resistance—the Corinthians in this situation must resolve to flee from idolatry (10:14). Paul thus encourages his auditors "by affirming a perseverance that does not diminish the dangers of apostasy or personal responsibility. For Paul, perseverance here implies divine assistance plus human endurance. He is conveying to the Corinthians that apostasy is a real danger, while perseverance is a real hope."[131]

---

123. See further, Oropeza 2007:192–206; 2012a:98–101.

124. E.g., SVF 1.53.1–2 [216]; Fitzgerald 1988:138–39.

125. See other examples of this in 3:17, 21–23; 6:9–11; 11:30–32; 15:12, 58.

126. See this meaning for humanity (ἀνθρώπινος) in Ciampa/Rosner 2010:466–67. Πειρασμός ("temptation") here refers to allurement to commit vice rather than sufferings or hardship.

127. Similarly, Weiss 1910:255.

128. Though as Deut 32 evinces, God's people are not always faithful.

129. On ἔκβασις as "result/outcome" see Arzt-Grabner et al. 2006:370–71; as "end" see Fee 1987:461. Alternatively, it could mean the "way out" (BDAG 300§3) but Weiss 255, says this makes the need to bear up under it seem unnecessary.

130. Notice Barrett 1968:229: "The *way out* is for those who seek it, not for those who (like the Corinthians) are, where idolatry is concerned, looking for the way in."

131. Oropeza 2007:222.

Third Supporting Proof (8:1—11:1)

Fleeing Idolatry and Demons (10:14-22)

The inferential **therefore** in 10:14 begins a new pericope that opens with Paul's command to **flee from idolatry**. This warning parallels 6:18, though idolatry replaces fornication as the vice, and a cultic setting is the imagined location. The strong members are envisioned eating idol food there. Our apostle appeals to their sensibility to **judge** for themselves what he says. He is confident they will agree with him as he amplifies the need for this flight by way of eight questions that prompt the answers he wishes to hear as he argues by use of example (10:16), application (10:17), analogy (10:18), contrary (10:19-20), and then a conclusion (10:20-22).[132]

The repetitive idea of **sharing** (κοινωνία) in this passage suggests both participation and partnership, and may be understood as "communion with someone by communally partaking in something."[133] Paul highlights both fellowship and eating with others inclusive of spiritual entities related to the dining experience. The Corinthians are to say "yes" to Paul's questions related to their sharing the **one cup** and **one bread** that connects believers with **the blood** (death), redemption, and presence of **the body of Christ** through their celebration of the Lord's Supper (10:16-17; cf. 11:17-34).[134] The members reconfirm their solidarity as the collective body of Christ by sharing in this meal (cf. 5:6-7; 12:13). The auditors are then prompted to affirm this type of sharing again as Paul compares it with **Israel according to the flesh** (i.e., as an ethnic people: Rom 4:1; 9:3-4; Gal 4:23). The Israelites eat and participate of cultic offerings at **the altar** of sacrifice in Jerusalem's temple (10:18; cf. 9:13). They eat in the Lord's presence and have a relationship both with the Lord and with those at the altar (Exod 18:12; 29:11-23; Lev 3:12—4:24; Deut 12:5-18; 14:23-26). Communion at the altar thus has horizontal (with other humans) and vertical (with God) dimensions.[135] Israel's covenant with God was also confirmed by God being present and eating with members of the covenant (Exod 24:1-11). What is pictured by Israel's cultic eating, similar to the Lord's Supper, is that worshipers enjoy mutual fellowship and eat together with the Lord being present. This activity marks an ongoing reconfirmation of their covenant relationship.

---

132. See Eriksson 1998:167-68.

133. Tilling 2012:97. This meaning perhaps arises from Hellenistic-cultic use (see Gäckle 2005:267). "Sharer" (κοινωνός: 10:18, 20) has a similar nuance, and to "share" (μετέχω: 10:17, 21), may emphasize partaking and participating.

134. "Cup of blessing" may be adopted from the third cup of Passover meals, the cup of redemption (*m.Pes.* 10.7).

135. Stressing the former, Woyke 2005:245-47, stressing the latter, Tilling 2012:97-99.

Third Supporting Proof (8:1—11:1)

The idea of cultic eating in the Lord's presence then prompts rhetorical questions relevant to the Corinthian situation—**What then am I saying? That a thing sacrificed to an idol is anything, or is an idol anything?** Paul agrees with the strong members that idols are nothing (8:4); hence, the expected answer is "no," which is quickly qualified: **But the things which they sacrifice, they sacrifice to demons and not to God.** Gentile idolaters are primarily in view.[136] All the same Paul's "they" may be deliberately vague in order to evoke on another level the Corinthians' "forefathers" (10:1). His words allude to Israel's past idolatry of sacrificing to demons (Deut 32:17; cf. Ps 106:36–37), which implicitly warns the Corinthians again not to follow in the wilderness generation's footsteps. They should not be partners with idolaters and participate in idolatrous meals (10:5–11).

For Paul, there may be a distinction between eating foods in an idol's temple, which the strong are not warned against (see 8:10), and participating with idolaters in their cultic sacrifices that accompany eating idol foods.[137] The Corinthians are warned against the latter, which involves partnering with demons. These δαιμόνια appear to be malignant spirits understood by Paul as angelic beings in league with Satan and existing since Israel's archaic past (2 Cor 12:7; Rom 8:38; cf. Deut 32:17).[138] Paul confronted similar spirits according to Acts 16:16–18 (cf. 19:11–12; 2 Cor 12:12; Rom 15:19). As such, it is incompatible for the Corinthians to participate at **the table of the Lord** (the Lord's Supper) and participate at **the table of demons**.[139] Although demons are not the actual deities whom idolaters intend to worship, Mody is right when affirming that "the act of sacrifice/worship/homage of idols is the *key act* by which evil powers are related to idols and are able to co-opt or divert what is intended for idols so that the idolaters serve *daimonia* [demons] by coming into the sphere of power of evil powers."[140]

---

136. In 10:20 τὰ ἔθνη ("the Gentiles") is missing in some important manuscripts (e.g., B, D) and is probably a gloss attempting to provide the verse with a subject (Metzger/United Bible Societies 1994:494). Even so, the present tense "they sacrifice" (θύουσιν), altered from the aorist "they sacrificed" (ἔθυσαν) alluded to in Deut 32:17, suggests Gentile idolaters contemporary with Paul's time are in the foreground. Contemporary Israelites in Jerusalem could hardly be meant if Christians still worshipped at the temple.

137. See Newton 1998:198–99, 363–70; Horrell 1997:101, 103; Borgen 1995:56.

138. Hence, they are probably the same type of beings exorcized by Jesus and his disciples (Luke 9:1; 11:14–21), and not, or at least not merely, the genius of the Roman emperor, as Winter 2015:214–25, proposes.

139. Τράπεζα ("table") can also mean "altar" (e.g., Mal 1:7, 12; Schrage 1994:2.446–47). The "cup of demons" may refer to libation offerings: e.g., libations to Dionysius, god of wine, who was known as "the Good *Daimon*" (Fotopoulos 2003:177).

140. Mody 2009:296.

Third Supporting Proof (8:1—11:1)

Communion with demons can happen by partnering with idolaters and sharing their cultic food as they make offerings to deities that demons co-opt. If the Corinthians participate in such cultic meals repeatedly, this may desensitize them to the peril they face.[141] This inadvertent devotion to demons is idolatry and a breach of covenant faithfulness to God.[142]

Paul follows up with two rhetorical questions. The first, **do we continue to provoke the Lord to jealousy?** expects no for an answer.[143] The auditors are to recognize that eating idol meats in this predicament incites the Lord to respond with judgment. These words allude to Israel provoking the Lord to jealousy by their idols and worship of that which is not God (Deut 32:19-21; cf. Num 25:10-17; Ps 106:28).[144] The provocation assumes a violation of God's covenant and commands for his people to have no other gods and no graven images (Deut 5:7-9; Exod 20:3-5). Divine punishment ensues from the Lord because of this. The second question, **we are not stronger than he, are we?** is written with irony directed at the strong members and expects the reply, "No we are not." The question has the goal of putting them to shame since they presently think too highly of themselves as being immune to idolatry. In Paul's ironic twist, they have so much knowledge and power that they can even dispute the Lord![145] Realistically, though, Paul knows through the subtexts he uses that the Lord shows himself as a strong rock while the people and all other forces are impotent by comparison (Deut 32:30, 36-39).[146] The Lord and king of glory is "strong and mighty" and the whole earth belongs to him (Ps 24:1, 8, 10; cf. 1 Cor 10:26).

Further Circumstances Regarding Idol Foods and a Recapitulation (10:23—11:1)

Paul appeals to common advantage as he responds again to the Corinthian assumption that **all things are permissible** for them (see 6:12). He qualifies their saying by claiming that **not all things are beneficial**. Even though eating idol foods is permissible for strong members, it may not be expedient

---

141. See Works 2014:113-14.

142. Phua 2005:170 is similar and adds that idolatry can also be "dishonouring the true God through the cognitive error of mixing or confusing God" with other deities or demons, along with "wrong kinds of worship."

143. With "we" Paul rhetorically includes himself among the strong.

144. See Waters 2006:132-48. On divine marital jealousy, see Ezek 16:38; 23:25; Gardner 1994:171.

145. Contrast Isa 45:9; Eccl 6:10; Job 9:32.

146. See Ciampa/Rosner 2010:483-84.

Third Supporting Proof (8:1—11:1)

since it can lead them to idolatry and cause weaker members to fall away. He adds that **all things do not build up**. What must be built up is the Spirit's temple, the body of believers in Christ, and the way to do this is by members edifying one another in love (8:1).[147] By insisting on their freedom to eat idol meats, the strong tear down rather than build up weaker members. They ought to follow Paul's maxim instead: **Let no one seek his own advantage, but the advantage of others** (10:24). This saying resembles Seneca's friendship language: "The one wants a friend for his own advantage; the other wants to make himself an advantage to his friend" (*Lucil.* 48.4). Paul, however, encourages what is advantageous not just for friends but also for the "other," suggesting for the Corinthians someone unlike themselves.[148] For the strong this includes not only seeking what is beneficial for weak believers but also unbelievers (10:27, 32). With his principle intact Paul now presents two scenarios related to idol foods—buying it in the market place (10:25–26) and eating it when invited to an unbeliever's home (10:27–29a).

The first circumstance imagines congregation members in the *macellum*, the city's **meat market**. John Fotopoulos locates the Corinthian market at "the Peribolos containing the statue of Apollo," a sacred site close to many temples including the imperial cult.[149] Its proximity to these places suggests that much of the meat for sale had been offered to idols, which perhaps prompted certain congregants to inquire about the meat they wanted to purchase.[150] For Paul, believers are free to purchase and eat market meat so long as they are **asking no questions** to the butcher regarding whether it has been offered to idols. To assure confidence in what they eat, Paul affirms from scripture that **the earth is the Lord's and the fullness of it** (Ps 24:1). The psalm proclaims the Lord as mighty creator of the earth. One may adduce from the text that meat is good because the Lord created all the animals from which it comes. For the unknowing believer it remains wholesome and free of demons even if it was used in an idolatrous ritual. The notion of refusing such meat if informed about its idolatrous connections is **for the sake of conscience**. In 10:25 this may assume that some weak believers, whose conscience is easily damaged (see 8:7, 10), can purchase meat if they do not ask questions about it. Then again, the strong can also appreciate these words since in 10:29 the conscience turns out to be not their own but another's (at least in the situation described in 10:27–28).

---

147. Hays 1997:175.

148. Barrett 1968:240. Here "other" is ἕτερος not ἄλλος.

149. Fotopoulos 2003:240.

150. Similarly, dietary laws prompted Jews to inquire about meat (*m.* Hul. 1:1; *m.* 'Abod. Zar. 2:3; Fitzmyer 2008:399–400).

Third Supporting Proof (8:1—11:1)

The second circumstance involves mixed dining and imagines at least three persons beside the believing guest—the host who invites the believer for dinner, the informant who tells the guest about the sacrificial food, and another whose conscience might be adversely affected by the guest eating idol food. The host is a Gentile, **one of the unbelievers**, whether patron, colleague, friend, or relative. Congregation members of more prestigious backgrounds might receive such invitations rather than the lower classes and slaves. Paul encourages these dining guests to **eat whatever is set before you, asking no questions** about the food. But if someone there says to the believer that the food is **offered to a god**, Paul charges believers, **do not to eat for the sake of the person who informed you**. The informant is another unbelieving Gentile; this person uses the more reverential ἱερόθυτος ("offered to a god") rather than the pejorative εἰδωλόθυτος ("sacrificed to an idol") that Paul and other emergent Christians use (Acts 15:29; Rev 2:14; *Did.* 6.3). The believer is to refrain from eating because unbelievers who are present might think the believer is hypocritical by claiming to worship one God and yet eating in honor of another (cf. 10:30). From the unbeliever's perspective, the believer's acceptance of idol food might be tantamount to endorsing the god to whom it was offered.[151] The unbeliever might also feel justified in worshipping other gods because of this.[152] Upon hearing that he is eating idol food, the believer is to refrain also **for the sake of** another person's **conscience** (10:28c–29a), which may assume a weak believer is present. Were other people invited to this dinner? Are any of the slaves who serve the meal believers? Will weak congregation members see or hear about this dinner? Any of these cases might result in consequences similar to 8:7–13; hence, the believing guest should not eat the food.

Typical of deliberative rhetoric the conclusion in 10:29b—11:1 recapitulates themes discussed earlier in the discourse.[153] Two leading questions reiterate the points of strong members. The first one—**why is my freedom judged by another's conscience?**—seems to protest consideration for weak members. The second—**if I partake with thankfulness** (i.e., I give thanks to God for the food), **why am I being maligned for that which I give thanks?**—seems to protest unbelievers at the dinner invitation in 10:28 who might slander them for being inconsistent in their beliefs and practices.[154] The answers to these questions come by way of summing up chapters 8–10. Three imperatives guide the ending.

---

151. See Garland 2003:497.
152. Conzelmann 1975:178.
153. See Watson 1989:301–18.
154. Thiselton 2000:790.

First, all the Corinthians' endeavors must be done **to the glory of God**. Christ's followers must acknowledge and honor God in everything they do, giving thanks for the good gifts of food, drink, health, life, and so on. This recalls 8:1–6 and the importance of believers loving the one true God who created all things through Christ. We also notice that **all things** to God's glory (10:31) replaces the Corinthian assumption of "all things permissible" (10:23). Paul replaces anthropocentric thinking with a theocentric one, "from an emphasis on rights to an emphasis on obedience and service."[155] If the strong consistently put God instead of themselves first, they could avoid idolatry and partnering with demons. Second, the Corinthians must **not be the cause of stumbling either to Jews or Greeks or the church of God**. They should love others enough to be concerned that no believer falls away from the gospel, and no unbeliever is hindered from accepting the gospel, because of what they eat (8:7–13; 9:19–23; 10:27–29a). Third, Paul again charges the Corinthians to **be imitators of me just as I am also of Christ** (11:1; cf. 4:16; *T.Benj.* 4.1). He presents himself as an example to follow since he tries to **please all people in all things, not seeking** his **own advantage but the advantage of many, so that they may be saved** (cf. 9:19–22; 10:24). The factors of flexibility, appropriate conduct, purposeful gaining of others, and imitating Christ who gave his life for the sake of others (Rom 5:8; 1 Thess 5:9–10) reflect the apostle's "salvific intentionality" as a missionary.[156] His adaptability reflects neither ethical compromise nor flattery but a refusal to exercise his own rights and privileges for the sake of saving others. The Corinthians ought to follow this example.[157] In essence the closing imperatives encourage Corinthians to love God, love their neighbor, and imitate Christ as seen by the apostle's example.

FUSING THE HORIZONS: AMBIGUITY IN IDOL FOODS THEN AND NOW

Paul ends his discourse in 10:31—11:1 with imperatives that will help his auditors make wise decisions when facing diverse situations related to idol foods. When these stand *in nuce* for the entire discourse, tensions between Paul permitting the consumption of idol foods under certain circumstances

---

155. Hays 1997:179.

156. Quote from Barram 2011:237–41.

157. As Ehrensperger 2009:154, rightly affirms, "the call to imitation, rather than being an imposition of a domination pattern which has to be copied, refers to examples of those who at least have attempted to embody the message of the gospel and its alternative values." Contrast Castelli 1991:116.

(8:7–13; 10:23–29) and prohibiting it as leading to idolatry in others (10:1–22) are less abrasive. Regarding 10:1–22 we do not need to suggest that a stronger opinionated Sosthenes wrote this section as co-author in a later draft (1:1),[158] or that this section is a different letter fragment or interpolation,[159] or that Paul is condemning idol foods only when eaten in idol precincts,[160] or that he condemns all idol food consumption unless it remains unknown.[161] Paul, recognizing the complexity of circumstances in which believers might encounter idol foods, provides warnings (8:9; 10:12, 14, 21) and ethical precepts based on love and imitation (8:13; 9:22b; 10:24, 31–11:1) that will help Corinthians discern the right course of action needed for their unique circumstances. The strong members' consumption of idol food, even if eating it knowingly, will *not necessarily* result in idolatry or apostasy.[162] And yet the situation is dangerous enough that, in practice, Paul's imperatives rule out almost every opportunity for the strong to eat such food knowingly, unless they do so incognito or only with other strong believers in the privacy of their own homes.

Our apostle's warnings and principles in relation to idol foods, though largely unappreciated in modern western societies, are still relevant in other parts of the world. Derek Newton, for example, presents similar problems that exist among Chinese, Japanese, Korean, and Indonesian (Torajanese) churches, the members of which grapple with participation in religio-indigenous shrine ceremonies, meals related to ancestor worship, and so on.[163] As with Paul and the Corinthians, there is ambiguity on what exactly constitutes idolatry in such practices, and boundaries must be negotiated for determining what is permissible and what is not for these Christians. Under such conditions, loving and honoring God, loving one's neighbor, and imitating Christ go a long way. Generally the issue of stronger believers causing new or weak believers to fall away from faith is entirely relevant. It is quite possible, for instance, that a new convert who struggles with pornography will stumble over what a "stronger" believer permits himself or

158. Richards 2004:116–17. In response, the same or similar phrases from 10:1–22 are used elsewhere by Paul: e.g., 12:1 (cf. 10:1); 1:9 (cf. 10:13); 6:18 (cf. 10:14); Rom 15:4 (cf. 10:6, 11).

159. E.g., Yeo 1995:83; Cope 1990:114–23; see responses in Smit 2000a; Oropeza 1998a:57–68.

160. E.g., Fee 1987:359–61; see response in Fisk 1989:49–70.

161. E.g., Cheung 1999:162; see response in Horrell 2007:120–40.

162. See Oropeza 2012a:93–94.

163. Newton 1998:393–99.

herself to watch on theatre and television screens or the Internet. A former alcoholic might stumble if incited by other believers to drink. In certain circumstances, then, it is still advisable to give up our freedom and "right" to do as we please for the sake of others. Guided by love and unselfishness, Christians should always be sensitive to the well-being of others.

Order and Solidarity When Assembling Together: Fourth Supporting Proof (11:2—14:40)

The fourth proof related to Paul's appeal for solidarity focuses on the Corinthians *coming together* as a church (11:17, 34; 14:26). His deliberative discourse attempts to persuade congregation members to conduct themselves in an orderly manner for worship as the unified body of Christ. After addressing gender distinction related to head coverings (11:2–16) and protocols related to their practice of the Lord's Supper (11:17–34), the apostle discusses spiritual gifts:

A Spiritual Gifts and Solidarity in the Body of Christ (1 Cor 12)

   B Love as Better than Spiritual Gifts (13)

A^1 Spiritual Gifts of Prophecy and Tongues (14)

The center of this pattern suggests the Corinthians must operate with love as their primary ethic when assembling together. Use of spiritual gifts should be for edifying others rather than distracting or confusing their solidarity in worship.

GENDER DISTINCTION WHEN PRAYING AND PROPHESYING (11:2–16)

Paul seems to structure this passage in the form of a chiasm:

A. Instruction based on church traditions and teachings (11:2–3)

  B. Male and female distinction related to coverings and reflecting honor/shame (11:4–6)

    C. Male and female distinction based on the original creation (11:7–9)

      D. Women's authority over their heads (11:10)

    C^1. Male and female distinction based on original and new creation (11:11–12)

Fourth Supporting Proof (11:2—14:40)

B¹. Male and female distinction related to nature and reflecting honor/shame (11:13–15)

A¹. Custom based on tradition in all churches (11:16)

Strategically the beginning and end of this discourse provide the Corinthians with an example of personal instruction compatible with other churches in Christ. In the chiasm's center, Paul draws a conclusion about what should be done at the intersection of public and private spaces. Based on the multiple times women/wives and men/husbands appear in this text (sixteen and fourteen, respectively), it is evident that an issue regarding gender distinction is at stake. But without knowing the details, we are left with the frustrating task of working on a puzzle without all its pieces.[1] We might also be tempted to read the text anachronistically, since its message does not fit well with our own cultural norms.[2] Our apostle works within a classification system entrenched in a patriarchal world that knows nothing about today's ideologies. Such problems compel us to approach this text with great humility.

Paul begins praising his auditors because they remember him **in everything and hold firmly the traditions just as I delivered them to you**. They maintain his instructions from his earlier visit, though his words are hyperbolic in an effort to build rapport. As the texts unfold, there are problems with the way they carry out certain apostolic traditions. Relevant to 11:2–16 may be a tradition that the apostles encouraged prophetic enablement for both genders (Acts 2:17–21).[3] When in Corinth, Paul and his colleagues probably exemplified according to gender what it was to pray and prophesy with head coverings (e.g., Priscilla) and without them (Paul, Aquila). Perhaps certain members noticed how other members did not maintain this custom after Paul left Corinth, and in their letter to Paul they raised questions about it to which he now responds.

Three heads are mentioned in 11:3—**the head of every man is Christ, and the head of the woman is the man, and the head of Christ is God**. Paul uses head (κεφαλή) metaphorically in this verse, but in what sense? Three common interpretations are that it refers to "authority over," "source/origin," or "that which is most prominent, foremost, upper-most, pre-eminent."[4] The first option may work well with the idea of submission,

---

1. Some suggest a non-Pauline interpolation here (e.g., Mount 2005:313–40; Crocker 2004:158–59), but this view lacks ancient manuscript support.

2. This point is addressed by Lakey 2010.

3. See Thiselton 2000:811.

4. See, respectively, Grudem 1985:38–59; 1990:3–72; Fee 1987:502–5; Perriman 1994:618.

Fourth Supporting Proof (11:2—14:40)

but this passage is not about submission but gender *distinction*.[5] Although the meaning as "source" promotes gender equality, it lacks well-established lexical support.[6] The third choice finds sufficient support. It is in keeping with metaphors of the ancient body—the head often conveys the "topmost" and leadership of the body (Philo *Mos.* 2.30; Seneca *Clem.* 1.3.5; Galen *De Usu Partium* 1.445.14–17).[7] Nonetheless, the position of prominence or "top" seems to include the idea of authority related to leadership in many source instances, a point that A. C. Perriman admits but adds that κεφαλή "cannot be thought to introduce in any *a priori* or necessary manner ideas of authority or sovereignty into the text."[8] While his point may be valid, headship in 11:3 includes God and Christ, and so the idea of them being topmost or preeminent cannot be easily divorced from the notion of leadership, which in turn cannot be easily divorced from some sense of authority. I doubt that Paul's ancient audience would differentiate and exclude certain of these nuances from the term the way we do today, or attribute the nuances only to Christ and God but not the man. Moreover, it is difficult to accept that headship as "source" can be entirely extricated from this passage given that Paul affirms that the woman originates from the man, and vice/verse (11:8–9, 12).[9]

I suggest, then, that Paul's use of the metaphor "head" in 11:3 is multivalent; it is an image to be visualized, and though it best represents the nuance of *topmost*, this does not necessarily exclude other meanings. We can acknowledge that in Paul's patriarchal world, and in agreement with Paul's gender order from Genesis, it made perfect sense to have the man as the head (topmost and prominent person) of the home. If this idea also carries with it any sense of leadership and authority, we should remember that this ancient world for most people, unlike westerners today, was one in which survival and provisions could not be taken for granted. Since husbands and fathers had more brute strength than their wives and children, and were normally more skilled and educated, they were the most fit to lead, protect, and provide for their family and ensure its survival. Even so, like the Jesus tradition that probably informs him, Paul regards the notion of leadership in terms of serving others rather than being served (3:5; 4:1; cf. Mark 9:34–35; 10:42–45; Matt 23:11–12), and headship similarly involves a concentrated

---

5. See criticisms of the authority view in Perriman 1994:602–10; Garland 2003:514–15.

6. See Perriman 1994:610–19, and discussion in Johnson 2009:35–57.

7. Lee-Barnewall 2013:603–5. Further, Perriman 1994:618.

8. Perriman 1994:616–17.

9. Though technically for Paul, *God* is the source of man and woman (Gen 2:7, 21–23).

Fourth Supporting Proof (11:2—14:40)

effort of honoring other members who are not the head (12:21-24).[10] Without this understanding of leadership, we risk falling into a deplorable legacy of Christians who misinterpret Paul as if he were enslaving the female body for the express service of the male head!

Whatever else the man as the woman's head might mean, it does not follow that this relationship correlates *exactly* to the way Christ is the head of the man or God is the head of Christ. Christ's headship probably implies his preexistence and lordship as creator of all things (8:4-6). The headship list starts with the man's head as Christ, then the woman's head as the man, and then again Christ is mentioned, whose head is God. The second mention of Christ in this link perhaps envisions him as the second Adam who now ushers in the new creation (15:21-22, 45-49). God is mentioned *last* rather than first in this list so as to stress God not as the creating head of all things but the *goal* of all headship.[11] This anticipates the eschatological reign of God as the head with Christ as the vizier over the cosmos when Christ returns and death is defeated (15:21-28; cf. 8:6). This fully realized end, incidentally, will do away with the gender problems Paul and the Corinthians currently face.

The issue at hand centers on the outward gender appearance in worship gatherings. **Every man who prays or prophesies having something on his head dishonors his head.** A head covering is that "something."[12] Although we cannot know the situation for sure, a plausible one for the male covering was the toga, which is normally draped over the head of pious and priestly Romans.[13] The importance of such coverings are entrenched in perhaps the most important Roman myth. Helenus the prophet charges seamen destined to be Romans regarding paying vows and devotion to the gods—they are to veil their hair with a purple robe: "This mode of sacrifice do thou keep, thou and thy company; by this observance let thy children's children in purity stand fast" (Virgil, *Aen.* 3.403-9).[14] Faithful citizens thus wore head coverings as a sign of religious piety, and Roman Corinthians were constantly reminded of this whenever seeing the statues of emperors

---

10. See Lee-Barnewall 2013:605-14.

11. This does not deny God as creator (11:12c) but it does highlight that God created all things through Christ.

12. E.g., Petrovich 2015:113-16. On "(having) on/down the head" (κατὰ κεφαλῆς [ἔχων]) compare Dionysius Halicarnassus 3.71.5; 12.16.3-4[23]; Plutarch *Quaest. rom.* [*Mor.*]267C; Edsall 2013:135; Massey 2007:502-23.

13. See in Ferguson 2014:231-32; Oster 1992:68; Gill 1990:246; Thompson 1988:101-4. On Jewish male cultic coverings, see Blattenberger 1997:44.

14. Finney 2010:37-38. Such coverings represent self-abasement, concealment, and deference (40).

Fourth Supporting Proof (11:2—14:40)

Augustus and Nero in their city depicted in pious gesture with head coverings.[15] The toga likewise is emblematic of high Roman status and elitism.[16] If certain male congregants wore the draped toga over their heads when worshipping, this would exhibit before other members their prominent social status, and perhaps draw much attention to themselves. In addition, if such coverings signaled respect for other deities, then Paul, having just discussed idolatry, might be prompted to present a viable alternative.[17] Our apostle perhaps subverts the famous tale from Virgil with the story from Genesis, as we notice below.

More immediately he claims that such a covering brings dishonor to the man's head, which may be understood either as Christ, or the man's own head (a synecdoche for the man's own body and person), or both. If to his own head, this dishonor may be understood by Paul in relation to confusion of gender protocol. A head covering, something women normally wear, takes away from male distinctiveness, and since gender identity is something God has decreed,[18] dishonor is attributed to the man who covers himself like a woman. If dishonor is to Christ as the man's head, the man's toga tends to bring honor to himself rather than Christ,[19] and as such, this head covering dishonors Christ. Thiselton distills the problem more thoroughly as "that which distracts attention from God or Christ in public worship by generating a discordant, semiotic clothing code or hairstyle code which inevitably draws attention to the self in a way which makes the person's head a source of shame for his or her own self-respect, the respect of congregation, and the honor of the Lord who in public worship should be the central focus of thought and attention . . . it constitutes attention-seeking behaviour which thereby dishonor God and shames the self."[20]

Similarly, **every woman who prays or prophesies with her head uncovered dishonors her head**, namely, her husband and perhaps her own person also. The woman is married (though Paul will include all women as the text unfolds), and it is almost as though her head covering were symbolic of a wedding ring; with it on she is protected from invasion and penetration.[21] Incidentally, the assumed covering is probably not her long hair,

---

15. See Sanders 2005:23; Belleville 2003:221; Oster 1992:68–69; Thompson 1980:101–2.
16. See Winter 2001:121–23.
17. Cf. Finney 2010:45.
18. See Thiselton 2000:830; Ciampa/Rosner 2010:514–15.
19. Schnabel 2006:601.
20. Thiselton 2000:827–28.
21. Martin 1995:235.

whether bound up or let down, but an actual veil or head covering perhaps made of textile.[22] In Paul's world hair often conveys sexuality, fertility, and may even symbolize the female's genitals. Tertullian's *On the Veiling of Virgins* would later indicate that as the woman's "lower parts are not made bare have her upper likewise covered" (*Virg.* 1.12).[23] Without headgear she risks self-advertisement conveying sexual attraction, availability, immodesty, and sexual unfaithfulness (Philo *Spec.* 3.51–56; Apuleius *Met.* 2.8; Num 5:11–31). She also diverts congregation members' attention away from God. Her covering honors her fidelity to her husband in contrast to uncovered hair that dishonors him, God, gender distinction, and connects her to what is disreputable. What would encourage women in the congregation to discard their coverings? One possibility is that they confused private and public spaces when worshipping together. Paul's churches normally met in houses rather than temples, sanctuaries, or synagogues (16:19; Rom 16:5; Phlm 2; Col 4:15; Acts 5:42; 12:2).[24] Whereas respectable wives and women might normally cover themselves in public settings, they did not do so when in the privacy of their own homes. Hence, since worship gatherings were conducted in homes, they may have thought it unnecessary to wear headgear, especially if it was their own home.[25] They interpreted church meetings as private rather than public spaces, and among a family of believing "brothers and sisters" in which Paul's motto "nor male and female" (Gal 3:28) was embraced, they confused gender equality in Christ with *sameness* and felt no need to be covered.[26] This would warrant why Paul, discerning that their uncovered heads distracted men in the congregation as well as sent the wrong symbolic messages to outsiders who visited their gatherings, stresses the importance of gender distinction related to head coverings.

Paul's graphic resolve is for the woman who does not cover her hair to have it **cut off** or her head **shaved** (11:6). The assumption might be that if her hair were short and uncovered, men in the congregation at least would

---

22. See Massey 2007:502–23.

23. Cited in Martin 1995:246.

24. Such homes become "sanctuary space" rather than household space (Cameron/Miller 2011:277). This does not preclude, however, their meeting in other places also (see 11:17–34).

25. See Massey 2013:39–56.

26. On sameness, see Thiselton 2000:829. Another possibility is that Corinthian women were encouraged to adopt the "new" type of Roman woman who was more promiscuous and provocatively dressed than her predecessors (Winter 2003). A third opinion is that certain women converts used to participate in mystery cults (e.g., Dionysian) and brought that worship style into the church, inclusive of unbound and disheveled hair when prophesying (Kroeger 2002:659–60; Kroeger/Kroeger 1978:331–38; Schüssler Fiorenza 1983:228). A combination of these is also possible.

Fourth Supporting Proof (11:2—14:40)

not be ogling over her since her head would be signaling masculinity instead of femininity. The short unveiled hair, however, may also convey a wrong message about her, one of shame whether related to humiliation, punishment for adultery, or a taking away from her femininity (11:5b; Aristophanes *Thesm.* 837–38; Tacitus *Germ.* 19; Dio Chrysostom *Or.* 64.3; Lucian *Fug.* 27).[27] The solution of a shaved head, then, seems to be said almost as a *reductio ad absurdum* to persuade them to the more sensible alternative of wearing head coverings.

Paul alludes to the story of Adam and Eve, not to address the woman's subordination to the man,[28] but to show gender distinction as part of the created order. The **man ought not to cover his head since he is the image and glory of God, but woman is the glory of man**. This sounds similar to Gen 1:26–27, but in the passage "glory" is not mentioned and "man" (ἄνθρωπος) refers to human beings, male and female, who both are created in God's image.[29] Paul seems to adopt the "image of God" from this passage and then reads into it the meaning of Adam being created first and then Eve afterward from Adam's rib (Gen 2:7, 18–23). He apparently interpreted Gen 2 as further explication of Gen 1.[30] From this perspective it seems that Adam is unique among humans because he was made from the dust of the earth without any human contribution, unlike Eve, and God's image was then passed from Adam to Eve and to their children afterward (11:8–9; cf. Gen 5:1–3).[31] This image may be understood as a visible representation of the otherwise unseen God, and glory may depict that manifestation in terms of certain divine attributes (e.g., power, mercy, love); the man mirrors the divine by exhibiting God's attributes.[32] This glory is also a sign of honor (see Mal 1:6). As Fee suggests, "the existence of the one brings honor and praise to the other. By creating man in his own image God set his own glory in man. Man, therefore exists to God's praise and honor, and is to live in relationship to God so as to be his 'glory.'"[33] Since man (Adam) was

---

27. See Ciampa/Rosner 2010:521; Garland 2003:520.

28. *Pace* Schottroff 2012:732.

29. Possibly Paul includes "glory" because he, like LXX translators, interprets the "likeness" (תְּמוּנָה) of God from Hebrew as "glory" (δόξα) in Greek (Num 12:8; Ps 17[16]:15; Wire 1990:120, 279). Gen 1:26, however, uses דְּמוּת and ὁμοιόω, respectively, for "likeness." On the divine image in Jewish sources, see van Kooten 2008:1–91.

30. Paul does not seem to read Gen 1 and 2 here as two distinct creation sources.

31. See Ciampa/Rosner 2010:524. Alternatively, Paul knew the woman was created in God's image but does not mention it because it would obstruct his argumentative goal (Gundry-Volf 1997:156).

32. See Feuillet 1973:159–61; Thiselton 2000:834–35.

33. Fee 1987:516.

Fourth Supporting Proof (11:2—14:40)

first to reflect God's likeness and glory, this first-hand reflection is somehow deflected by his wearing a head covering in worship. Ciampa and Rosner try to make sense of this by suggesting that "nothing should happen in worship that would detract from God's glory, including behavior that would draw attention to the glory of man," and since the woman is the glory of man, that glory should be covered when worshipping God.[34]

A climactic moment in the pericope, as evinced by its location in the chiasm's center (see above), is when Paul writes, **for this reason, the woman ought to have authority** (ἐξουσία) **over her head** (11:10a).[35] This authority is not placed under someone else's power (i.e., that of her husband or another man; such an idea finds no lexical support). Rather, the woman exercises this authority herself.[36] She has the right to be in charge of her own head, and that means she should control her hair and make it respectable for public viewing. Paul's expectation is that she will take responsibility herself to wear a covering and thus avoid exposing her head to indignity. This would honor gender distinction, demonstrate faithfulness to her husband, and prevent other males from lustfully looking at her as she prays and prophecies.[37] This approach is in keeping with Paul's concern for correcting the Corinthian perspective of authority "precisely in the sense of rights or freedoms claimed by his readers which he seeks to have them voluntarily subordinate to broader community values."[38]

The next phrase, **because of the messengers** is bewildering only if, as many Bible versions do, ἄγγελος is translated as "angels" rather than "messengers." If referring to supernatural beings, interpretations run the gamut from good angels who might be offended by the disorder of unveiled women, to bad angels who might lust after the unveiled women akin with the myth of the heavenly Watchers who birthed giants through female earthlings (e.g., 1 *En.* 6–7; *T.Reub.* 5.5–6).[39] If the phrase is adopted from the Corinthians' own vocabulary, we could only speculate blindly about what they, let alone Paul, might have meant by these angels. Perhaps a more viable option is Winter's understanding of τοὺς ἀγγέλους as "the messengers," i.e., human messengers, not angels (Gen 32:4; Luke 9:52; Epictetus, *Diatr.* 3.22.23). In

---

34. Ciampa/Rosner 2010:527; cf. Hooker 1964:415.

35. "For this reason" ("διὰ τοῦτο") can point forward to "because of the ἄγγελος" (Schrage 1994:2.513) or in both directions (Fee 1987:518).

36. BeDuhn 1999:302–33, provides evidence and affirms that "Paul *always* employs the term to mean authority held by the subject."

37. Ibid. 303–4; Garland 2003:525–26.

38. BeDuhn 1999:303.

39. See various options in Tolmie 2011:4–5; Stuckenbruck 2001:220–34; Fitzmyer 2008:417–19.

Fourth Supporting Proof (11:2—14:40)

his view, *inter alia,* since Christian assemblies met weekly instead of the standard annual festival for civic gods or the monthly meetings prescribed by Roman rules for association meetings, this may have raised questions for the latter of possible political sedition.[40] Since Christian homes were open to visitors (14:23), political informants might be sent to observe the peculiarities of this sect that, like the Jews, worship one invisible god, but unlike the Jews, had no legally exempt status to do so. Likewise, anyone with "civic status or wealth whose curiosity was aroused about Christian faith would not go to any meeting without having a client or others first carry back reports of its activities."[41] By women not covering themselves and thus symbolizing disregard for their marital status—and men wearing coverings like elitist priests to draw attention to their status—Paul was concerned that outsiders and messengers might get the wrong impression of Christian gatherings.[42] With this understanding intact, although these messengers might find that covered Christian men resembled Roman piety (though unacceptable for Paul, as we addressed above), they might also interpret the women's lack of headgear as defiant toward marital protocols. Paul thus encourages the women worshippers to exhibit themselves in a way that dismantles potential criticisms from outsiders and invites these outsiders instead to be more open to receive their prophecies (14:24–25).

The qualification, **nevertheless, neither is woman independent of man nor man independent of woman in the Lord** reaffirms earlier teachings about gender equality *in the Lord* Jesus Christ (see Gal 3:28).[43] Such equality anticipates life in the new creation, an era that when fully realized will do away even with the old creation in which Adam was prior to Eve. Paul affirms that neither gender exists apart from the other (11:11–12); man and woman in the present are mutually dependent for procreation, and they are distinct and divinely created that way since **all things are from God**.[44] Our apostle then prompts the Corinthians to say "no" to his question, **is it proper for a woman to pray to God uncovered?** And they are to say "yes" to his question that asks whether **nature itself** teaches that

---

40. Winter 2001:133–34. Although the magistrate Gallio saw them as no threat (Acts 18:12–17), his appointment ended a few years before Paul wrote 1 Corinthians (135).

41. Ibid. 137.

42. Ibid. 138–140.

43. However, 11:11–16 does not demarcate Paul's view as opposed to the Corinthians' alleged view in 11:3–10 (*Pace,* Peppiatt 2015:66–84, 102). Nowhere in Paul do we find such a prolonged oppositional viewpoint, and there are no clear indicators for it (e.g., positing an inquiry and then refuting it with μὴ γένοιτο: 6:15; Rom 6:1–2).

44. See Gen. 1:31; Isa 45:7; Amos 5:8; Heil 2005:175.

long hair on a man **is a dishonor to him** but a woman's long hair **is a glory to her**. For Paul both propriety (πρέπω) and nature (φύσις) lay claim to what is observationally self-evident. The former may connote here what is conspicuously fitting "on the eye."[45] The eye of the beholder in this case is relative to Roman custom in which men's hairstyles were generally shorter than women's, and long hair might take away from masculinity. Of course, Paul knew of exceptions to this custom, such as long-haired men honoring Nazirite vows (e.g., Judg 13–16), and so we suspect his words are at least partially a rhetorical attempt to discourage congregants obsessed with sophists who had long and elaborate hairdos and looked effeminate (Philo *Spec.* 3.37–38; *Ps.-Phoc.* 210–12; Philostratus *Vit. soph.* 1.8.489; Epictetus, *Diatr.* 3.1.1–45; see 1 Cor 2).[46]

Unlike his argument from propriety, however, Paul's argument from nature expects uniform agreement.[47] It connotes for Paul what is endowed by God's creation. Nature, of course, does not determine hair length, but it does exhibit gender differentiation regarding sex organs, voice, and (relevant to hair) beards and bald heads for males (cf. Epictetus *Diatr.* 1.16.9–14). His argument from nature would likely be understood by the Corinthians as self-evident. Branson Parler shows that the ancient physiological models of Aristotle and Hippocrates teach gender differentiation inclusive of hair on one's head, which was believed to draw moisture and semen upward:

> Men expel seed and women receive it in order to produce new life. . . . Short hair on a man would mean less suction power to hold the semen in the man's body thus enabling him to better fulfill (part of) his natural, teleological function of procreation. Likewise, long hair on a woman would mean more suction power to draw the semen into her uterus and thus enable her to better fulfill (part of) her natural, teleological function of procreation. In this physiological paradigm, hair is not merely a marker of socially constructed gender roles (though it may be that as well) but an essential part of the procreative difference between male and female.[48]

The man's long hair, then, may signal infertility and less masculinity, whereas the woman's long hair signals fertility and more femininity. Her unveiled hair is doubtless beautiful and an honor to her and her husband in private

---

45. LSJ 1461.
46. With Witherington 1995:237.
47. See examples of φύσις in Arzt-Grabner et al. 2006:390–92.
48. Parler 2016:130; e.g., Hippocrates *Nat. puer.* 9; *Generation* 1–2; Aristotle *Gen. an.* 747a.5–20.

Fourth Supporting Proof (11:2—14:40)

spaces, but Paul's reason for it being glorious is that **long hair is given to her as a covering**. That is, her long hair is as a garment that covers her head and is provided by nature. Her hair nonetheless does not replace her veil in public spaces (see 11:5–6); rather, it "is *analogous* to the additional covering represented by the veil."[49] As P. T. Massey affirms, the woman's hair is still to be covered, and "veiling is a reflection or extension of long hair. . . . The veil thus follows the contour of a woman's long hair and accentuates the glory (δόξα) of her natural beauty without creating the social stigma of either immodesty or ostentatiousness."[50]

The closing remark, **but if anyone who wants to be contentious**, anticipates congregation members who might object to Paul's instruction here. He responds that the Corinthians stand alone in their novel practice of worship with men's heads covered and women's heads uncovered—none of **the churches of God** have such a **custom**.[51] The implication is that they should be in solidarity with other churches and willing to change their practices.

Fusing the Horizons: Custom and Modesty

Although the topic of head coverings seems relegated to the socio-cultural mores or "custom" of a given society,[52] its promotion of gender differentiation remains entirely relevant for the interim between the old creation and fully realized new one. Namely, we can still appreciate today that gender distinction is a good gift from God and should not be defaced regardless of what one's culture might think. This does not mean that women in postmodern western societies must still wear headgear; males at these churches do not normally drool over uncovered female hair. Rather, modesty in dress and propriety in worship are timeless values that should always be honored, and that may look different depending on the church and its respective socio-cultural milieu. Paul's cultural taboos can be posed analogously to some

---

49. Watson 2000b:87. Here the preposition ἀντί means "as" (a "corresponding counterpart": Massey 2011:53), and περιβόλαιον (Exod 22:26; Deut 22:12; Dionysius Halicarnassus, 3.71.5), probably refers to a textile covering known as the *himation* or *palla* (Massey 2007:522; Edsall, 2013:139), rather than a wraparound hairstyle (Murphy-O'Connor 1983:179–81; see response in Edsall 2013:136–38) or testicles (Martin 2004:83; see response in Goodacre 2011:391–96. Martin 2013:453–65, rejoins but with few sources and their meaning for our text remains quite questionable).

50. Massey 2011:72.

51. ISV is correct: "we do not have any custom like this"; *contra* "we have no other practice" (NIV, NASB).

52. On συνήθεια ("custom": 11:16), see John 18:39; Plato *Rep.* 516A.

Fourth Supporting Proof (11:2—14:40)

of our own. If several women today came to church wearing see-through negligees, the usher might cover them with choir robes and advise them to dress more modestly for church. And as Richard Hays says, men wearing baseball caps to a formal dinner or church would be perceived as "rude and irreverent."[53] These norms, too, might change one day, but as long as church attendees get distracted or are tempted to gaze on the creature rather than Creator, issues involving gender sensitivity, propriety, and modesty in appearance will remain important.

DIVISIONS WHEN COMMEMORATING THE LAST SUPPER (11:17-34)

The next issue centers on the congregation commemorating the Lord's Supper. In contrast to his praise in 11:2, when they **come together** for this meal Paul says, **I do not praise you**. Their celebration turns out to be **for the worse**: there are **divisions** among them related to this meal, which has become disadvantageous for certain members.[54] He expresses displeasure with epideictic blame employing irony, pathos, and four rhetorical questions building up to a second and louder, "I do not praise you!" (11:18-22). He then instructs from the Lord's Supper tradition handed to him (11:23-26). The various words related to judgment, examination, and discernment in 11:27-32 sound similar in Greek, suggesting the use of paronomasia. He then concludes with an attempt to resolve the problem (11:33-34).

Paul believes the report of their misconduct **in part**. There is no reason to doubt it, however, and so this is probably said in irony as a type of mock disbelief based on what follows.[55] In keeping with this irony, Paul continues in 11:19, **for of course there must be discriminations among you, so that those approved among you** as dignitaries **may be recognized!**[56] The "for"

---

53. Hays 1997:184.

54 The enumerative "in the first place" (πρῶτον μὲν) is apparently broken off from a subsequent "Secondly": Fee 1987:536-37.

55. See Mitchell 1991:152. Alternatively, μέρος τι could mean "a certain matter/report" (Winter 2001:159-63).

56. The schisms are described as αἱρέσεις, which may be understood as factions, or perhaps more relevantly, *discriminations* (Horsley 1998:159; cf. Philo *Gig.* 18.6; Josephus *Ant.* 7.321). Last 2013:365-81, posits the meaning as "elections" of appointed officers administrating the meal, a view contested by Brookins 2014:423-32.

serves to explain the reason for his displeasure described in 11:17–18.[57] Verse 19, then, conveys something negative about those who are approved, and as such it could hardly be referring to divine election or to the divine necessity of divisions in light of prophecy (e.g., Matt 10:35–36).[58] Paul is being sarcastic by presenting the approved ones (δόκιμοι) as elitists or dignitaries (see Philo *Jos.* 34[210]).[59] Similar uses of approval are found in voluntary associations and comparable with members gaining honor and positions in these associations.[60] In this manner Paul once again attempts to shame their overestimation of themselves that is instigating divisions, similar to his inflated description of them as kings in 4:8. His irony makes the rebuke that follows all the more pointed—**Thus, when you come together in the same place, it is *not* to eat the Lord's Supper!**[61] They have turned the sacred meal into something selfish and status seeking. Paul's rebuke along with his lack of praise elicit the auditors' pathos by amplifying their practice as disgraceful.

Their commemoration of Jesus's Last Supper appears to be celebrated as a full dinner, apparently in the manner of an *eranos,* a picnic-like or contributed meal in which each person eats what he or she brings.[62] Thanksgiving and breaking of shared bread perhaps commenced the dinner in a manner recalling Jesus's final dinner, and special significance was attributed to drinking from one cup of wine, which may have taken place at the meal's end (10:16; 11:25).[63] After the dinner, too, proclamations, teachings from scripture, and oral traditions related to Jesus may have continued (see Acts 20:7–8). This meal might be similar to the structure of a symposium in Greco-Roman parlance, though in the latter case rhetorical speeches, philosophical discussions, music, and entertainment, along with more drinking that often devolved into debauchery and sexual improprieties, took place.[64]

57. Or the reason why he cannot praise them (Garland 2003:538).
58. Barrett 1968:262 rightly contests the former but accepts the latter.
59. Campbell 1991:65–70.
60. See McRae 2011:179.
61. The "Lord's Supper" (κυριακός δεῖπνον) at this time may not have been known as a technical term, if McGowan 2015:503–21 is correct. But even if so, commemoration of Jesus's last supper still seems to be celebrated in the language of a fellowship meal (10:16), the "Lord's table" (10:21), and perhaps included in meals related to the breaking of bread (Acts 2:42–46; 20:7–11; Keener 2012:1.1003–4).
62. This is not quite the same as a "potluck" in which each one contributes to the one meal that everyone eats. See Homer *Od.* 1.226–27; Athenaeus *Deipn.* 8.365AB; Coutsoumpos 2005:46–51; Lampe 1994:38–39.
63. See Furnish 1999:79; Hofius 1993:80–88.
64. See e.g., Aristophanes *Ach.* 1085–94; Lucian *Lex.* 6–13; Fotopoulos 2003:160–74; Taussig 2009:21–85, 131–39; Smith 2003:1–12, 147–58.

Fourth Supporting Proof (11:2—14:40)

The problem in Corinth centers on certain members bringing and consuming larger portions of food and drink than poor members.⁶⁵ Paul addresses the problem to the entire church as it comes together, which suggests that quite a few members were in the "have" category and causing this problem for those who "have not."⁶⁶ Some have imagined this gathering at a villa-styled home with a *triclinium* room that seated nine to twelve honored guests, set apart from the atrium and other areas in which less prominent and poorer members ate.⁶⁷ The best positioned members would eat the best portions. The meaning of προλαμβάνω in 11:21 as "take beforehand" ("eat ... without waiting for anybody else" NIV) complements this view with the inference that slaves and poorer members arrived at the dining house later, presumably because these had to work long hours. By the time they arrived, and since they had no place in the triclinium, little or no food remained for them (see also 11:33 below). David Horrell, however, aptly challenges the triclinium setting as lacking clear and correctly timed archaeological evidence from Corinth, opting instead for the supper taking place in a workshop building with an upper room akin with discoveries east of the Corinthian theatre.⁶⁸ Differently, David Balch, noticing that members sat rather than reclined (14:30), suggests *inter alia* from Roman domestic art their gathering at a peristyle garden or tavern with benches for seating.⁶⁹ A poor member's location at the gathering, then, may have been right next to a more well-to-do member. Moreover, with this view, the term προλαμβάνω does not mean to "take beforehand," but to "take" the food in the sense of intense consumption so that **each one devours his own supper** "without sharing with others" (NLT). This meaning suggests that since the wealthier members bring bigger and better portions of food with them than the meager amounts (if any) that the poor might bring, the latter remain hungry at the meal while they haplessly look at the well-to-do members consuming sumptuous foods and wine. This problem is taking place **during the eating** (ἐν τῷ φαγεῖν) with the poor being present at the meal; they are not arriving late.⁷⁰

---

65. See scenario surveys in Smith 2010:521–27; Klauck 1982:291–95.

66. This suggests that the wide-scale poverty of members posited by Meggitt 1998:120 and Friesen 2005:351–70 is overdrawn. See Introduction.

67. E.g., Murphy-O'Connor 1983:153–61. Gaius's home is sometimes proposed (Rom 16:23). Pompeii trinclinia fitted only six to nine persons (Perkins 2012:142), whereas in Pergamon an association for Dionysiac "cowherds" had two that together fitted up to seventy (Ascough 2012a:24; Ascough/Harland/Kloppenborg 2012b:B6).

68. Horrell 2004:349–69.

69. Balch 2015:311–43.

70. See Winter 2001:148–51.

Fourth Supporting Proof (11:2—14:40)

The outcome is that **one is hungry and another is drunk**. Poor members do not get enough to eat while other members eat and drink so much that they get intoxicated.[71] Paul's exasperated questions that follow rhetorically shame them and substantiate his refusal for praise. They could **eat and drink** at home to curtail their appetites once gathered together, but they have not done so. Their actions show that they **despise the church of God** because they **shame those** members **who have nothing**. Paul might agree with Pliny that impropriety toward guests at meals and unequal portions of food connote stinginess and extravagance (*Ep.* 2.6); and with Seneca he might concur that intoxication is offensive and a type of madness that casts off restraints to wrongdoing (*Lucil.* 83.9-27). Our apostle would add, however, that drunken and greedy persons might jeopardize their inheritance in God's kingdom (6:10).

His version of the Last Supper is comparable with what is written later in the Gospels (11:23-25; Matt 26:17-28; Mark 14:12-25; Luke 22:17-23).[72] Even though Paul **received** these words **from the Lord**, it does not appear to be from direct revelation but a recollection of Jesus's words passed on to him orally by the Lord's earliest disciples. That this happened **on the night he was betrayed** (παραδίδωμι) grounds the tradition in an actual event—Jesus's arrest that led to his crucifixion.[73] All four Gospels describe his betrayal and arrest repeatedly using παραδίδωμι, the same word Paul uses (e.g., Mark 14:10; Matt 26:15; Luke 22:4; John 18:5).[74] Among the various types of meals that might have influenced this tradition, the Passover is the most significant (Exod 12).[75] Paul himself is informed by this feast as he calls Christ the Passover lamb and associates the third cup of wine at the Seder meal **after supper** with the "cup of blessing" served at the Lord's table (see 5:5-7; 10:16; *m. Pes.* 10:1-7). Likewise, the repetitive command of Jesus

---

71. Smith 2010a:527, suggests drunkenness here is a metonymy for gluttony, but wine appears to be plentiful at the meal and drunkenness is stressed as a vice (5:11; 6:10).

72. See theories related to parallel wording in Marshall 1993:30–56. Unique idioms suggest Paul did not originate this tradition (Jeremias 1966:101–5).

73. On the Last Supper's historicity, see Fitzmyer 2008:430.

74. God "handing over" Jesus to redemption on the cross is not the primary meaning, *pace* Works 2014:94; Smith 2003:188; the crucifixion did not happen on that *night*. See problems with other interpretations of παραδίδωμι in Oropeza, 2010:342–45. Paul likely knew the betrayer's name, but the tradition he unfolds centers on *Jesus* (not Judas) and what Jesus says about the last supper. Hence, for this tradition (and Paul) to include Judas's name would be digressive. Moreover, the shame of mentioning an apostate who was formerly one of Jesus's closest disciples may have also been another deterrent for not including Judas's name (see Oropeza 2011:144–45).

75. See Thiselton 2000:871–74; Oropeza 2004:49–57.

to **do this** (i.e., eat unleavened bread and drink from the cup of wine) **in remembrance of me** (11:24c, 25c) recalls Passover observances in remembrance of Israel's redemption from Egyptian slavery (Exod 12:14; 13:9; Deut 16:3; *Jub* 49:7-23).[76] Through the Lord's dinner, however, remembrance is centered on the redemption that Jesus's death brings.

Other scriptural traditions are echoed in Jesus's words, **This is my body which is for you** (11:24b) and **This cup is the new covenant in my blood** (11:25b). In the first saying, "for you," reflects Isa 53:5, which suggests a sacrificial expiation anticipated in body of the suffering servant (52:13—53:12), whom emergent Christians interpret as Christ. It became, as Ben Meyer convincingly argues, part of early faith formulae that predate Paul.[77] Through such language Christ's crucifixion was linked with redemption and expiation from sin.[78] Paul associates these thoughts with the sacrificial notion that Christ died "for our sins" according to Scripture (15:3). The second saying recalls Moses establishing the covenant of the Law by sprinkling blood and sharing a meal with the leaders of Israel in God's presence (Exod 24:8-11). Similarly, Christ establishes a "new covenant" with his own blood represented by the wine shared with his disciples. These words also may recall Jeremiah's new and everlasting covenant (Jer 31:31-33; 32:38-40). Through Christ's death, Paul and other Christians believed they were living in the era predicted by Jeremiah in which God's relationship with the faithful was characterized by inner transformation, laws written on their hearts, and the forgiveness of sins (2 Cor 3:3-6).

Christ's story is retold by his community as they visibly reenact the Lord's death by partaking of the bread and wine. This death becomes the story of their own redemption not from Egypt but from the fallen present age infested by sin and Satan which once enslaved them. After their redemption, the followers of Christ embark on their own prophetic exodus-wilderness journey that finds its rest in God's heavenly kingdom (10:1-11). Until that rest is realized, the Corinthians along with all Christ's followers are to **proclaim** through their enactment of this commemorative meal **the Lord's death until he comes**. By sharing in the Lord's death this way, they will also share in his resurrection at his second coming (15:20-24). Participation in this meal, then, "becomes a focal point where past deliverance, present sustenance, and future hope intersect."[79] Paul's review of this meal aims to instill his Corinthian auditors both with the sacredness of this meal

---

76. See Hofius 1993:104.
77. Meyer 1993:18-19.
78. Rom 3:25; Col 1:20; Heb 9:14; 1 Pet 2:13; 1 John 1:7; Rev 1:5.
79. Oropeza 2004:57.

and with Christ's unselfish giving as a model for them to follow in relation to poor members who attend the supper.

Seeing, then, that the meal proclaims Jesus's death, those who consume these elements **in an unworthy manner will be held accountable** for the Lord's body and blood. Garland rightly suggests that "those whose behavior at the Lord's Supper does not conform to what that death entails effectively shift sides. They leave the Lord's side and align themselves with the rulers of this present age who crucified the Lord."[80] If Christ is spiritually present as the Lord honored at this meal (see 10:16-21), the Corinthians are to discern the reality of Christ's **body** present with them (11:29). Though as Peter-Ben Smit affirms, the term is multivalent: "The 'body' is both a designation of the bread broken at the Lord's Supper, a reference to Christ's body, and a designation of the community *qua* body of Christ.... Whoever shames the poor members . . . offends both the community as a body and Christ, whose body is at stake as both the content (the bread broken) and the context (the community) of the Lord's Supper."[81] The Corinthians, then, must not regard the bread and cup in a mundane sense as merely food and drink.[82] Before they partake, they must **examine** themselves. Examination was crucial for sacred meals, as an Athenian inscription from the second century (CE) evinces: "It is not lawful for anyone to enter this holy assembly of banqueters before being examined to see whether they are holy and godly and good."[83] Paul, however, hires no church policeman to do this; rather, each worshipper is to examine themselves to determine their own character, deficiencies, and state of righteousness.[84]

Self-examination should have the result of a positive change of behavior,[85] and would help avoid the Lord's **judgment**. Many are physically **weak and sick, and a number** of them are **falling asleep** in death.[86] Some possible culprits for these calamities include the current food shortage (see 7:26), drunkenness, gluttony, food poisoning, or a plague.[87] But Paul, along

80. Garland 2003:550.
81. Smit 2013:84.
82. Ciampa/Rosner 2010:555.
83. Malcolm 2013b:116.
84. See similarly 2 Cor 13:5; Cicero *Off.* 1.32.114.
85. Stein 2008:150.

86. The adjective ἱκανός ("many" NKJV) might suggest a large amount of deaths, possibly from an epidemic (Murphy-O'Connor 2009:228-29). But if rendered "a number" or "enough," the amount is unspecified (see options in LSJ 825). I suggest that some already died while others might be close to death. With ἱκανός perhaps Paul plays up the number for rhetorical effect.

87. See possibilities in Perkins 2012:145-46; Thiselton 2000:894-97; Garland

Fourth Supporting Proof (11:2—14:40)

with many ancient people, simply assumed that physical maladies may be caused by divine and supernatural powers (5:5; Mark 2:3-5; John 9:2; Jas 5:14-15; Rev 2:21-23). He interprets this present judgment as being **disciplined by the Lord** (cf. Heb 12:5-11), and its purpose is **so that we may not be condemned with the world** on judgment day and excluded from God's kingdom.[88] One possible interpretation of 11:32 assumes that this condemnation is conditional. Paul anticipates that the physical sufferings of those who are being disciplined would cause them to repent and in this manner they will avoid future condemnation (see 5:5).[89] This either implies that those who already died will be condemned (and so it appears their discipline was unsuccessful),[90] or this judgment is corporate (it affects certain congregation members regardless of whether they participated in the wrongdoing or not).[91] A second possibility is that the Corinthians' judgment and discipline extends only to illness and physical death in the present but not to future condemnation on judgment day. This is quite exceptional when compared with the final judgments warned against earlier (e.g., 3:16-17; 10:5-12)—their behavior at the supper may not be considered as heinous as some of their other vices. If this view is correct, then believers who occasionally commit vice do not necessarily suffer final judgment as do those whose lifestyle is *characterized* by vice (6:9-10; Gal 5:19-21).[92] A third option is that **we** in 11:31-32 suggests corporate judgment; hence, the church as an elect corporate entity is disciplined by these maladies but escapes final judgment, whereas individual members who commit vice and eat unworthily are still in jeopardy of condemnation.[93] Paul mentions illness and death as a way to prompt them to correct their behavior, and thus repentance is implied with any of these options.

Our apostle closes in 11:33-34 with some final instructions on resolving their conflict, similar to 11:22 but without shaming the members. They

---

2003:553-54. Robertson/Plummer 1925:253, suggest that much sickness in the church prompts Paul to point out what he thinks is its cause, though his inference is not necessarily by special revelation.

88. In 11:32 κατακρίνω is a future final judgment whereas κρίμα in 11:29, 34 is a present judgment.

89. See Allo 1956:283; Keener 2005:99.

90. Marshall 1975:115-16. Ramelli 2011:145-63, argues for spiritual illness and death. However, auditors in this letter are only familiarized with *physical* death as "sleep" (7:39; 15:18).

91. Konradt 2003:442, 449-50; cf. Schnabel 2006:669.

92. See Oropeza 2012a:103-4.

93. On Pauline corporate/individual distinction, see further, Oropeza 2007:182-84, 204-10.

Fourth Supporting Proof (11:2—14:40)

must welcome or **receive one another,** especially those who have less to eat, when coming together.[94] If poorer members have little to eat, hospitality means that other members should be willing to share with them their own food. And if those who "have" are in the habit of getting hungry before the sacred meal, they should eat privately at home first rather than selfishly horde up all their food in front of the poor. This way they might be more willing to share the food they bring. Other issues related to this situation Paul does not address but says **I will give directions when I come** again to Corinth (cf. 4:18–19; 16:3–4). Perhaps he wished to implement some rules for the poor in Corinth, or maybe some private conversations were in order, especially for the host of these meals.[95]

GIFTS OF THE SPIRIT AND SOLIDARITY IN THE BODY OF CHRIST (12:1–31)

Paul continues on the subject of proper worship when coming together. He addresses spiritual gifts and encourages the maintenance of order and solidarity for the benefit of all members (12:1–7). Nine gifts appear in 12:8–10, and then eight are ranked in 12:28. Five questions are posed regarding body members (12:14, 15, 17, 19), and talking body parts add some humor while discouraging divisions (12:15–16, 21). Seven more rhetorical questions are then posed (12:29–30). The passage includes repetitive wording (anaphora) (12:4–10, 13) and asyndeton with the successive omission of "and" (12:27–30).[96] These features help foster Corinthian members to regard themselves as distinct but complementary parts of the collective body of Christ via God's Spirit (12:7, 25a–26). Paul's discussion may be outlined as a chiasm:

    A. Variety of spiritual gifts apportioned (12:4–10)

        B. Solidarity of members as one body in the Spirit (12:11–14)

            C. Questions denying the unsuitability of certain body parts (12:15–16)

---

94. Cf. ἐκδέχεσθε ("receive") in 3 Macc 5:26; Josephus *Ant.* 7.351; Hofius 1993:89–91; Winter 2001:144–54. Paul similarly discourages divisions among the Romans by charging them to make weak believers feel *welcome* when eating together (Rom 14:1; 15:7: though here προσλαμβάνω), and there also he establishes Christ as their example for solidarity and unselfishness (15:1–6). The alternative meaning is "wait" for one another before eating (Theissen 1982:151–53; Lampe 1994:37). See 11:21.

95. Walters 2010:363–64, posits that Paul's words undermine the host's authority. Perhaps so (see also Smit 2013:188), but *pace* Walters (353–54), neither Apollos nor alleged opponents appear to be the problem (see 1:12 above).

96. Bullinger 1898:142, 199.

Fourth Supporting Proof (11:2—14:40)

    D. Questions prompting explanation of many members in the body (12:17-20)

   C¹. Statements denying the unsuitability of certain body parts (12:21-24)

  B¹. Solidary of members as the one body of Christ (12:25-27)

 A¹. Variety of spiritual gifts semi-ranked (12:28-30)

The center of the chiasm stresses that members comprise the one body of Christ and are placed in their respective locations by God and not themselves. Hence, they should neither boast nor be ashamed of their place or gifts in the body.

Paul's opening words, **now concerning spiritual things** (πνευματικός), may suggest he is responding to another correspondence question from the Corinthians (see 7:1). His stress on mutuality, bodily edification, and ranking of spiritual gifts betrays a competitive atmosphere among members who probably boast of their spiritual endowments (14:36-37).[97] Another problem includes disorderliness (14:33, 40). Other issues, if Chris Forbes is correct, center on their speaking in tongues without intelligible interpretation, their continuing this practice before outsiders, and their prophesying in a manner that discourages discernment of what is spoken (e.g., 14:1-5, 23, 29).[98] The term πνευματικός may be the Corinthians' preferred word for manifestations of spirituality, whereas Paul prefers using "spiritual gifts" (χαρίσματα 12:4, 9, 28, 30-31), which highlight spiritual manifestations as graciously given by God.[99] God is the benefactor of those to whom these gifts are given, and the clients are expected to reciprocate honor, praise, and gratitude to the gift-giver and likewise reflect generosity by sharing what was given with others.[100]

Paul writes, **I do not want you to be ignorant** about spiritual matters, which is a humbling reminder that his auditors need spiritual direction.[101] They were **at one time Gentiles**, formerly idolaters who did not know God. But as believers they (should) no longer do things that characterize unbelieving Gentiles (cf. Eph 2:1-3, 11-12; 4:17-19). They formerly **were (led away) to mute idols**, descriptive of the idols' lifeless incommunicable state

---

97. Garland 2003:558, suggests their question is, "What spiritual gift is highest and best?"
98. Forbes 1997:171-72, 260.
99. See Harrison 2003:80-81. Cf. 1:4, 7; Rom 12:6; Philo *Leg. All.* 3.78.
100. See deSilva 2000:142-48.
101. With Starling 2014:275.

Fourth Supporting Proof (11:2—14:40)

in antithesis to the living God. With this language Paul may be imagining a *pompe* or cultic procession celebrated in cities like Corinth in which devotees were "marched away" in public viewing to arrive at a sanctuary where cultic images are seen and sacrifices made.[102] Another possibility is that they are imagined being led away (ἀπάγω) as slaves or prisoners.[103] If so, this may suggest the Corinthians were formerly entrapped by idolatrous and evil spiritual powers (10:20; Gal 4:3, 8–9).[104] But now they are to be led by God's Spirit (Rom 8:14; Gal 5:18).[105]

Since the Corinthians should not be ignorant about spiritual matters, they are informed in 12:3 that **no one speaking by** the agency of **God's Spirit says, "Jesus be cursed!"** Winter suggests from curse tablets uncovered near the Demeter and Persephone cult precincts in Corinth, among other sources, that the curse reflects an invocation of Jesus to curse one's enemies.[106] Some of the believers were practicing this, and Paul condemns it. On this view Ἀνάθεμα Ἰησοῦς means "Jesus [gives or grants] a curse."[107] But this is rather questionable since Paul himself has no problem invoking a curse on those who do not love Jesus (16:22). Another possibility is that, prior to conversion, a congregation member once either blurted out this curse or heard someone else do so in an idolatrous setting or local synagogue.[108] I suggest instead that Paul may be recollecting his own experience. Prior to his transformation, as a persecutor of Christ's followers, he used to compel believers to utter this curse and revile the name of Jesus. It became proof of renouncing one's faith in Christ (Acts 26:11; cf. Gal 3:13; 1 Tim 1:13).[109] In later decades, those accused of being Christians under Emperor Trajan were compelled to revile the name of Christ since no genuine Christian would ever do this (Pliny *Ep.* 10.96). Paul may be contrasting de-conversion (apostasy) with conversion. The phrase, "Jesus be cursed," stands in antithesis to the claim, **"Jesus is Lord"** that is part of one's confession at conversion (6:11; Rom 10:9–13; Col 2:6; cf. Acts 2:21, 38; 22:16). This confession invites the Spirit to dwell with the neophyte and ushers that person into the corporate

---

102. See Paige 1991:57–65; Horsley, 1998:168; on the quote: Collins 1999:447.

103. Arzt-Grabner et al. 2006:410–12. Is Paul once again imagining prisoners of war (or animals: Paige 1991:63) in a triumphal procession being led away to be killed? Whatever the case, ἀπάγω does appear to connote an ecstatic state (see Schnabel 2006:683–86).

104. See Zeller 2010:386.

105. Ibid. 387.

106. Winter 2001:164–83; see further curse tablets in Stroud 2014:187–202

107. Winter 2001:176; similarly, Mgaya 2009:79–89.

108. See the range of options in Thiselton 2000:918–27; Garland 2003:570–71.

109. Oropeza 2011:36, 134–35; 2012a:72.

body of Christ (see 12:13; cf. Rom 8:9). Paul's response that **no one can say Jesus is Lord except by the Holy Spirit** assumes that conversion is at stake. The confession is public, declaring before other witnesses one's absolute allegiance is to Jesus's lordship—it sets oneself apart from non-Christian Jews, for whom these words would sound blasphemous, and non-Christian Gentiles, who might find the claim subversive to Caesar.[110] In such milieu this confession has far more meaning than a charlatan would dare parrot in deception!

Paul's words have at least three corollary implications. First, once God's Spirit dwells in and with the confessor of Jesus as Lord, the Spirit will apportion spiritual gifts to each believer as the Spirit sees fit (12:11, 13). Second, there seems to be no waiting period or subsequent outpouring of God's Spirit that must take place before a believer could operate in spiritual gifts. Every baptized believer is spiritual.[111] Third, since not every utterance or spiritual phenomenon comes from God's Spirit, there is need for discernment among congregation members regarding their use of speaking gifts (cf. 14:26–29). Discernment is all the more necessary if a person who is relatively a new believer makes spiritual utterances. Such manifestations must not be fabricated, manipulated, or expected to come by a self-induced emotional state. Likewise, there is no compelling reason to assume the Spirit's manifestation and gifts center on the notion of "ecstatic" phenomena, or a state of trance caused by spirit-possession, or Christian "spiritism" in which believers become mediums of a plurality of good spirits.[112] The phenomena Paul promotes comes from **the one and same Spirit** (12:4, 11), who, to be sure, could overwhelm believers with a vision or extreme joy, but does not necessarily or even characteristically do so as they operate in prophecy, tongues, and other spiritual gifts. The person is still in control of his or her own faculties (14:32–33).

In 12:4–11 several points are noteworthy. First, the **same Spirit ... Lord ... and ... God who empowers all** are involved in the various apportionments, ministries, and activities of believers. This proto-Trinitarian language of Paul grounds diversity in unity as the appropriate model for all Corinthian members to emulate regarding their service and gifts. The Spirit is viewed as a divine personal entity here, sovereignly bestowing gifts

---

110. Similarly, Fee 1987:581–82.

111. Cf. Eriksson 1998:217.

112. *Pace* respectively, Conzelmann 1975:204; Mount 2005:317–18, 327; Tibbs 2006:69–72, 271–72, 279. Tibbs's "a holy spirit" (12:3) is unlikely given the Spirit's uniqueness in 12:4, 11 and the article τό used with πνεῦμα in e.g., 2 Cor 1:22; 13:13[14]; Gal 5:22; Rom 8:27; etc.

Fourth Supporting Proof (11:2—14:40)

and **distributing to each one individually as He wills** (12:11).[113] Second, the various members each have different gifts (**to one ... to another ...**) but are to work together **for what is beneficial** for the entire body of Christ (12:7; cf. 10:33).[114] Our apostle challenges the Corinthians to turn from a status-seeking orientation to one of voluntary self-giving for the edification of others. Third, the gifts mentioned here are not an exhaustive list (cf. 12:28; Rom 12:4–8; Eph 4:11–12; 1 Pet 4:10–11). They reflect those with which Corinthians are familiar, and some that Paul wishes they would emulate more. Fourth, there seems to be no standard limit to the amount of gifts in which each believer is able to operate; otherwise, Paul would not encourage members to desire the "greater gifts" and prophesying (12:31; 14:1). Fifth, these gifts are not a magical manipulation of forces. God's Spirit has the ultimate authority to permit or deny the human experience of what we today might identify as supernatural occurrences. There may be cases, for example, in which a person who operates in the gift of healing will not be able to heal the sick. Paul's colleagues Timothy and Trophimus were not healed miraculously of their illnesses despite the charismatic gifts of their apostolic colleagues (1 Tim 5:23; 2 Tim 4:20). Finally, these gifts are not merely natural skills or talents; as gifts from God's Spirit they can enhance natural abilities, or be newly added abilities, or both.

Nine gifts are mentioned in 12:8–10. The **word of wisdom** and word of knowledge are gifts related to speaking.[115] The Corinthians are drawn to wisdom, especially as it relates to eloquent speaking (1 Cor 1–4); like Pliny, they might think that talented orators are divinely inspired (*Ep.* 1.20). Paul's slant on wisdom as a gift emphasizes less the skill of articulation and more the enablement of a believer to understand divine revelation and mysteries known by God (2:6–16). Exactly how disclosure of mysteries is different than prophecy is not explained, but they are distinguished (13:2; 14:6, 26). Perhaps this gift's main model is Daniel, the interpreter of dreams, visions, and prophetic and apocalyptic discourse (e.g., Dan 1–2). A more practical application of communicating wisdom may relate to Solomon (e.g., Proverbs). It is sometimes assumed that the **word of knowledge** may involve

---

113. The "spirit [world]" for πνεῦμα in 12:4, 7–9, 11 (Tibbs 2006:279) is hard to reconcile with 12:4–6 where the "Spirit" appears to be a personal entity, not realm, who is in unity with the personal "Lord" and "God."

114. For "another," Paul switches between ἄλλος and ἕτερος. Such is found in other lists (BDAG 399) and may simply substitute the contrastive "μέν ... δέ" (12:8) to highlight a different person (Thiselton 2000:944).

115. See options in Tibbs 2006:202. Isaianic discourse may inform Paul here; the Messianic "root of Jesse," with the Spirit resting on him, operates with the "spirit of wisdom and understanding" and with "the spirit of knowledge" (Isa 11:1–2, 10; cf. Rom 15:12 = Jesus).

extra-natural awareness of thoughts, activities, locations, or circumstances of another person, thing, or group (5:3-4; Acts 5:1-9; Mark 2:6-8; John 1:42, 47-50). Such phenomena, however, seems to be understood by Paul as one aspect of prophecy, or at least overlapping with it (14:24-25). Hence, the gift of knowledge may include or perhaps center on the special ability through the Spirit to communicate truths, insights, and instruction from or relevant to Scripture and the gospel of Christ (13:2; 14:6; cf. 2 Cor 11:6).[116] The word of wisdom and knowledge may begin Paul's gift list to stress that those endowed with such communication have nothing to boast about (8:1-3). They were given these gifts by God's Spirit.

The gift of **faith** means something different than saving faith; otherwise, all believers would have this gift rather than just some. This gift highlights extraordinary trust in God that eventually experiences the thing hoped for, often resulting in the miraculous (cf. 13:2; Mark 11:20-24; Matt 8:23-27; Heb 11). In addition, the ability to work wonders in nature, such as Jesus calming a storm and feeding 5,000 with a few loaves and fishes (Mark 4:35-41; 6:35-44), may be meant. A group that earnestly and persistently prays together in faith may also experience extraordinary answers to their requests (Jas 5:15; Acts 12:5-16). **Gifts of healings** would be especially relevant in Corinth where one of the temples of Asclepius, the savior and god of healing, resided. Divine healing for early Christians confirms the Messianic era has arrived in which those who are sick, blind, lame, or suffer some other infirmity can be made whole again (cf. Luke 7:21-22). The plural "gifts" perhaps suggests diverse ways and conditions in which God might heal through various individuals or communities.[117] Not all healings need to be physical.

The **workings of powers** may overlap in content with other gifts, but unique here may be the "curse" miracles, such as Peter revealing the sin and impending death of Ananias and Sapphira or Paul cursing the false prophet Elymas with temporary blindness (Acts 5:1-11; 13:11).[118] Differently or in addition to this function, some suggest this gift refers to authority *over* these "powers," which are malicious. Hence, this gift is the "effective acts over evil spirits" (15:24; Rom 8:38).[119] Exorcisms similar to the ones Jesus and his disciples performed might fall into this category (Mark 3:14-15; Luke 9:1-2; Acts 16:16-18), and perhaps even raising the dead, which exemplifies power

---

116. Although gifts of knowledge and teaching might overlap (12:8, 28), they are distinguished in 14:6.

117. Godet 1893.2.197; Thiselton 2000:949.

118. See John Chrysostom, *Hom. 1 Cor.* 29:5; Thiselton 953.

119. Tibbs 2006:205-6; cf. Wolff 1996:291.

over death (Mark 5:35–43). Exorcisms would not entirely overlap with **discerning of spirits**. The latter's placement between prophecy and tongues may be due to its primary role of determining whether prophetic and spiritual utterances truly originate from God's Spirit (cf. 14:29). This is apparently discerned subjectively and extra-naturally, though wise criteria may assist. The righteous lifestyle of the prophet (Matt 7:14–21), his or her predictive accuracy (Deut 18:15–22), the prophecy's benefit to other members (1 Cor 14:3), and whether an utterance complements or contradicts apostolic teachings and traditions (15:1–4; cf. Gal 1:6–9), were doubtless among early criteria. God's Spirit must be discerned and distinguished from the prophet's human spirit and demonic spirits (1 Thess 5:19–21; 1 Tim 4:1; 1 John 4:1, 6). This gift is sorely needed by the strong members who seem oblivious to the possibility of demons being present in idol precincts (10:21–22).

Prophecy may involve predicting the future (Acts 11:27–28; 21:10–11), but more centrally it is "the proclamation of a revelation imparted by God, not by human wisdom."[120] The gift's spontaneity is evident in 14:29–32, but this should not be equated with ecstatic irrationality.[121] **Tongues**, or glossolalia, is the "ability to speak some kind of language unknown to the speaker."[122] Paul mentions **various kinds of** tongues, which suggests there is more than one species of Spirit-led voices. Hence, we do not need to decide here between tongues as a human foreign language, a language similar to but not the same as a foreign language, a sub- or non-linguistic utterance, or heavenly languages of angels.[123] Nevertheless, more than mere aptitude for speaking foreign languages *known* to the speaker is meant here given that tongues is in a list of miraculous gifts endowed by God's Spirit. Dale Martin may be right that for the ancient world of Corinth, speaking in tongues implied high status since it was assumed to be the language of angels and gods (*T. Job* 48–50; Dio Chrysostom *Or.* 11.22).[124] If so, then perhaps status-seeking congregants interpreted the gift this way and excelled in it, which may be one reason why Paul encourages prophesy over tongues (1 Cor 14). He promotes that the Spirit distributes gifts as the Spirit sees fit, which among

---

120. Ahn 2013:179, and for discussion, 175–84. Although prophecy includes revelation, not all revelation is prophecy (see word of wisdom in 12:8; 14:6, 26; Hiu 2010:128).

121. With Ahn 2013:182–84; Fee 1996:171.

122. Turner 2006:13.

123. See respectively, Forbes 1997:63; Garland 2003:584; Thiselton 1979:15–36; Fee 1987:598, 630–31. Not every human expression prompted by God's Spirit should be automatically relegated to either human or heavenly intelligent languages (Acts 2:5–12; 1 Cor 13:1), as the spiritual groaning in Rom 8:26 exemplifies.

124. Martin 1995:87–92.

other things implies that these gifts are neither for status elevation nor the exclusive possession of the spiritually elite.[125] The **interpretation of tongues** does not necessarily need to be a verbatim translation of the utterance, but a spoken disclosure of what was said or expected by the utterance; it provides meaning to the experience (cf. 14:5, 13, 26).[126] This gift also may bring into articulation what is unintelligible, and perhaps even sub- or unconscious.[127]

Paul shifts from this list to compare solidarity of the human body with church members as the **body of Christ** (12:12–27). Although congregation members function metaphorically as body parts in this discourse, their connection with Christ is real because they all share the same Spirit of God who dwells with them as with the risen Christ: **for just as the body is one and has many members . . . so it is with Christ**. Bodily solidarity was reflected also in Stoic thought that observed the universe as a body in which unity with deities provides the background for ethical modes of unity for humans, who are in obligation to one another (Marcus *Med.* 2.1; 7.13; Seneca *Lucil.* 95.52).[128] Such analogies were widespread in the Greco-Roman world, and they frequently promote social and political unity (Xenophon *Mem.* 2.3.18; Cicero *Off.* 3.5.22–23; Dio Chrysostom *Or.* 3.104–7).[129] The fable of Menenius Agrippa is well-known in which the mouth, hands, and teeth rebel against the belly. They refuse to give it food, but for obvious reasons this turns out to be detrimental both for themselves and the whole body (Livy *Hist.* 2.32.12–33).[130] Mitchell observes that Paul's metaphor of the body applies to those of political writers, including the use of body parts, their personification, gift differentiation, and community contributions, gifts for the "common advantage," and the sharing of one soul or spirit. These common political topoi used for combating factionalism in social organisms Paul transfers over to the social body of Christ for the purpose of unity in response to divisions in the community.[131] A major distinction for Paul is that he connects such topoi with baptism into Christ.

The one Spirit unifies and connects all these believers as one body (12:13; cf. 6:17),[132] which may suggest a mystical union in which Christ lives

---

125. See Bryan 2008:98–99.
126. Cf. Collins 1999:456; Garland 2003:586.
127. So Ahn 2013:162; Thiselton 2000:17–24; Theissen 1987:292–340.
128. See further, Lee 2006:101. Kim 2008; 2013:29, stresses an ethical dimension for the corporate body of Christ, though (unlike Kim) the Spirit's activity highlights Christ's resurrected rather than crucified body (e.g., Rom 8:11).
129. Martin 1995:92–93.
130. Horsley 1998:171.
131. Mitchell 1991:159–61.
132. With Liu 2013:160–61.

Fourth Supporting Proof (11:2—14:40)

in them and they in Christ (Gal 2:20; 3:27; Col 3:17).[133] In this collective body every member counts regardless of ethnic (**whether Jew or Greek**) and status differentiations (**whether slave or free**).[134] Baptism here doubtlessly refers to conversion-initiation since those who participate in it become members that belong to the body of Christ. Although in the parallel passage of Gal 3:27-28, in which water baptism is in view, Paul finds no problem using the term *baptize* for both the water ritual and conversion-initiation in the Spirit (see 10:2). He focuses on the latter here—**in one Spirit we all were baptized into one body** of Christ.[135] Spirit baptism for Paul may be viewed both as a conversion event (12:13) and indwelling (Rom 8:9). This picture is not much different than the baptism in the Spirit mentioned in Acts 10:44—11:18 in which the first uncircumcised Gentile converts, Cornelius and his household, are baptized in Spirit and speak in tongues (prior to water baptism), though for Paul tongues is only one of many spiritual gifts, and not everyone has this gift (12:28-30).[136] Rather than water, the Spirit is the element in which believers are baptized. They have been drenched with the Spirit, similar to plants that are **watered** (3:8) or as a cloud burst that soaked them with a downpour of the Spirit (Isa 29:10; Ezek 32:56).[137] This imagery is compatible with and perhaps originates from Joel 2:28-32 (3:1-5LXX).[138] The text of Joel is a bedrock for emergent Christians who identify themselves as the "church" (see 1:2). It anticipates an era in which God would pour out the Spirit on the faithful, and they will call on the name of the Lord; the latter idea perhaps prompts Paul's expression "Jesus is Lord" in 12:3. This outpouring would result in God's people experiencing visions, dreams, and prophecy. For Paul, when the saints assemble together, spiritual manifestations concomitant with Joel's message take place.

Our apostle embarks on discussing various body parts in relation to the corporate body of Christ. The Corinthians would not seem to be unfamiliar with such imagery since local legends include stories about Medea, the

---

133. See Meyer 1877.2.84. The "in Christ" model (Schrage 1999:3.214-15) is more explicit in Rom 12:4-6. For various interpretations, see Schnabel 2006:723-25.

134. Unlike the parallel Gal 3:28, male/female is missing in 12:13, perhaps deliberatively since inclusion might have served as a catalyst for the Corinthians' lack of gender distinction (11:2-16).

135. Alternatively, Rabens 2013:107, suggests with Spirit-initiation the use of synecdoche in which "a part is being used as reference to the whole" of conversion that includes other elements such as water baptism (cf. 6:11).

136. On distinctions between Luke-Acts and Paul on Spirit phenomena, see Dunn 1970; 1975.

137. See Dunn 1998:418, 421.

138. See further, Zeller 2010:399.

Fourth Supporting Proof (11:2—14:40)

infamous wife of Jason, who was responsible for cutting into pieces the bodies of her brother and Jason's uncle (see Introduction).[139] Paul, however, personifies body parts humorously to instruct about solidarity. The **foot** and **ear** feel unworthy because they are not the **hand** and **eye**, respectively, and Paul asks rhetorical questions about whether the foot and ear are any less part of the body because of this. The expected answer is "no." Similarly, the body parts that think too highly of themselves, the **eye** and **head**, cannot say to the **hand** and **feet**, respectively, **I have no need of you**. The questions posed in 12:17, 19 imagine the monstrosities of a single body part becoming the entire body, whether one gigantic eye, ear, or another part. These questions prompt his auditors to agree that each member of the body is necessary for the whole to function properly. The center of Paul's chiasm drives home the points that there are **many parts and yet one body**, and that **God** has sovereignly **placed the members, each one of them in the body, just as He wanted**. Paul teaches interdependence contrary to the claim of not needing other parts; the body depends on the diversity of its members.[140]

The solidarity promoted in this body celebrates the members that might seem to be **less important, insignificant,** and **unpresentable** (such as genitalia). These members, the apostle insists, are **necessary**, should be given **honor**, and receive **greater presentability**, respectively (12:22–24). God has composed the body together **giving greater honor to the member who feels inferior**. Such disposition turns out for the greater benefit of the entire body. Along this line, Aesop relates a fable in which the eyes blame the human they belong to for having the mouth gain pleasure from many things, especially honey. The human then gives the eyes honey, which makes them cry in pain as they learn that honey is unpleasant for them (Dio Chrysostom *Or.* 33.16). Paul's social body, moreover, calls into question assumptions of political bodies that favor those who are considered by society to be significant: the elitists and upper classes. Honor instead goes to those considered less honorable.[141] This is the way God operates in the body of Christ—status does not matter. The elevated recognition of the lowly will help prevent schisms in the congregation, and Paul suggests a new order in which members do not boast and compete against each other but recognize their mutual dependency and **care for one another**. As one body in Christ they are to **rejoice** together with those who are honored, and **suffer** with

---

139. Corinth's sanctuary for Asclepius also had grateful devotees offer various replicas of body parts that had been healed by the god, but these votive offerings date back to the fifth and fourth centuries BCE (Wickkiser 2010:43–44, 53), making it rather questionable that they were still visible to the Corinthians of Paul's day.

140. Cf. Lee 2006:150.

141. See Martin 1995:94–96.

Fourth Supporting Proof (11:2—14:40)

those who suffer (12:26). The latter especially embarks on what it is to be a caring community that empathizes with others (cf. 2 Cor 1:3–7). To be one body is to stand in unity with every body part.

This chapter closes with Paul listing church positions of **apostles first, prophets second, and teachers third**, and then those who operate in various spiritual gifts (12:28–31a). The three offices are appointed by God, and perhaps this ranking reflects the way earliest churches were originally founded. Jesus's disciples first established his church as apostles (Acts 1–2), and later on the offices of prophets and teachers were called to continue nurturing churches that had been established (Acts 13:1–3). Even so, one could hardly deny that such positions identify church leaders. They head this list not so that people in this position could "rule" over other members, but that they could serve others, similar to Christ's teaching that the disciple who is first must become the servant of all (Mark 9:33–35). The apostles are witnesses of Christ's resurrection and sent-out as missionaries proclaiming the gospel and establishing churches (1 Cor 9:1–2). Prophets, as Thiselton identifies, "perform speech-acts of announcement, proclamation, judgment, challenge, comfort, support, or encouragement."[142] In certain verses the prophet seems to be indistinguishable from anyone with the gift of prophecy (14:29–31). The former, however, also appears to have some sort of leadership position or authoritative role in the church, similar to Agabus and the prophets in Antioch (Acts 11:27–28; 13:1–2; 21:10–12).[143] Teachers "perform speech-acts of transmission, communicative explanation, interpretation of texts, establishment of creeds, exposition of meaning and implication, and, more cognitive, less temporally applied communicative acts."[144]

Two gifts are mentioned for the first time in 12:28 including **helps** and **administrations**. "Helps" seems to be for those endowed with the ability to serve well in various capacities in the congregation, often doing menial but absolutely necessary tasks behind the scenes that rarely get recognized, such as cleaning and running errands. "Administrations" conveys the idea of steering a ship, directing, or governing, and here perhaps it reflects the gift of guiding and counseling others (cf. Rom 12:8). Together, these gifts perhaps involve doing the functions of deacons and overseers, respectively.[145] To what extent these two may be considered Spirit-given or supernatural is not mentioned. The gifts on this list appear to be in order of prominence,

---

142. Thiselton 2000:1017.

143. See further distinctions in Forbes 1997:246.

144. Thiselton 2000:1017. Thiselton's mention of creeds seems anachronistic unless understood simply as the earliest basic statements and traditions of emergent Christian beliefs.

145. See Dunn 1975:252–53.

or at least tongues and the interpretation of tongues, which are placed last (12:30; cf. v.10). It so happens that Paul considers prophecy to be greater than tongues (1 Cor 14), and the Corinthians should seek greater gifts. The gifts may be ranked on the basis of how they benefit others (14:6),[146] and if so, then the greater gifts require greater utilization for edifying others rather than boasting in one's spirituality. Perhaps the gifts of wisdom, knowledge, and prophecy are assumed to be operating through the offices of apostle, teacher, and prophet. These tidy distinctions, however, tend to overlap since Paul and other individuals may operate in much more than one gift.

Paul ends the chapter with rhetorical questions posed to reinforce auditors to recognize the importance of gift diversity and dependency on those who have them. They are to reply, "no, not all are apostles, prophets . . . .or possess gifts of healings, or speak in tongues," and so on. Although the Spirit distributes gifts as the Spirit wills, Paul encourages congregants to **earnestly desire the greater gifts**. This suggests that fervent prayer, the action behind earnest desire (14:12–13), might result in a divine willingness to grant petitioners their requests for new spiritual endowments.

LOVE AS THE SUPERLATIVE WAY (13:1–13)

Paul explicates love's role at the center of his discussion on spiritual gifts. It is **a more superlative way** than pursuing greater gifts (12:31b).[147] He discusses love (ἀγάπη) more as a "way" than an emotion, which Hays distills as "a manner of life within which all the fits are to find their proper place."[148] Thiselton rightly asserts here that love "denotes above all a stance or attitude which shows itself in acts of will as regard, respect, and concern for the welfare of the other. It is therefore profoundly christological, for the cross is the paradigm case of the act of will and stance which places welfare of others above the interests of the self."[149] Paul already stressed the importance of God's love and loving one's neighbor (8:1–3), and now he exhibits love using epideictic rhetoric, more specifically an encomium in praise of love (esp. 13:4–7).[150] Encomia personifying virtues were well known (1 Esd 4:33–41;

---

146. So Garland 2003:598; Smit 1993:224.

147. Thurén 2001:101 posits that καθ᾽ ὑπερβολὴν is "by means of hyperbole." Although there is hyperbole (e.g., 13:2), it does not characterize the entire discourse, and elsewhere Paul uses καθ᾽ ὑπερβολὴν in a superlative sense (2 Cor 1:8; Gal 1:13; Rom 7:13).

148. Hays 1997:222.

149. Thiselton 2000:1035, italics in the original.

150. E.g., Smit 1991:193–216 on former; Sampley 2002:950, on latter. For various interpretations of the discourse, see Focant 1996:211–15; Wischmeyer 1981:191–223.

Fourth Supporting Proof (11:2—14:40)

Aphthonius *Prog.* 8[38.25R–40.27R]; Aristides *Or.* 24.42).[151] Paul, however, presents himself as an example regarding love and thus keeps the encomium serving the purpose of deliberative rhetoric.[152] Although similar love lists were known,[153] Paul shows no dependence on these or other traditions. Our apostle presents the futility of spiritual gifts without love (13:1–3), identifies two descriptors of what love is (13:4a), and then using anaphora (repetition) he enlists eight things that love does "not" do and four things love "always" does (13:4b–7). The temporal and incomplete state of spiritual gifts is then set in antithesis to love's enduring and complete character (13:8–12). The conclusion uses asyndeton (no conjunctions) to exhibit love as the greatest way. In keeping with Paul's appeal for unity, love promotes concord and combats against factions.[154] Without love, members in the body of Christ would be using their gifts for selfish purposes and not for the care and edification of other members. The importance of love in 1 Cor 12–14, then, is essential—spiritual gifts have no value without it.[155]

Paul presents himself hypothetically as a person excelling in spiritual gifts but failing to operate in love (13:1–3). He takes the gifts in these verses to their full potential in order to make their uselessness without love all the more amplified. The **tongues of humans and of angels** together probably refer to both human languages, as in Acts 2:1–13, and heavenly languages.[156] Such glossolalia are included among the "varieties" of tongues in 1 Cor 12:10. Daniel Wallace claims in 13:1–3 that Paul moves from the actual (e.g., gift of prophecy) to hypothetical (e.g., Paul does *not* understand all mysteries and knowledge): "It is therefore probable that Paul could speak in the tongues of human beings, but *not* in the tongues of *angels* (v. 1)."[157] Although the hypothetical seems impossible to achieve if promoting omniscience in v. 2, it *is* achievable with the gift of sacrificial giving in v. 3. Hence, Wallace's model is not entirely consistent. Moreover, since Paul and the Corinthians' tongues are not understood (see 14:2, 6, 15–16, 18), and other Jews believe that humans could speak in heavenly languages (*T.*

---

151. Sigountos 1994:255–56.

152. See Collins 1999:474, though negatively in 13:1–3, then positively in 13:11–12.

153. E.g., Plato *Symp.* 197C–197E; Maximus of Tyre *Diss.* 20.2; Conzelmann 1975:219–20.

154. E.g., Polybius 23.11.2–3; Ps-Phocylides *Sent.* 219; Mitchell 1991:166–69.

155. See Aguilar Chiu 2007:328.

156. Possibly, human tongues includes "new" tongues (Mark 16:17[A, TR]). Tongues of angels is probably not hyperbole for eloquence; Paul associates eloquence with wisdom (1:17; 2:1, 4). Perhaps he heard angelic voices during his third heaven experience (2 Cor 12:3–4). On esoteric-angelic languages, see Poirier 2010:81–140.

157. Wallace 1996:698.

Job 48–50; *Apoc. Zeph.* 8.3–4),[158] it is more plausible to surmise that Paul thought such languages were not only attainable but that he himself could speak in them.[159] Max Turner perceptively suggests that "like most modern Pentecostals/charismatics without linguistic expertise, [Paul] would simply assume that utterances that sounded like unknown languages (and were capable of charismatic 'interpretation') *were* kinds of languages (earthly or heavenly)."[160]

Without love, in any case, the most sublime tongues are reduced to the sound of **reverberating bronze or a clanging cymbal**.[161] These sounds might be heard at cultic processions such as with Bacchic/Dionysian or Cybele festivities.[162] Paul's point, however, is not to compare tongues with cultic instruments but with sounds from something that is lifeless.[163] Likewise, these sounds are simply noise without melody (14:7–8). One application of this is that without love, those who utter unknown tongues in public will not bother to seek an interpreter; they only want to edify themselves and not others. As such, their tongues are merely noise.

Prophecy itself either discloses **all mysteries and all knowledge**, or these are three distinct spiritual gifts. Since the revelation of "mysteries" may refer to the word of wisdom, and "knowledge" refers to the word of knowledge (12:8; 14:6, 26), three gifts is the preferable view. These gifts are totally deficient without love, but when operating in love they seek to edify others (14:3, 26).[164] The gift of **faith** is exemplified by Paul's metaphoric ability **to remove mountains**, echoing what Jesus taught (Matt 17:20; Mark 11:22–24). Without love, however, these gifts result in him saying, **I am**

---

158. The former mentions Job's three daughters given sashes and enabled to speak in "angelic dialect," the "dialect of the archons," and the "dialect of those on high," respectively (OTP 1.85–66).

159. If for the sake of argument, he is agreeing with the Corinthians' own belief that their tongues include angelic languages but disbelieves it himself, his claim to speak in tongues more than all of them (14:18), and his command for them to not prohibit tongues (14:39), seem disingenuous.

160. Turner 2006:16–17.

161. Paul's use of χαλκὸς ἠχῶν may refer to an acoustic bronze jar that amplifies one's voice in theatre (Klein 1986:286–89), a gong (ISV), or a "ringing bronze-thing" further explicated by Paul as a "loud-sounding cymbal" (Portier-Young 2005:101; Ciampa/Rosner, 2010:629).

162. Ovid *Fasti* 3.740–42; Pliny *Ep.* 2.14; Philostratus *Vit. soph.* 1.520; Schrage 1999:3.286–87; Wolff 1996:314–15. See responses in Schnabel 2006:761; Forbes 1997:124–48.

163. See Zeller 2010:408.

164. Grudem 1988:155, adds further elements combining prophesy and love.

Fourth Supporting Proof (11:2—14:40)

nothing—I am "spiritually zero."[165] The gift of generosity (Rom 12:8) is described in sacrificial terms and enables Paul to **dole out all my possessions** to the poor and **surrender my body that I may boast**.[166] Paul speaks of his body becoming a living sacrifice for the gospel's sake, which entails suffering (Rom 12:1; 2 Cor 11:23–33), and his boast anticipates a reward for his labor at the second coming (3:14; Phil 2:16–17).[167] This is reminiscent of Jesus's promises that those who give up their possessions to follow him will be rewarded, whether in this life or the next (Mark 10:28–30; Luke 12:32–33; 18:22). All the same, sacrificial giving without love provides no such benefit for the giver.

Love is personified and stands for someone characterized by love in 13:4–7.[168] The placement of the phrase **love waits patiently and shows kindness** at the beginning of Paul's list underscores Corinthian necessity to behave with such virtues when gathering together for church and operating in spiritual gifts. They must be patient and kind, for example, to every member and wait their turn to share a spiritual word (14:26–31), along with being courteous to weak and poor members (8:7–13; 11:33–34; 12:21–24). More generally, patience is required through suffering and working with others (Rom 12:12; 1 Thess 5:14–15).[169]

The next eight descriptors each use a negative particle (οὐ) and may aim to discourage various shortcomings in the congregation. That love does **not stir envy** challenges their discordant behavior in 3:3. Love **does not brag** and is **not puffed up** discourages their attitude of arrogance and thinking themselves superior to others (4:6–7; 8:1–2). Love does **not behave indecently** confronts sexual impropriety (7:36), and love **seeks not its own** recalls their need to alter selfishness ways in table fellowship (10:24, 33; 11:33–34). If love were the Greek word ἔρως, perhaps it would desire to seek its own, as in myths of the god *Eros*, who as a suitor seeks to possess objects for self-gratification. Paul instead identifies love in opposition to self-love.[170] The idea of love **not** being **provoked** to anger may discourage irritability

---

165. Spicq 1963:2.147; Thiselton 2000:1042.

166. Certain manuscripts have "that I should be burned" (ἵνα καυθήσομαι: e.g., C, D; cf. NKJV, ESV), which emphasizes persecution and martyrdom (e.g., 2 Macc 7:4–5). However, "that I may boast" (ἵνα καυχήσωμαι) has more reliable manuscript support (see Malone 2009:401–6), and it makes better sense to suggest that later scribes had altered the perplexing "boast" to "burn" rather than the reverse (Hays 1997:225).

167. Ciampa/Rosner 2010:637, are similar but highlight that martyrdom is still meant (2 Tim 4:6).

168. Anderson 2013:556.

169. See Montague 2011:226.

170. See Nygren 1957:130; Thiselton 2000:1050.

Fourth Supporting Proof (11:2—14:40)

that engenders rivalry and grumbling in the congregation (1:11; 3:3; 10:10). That it does **not take account of wrongs done** seems related to their taking other members to court (see 6:7–8). If so, then it may be implied that the plaintiff should show forgiveness, refuse to harbor resentment, and relent from "getting even." The notion that love **rejoices not in injustice but co-rejoices with the truth** may be relevant especially for deterring those who do wrong to other members and thus provoke them to battle in court. Instead, they should stand for the truth of a matter and not bear false witness.

Many of love's qualities in this encomium are multifaceted and should not be limited *only* to things immediately relevant to the Corinthian situation. The notion of co-rejoicing, for example, is important for the body life of any church (12:26), and truth may include one's perception of God, Christ, and the gospel (Rom 1:18; 2 Cor 11:10; Gal 2:5).[171] The exercise of love would seem to be key in resolving many conflicts in a church.

Four further descriptors enhance the virtually limitless extent to which love perseveres and never fails—it **bears all things, believes all things, hopes all things, endures all things**. The first phrase is inclusive of putting up with the faults of others, not giving in to ungodly ways, and not permitting discouragement to fester on account of afflictions and disappointments. It forms an *inclusio* with "endures all things" and overlaps in meaning.[172] The latter, though, stresses love's final perseverance and sets the stage for the next verse that declares, **love never falls away** (13:8a). The statements between the *inclusio* are repeated again as faith and hope in 13:13. Rather than conveying naivety, belief and hope are the means by which endurance is supplemented—they persist despite whatever obstacles and hardships might come their way. These virtues eventually point to the idea that love is supreme and remains forever; it "conquers all things" (Virgil, *Eclog.* 10.86).

Love's permanent stability is then set in contrast to three spiritual gifts, each of which will eventually fail (13:8–12). This stresses again that love is greater than any spiritual gift. **Prophecy, tongues** and **knowledge** have temporal value; in the present era they contribute partially to the full knowledge that will be revealed **when what is complete has come**. This completion or perfection (τέλειος) does not refer to the close of New Testament canonical revelation (a view that is anachronistic since Paul, and especially the Corinthians, would not even understand what this means).[173] Nor does

---

171. Cf. Wischmeyer 1981:102–3.

172. See Ciampa/Rosner 2010:649–50, in which the former is "never give in" (to worldly pressure) and the latter is "never give up."

173. Wallace 1996:422, distinguishes between tongues that *die out* (παύω in middle voice) and prophecy/knowledge that will be *done away* (καταργέω in passive voice) to suggest that tongues may have died out before the time when the "perfect" comes. But

Fourth Supporting Proof (11:2—14:40)

it refer to Christian maturity in love (Paul had such maturity yet still speaks in tongues: 2:6; 14:18).[174] It refers to the completion of the ages at the second coming of Christ. Spiritual gifts, then, inclusive of tongues, are expected to operate until Christ returns (1:7).[175] In 13:9, "**For**" introduces the explanation of when and why these gifts will end.[176] In the verses that follow, the repetitive use of **now** at the present time and **then** at that future time supports that the present age has these spiritual gifts as a partial revelation, and the coming age does away with these gifts since at Christ's return the full revelation will be present with believers. Paul uses two illustrations to support the idea of eschatological completion. First, the words, **when I was a child** invites auditors to recall earlier years when they spoke, thought, and reasoned like a child, but this was all prior to their coming of age when they **set aside childish things**. This is likened to spiritual gifts in the present age in relation to the future age of completion when believers will set aside their gifts as though toys.[177] Presently they can only communicate knowledge and prophecy **in part**, which suggests that such communication is incomplete and fragmentary, providing only glimpses of what is up ahead.

Second, the believers' perception of spiritual things and God in Christ are compared with looking **by means of a mirror indirectly or in a riddle**.[178] Such imagery would be entirely relevant for recipients familiar with bronze mirrors produced in Corinth.[179] Mirrors made of this material needed to be polished regularly to see one's image clearer. Paul may be assuming a well-known Jewish and Hellenistic sentiment that what is divine can only be seen or known indirectly, as it were, through things that "represent the divine and which are to be regarded as 'signs' or 'images' of God."[180] If so, then knowing **face to face** means the mirror will be set aside and believers will see

---

this interpretation overlooks how verb use forms a chiastic pattern of prophecy (A), tongues (B), and knowledge (A1) in 13:8 that stylistically helps avoid "tedious repetition" (Fisk 2000:89) instead of imply an earlier cessation of tongues than the other two gifts. There is no evidence in the NT to support that Paul or any apostle knew or taught that tongues would cease before other gifts.

174. And if referring to this maturity for the church worldwide, when could that ever take place except at the second coming?

175. See further arguments in Oropeza 1/2017; Schnabel 2006:775–76.

176. Ciampa/Rosner 2010:655.

177. Καταργέω ("set aside," "abolish") describes both the ending of gifts (13:8, 10) and childish ways (13:11).

178. Αἴνιγμα ("riddle," "indirectly") may be another example of Paul's use of double entendre (see 4:6 Excursus).

179. See Arzt-Grabner et al. 2006:442.

180. Hollander 2010:397; cf. Philo *Leg. All.* 3.101; Plutarch *Is. Os.* 76[383A–B]; Lindemann 2000:291.

directly God or Christ or both. This phrase alludes to Moses knowing God face to face (Exod 33:11; Deut 32:10). In Num 12:6-8, from which Paul's word "riddle" seems developed, God speaks to Moses "mouth to mouth" and not in riddles. He receives direct words from the divine Presence in the cloud, and not in dreams and visions as do other prophets. Moses is also able to see the very "glory" of the Lord. Later Jewish debates try to distinguish how Moses had clearer access to God than the prophets. For instance, Rabbi Judah bar Ilai, using Num 12:8 as one of his texts, believes the prophets saw God though nine mirrors but Moses only through one (*Lev. Rab.* 1:14). Other sages suggested the prophets saw God in a blurry or tarnished mirror whereas Moses saw God through a clear or polished one.[181] In the age to come, however, all flesh will see the glory of the Lord (Isa 40:5). Paul may have known similar interpretations in his own day.[182] For him the mirror's image in 13:12 is not one's own face but the face of God, though known indirectly as from spiritual speech gifts. Believers perceive that face and glory only partially and indirectly. When the future culmination of all things takes place, the glorious image of God in Christ will be seen directly. Then Paul (along with the faithful) will know the Lord **face to face** and fully **know just as also I am known** by the Lord (cf. 2 Cor 3:18; 4:6, 14; 1 John 3:2; Rev 22:4). The second coming of Christ, then, is that time when full knowledge, revelation, and recognition of God in Christ reaches its completion. Partial recognition, characterized by the gifts of tongues, prophecy, and knowledge, will then become obsolete.

Until then, **faith, hope, and love** remain prominent in the present age. This triad presents an alternative to the triad of tongues, prophecy, and knowledge.[183] Paul perhaps selected these virtues since they identify well what it is to be in Christ.[184] They also have special relevance to enduring affliction (1 Thess 1:3-8; 5:8; Rom 5:1-5). If we can repeat Horsley's perceptive ideas, faith inaugurates and enables the new life in Christ in the present age; hope enables those in Christ to endure problems of this age; and love holds together those in Christ as a community "in anticipation of the completion of God's fulfillment . . . into the kingdom."[185] In the age to come Paul implies that faith and hope will be set aside since recognizing God face to face will replace belief in what is not seen (2 Cor 5:7), and with

---

181. See Fishbane 1986:71

182. Ibid. 74; Ciampa/Rosner 2010:659-60.

183. Malcolm 2013b:124. Similarly, the "fruit of the Spirit" (Gal 5:22-23) is more important than "gifts of the Spirit."

184. See Lang 1994:188.

185. Horsley 1998:179.

Fourth Supporting Proof (11:2—14:40)

the future hope having finally arrived, there is no need to hope anymore (Rom 8:23–25). What remains perpetually is love, which is to characterize the intimate relationship believers have with God and each other both now and forever.

Prophecy as Greater than Tongues (14:1–19)

Now that Paul has expounded on spiritual gifts as beneficial for the solidarity of members (1 Cor 12), and their value as worthless without love (13), he proceeds to address their ability to build up members when they assemble together (14:3–5, 12, 17, 26).[186] Their coming together is reminiscent of language used when participating in the Lord's Supper (14:26; cf. 11:17–18, 33) and perhaps is suggestive of speech-acts that take place after dinner, as though at a Christian symposium. This chapter compares tongues and prophecy (esp. 14:1–5), which suggests a use of *synkrisis* in which two gifts rather than persons are being compared, and prophecy turns out to be the greater gift.[187] Paul also employs rhetorical questions (4:6–8, 9, 16, 23, 36), illustration (14:7–8), paranomasia (word plays: 14:10, 38), hyperbole (14:18–19), and Scripture citation (14:21). His designation "brothers and sisters" breaks the discourse into four parts (14:6, 20, 26, 39), and evokes images of a family being taught wisdom in relation to building up one another (as well as outsiders), which is done through the harmonious and orderly use of speech gifts. The importance of speaking the same thing (1:10) rather than speaking in a disharmonious and unintelligible manner, fosters unity and edification. Dio Chrysostom promotes a similar rhetorical tact by advancing the significance of an assembly having a common language for the sake of concord (*Or.* 32.29; 39.3).[188] In keeping with deliberative rhetoric, Paul presents himself as someone to imitate, hypothetically speaking (14:6, 11, 14–15, 19). A string of imperatives related to proper conduct when assembling together reinforces that what Paul says here is the "command of the Lord" (14:37; cf. 1, 12–13, 20, 26–30, 34–35, 37, 39–40).

The Corinthians foremost are to **pursue love and earnestly desire spiritual things, and in particular (earnestly desire) that you may prophesy**.[189] This is not because prophecy is the greatest of all spiritual gifts. It

---

186. See Fee 1987:652.

187. On synkrisis, see further, Aristotle *Rhet.* 1.9.36–41; Theon *Prog.* 10[9].112–15; Oropeza 2016:227–28, 637–41.

188. See Witherington 1995:275.

189. On μᾶλλον δέ as "particularly"/"even more," see examples in Arzt-Grabner et al. 2006:446.

in fact lacks preeminence in the list of 12:8–10, is only one of a number of "greater gifts" at best (12:31a), and *interpreted* tongues has virtually the same benefit (14:5).[190] Paul encourages prophecy because it edifies congregation members, whereas speaking in tongues, if uninterpreted, does not. Our apostle instructs them thusly to curb the tide of their apparent obsession with tongues. He explains that **the one who speaks in a tongue . . . speaks mysteries in spirit**. This phenomenon involves the believer's human spirit being connected to, drenched with, and empowered by the Holy Spirit to speak thusly. The Spirit is the giver of the gift (12:7–11) and also plays an intercessory role in prayer (Rom 8:26–27). This person utters mysteries in that what is spoken is unintelligible to both the speaker and hearers—this person **speaks not to humans but God, for no one understands** the language (14:2; cf. 14:14).[191] The utterance is directed to God and is thus a prayer or praise, and it also **edifies** the self not because the speaker understands the language spoken, but because the speaker's spirit communes with God's Spirit (14:4, 14–15; cf. Jude 20).

Although Paul's earlier references may be inclusive of human foreign languages as one species of tongues (12:10; 13:1a), this variation does not fit his description in 14:2 since neither he nor anyone else seems to recognize the language. It is remotely possible that he means, *generally speaking*, no one understands it, but this possibility becomes even more remote when we read that Paul assumes the Corinthians would not understand him if he came speaking in tongues to them (14:6). If he were speaking a human foreign language, it is very likely that *someone* in a multilingual center like Corinth *would* understand him and be able to translate.[192] At least one study that records and examines contemporary tongues considers it a unique dialect or "pseudo-language" without definite linguistic structure.[193] Along this line it can be said that the Spirit does not need a real language to prompt sounds and utterances through humans.[194] But we simply do not know that contemporary glossolalia has the same structure as Corinthian glossolalia, nor yet that all contemporary glossolalia uniformly fits the description

---

190. Also, ἵνα ("that") in 14:1, 5, is not understood in the final sense of "in order that," but as a marker for an object clause in which the ἵνα-construct functions as a substitute for an infinitive (see 4:2; 14:12; BDAG 476). Hence, tongues and other spiritual things are *not* for the purpose of prophesying.

191. In 14:2 ἀκούω does not mean to "hear"—others *do* hear the tongues (e.g., 14:9, 16, 23, 27–28); it means to "understand" (cf. Mark 4:33; BDAG 38). See options for μυστήρια ("mysteries") in Schnabel 2006:792–93.

192. Garland 2003:584.

193. Samarin 1969:60–64.

194. See Thiselton 2000:1100.

Fourth Supporting Proof (11:2—14:40)

of "pseudo-language."[195] That Paul identifies the content of tongues with "words" in 14:19 may suggest something more than sub-linguistic utterances or groanings as in Rom 8:26–27.[196] In this chapter, if tongues are human foreign languages, they must be very unique ones. More plausibly, they are "new" languages (Mark 16:17[A, TR]), or angelic languages (13:1b), or a combination of these.

Paul's **I wish you all to speak in tongues** does not necessitate that everyone does or should have this gift. Since the Corinthians already excel in it, Paul concedes to its value,[197] and he tries to build rapport with them this way so as to be more persuasive when saying, **even more I wish you would prophesy**. Prophecy is preferred over tongues since it is comprehensible and thus beneficial for the **edification** (14:5, 12, 26) **and exhortation** (Rom 15:4; Heb 13:22) **and consolation** of church members (1 Thess 2:12; 5:14). Important prophetic aims include the advancement of ethical conduct and deeper understanding of the confessed gospel.[198] The extra-natural aspect of this gift seems emphasized (e.g., 14:24–25) in which words are "given by the Spirit in a particular situation and ceases when the words cease."[199]

The first instance of **brothers and sisters** in this chapter helps delineate a structural turn in which the conditional conjunction ἐάν (normally "if") plays a significant role. It appears seven times in 4:6–19 and often guides hypothetical questions that prompt auditors to agree with Paul's reasoning. His first question asks whether it would benefit them **if I came speaking in tongues**. The expected answer is that he would not benefit them unless he were to use an intelligible speech gift such as **revelation . . . knowledge . . . prophecy or teaching** (4:6; cf. 12:8, 10, 28).[200] He then poses two more questions regarding the musical instruments of **flute . . . lyre . . . trumpet**.[201] The anticipated answers are that if these instruments fail to make distinctive sounds, it will not be known what is being played and, for the trumpet, no one will prepare for war. In essence, unless musical sounds have recognizable melodies, they are similar to the modern analogy of a cat walking on a piano. Similarly, a fourth question poses that unless the Corinthians utter

---

195. E.g., Keener 2011:1.328–29, documents a number of modern cases of the miraculous use of foreign languages similar to Acts 2:1-11.

196. See Ciampa/Rosner 2010:695.

197. See Hovenden 2002:120.

198. See Gillespie 1994:144–49.

199. Dunn 1975:228.

200. Though "revelation" is not named as a gift, it perhaps refers to the word of wisdom (see 12:8) or more generally as any Spirit-prompted speech (14:26–30).

201. This first two are found in 1 Sam[Kgdms]10:5 and in religious Hellenistic practices (Collins 1999:496). On the trumpet's use in the LXX, see Hiu 2010:57.

Fourth Supporting Proof (11:2—14:40)

clear and intelligible speech, **how will it be known what is spoken?** Though they may be speaking to God, for others it is as though they are **speaking into the air**—their voices serve no purpose.

His word-play on **many kinds of *sounds* in the world, and none is without sound** (φωνῶν ... ἄφωνον) is inclusive of but not limited to human languages. These words may evoke sounds in the city, and perhaps Paul's recollection of noises he heard at his workshop in Corinth. These include the sounds of workers, vendors, haggling, yelling, Greek, Latin, Aramaic, sophists preaching, drunks singing, children playing and screaming, others crying, and musical instruments in the background.[202] The **force** or significance of those sounds, which are all meaningful in their own right, must be recognized and understood by hearers or else, as Paul asserts, **I will be a barbarian to the speaker, and the speaker a barbarian to me**. This individual characterizes the foreigner from the outskirts of Roman civilization. If a barbarian were in town, his native language would rarely be known (e.g., Ovid *Tristia* 5.10.37; Herodotus *Hist.* 2.57).[203] Tongues, like the barbarian's language imagined by Paul, are incomprehensible to those who hear them. Since the Corinthians desire the manifestation of **spiritual realities**,[204] they should **desire to excel for the edification of the church**—those who speak in a tongue should **pray** for the ability to **interpret** it.[205]

Paul continues that if he prays in tongues, **my spirit prays but my mind is unfruitful**. Here the human mind (1:10; 2:16; 14:19) and human spirit (2:11; 5:3–5; 7:34; 16:18) are contrasted. "My spirit" has Paul as possessor and therefore does not mean another spirit other than Paul's own, though the Holy Spirit communes with his spirit. The dichotomy between spirit and mind has little to do with irrational and rational; divine inspiration does not have to mean losing one's reason or volition as though in a trance or possessed (cf. 14:32).[206] When Paul's spirit prays, his mind (i.e.,

---

202. See a prime example in Seneca *Lucil.* 56:1-4.

203. Fitzmyer 2008:514.

204. Collins 1999:499. Differently, Tibbs 2006:51–53, 236–42, in 14:12 interprets the plural πνευμάτων as *spirit beings* to argue for good spirits possessing believers to enable the tongues. It is not impossible to suggest that Paul's term is borrowed from the Corinthians and thus may reflect their own assumption that angels (as spirits) enable them to speak in tongues (cf. 13:1). Regardless, Paul assumes the one Spirit of God distributes spiritual gifts and empowers believers to operate in them (12:7, 11).

205. Contrast Zerhusen 1997:139–52; Riddlebarger 2013:377, 382–83, who argue that the speaker knows the foreign language. But if so, there is no reason to *pray* for an interpretation that is already supposedly known (see Garland 2003:584 fn. 12). Tongues is an extra-natural "spiritual" ability having little to do with natural language skills (14:1–2). See also comments in 12:10; 13:1; 14:2, 14–15, 27–28.

206. See further, Forbes 1997:64. Martin 1995:100–101; Thiselton 2000:1112–13.

understanding) may be inactive but not absent. Clear thoughts are needed to produce intelligible words, but tongues are not intelligible.[207] Thus, when he prays in tongues, it does not benefit his own mind nor the minds of others.[208] His follow-up question asks for a conclusion to the matter (14:15a),[209] which is, **I will pray with the spirit and I will pray with the mind also**. Both unintelligible and intelligible prayer edifies Paul's spirit, but the latter can also edifying others. He adds charismatic singing to this: **I will sing with my spirit**, which is apparently done non-cognitively and in tongues, perhaps similar to the hymnic style of angelic worship performed by Hemera, Job's daughter (*T.Job* 48.3).[210] This contrasts, **I will sing with my mind also**, which doubtless means to sing cognitively with understandable lyrics, which was part of ancient worship (14:26; Eph 5:19; Col 3:16). Paul encourages both types of prayer and singing, but when congregants worship together, comprehensible worship is reinforced by another hypothetical situation in which an outsider visits the congregation. This is someone who **takes up the place of the uninformed** and does not know or has not experienced tongues and spiritual gifts (14:16).[211] Who is this visitor? He or she can potentially say, **Amen**, and thus seems familiar with emergent Christian jargon (see 16:24). Maybe this person is an unbaptized attender open to the gospel. In any case, Paul expects the answer that, due to incomprehension, this visitor will not be able to respond in confirmation of the tongue-speaker's blessing and thanksgiving. The visitor remains unedified.

Our apostle gives thanks, saying that **I speak in tongues more than all of you**. He gives credit not to himself but to God for this enablement. Perhaps he assumes quantitatively that in private he prays in tongues more than they do, or maybe his speaking is qualitatively better because he "understands, appreciates, and experiences this gift more intensely."[212] Then again, it is not clear how he would know of this either way. The claim is therefore hyperbole with the rhetorical aim of eliciting ethos, an appeal to his spiritual character. It also helps amplify his next point, which is also hyperbole. Even though he exercises this gift more than they do, when **in church, I wish to speak five words with my mind, so that I may instruct others also, than ten thousand words in a tongue**. Paul's ability to communicate anything

---

207. Schnabel 2006:808.
208. See Fee 1987:669.
209. Cf. 14:26; Conzelmann 1975:233.
210. Ciampa/Rosner 2010:690.
211. The "uninformed" (ἰδιώτης: 14:16) appears again with an unbeliever in 14:23.
212. Garland 2003:642.

productive to a congregation in one small sentence, so long as that sentence is intelligible, is more beneficial than unintelligible tongues.

Tongues and Prophecy for Believers and Unbelievers (14:20-25)

Now that Paul has provided the rationale for their desiring prophecy over tongues, he reinforces it with Scripture and two situations related to assembling together—one hypothetical situation in which uninterpreted tongues is disadvantageous, and one ideal situation in which prophesy is advantageous.[213] This unit opens with the designation, **brothers and sisters**, and charges them with three imperatives: **be not children in things pertaining to understanding, but in reference to evil be babes; in things pertaining to understanding, be mature adults.**[214] Earlier contrasts between mature and immature centered on wisdom (2:6; 3:1), but here it centers on orderly worship. He relates tongues to what is written in Scripture, identified as **the Law** to reinforce its authority.[215] He loosely cites or paraphrases Isa 28:11-12: **"With other tongues and other lips I will speak to this people, and not even this way will they listen to me, says the Lord."** This quote does not follow closely extant Hebrew or Greek versions of this text:[216]

> For with stammering lip and another tongue he will speak to this people ... and they were not willing to hear. (MT)

> Because of contempt of lips, through another tongue, because they will speak to this people ... and they did not want to hear. (LXX)[217]

Even though Paul normally cites from the Greek text, on the balance, his words follow the MT more than LXX here.[218] Our apostle may have been contextually attracted to this text because he interpreted the cornerstone

---

213. See Gillespie 1994:161.

214. Paul's mention of children seems informed by Isa 28:7-12, though he interprets the text differently (see below).

215. Sometimes "Law," as here, refers to Scripture as a whole rather than only the Pentateuch (Rom 3:19; John 10:34).

216. If Paul follows Aquila's translation (Origen *Philocalia* 9.2; Wilk 2005:142), the text is unavailable.

217. Paul has "I will speak," whereas the MT has "he will speak," and the LXX, "they will speak." He also omits a portion of Isa 28:12 as not relevant to his point on tongues. See further differences in Stanley 1992:197-205.

218. See Aernie 2012:98-100.

Fourth Supporting Proof (11:2—14:40)

laid in Zion as Christ (Isa 28:16; cf. Rom 9:33). He probably thinks of Christ when adopting the phrase "says the Lord."[219] In Isaiah's discourse the Lord's spokespersons, the priest and prophet in Jerusalem, are portrayed as erring in their communication of God's message, being confused with drunkenness. Their drunken speech is compared to baby talk that is incomprehensible, or alternatively, they mock Isaiah's prophecy as that of an infant's (28:7–10).[220] The outcome is the same either way—as a form of judgment, God will permit incomprehensible speech to be heard by these people (28:11), whether from their drunken infantile leaders (LXX?) or a foreign country (MT). The MT is clearer, though we do not know to what extent Paul follows its context. If his source is similar, it suggests that since these people do not want to hear or obey the Lord's messages through His prophet, the Lord will "speak" to this people indirectly by permitting invasion by a foreign country to take place in which this people will be forced to hear invaders communicate in a foreign language to them. They will be ensnared and taken captive by their enemies (28:12–13). The importance of God's people as "my people" in 28:5 and "this people" in 28:11 should not be missed. This switch connotes God, as it were, temporarily disowning the people by bringing judgment on them due to their refusal to listen and obey divine words.[221]

Our apostle has taken this theme of judgment and reconfigured it so that the incomprehensible language of foreigners, which perhaps to the people sounds like the gibberish of babies and drunkards, is compared with the Corinthians speaking in tongues. If speaking in tongues sounds like the voice of drunkards and foreigners, this may disclose that Paul was not the only one comparing Isa 28 with the phenomenon (see Acts 2:13). Perhaps he adopts this comparison orally from an earlier apostolic tradition, which might explain why Isaiah is so loosely referenced and similar to the Hebrew text. We do not need to decide, however, on whether the Isaianic and Corinthian comparison of tongues *literally* refers to a human foreign language or is merely analogous to it. If we press the comparison too far, we would have to conclude that speaking in tongues amounts to speaking in Assyrian, since this is the language of the foreigners of Isaiah's text! Paul's point of citing Isaiah, even if thought to be prophetic fulfillment, is merely to demonstrate tongues as a *sign* rather than probe the exact *nature* of tongues.

---

219. So Nagel 2013:46–47.

220. For the latter, see Aernie 2012:95–96. The words, "כִּי צַו לָצָו צַו לָצָו קַו לָקָו קַו לָקָו" (28:10) often translated as "precept upon precept . . . line upon line" (NRSV), are actually nonsensical words (BDB 846, 875), not unlike the perception in Acts 2:13 or a baby's "goo goo gah gah." NET's "meaningless gibberish, senseless babbling," is better.

221. Compare Isa 6:8–10 with 1:3; 5:13; Vriezen 1962:128.

Fourth Supporting Proof (11:2—14:40)

For Paul the foreigners prefigure the Corinthians who speak in tongues, whereas "this people" for Paul has now become the outsiders and unbelievers. This may have sounded rather strange to the most informed congregation members. They might know that Isa 28 identifies "this people" as Israelites, but in Paul's reconfiguration of the passage, "this people" now prefigures uninformed and unbelieving outsiders who currently visit the church in Corinth.[222] Most congregation members, however, probably were not familiar enough with the passage to know this.[223] This launching pad from Isaiah, then, is at least understandable as Paul asserts that **tongues are (meant) for a sign not for the believers but for the unbelievers**. Tongues are a visible token of judgment, a sign symbolizing the "inaccessibility of divine revelation."[224] This sign is negative. If all in the church, hypothetically speaking, spoke in tongues **and there came in those who are uninformed or unbelievers**, Paul asks, **will they not think you are mad?** The unspoken answer is "yes," this is how outsiders would *perceive* them. They might conclude that Christ's followers are just another mindless cult whose worship resembles the ecstatic frenzies among followers of Dionysus or Cybele.[225] Such visitors might reject Christ and the church. Unintelligible tongues, then, serve as a negative sign for unbelievers—they remain in their unbelief after hearing the cacophony. Conversely, tongues are not a negative sign for believers since they understand that tongues are self-edifying and a spiritual gift from God even though they may not understand what is being said.[226]

The next sentence, **but prophecy is not for the unbelievers but for the believers**, is extremely difficult to explain given that, subsequently in 14:24–25, unbelievers confirm rather than deny God's presence in the congregation when hearing prophecy. As is occasionally suggested, one wonders if Paul's secretary or an early copyist accidentally made the blunder. Or is it that Paul reiterates a Corinthian saying in 14:22b (similar to 6:12), which he then proceeds to correct in 14:24–25? Problematic with this is that "so then" (οὖν) in 14:23 does not intend to contradict what precedes it.[227]

---

222. For Paul, however, this does not nullify Israel as God's people; he elaborates elsewhere that even though Gentiles in Christ are now included among God's elect people, Israel is still that people (e.g., Rom 9–11).

223. See audience familiarity with this scripture in Stanley 2016:59–61.

224. Hays 1997:240.

225. See Smit 1994:183; Hays 1997:238–39. Chester 2003:116–17; 2005:417–46, interprets the madness as a positive sign in which Greco-Roman outsiders will think the church is divinely inspired. This interpretation, however, seems to defeat Paul's aim to discourage congregants from publicly speaking with uninterpreted tongues.

226. So Garland 2003:650.

227. Garland 2003:649, in response to Talbert 1987:87–88; Johanson 1979:180–203.

Fourth Supporting Proof (11:2—14:40)

However, if the structure follows the A, B, A, B pattern below, "so then" in A explicates tongues only in A¹, whereas prophecy in B is corrected by the "but" in B¹:

> A "So then" (ὥστε) connects the citation with tongues as a negative sign for unbelievers (14:22a)[228]
>
> B "But" (δέ) guides what the Corinthians' (incorrectly) believe: that prophecy is not for unbelievers (14:22b)
>
> A¹ "Therefore" (οὖν) guides an elaboration on tongues as a negative sign for unbelievers (14:23)
>
> B¹ "But" (δέ) guides an elaboration on prophecy that amends Corinthian belief in B: Prophecy *can* make unbelievers become believers (14:24–25)

Among other explanations,[229] another possibility worth mentioning is the view that Paul did not intend that the effects of prophecy and tongues be mutually exclusive in relation to believers and unbelievers. His rhetorical momentum leaves behind tight logic as he makes 14:22b symmetrical with 14:22a. Hays suggests that Paul is really saying that "prophecy is not [primarily] for unbelievers but for believers."[230] If the word "sign" is implied in 14:22b as an ellipsis, then prophecy is also a sign, but unlike tongues, it functions as a positive sign.[231] It confirms to believers that the eschatological fulfillment in which Gentiles will worship with Jews, alluded to by the unbeliever's presence and confession in 14:25, has arrived. God is present in the midst of them (Isa 45:14; Zech 8:23; Dan 2:47; cf. Joel 2:28–32), and *even the unbeliever* confesses this to the believers.[232]

With either interpretation above, Paul still seems to qualify 14:22b by showing in 14:24–25 that prophecy can benefit unbelievers, too. If,

---

228. ὥστε does not signal a question here, *pace* Johanson 1979:193–94, but focalizes a preceding argument in a conclusive way, as Long 2013:149–57, shows (though, differently than Long, I maintain that ὥστε in Paul *does* function sometimes with preceding traditional material; e.g., Gal 3:9; 1 Cor 10:12 and 14:22 [see comments *ad. loc.*]).

229. E.g., Prophecy is meant to benefit believers so that its use in church will benefit unbelievers incidentally (Hiu 2010:100). Prophecy is a sign not *resulting* in unbelievers but *resulting* in believers (Gladstone 1999:185–92; Heil 2005:200). Tongues are (mistakenly) *recognized* by the ordinary person as pagan mania and so are *proper to* unbelievers, but prophecy is a refutation to the public that God speaks to them through believers (Smit 1994:184–89).

230. Hays 1997:240. Similarly, notice John 6:27; 12:44: "not only"/"not primarily."

231. On signs as having both negative and positive effects, see Aernie 2012:103–8.

232. See Dunn 1975:231; Forbes 1997:179–81.

Fourth Supporting Proof (11:2—14:40)

idealistically speaking, everyone prophesies and outsiders visit the church, such a person is **convicted by all,** and **called into account by all** because **the secrets of his heart are revealed.** But this does not happen as a result of all the prophets directing their prophecies to the outsider. Rather, the outsider overhears prophecy in the church, is inwardly convicted by what is heard, and realizes that God may be indirectly speaking to him. This causes the outsider to fall on his face, suggesting reverence before the divine presence because of a miracle or manifestation (Gen 17:3; Num 16:22; 1 Kgs 18:39). The person will then **worship God declaring that "God is really among you!"** Paul may have derived the expression from prophetic passages that depict foreigners making similar declarations of belief (see above). Especially relevant is Isa 45:14, which depicts restoration in which the nations will acknowledge God. When we combine this thought with the picture behind Isa 28, it turns out that tongues points to judgment and exile of God's people, whereas prophecy points to their restoration inclusive of Gentiles.[233] Paul's interpretation is mission driven.[234] Since the outsider is convinced of God's presence in the congregation, he would doubtless believe the gospel message. One finds a similar pattern at Pentecost in Acts 2:5-13 when some in the crowd did not understand the meaning of the tongues and became mockers.[235] It was not until Peter explains the phenomenon that the crowd was convicted and converted to faith in Christ (2:37-41; cf. 2:14-36). It is rather likely that Paul had taught the Corinthians oral traditions related to such apostolic use of tongues.[236] Since this congregation excelled in the gift, members almost certainly would have asked him about its origin, and Paul was probably not the originator of its use; but those who were apostles before him were.[237]

ORDERLY SPEECH GIFTS WHEN COMING TOGETHER (14:26-40)

This chapter's third mention of **brothers and sisters** begins a pericope guided by Paul's instructive commands. His first imperative provides a guiding principle for the discourse (14:26). The following set of imperatives give protocols on tongues (14:27-28) and the next set on prophecy (14:29-33), and the next on the silencing of wives (14:34-35). The authority behind his

---

233. Aernie 2012:110.
234. Ciampa, 2013:15; Schrage 1999:3.409-10.
235. On language in Acts 2 as signaling judgment, see Charette 2005:173-205.
236. Notice footnote on 16:8.
237. Wilk 2005:143, adds that Paul read Isa 28:11-12 as prophecy in light of Pentecost manifestations.

Fourth Supporting Proof (11:2—14:40)

commands is then disclosed (14:36–37). Paul's first imperative—**when you assemble together . . . let all things be done for building up** others—presents an ideal procedure of worship that can be implemented into the way the congregation already does worship. Members must aim to edify others with their speech gifts, whether by **song, teaching** (see 12:28–29), **revelation** (14:6), or **speaking in a tongue** that requires **interpretation** (12:10; 14:5). The **song** (ψαλμός) may refer to singing and playing a stringed instrument or reciting/singing a psalm from the Scriptures.[238] Playing an instrument without the aim of promoting singing or inspired speech may not have been on Paul's agenda here since he emphasizes speech gifts. There is no reason, however, why musical instruments should not be played in such gatherings, and given Paul's Jewish roots, it is very likely that he thought musical instruments would be conducive for praise, worship, and prophecy at these gatherings (Ps 150:3–5; 2 Kgs 3:15–16). The song could be learned or spontaneously inspired as in 14:15b. If a member were to sing in tongues, Paul would doubtless encourage an interpretation.

When members speak in tongues Paul charges that **two or at most three** should speak, not all at once but **in turn, and let one interpret**. The person who interprets may be among the three who speak in tongues (14:5),[239] or more likely another member with the gift of interpretation (12:10). It is evident that not all those who speak in tongues are able to interpret their own tongues (14:13, 28), and Paul stresses diversity related to gift distribution, distinguishing between members with the gift of tongues and those with the gift of interpreting tongues, similar to how the gift of prophecy is distinguished from discernment of prophecy (see 12:10–11, 30). If there is no interpreter present, those who speak in tongues must **be silent in church**, and they should pray in tongues quietly or privately (14:28).

Regarding prophecy our apostle gives direction to **let two or three prophets speak and others discern** what is spoken. The prophets take turns **one by one** uttering what they are prompted by the Spirit to say (14:31), and other members determine the validity of the prophecy, especially those with the gift of discernment. That others (more than one) are required to discern safeguards against false prophecies. Even though prophets are highly ranked in the body (12:28), their words should be tested and not naively accepted by virtue of the prophet's authority. The one who first prophesies is to **be silent** if another **one sitting down** starts to prophecy. Such conduct avoids the confusing scenario of multiple speakers prophesying at the same time as well as

---

238. See discussion in Schnabel 2006:830–33.

239. But it probably does not mean that *each one* interprets: see Ciampa/Rosner 2010:711–12, *pace* Thiselton 2000:1131.

prevents the long-winded prophet from taking up too much time.[240] It also assumes that the prophecy is spontaneous; they are prompted by the Spirit to speak.[241] Paul emphasizes prophecy in relation to teaching and exhortation: **that all may learn and all may be encouraged** (14:31 cf. 14:3).

By his claim that the **spirits of the prophets are subject to the prophets**, Paul means again the human spirit of each prophet, the innermost self (see 14:14–15).[242] The human spirit is the primary modem through which God's Spirit prompts inspired communication. This makes perfect sense of the necessity for prophets to control themselves and be silent while letting another person who is prompted by the Spirit to speak. The person who prophesies is in control of his or her own spirit so that there is no basis for a lack of self-control or excusing one's disorderly conduct by saying, "I couldn't help myself; the Spirit takes a hold of me, and I'm not in control anymore!"[243] Orderly worship is confirmed in 14:33a: **For God is not (the God) of disorder but of peace**. A tumultuous zoo of disorderly worship is not honoring to God who characterizes peace, a virtue which for the Corinthians in this situation suggests a state of harmony and "good order."[244] The tag, **as in all the churches of the saints** (14:33b), probably goes with the preceding rather than subsequent thoughts. Elsewhere, Paul connects similar phrases to concluding statements rather than commencing new ones (4:17; 7:17; 11:6).[245] Hence, orderly worship typifies the behavior of all churches, and the Corinthian congregation should be no exception.

Many interpreters question how Paul could write about silencing women in 14:34–35, when in 11:5 he permits women to prophesy. Some argue that these verses are an interpolation added by a later editor.[246] Indeed, certain Western manuscripts place these verses after 14:40, enabling the possibility that they were added originally as a marginal gloss in one of the letter's copies, and that gloss was eventually added to the main text. Antoinette Wire, however, evinces that the variant manuscripts all seem to have "originated from a single displacement" that may have originated from

---

240. Forbes 1997:262.

241. Hiu 2010:102; Dunn 1975:228.

242. *Pace* Tibbs 2006:52; Thiselton 2000:973.

243. Such claims indeed were used to justify charismatic disorder in the 1990s (see Oropeza 1996; 2002b:137–50).

244. BDAG 287.

245. See further points in Hiu 2010:136–37; Fee 1987:697–98. Hiu affirms that "as" (ὡς) typically does not begin a new sentence when it belongs to a dependent clause without a verb.

246. E.g., Payne 2009:217–67; Barnes 2014:168–69; Schottroff 2012:736; Schrage 1999:3.481–87; Fee 1987:699–705.

Fourth Supporting Proof (11:2—14:40)

an editor attempting to improve Paul's style or alter his words.[247] When we combine Wire's study with evidence that longer NT text displacements are normally authentic, and that the authentic text is widely witnessed geographically, and that *no* ancient manuscript omits these verses, this warrants skepticism regarding an interpolation here.[248] We are best served explaining the apparent discrepancy another way.[249] Armin Baum studies relevant Greco-Roman and Jewish sources and suggests that, similar to the sentiments of that time, the principle behind both 11:5 and 14:34-35 "was that female public speaking without male consent is unacceptable whereas female public speaking with male consent is unobjectionable."[250] Indeed, though diverse attitudes regarding women in public are evident,[251] Paul's patriarchal world is generally unfavorable toward women speaking in public, and cultural assumptions include women being subject to their husbands and speaking through them (Plutarch *Conj. praec.* 142C-E; Livy *Hist.* 34.1.5; Aristotle *Oec.* 3.A-C[1-135]; Euripides *Suppl.* 40-41).[252] But as we noticed earlier, the issue in 11:2-16 does not *center* on male consent but gender distinction, and in 14:34-35 I hope to demonstrate that Paul's command for women again is not based primarily on male consent. Together these passages may even assume that wives and other females could speak publicly in worship gatherings *if* they are gifted and inspired by God's Spirit to do so.

My rendering of 14:34, **Let the wives in your assemblies be silent, for they are not permitted to be talking but to be in submission, just as the law says also**, understands women as wives (γυναῖκες) as the context clarifies. The plural "assemblies" probably does not refer to churches universally but the various houses and facilities where the Corinthians gather for worship. Paul's use of λαλέω in this verse is better understood as "talking" or even "chatting" instead of "speaking."[253] A prominent key to this word choice comes from 14:35a—if the wives **wish to learn anything, let them**

---

247. Wire 1990:151; cf. 149-52. Haplography may account for the displacement: the copyist's eye might have skipped from "churches" in 14:33 to "churches" found in Western versions of 14:35. See also Niccum 1997:242-55; Miller 2003:217-36; Garland 2003:675-77.

248. See Ross 1992:153-56; Niccum 1997:253-55.

249. Are the words in 14:34-35 the Corinthians' own words that are rejected in 14:36 (e.g., Janzen 2013:55-70)? Such a slogan would be too long and it is not evident that 14:36 rejects 14:34-35 (Ciampa/Rosner 2010:719-20).

250. Baum 2014:274.

251. E.g., Cornelius Nepos *De viris illustribus* pref. 7; Oster 1995:358-59.

252. Massey 2013:252-54; Hiu 2010:149-50; Wire 1990:156.

253. See Plato *Euth.* 287D; Plutarch *Garr.* 503F-504A; Eph 4:25; Acts 23:18; 2 John 12; LSJ 1025-26; Arzt-Grabner et al. 2006:120-21.

ask their own husbands at home.[254] This implies that the wives were asking questions at church, apparently disrupting the inspired speaker's message by uninspired inquiries. Certain scholars suggest this activity involved "sifting" the prophet's words and cross-examining them with questions regarding their lifestyle or beliefs in public, and this would be especially controversial if wives were probing their prophetic husbands this way.[255] At least some questioning of prophecy, however, doubtless included the gift of discernment (14:29; cf. 12:10), and one is hard pressed to affirm either that only men could use this gift publicly or that a wife's evaluation could never pass for such discernment. Another problem is that Paul's recommendation for wives to learn from their husbands privately has little to do with evaluating and challenging the speaker.[256] Her questions must have been understood as uninspired. Perhaps some of them interrupted the speaker, not to challenge him or her but to ask for clarification of what was being uttered. Moreover, they may have been asking questions to their husbands *about* what another speaker was presently saying. They may have been asking husbands or other wives nearby such things as, "What do you think he means? Could he be saying that . . . " "Is she referring specifically to me? What she's saying actually happened to me this week when I . . . " which presumably sparked brief chatting instead of listening.[257] The confusion perhaps originated because many gatherings met in homes.[258] Whereas chatting and asking questions might be acceptable in the privacy of one's own home, it was not to be done in homes and other facilities used for public sacred gatherings. *Paul is forbidding wives from uninspired talking when others are inspired to speak.*

Barrett dismisses λαλέω as meaning uninspired speech and "chatter" by claiming that "in the New Testament and in Paul, the verb normally does not have this meaning, and is used throughout chapter xiv . . . in the sense of inspired speech."[259] But there are significant weaknesses with this argument. First, whereas other instances of λαλέω in this chapter are qualified as tongues, prophecy, or inspired speaking, we should not automatically subject this meaning to 14:34, especially when 14:35a seems to clarify that

---

254. That wives could learn intellectual things may be progressive for that time: see Keener 2005:119.

255. Witherington 1988:102; Thiselton 2000:1158.

256. So Greenbury 2008:726.

257. This problem would be compounded if house-churches were set up with men and women partitioned, similar to the Jewish Theraputae sect (Philo, *Contempl.* III.32–33; Simon 1967:124–25); then wives would almost need to shout at their husbands to get their attention.

258. See Massey 2013:252.

259. Barrett 1968:332; cf. Spurgeon 2011:323; Soards 1999:306.

Fourth Supporting Proof (11:2—14:40)

their speaking has to do with *learning* and *questioning* rather than teaching, proclaiming, and praying. Second, contrary to interpreting λαλέω in 14:34 as inspired speech, it is clear that elsewhere Paul does not forbid Corinthian women from such speech, whether prophesying or praying at church (11:5). Third, Paul's rhetorical wish that "all" would speak in tongues and prophesy becomes rather empty if he is precluding all the wives or women (14:5). Moreover, "each" person in the congregation would seem to include women who can speak in tongues, interpret, give a revelation, teach, sing, or use another speech gift (14:26). Such inspired speaking involves spiritual gifts that the Spirit distributes to each believer (12:7–11), and nothing suggests that these gifts are given only to men.[260] If Paul agreed with the early Christians who associate the Spirit's outpouring with Joel 2:28–32 (cf. 1 Cor 1:2; Acts 2:1–22), this would seem to confirm that prophetic and spiritual speaking are not just given to "sons" but also "daughters." *The gifts of the Spirit do not discriminate according to gender.* Hence, and despite how Paul might use λαλέω elsewhere, in 14:34 it does *not* seem to reference inspired speech.

Kenneth Bailey, who has extensive experience working with women in Mediterranean villages, says that chatting is *still* a problem in these church gatherings.[261] He attributes this to factors such as lack of education and social contacts, along with short attention spans that such things might induce. The problem in 14:34–35 may involve similar factors in which chatting becomes a way of learning. Hence, the chatting of these women, along with both genders inappropriately using tongues and prophecy, hinder orderly worship. Paul requests the culprits of all three to be silent in church (14:28, 30, 34). For the latter he essentially says, "Women, please stop chatting so you can listen to the women (and men) who are trying to bring you a prophetic word but cannot do so when no one can hear them."[262] The wives must therefore be **silent** and **submit** themselves to the speaker under divine guidance in reverence to God, whoever he or she might be (cf. 16:16, 18; Eph 5:18–21).

This silence and submission is in accordance with the **Law**, that is, Scripture (see 14:21). Genesis 1–3, or more particularly 3:16, does not appear to be what is referenced since silence and submission are foremost to the speaker rather than husband, and in any case, nothing is said about silence in Gen 1–3.[263] Aaron and Miriam's rebuke related to questioning

---

260. See Long 2007:99–100.

261. Bailey 2011:412–17.

262. Ibid. 416.

263. *Contra* Orr/Walther 1976:312. Gen 3:16 claims that as a result of the curse (far removed from Paul's new creation!) the woman's inclination will be toward the man/husband and he will exploit that (Bruce 1971:136).

Fourth Supporting Proof (11:2—14:40)

Moses's prophetic authority comes closer to what Paul means (Num 12:1–15).[264] Paul alluded to this story earlier (see 13:12), and if it is echoed here, then reverence to the prophet seems required of both genders. Elsewhere in Scripture the notion of silence is encouraged when hearing wise counsel (Job 29:21), and is also given in respect for those in authority (Judg 3:19).[265] Silence and reverence likewise are to be given to God (Hab 2:20; Zeph 1:7; Zech 2:13).[266] Commenting on worship in Habakkuk's context, O. P. Robertson writes, "One should wait upon him [God] in the awed silence that is often the most appropriate expression of true worship."[267] Marvin Sweeney affirms that Zeph 1:7 "constitutes the prophet's exclamatory demand for silence at the beginning of the presentation of YHWH's oracular statements that announce the coming Day of YHWH."[268] It seems to be standard protocol, then, that in the Scriptures which inform Paul, silence is required whenever a prophet speaks divine words. This idea is what Paul probably means by referring to Scripture. In Acts, Peter and Paul's motioning of the hand to silence their audiences assumes both commotion among their auditors and the necessity to be quiet as they speak (Acts 12:17; 21:40). Likewise in Qumran, talking during the discourse is forbidden (1QS 6.10–13).[269] Such texts evince that ancient audiences could be quite noisy. Men as well as women might be guilty of disrupting the speaker, and so we surmise that the only reason Paul does not silence men or husbands from chatting in the Corinthian setting is because they were not the problem.[270]

The additional phrase, **for it is shameful for a wife to talk in church,** equates this activity with what is unacceptable and dishonoring. It would surely be shameful according to cultural norms of the time for a wife to talk in a way that embarrassed her husband publicly.[271] Again, this was happening not necessarily because wives challenged their husbands as speakers, but because they were asking questions to their husbands about other speakers and interrupting or distracting those speakers and the ones who heard them. Plutarch considers it rude and disrespectful when audiences interrupt the lecturer or ask uneducated or irrelevant questions (*Rect. rat. aud.* 39C;

---

264. See Liefeld 1986:149–50.
265. Witherington 1988:103.
266. See Hiu 2010:148.
267. Robertson 1990:212; cf. Barker 1999:349.
268. Sweeney 2003:78.
269. Fitzmyer 2008:526.
270. Rightly, Witherington 1988:104; Hiu 2010:148.
271. See Garland 2003:668.

Fourth Supporting Proof (11:2—14:40)

42F–43C; 48A–B).²⁷² Anaximander's rhetorical handbook recognizes interruptions as a peril orators face. Among his solutions is that orators are to meet interruptions by showing them as contrary to justice, law, and what is honorable (καλός) and publicly advantageous (*Rhet. Alex.* 1433a.25–29; cf. 14–18). Paul would seem to agree with such sentiments by claiming that in Christian assemblies, the wife's distractive talking is shameful and runs counter to Scripture. As such, these women disrespect the speaker and the Spirit who inspires him or her.

FUSING THE HORIZONS: WOMEN SPEAKERS AT CHURCH

Sometimes 14:34–35 is read in tandem with 1 Tim 2:9–15 to make the claim that if Paul charges women to be silent, this means that churches today should not permit women speakers, teachers, or leaders. What prompts this discussion in both letters, however, arises from distinctive circumstances, and though there are some word similarities in both texts, they are applied quite differently.²⁷³ A unique situation arises in 1 Timothy in which false teachings are being perpetrated in part by widows in the house churches (5:5–16; cf. 1:3–7).²⁷⁴ In this situation Timothy, who is pastor of the church established in Ephesus, is told, "I am not permitting a woman to teach and to assume authority over a man" (2:12).²⁷⁵ These women are not to take on teaching roles and take over male leadership, Timothy's especially.²⁷⁶ The decision, it seems, was not meant to be perpetual but had the aim of safeguarding this congregation from the damaging teaching. It was doubtless compounded by the problem that (due to no fault of their own) many women in the patriarchal world were not afforded the level of literacy and education given to men. With this unfortunate setback, these women had become quite susceptible to false instruction. We notice that men who perpetrate false teachings in the Pauline churches are also to be silenced (Tit 1:11).

Genesis 2–3 is used in 1 Tim 2:13–14 to affirm Adam as "first," and Eve as the one "deceived" by the Serpent. To be sure, Adam is created

---

272. Cf. Hiu 2010:149.
273. See Marshall 2004:440–42.
274. See further, Oropeza 2012a:272–78.
275. On the present tense as timely and specific rather than universal, see Payne 2009:319–25; Witherington 2006:226–27.
276. On male leadership in the patriarchal world, see 11:3 comment.

Fusing the Horizons: Women Speakers at Church

first and has some sense of priority in this text, but the point derived from Genesis is that "as Eve was deceived by the Serpent, so the women in the Ephesian congregation are being deceived by the false teachers who are inspired by Satan (cf. 1 Tim 4:1–3; 5:13–15)."[277] As long as the Ephesian women are influenced by these teachers, they fulfill the hypothetical prerepresentation of Eve being deceived and leading Adam astray.[278] There is no indication that because of the creation story, no woman under any circumstance in any church should ever be permitted to speak, teach, or lead men. Our author was possibly incited to mention the creation story in order to refute a false teaching that influenced the congregation.[279] Although the old created order of the firstness of Adam is recognized, in Pauline thought this order is passing away in light of the new creation in Christ that will eventually come to realize fully "nor male and female . . . in Christ" (Gal 3:28; cf. 2 Cor 5:17). Consistent with the new creation model, Paul's churches enable and endorse women leaders such as Phoebe and Junia (Rom 16:1, 7), and teachers such as Prisca (1 Cor 16:19; Acts 18:26).

We know from Paul and the New Testament that women were permitted to prophesy and speak under the Spirit's inspiration (11:5; 14:26; cf. Acts 21:8–9; Rev 2:20). This was perhaps encouraged because in the new era of the Spirit's outpouring, which is to continue until Christ returns, "your daughters will prophesy" is to characterize the church era (Acts 2:17). This is compatible with the Jewish roots of Christian faith, which endorsed women prophets such as Deborah, Huldah, and Anna (Judg 4–5; 2 Kgs 22:14; 2 Chr 34:22; Luke 2:36–38).[280] Likewise, epigraphic evidence supports that women had leadership roles in ancient synagogues,[281] and Jewish texts do not preclude their participating in ancient synagogue worship.[282] It seems that neither 14:34–35 nor 1 Tim 2:9–15 intend to claim that women of all churches of all eras must not speak, prophesy, or teach adult males in the churches. We add to this that, unlike the ancient patriarchal world, women in our own era can receive the same biblical and theological education that

---

277. Oropeza 2012a:274.

278. On prerepresentation, see 10:6.

279. Marshall 2004:442, 459–60, claims this false teaching centered on female superiority over males.

280. For further women prophets in ancient Jewish, Christian, and Greco-Roman traditions, see Wire 1990:237–69.

281. See Van der Horst 1998:90–92.

282. See Crüsemann 2000:30–31; cf. *t. Meg.* 4.11.

Fourth Supporting Proof (11:2—14:40)

men do. They are just as competent as men, then, to lead a church, teach in a classroom, or preach from the pulpit.

Paul's rhetorical questions in 14:36—**Or did the word of God originate from you? Or were you the only ones it reached?**—expect the answer "no." This rebuke targets members who might be arrogant about their spiritual gifts and decide to disregard Paul's commands. He continues that if anyone thinks themselves **a prophet or spiritual, let that person know that the matters about which I write to you are the command of the Lord** Jesus. Paul appeals to ethos that prompts his auditors to recognize his apostolic authority.[283] He might be claiming that through inspired revelation he is writing these imperatives, but more likely he has in mind Jesus's command to love one another as the basis for his instructions (8:1–3; 13:1–13). If any prophet or spiritual person among them **does not recognize** the love command and Paul's instruction related to it, that person **is not recognized** by God, Christ, and the Spirit (14:38; cf. 8:3). This warning does not arise from Paul on a power trip, but as Thiselton rightly asks, "If a prophet's utterance contradicts *apostolic* utterances (let alone biblical tradition), does not that of itself disenfranchise the currency of the prophetic utterance?"[284] It seems that any allegedly inspired word from prophetic congregants must be false if their message contradicts what God, Christ, and the Spirit have already spoken, whether through Scripture or apostolic teaching. As such, this person is not recognized—his or her prophetic message does not come from God's Spirit. Moreover, these words may recall an oral tradition about false prophets who speak in the name of the Lord but will be not be recognized on judgment day; the Lord Jesus will say to them, "I never knew you" (Matt 7:21–23; cf. 10:33; 25:11–12).

The conclusion makes final appeals to the **brothers and sisters** regarding tongues, prophecy, and proper conduct in worship (14:39–40). They are to **earnestly desire to prophecy, and do not hinder speaking in tongues**. In the first clause Paul recapitulates the importance of seeking intelligent spiritual discourse when assembling together (14:1, 26). In the second clause he implies that even though prophecy is preferable to tongues at these gatherings, tongues should not be forbidden so long as they are interpreted in the way prescribed earlier (14:26–28). No doubt, private praying in tongues also should not be hindered. Inclusive of the

---

283. Collins 1999:517.
284. Thiselton 2000:1163.

Fourth Supporting Proof (11:2—14:40)

entire content of chapters 11–14, Paul ends by directing auditors to **let all things be done appropriately and in an orderly manner**, which will foster the building up rather than disruption of solidarity among congregation members (cf. 14:26, 33).

Solidarity in Belief of the Resurrection: Fifth Supporting Proof (15:1–58)

Paul's final proof supporting solidarity discourages the view of "some" who deny a future resurrection (see 15:12). The inclusive and repetitive "all" rallies for unified beliefs (15:7, 22–23, 28, 51). Although he collects witnesses supporting Christ's resurrection, thus engaging with what is forensic, his rhetorical aim is still deliberative.[1] He tries to convince his auditors to accept bodily resurrection, and his use of "in vain" highlights what is disadvantageous for them (15:2, 14, 17; cf. 15:10, 32, 58).[2] Paul presents evidence from the past (15:1–11) and blends forensic and deliberative elements in hypothetical arguments (15:12–19), all to persuade the Corinthians to accept his point-of-view and live in a manner conducive to it (15:20–34, 58). Our apostle first presents traditional material distilling the heart of the gospel message (5:1–11). Two leading questions in 15:12 and 15:35 help formulate the subsequent structure, and their sections end with ethical imperatives.[3]

> A. Leading statement and question followed by hypothetical arguments showing disadvantages of the denial of resurrection (15:12–19)
>> B. Adam/Christ comparisons showing advantages of the resurrection (15:20–22)
>>> C. Christ's return and defeat of death and other powers based on Scripture (15:23–28)
>>>> D. Concluding exhortations with rhetorical questions showing disadvantages of denying the resurrection (15:29–34)
> A¹. Leading questions followed by examples supporting the nature of the resurrected body (15:35–44)
>> B¹. Adam/Christ comparisons supporting the resurrected body (15:45–49)

---

1. Cf. Saw 1995:183–98. See forensic elements in Wegener 2004:441–42; Brown 2014:129
2. Eriksson 1998:245.
3. On the text's repetitive nature, see Nash 2009:394–95; Brown 2014:111.

Solidarity in Belief of the Resurrection: Fifth Supporting Proof (15:1-58)

    C¹. Christ's return and defeat of death based on Scripture
    (15:50-57)

    D¹. Concluding exhortation (15:58)

This parallelism suggests that the most relevant issues include the nature of the resurrected body, ethical imperatives in light of it, Adam/Christ explications, the defeat of death, and arguments of disadvantages if denying the resurrection.

Proclamation of Christ's Resurrection (15:1-11)

Paul's words imagine a courtroom setting where he, as advocate for the resurrection, unfolds his statement of facts from the past and presents Scripture and witnesses as evidence of Christ rising from the dead. Such evidence may be considered inartificial proofs; they are not invented by the orator and can persuade without rhetorical argumentation (Quintilian, *Inst.* 5.1; Aristotle, *Rhet.* 1.15). Although Paul writes, **I make known to you ... the gospel which I proclaimed to you**, this message is not new to them. They already **have taken a stand** in the gospel, and by it they are presently **being saved**. Paul challenges them to remember his early proclamations, and he implicitly chides them for forgetting them in practice. This gospel relates to prophetic discourse about the good news of a coming era in which God's anointed one, whom Paul interprets as Jesus, would bring deliverance (Isa 61:1-2; cf. 40:9; 52:7).[4] The Corinthians have received this message and are being saved by it, unless they **believed in vain**.[5] This implicit warning suggests that if they abandon their belief in the gospel, they would jeopardize their salvation. It evokes *pathos* by stirring the emotions of his auditors with hope and fear.[6] The stakes could be no higher than the hope of eternal gain or fear of its loss.

    Of primary importance is the gospel Paul received from earlier apostles, which he passes on to the Corinthians (15:3-5). The creed-like statement that Christ **died ... was buried ... rose ... and appeared** to witnesses reflects apostolic oral tradition based on very early proclamations.[7] Although Paul considers his view to be entirely consistent with these apostles, he

---

    4. See Thiselton 2000:1184.

    5. "In vain" (εἰκῇ: Gal 2:21; 3:4; 4:11) is virtually synonymous with μάταιος (1 Cor 15:17) and κενός (15:10, 14, 58), all of which suggest uselessness or ineffectuality (see Oropeza 2009:148).

    6. Eriksson 2001:115-26.

    7. The Greek here is not typical of Paul's, as Jeremias 1966:101-3 demonstrates.

Solidarity in Belief of the Resurrection: Fifth Supporting Proof (15:1-58)

brings together select resurrection traditions in a unique way.[8] According to Gal 1:15—2:1 he met with the apostles Peter and James in Jerusalem three years after his transformation.[9] He mentions both as witnesses of the resurrection (15:5, 7), and it is quite possible that he received his "creed" from them. This implies that rather than Paul shaping the traditions written later on in the canonical Gospels, the oral traditions behind the Gospels shaped Paul's own understanding of Christ's death, burial, resurrection, and appearances. Birger Gerhardsson rightly discerns the importance of prior traditions:

> Elementary psychological considerations tell us that the early Christians could scarcely mention such intriguing events as those taken up in the statements about Jesus' death and resurrection without being able to elaborate on them. Listeners must immediately have been moved to wonder and ask questions. Regarding our text there must have existed in support of the different points in the enumeration [of 15:3-8] ... narratives about how they came about. Our text ... cries out for elaboration.[10]

The first confessional statement **that Christ died for our sins** presupposes Jesus as the anointed savior who would deliver his people according to prophecy (e.g., Isa 61:1-3).[11] His death on the cross has redemptive value and is reminiscent of the expiation of sins declared at the Lord's Supper (11:24; cf. 2 Cor 5:21; Rom 3:25; 4:25; 5:9). His efficacious death is **according to the Scriptures**, and may assume a passage such as Isa 53:5 in which the suffering servant, whom believers identify as Jesus, is wounded and weakened "on account of our sins" (52:13—53:12).[12] It seems best, however, not to reduce these confessions to only one scripture referent, especially since "scriptures" is plural. More broadly, Paul perhaps understood Jesus to be fulfilling the Law, prophets, and psalms (Luke 24:25-27, 44-46). If so, then the suffering servant discourse may presuppose an understanding of atonement from sin captivated in Israel's ancient sacrificial system, which Paul sees as foreshadowing Christ's sacrificial death (e.g., Lev 1-5, 16).

---

8. See Coppins 2010:286. The repetitive "then ... then ... .then" (15:5-7) may suggest chronological order (Lietzmann/Kümmel 1949:77).

9. MacGregor 2006:226-27, dates this event at 35 CE, and the "creed" Paul cites even earlier since it would already be formed prior to his meeting these apostles.

10. Gerhardsson 2003:89.

11. On Paul's development of Χριστός as a cognomen for Jesus, see Schnabel 2006:877-88.

12. Meyer 1993:18-19; Hofius 2004:177-80.

Solidarity in Belief of the Resurrection: Fifth Supporting Proof (15:1–58)

The second statement, **and that he was buried**, confirms that Christ died, which stands as the prerequisite for resurrection. The burial assumes that the dead body of Jesus was laid in a tomb and then vacated it after he rose again. There is no reason to deny that this is what our apostle meant by burial even if he does not technically use the phrase "empty tomb" as conceptualized from the Gospels.[13] Like Paul, later proclamations and creeds normally did *not* include any explicit mention of the empty tomb either; and yet these same sources make explicit mention of the resurrection of flesh.[14] This suggests that the empty tomb was mostly confined to full narratives, such as found in the Gospels, rather than brief confessional formulae that we find here. For the Corinthians, Paul's mention of Christ's burial would be sufficient to assume an empty tomb or grave site, since they were almost certainly familiar with longer narratives about his resurrection that included his body evacuating the burial site. If Christ's burial is to be understood "according to the scriptures," then perhaps texts such as Isa 53:9–11 and Ps 16:8–11 are assumed.[15] Psalm 16 is especially relevant since the psalmist speaks of the body not seeing corruption in the grave, and this reference characterizes early apostolic proclamations about the resurrection, inclusive of Paul's proclamation (Acts 2:24–32; 13:34–37).

The third confession is that after Jesus's death and burial, **he was raised . . . according to the scriptures**. This belief resonates with Jewish traditions anticipating the human body raised to life after death (Dan 12:1–3; Ezek 37:1–14; Isa 26:19; 2 Macc 7:10–11, 14; 1 *En.* 22:13; *T. Benj.* 10.6–9). The resurrection of Christ is the pivotal moment in Paul's history that confirms the arrival of the new era and assures the future resurrection of believers.[16] Christ rising on the **third day** is adopted from apostolic tradition as well as being in accordance with scriptures. Hosea 6:2 speaks of an anticipated restoration that includes God raising up his people on the third day. Perhaps Paul read this verse in a way similar to the Targum of Pseudo-Jonathan that associates this verse with resurrection from dead. Another referent may include Jonah being three days in the fish, which is said to be a sign related to Christ's death and resurrection (Jon 1:17[2:1]; cf. Matt 12:38–40; 16:4). Perhaps more relevant for Paul is Lev 23:1–16 in which the firstfruits of the harvest is offered on the "day after the Sabbath"

---

13. See Hengel 2001:120–83; Eriksson 1998:93; Lehmann 1968:78–86.

14. e.g., Acts 10:36–41; 17:31; 1 Pet 3:18–22; Ignatius *Smyr.* 1.1–2; *Trall.* 9; Justin *Apol.* 1.21.1; *Old Roman Creed* c. 175 CE; Ware 2014b:480–81.

15. On the former, see Hofius 2004:177–80.

16. The semantic range for ἐγείρω (to "rise," "get up") doesn't include the idea of elevation or ascension (Ware 2014b:494–95; cf. 487); i.e., Jesus rose in his own body rather than was merely assumed into heaven without his earthly body.

Solidarity in Belief of the Resurrection: Fifth Supporting Proof (15:1–58)

during the Feast of Unleavened Bread, two days after the Paschal lamb is slaughtered. He may have connected this offering and the sixteenth of Nisan with the same day Christ, the Paschal lamb (1 Cor 5:7), was risen. This would be the third day.[17]

The final statement claims that the risen Christ **appeared** to many (15:5–7). Bodily resurrection seems to preclude that these witnesses merely dreamed or saw spiritual visions of Jesus.[18] Unless prophetic and apocalyptic texts were never read in synagogues, first-century Jewish disciples would seem to know the difference between actually seeing a person and merely having a vision or dream of that person. By these appearances Paul means that Christ appeared to witnesses in a body that was recognizable as their rabbi who had been crucified a few days earlier. First, **he appeared to Cephas** (Peter), **then the twelve** disciples, though technically eleven if Judas abandoned them, though it is not impossible that Paul also knew of a tradition about Judas's replacement (Acts 1:13–29).[19] Paul seems to have a tradition similar to Luke that declares the risen Lord had appeared in a unique way to Peter (Luke 24:34; cf. Mark 16:7). John's Gospel has Peter visiting the empty tomb first among the eleven (John 20:2–10; 21:1–19).[20] Christ then appeared to **more than five hundred brothers and sisters**. No early source matches this number, though the witnesses in Matt 28:10 is sometimes suggested.[21] It seems that certain post-resurrection appearances, though communicated orally, were never recorded in the Gospels. This appearance, in any case, happens **at one time** and thus seems to rule out visions, dreams, or hallucinations, which are subjective and happen to individuals rather than multitudes. Should any Corinthian wish to contest these witnesses, the majority of them are still alive when Paul writes this letter over two decades later; they could confirm these claims. Paul does not need to specify which **James** he means, presumably because the Corinthians already know this is the "brother of the Lord" who as an apostle has seen

17. Cf. Thiessen 2012:389–90; White 2015:103–19.

18. The aorist passive ὤφθη probably means he "appeared" (BDAG 719[A.1.d.]). The alternative "was seen" may also be used if not reduced to implying non-bodily appearances.

19. On Judas, see 11:23 above.

20. Why doesn't Paul name Mary Magdalene and other women witnesses as do the Gospels? Oftentimes in patriarchal societies men were considered the only reliable witnesses (Aristotle *Ath. Pol.* 53.2; Josephus *Ant.* 4.219; Brown 2014:129–30). Although Paul mentions women via the "brothers and sisters" in 15:5, since 15:3–11 functions forensically with witnesses as inartificial proof (see above), perhaps he thought that his auditors would not find it any more persuasive for him to add Mary and the women's testimony (see also Gerhardsson 2003:82–83).

21. E.g., Schnabel 2006:892–93.

Solidarity in Belief of the Resurrection: Fifth Supporting Proof (15:1–58)

the risen Christ (9:1, 5). His witness is another oral testimony not found in the Gospels.[22] Paul considers him to be one of the "pillars" of the Jerusalem church (Gal 1:17–20; 2:9). Then Christ appeared to **all the apostles**, which seems to go beyond the Twelve, and perhaps suggests all other believers who encountered the risen Christ after James. With this extension Paul implicates himself among their number.[23]

Last of all, Paul claims that **he appeared to me also** (15:8). This probably refers to his encounter with Christ on the road to Damascus. The risen Lord appears to Paul in a bright light from heaven and speaks to him (Acts 9:1–19; 22:6–11; 26:12–18; cf. Gal 1:12–16). Paul fell down and heard the Lord's words and was stricken with temporary blindness, and those who were with him witnessed the phenomenon, though differently than Paul.[24] Jesus appeared to him in a glorified state similar to his transfiguration in Luke 9:29. This event, though similar to a theophany, was more than merely a vision. Paul could speak of it as an objective encounter distinct from the more subjective vision he had in 2 Cor 12:1–9.[25] Christ's appearance to Paul is also confirmed in Acts by Ananias (Acts 9:17), Barnabas (9:27), and Jesus as described by the Lukan Paul (26:16).[26] More importantly, Paul's own testimony reflects an objective encounter comparable with the other apostles (cf. 1 Cor 9:1). Hence, Paul's view of the resurrected Messiah does not seem to be very different than the Gospels which more specifically have Christ identified, touched, handled, and eating with his disciples after his resurrection (Luke 24:39–42; John 20:17, 27). Christ's glorified risen state maintains some sense of continuity with the body buried—the vacated burial site of Jesus suggests that Jesus rose in his own body with the same surviving "I." And as the firstfruits of the resurrection, there is continuity between his resurrected state and those who will rise again in the future (15:20–22).

He describes himself in relation to this encounter **as though to one untimely born**. This language reflects a metaphorical miscarriage pointing to his dead spiritual state given new life in Christ after he believed (cf. Eph 2:1–5).[27] Paul seems to adopt ἔκτρωμα from the story of Miriam's leprosy

---

22. Jerome (c. 347–420) quotes from the Gospel of the Hebrews about how the Lord first appeared to James (*Vir. ill.* 2), but this account is late, and so its reliability is quite questionable.

23. So Eriksson 1998:96.

24. On tensions and resolutions between Acts narratives, see Witherington 1998:302–15; Keener 2013:2.1598–1602.

25. See Keener 2013:2.1607.

26. See Wright 2003:389–90, 396.

27. See Hollander/van der Hout 1996:227–36. For a synopsis of other possible interpretations, see Garland 2003:692–93; Schnabel 2006:897–98.

Solidarity in Belief of the Resurrection: Fifth Supporting Proof (15:1–58)

(Num 12:12; see 1 Cor 13:12; 14:34). In the story, Aaron asks Moses to heal Miriam, as he pleads, "let her not be the same as though dead, as though an untimely born (ἔκτρωμα)." Likewise, the image of a small and unfit but living miscarriage seems proper to his claim as **the least of the apostles who is not fit to be called an apostle**. Paul, a persecutor of the church, spiritually dead and unfit to become a follower of Christ, astonishingly becomes an apostle for Christ! Such transformation he could only attribute to divine favor—**by the grace of God I am what I am**. And grace still works abundantly through his missionary efforts and lowly tent-making trade: **I labored more than all of** the other apostles. This is not self-boasting but recognition that divine grace takes effect in his meager human efforts.[28] His many toils and hardships is a boast in weakness that exercises God's power (2:1–5; 2 Cor 11:22–33; 12:9–10). The grace of God, through his proclamations, results in the Corinthians believing his gospel, though his words, **whether I or they**, recognize that some were converted by other apostles and missionaries.

Disadvantages of Denying the Resurrection and the Resurrection Forecast (15:12–28)

The leading question of this section arises from the previous proofs for Christ's bodily resurrection and conveys astonishment and reproach.[29] **Now if it is proclaimed that Christ has been risen from the dead, how say some among you that there is no resurrection from the dead?** Paul arouses pathos; the recipients are stirred to feel ashamed about this denial. Most scholars agree that they did not reject Christ's resurrection but their own. Beyond this, there is little agreement on the reason for their unbelief. Since the congregation has an acute problem with factions, we find it peculiar that most interpreters argue for a *unified* reason for these members' denial.[30] In all probability they denied the resurrection for different reasons, and this reflects the various competing beliefs about the afterlife in Greco-Roman culture of that time.[31] All the same, since Paul has stressed Christ's resurrection as bodily, this probably implies that Corinthian dissenters deny the importance of their own bodies rising again (see 6:13–14; 15:35).

---

28. Barclay 2008:377–78, says something similar.

29. Zeller 2010:477; Meyer 1877:2.50.

30. For a survey of various positions, see Brown 2014:66–79; Zeller 2010:456–59; Fitzmyer 2008:559–61; Schrage 2001:4.111–13; Tuckett 1996:251–60; Sellin 1986:17–37; Wedderburn 1981:229–41.

31. See Oropeza 11/2016.

Solidarity in Belief of the Resurrection: Fifth Supporting Proof (15:1–58)

What may have instigated this denial is that certain members had recently died (11:30), and other members expected them to rise again like Jesus. When this did not happen, they doubted bodily resurrection. They could accept that deification and bodily immortality may be for heroes like Jesus, Hercules, and Achilles. They doubtless heard stories that Asclepius became a god when Zeus struck him with lightning after Hades complained that the dead are diminishing due to Asclepius's cures raising them back to life.[32] Some also surely heard that Romulus, founder of Rome, vanished before death to be seen again as the god Quirinus; this belief was accepted by the masses (Plutarch, *Rom.* 27.3–28).[33] But such transformations, the Corinthians supposed, were for special heroes rather than regular people like themselves who become bodiless shades at death (Homer, *Od.* 11; Virgil, *Aen.* 6).[34] Such a belief would seem to be more acceptable for common folks like the Corinthians than elite philosophical speculations about the soul inhabiting another body after death (Plato, *Phaedr.* 245C–249D) or being absorbed at the conflagration of all things (Epictetus, *Diatr.* 3.13.4–5). Though given their diverse opinions, other members might believe that at death the soul escapes the body forever to live in the heavens and/or be set among the stars (e.g., Josephus, *Bell.* 6.46–47). At all events since the dead bodies of believers were probably cremated, as was often done in Corinth, this likely raised more doubts among the congregants that such bodies could return from the ashes.[35] Doubtless their denial increased rifts in the church, especially with the *some* who agreed with Paul's view of bodily resurrection.

Having presented inartificial proofs of Scripture and witnesses to the resurrection of Christ, Paul turns to the artificial proof of argumentation. He demonstrates that rejecting the resurrection leads to preposterous ramifications (15:12–19). These arguments exhibit disadvantages related to denying the resurrection.[36] The rhetorical proof type he uses is logos, which

---

32. See Diodorus Siculus *Bib. hist.* 4.71.1–4; Pausanius *Descr.* 2.26.5–6; 2.27.4; Homer *Il.* 2.729–33; Sextus Empiricus *Prof.* 1.261–62; Endsjø 2009:48, 57–58.

33. Plutarch (an elite Platonist), however, doubts the fable along with a few similar stories. See more examples in Endsjø 2009; 2008:417–36; Oropeza 11/2016, and Introduction.

34. Brown 2014:79–107, 233, opts for this view rightly evincing bodily immortality through Greco-Roman myths.

35. On cremation in Rome and Corinth, see Pliny *Nat.* 7.53[52]; 55[54]; Cicero *Leg.* 2.57; Thomas 2005:286–88, 301–2; Walbank 2005:261, 270. Similarly, Endsjø 2009:155–58, suggests the Corinthians would disbelieve that mangled and decomposing bodies could be raised again.

36. Appeals to disadvantage characterize deliberative discourse (Thiselton 2000:1214), and yet artificial proofs in this context highlight forensic rhetoric, thus

Solidarity in Belief of the Resurrection: Fifth Supporting Proof (15:1–58)

persuades by rational argumentation, such as by example or enthymeme.[37] A string of conditional clauses beginning with "if" rally against resurrection denials. Thiselton correctly distills Paul's reasoning: "If the universal principle has no currency, by deductive logic a particular instance of it has no currency either."[38] Anders Eriksson poses an argument from consequences in which the premise, **If there is no resurrection from the dead** (15:13a; cf. 16a) requires the missing premise to be, "And Christ is one of the dead." From this the conclusion follows, **neither has Christ been raised** (15:13b, 16b).[39] This conclusion then becomes a sorites posed as a condition from which arise further negative outcomes (15:14b–15, 17b–18, 19) so as to create two complementary structures built on previous premises stated or implied:

A. But if there is no resurrection from the dead, neither has Christ been raised (15:13)

  B. And if Christ has not been raised, then our proclamation is in vain (15:14a–b)

    C. (If our proclamation is in vain, then) your faith is in vain (15:14c)

  B¹. And (if Christ has not been raised) we are found also to be false witnesses concerning God because we testified against God that He raised Christ (15:15a–b)

A¹. When God did not raise (Christ) since the dead are not raised (15:15c–d)

A². For if the dead are not raised, neither has Christ been raised (15:16)

  B². And if Christ has not been raised, your faith is in vain (15:17a–b)

    C.¹ (If your faith is in vain) you are yet in your sins (15:17c)

      D. Then (if you and others who are in Christ are yet in sin) those who have fallen asleep in Christ have perished (15:18).

---

blending judicial and deliberative elements.

37. i.e., a rhetorical deduction often requiring audiences to fill out an abbreviated syllogism (cf. Aristotle *Rhet.* 1.2.2–8; Quintilian *Inst* 5.10.1–3; Eriksson 1998:38–43).

38. Thiselton 2000:1214.

39. Eriksson 1998:258–59.

Solidarity in Belief of the Resurrection: Fifth Supporting Proof (15:1–58)

The conclusion in 15:19 relates both to points A and D, and hence, the entire chain may be implied in this verse. The Lord's resurrection is the essential ground for faith and salvation (15:12–19; cf. Rom 4:25; 10:9).

There are five disadvantages, directly or indirectly, if Christ has not been raised from the dead. First, the apostles' **proclamation is in vain**. Since the gospel tradition proclaimed by Jesus' disciples is that Christ died for our sins, was buried, and rose again (15:3–4), without the resurrection, the central proclamation of the gospel becomes emptied of its power as a direct result of Christ not being raised. Without the objective fact of Christ's resurrection, the content of apostolic proclamation is compromised—it cannot be dealing with reality.[40] Second, since the Corinthians believed that proclamation (15:1–2), which is in vain if Christ is not risen, then it follows that their **faith** in the proclamation also **is in vain**. They have believed a false message. This is the direct result of a vain proclamation that arises from Christ not being raised.[41] Third, the apostles turn out to be **false witnesses concerning God**. They proclaim that God raised Jesus when God did not; thus, they testify against God by claiming God did something God did not do. Fourth, the Corinthians are still enslaved **in their sins**. This seems to follow directly from their faith being in vain. Their sins are not forgiven because their faith has been nullified by believing in a gospel that proclaims Christ is risen when he has not risen. Paul also may be inferring that without Christ's resurrection, the expiation related to his death as spoken through his own words and prophetic Scripture (11:24–25; 15:3) is invalidated. Christ's death has not been vindicated by God without the resurrection. In addition to this, since sin and death are inextricably bound together being generated from Adam's original sin (15:21–23, 54–57; Rom 5:12; 6:23), we can agree with N. T. Wright that "if God has overcome death in the resurrection of Jesus, then the power of sin is broken; but if he hasn't, it isn't."[42]

Finally, **those who have fallen asleep in Christ have perished**. This sleep refers to death (7:39; 11:30; 15:7). Paul's assumption, comparable with Jewish apocalyptic, is that the body sleeps in death and will wake up and rise again (15:20, 51; 1 Thess 4:13–15; cf. Dan 12:2; *T. Jud.* 25.4).[43] This hypothetical condition of the dead in Christ having perished is the outcome of the sorites of those still enslaved to sin as a result of useless

---

40. See Schnabel 2006:914.

41. Paul mentions a vain faith again in 15:17b, but here he omits the middle link of the vain proclamation of the gospel assuming the auditors already know this from verse 14.

42. Wright 2003:332.

43. See Brown 2014:142–43.

Solidarity in Belief of the Resurrection: Fifth Supporting Proof (15:1–58)

faith. They have perished in the sense of being "outside the gospel's saving power."[44] As such, they share the same fate as unbelievers being eternally lost and eschatologically destroyed (1:18; 2:6; 3:17; 2 Cor 2:15–16). Our apostle concludes with another condition and result that seems to be based primarily on the previous result (15:18) along with the main hypothetical statements in 15:13 and 16: **If we have hoped in Christ in this life only, we are to be pitied more than all humans** (15:19). The apostles suffer persecution and hardships in vain as gospel proclaimers if Christ is not risen. They are to be pitied since they are still in sin, and so apart from suffering in this life uselessly for their false belief, they also face eschatological destruction after death.

The previous hypothetical circumstances are then dismissed for the reality of Christ's resurrection, which assures the future resurrection of believers along with death's demise (15:20–28; cf. 6:14; Rom 8:23, 29; Phil 3:20–21). **But now Christ has been risen from the dead, the firstfruits of those who have fallen asleep** in death.[45] Christ's resurrection marks the pivotal point in Paul's apocalyptic framework—it reverses Adam's curse that brought about sin and death in the original creation (Gen 3; cf. Rom 5:12–20). All humanity exists in solidarity with this first human representative, and as a result, **in Adam all die**.[46] However, those who are **in Christ**, the second human representative, **will all be made alive** on account of his resurrection. Our apostle imagines two contrasting realms or domains for those who are *in Adam* and those who are *in Christ*.[47] The latter's realm is the new creation characterized by new life (2 Cor 5:17), which stands over against Adam's fallen creation characterized by death. The resurrection manifestations have their own divinely appointed **order**. Christ's took place first during his advent and is described as the **firstfruits**, which recalls festive offerings associated with the Feast of Weeks (Lev 23:1–22). The occasion marks the firstfruits of harvest offered on the third day after the Passover meal, a feast Paul interprets as foreshadowing Christ's death and resurrection (see 5:7; 15:4). What is offered as firstfruits is holy and representative of the quality and character of the entire harvest that must eventually follow.[48] Christ's risen body anticipates the holy harvest of those in Christ who will

---

44. Boer 1988:108.

45. "But now" (νυνὶ δὲ) introduces "profound statements" about the gospel (12:18; 13:13; Garland 2003:705).

46. On Adam's fall in apocalyptic discourse, see Boer 1988:111. For an Adamic survey, see Legarreta-Castillo 2014:5–31.

47. See Campbell 2012:347–49; Brown 2014:143.

48. See Holleman 1996:50; Weiss 1910:356; Thiselton 2000:1224.

Solidarity in Belief of the Resurrection: Fifth Supporting Proof (15:1–58)

also be raised bodily. Jacob Thiessen explains an early Christian tradition that Paul may assume:

> According to the account in Acts God's Spirit was "poured out" (cf. Acts 2:33) 50 days after Jesus' resurrection on the first day of Pentecost or Feast of Weeks (cf. Acts 2:1), the very day on which the "firstfruits" of the wheat harvest were to be dedicated to God (cf. Exod 34:22; Lev 23:16–25; Num 28:26ff; Deut 16:9f.) Since this "outpouring," God's Spirit is leading people to faith in Jesus and is gathering them as "firstfruits" (cf. 1 Cor 16:15; 2 Thess 2:13; Jas 1:18; Rev 14:4). He furthermore is the guarantee of their bodily resurrection (Rom 8:10f; 2 Cor 1:22; 5:5; Eph 1:14,19f) and thus of the eschatological "harvest."[49]

Those who are of Christ represent the harvest's remainder and are next in the order of events related to resurrection; they will be raised **at his** (Christ's) second **coming**. The dead in Christ apparently precede those who are still alive at that time (15:51–52; 1 Thess 4:13–17). Paul's use of this "coming" (παρουσία) imagines a pompous entrance of Christ as a king.[50] This depiction recalls another triumphal procession (cf. 15:57), but this time the Messiah is not the condemned criminal bearing his cross under the mighty power of Rome as in 1:18, but the triumphal general who subdues Rome, Caesar, kings, and all other rulers and authorities, whether in the heavens or on earth (15:24–28; cf. 2:6–8; Rom 8:38; 16:20; Col 1:16; Eph 6:12; Dan 7:10–14). For Paul this takes place at **the end** of human history.[51] If there is any time lapse between the second coming and the end, it would seem to be set aside for defeating every oppositional power, including death (15:53–55 cf. 1 Thess 1:10; 5:1–8; 2 Thess 1:6–10; 2:8). Presumably, judgment day also takes place at this time even though Paul does not mention it here (4:4–5; 6:2–3; 2 Cor 5:10).[52] A chiasm is detectable in 15:24–28:[53]

A "when . . . " (15:24a)

  B "when . . . all/every" (15:24b)

    C "for . . . all . . . under his feet" (15:25)

---

49. Thiessen 2012:388.
50. See in papyri sources on παρουσία in Arzt-Grabner et al. 2006:482.
51. Here τέλος should be interpreted temporally as the "end" (cf. 1:8; Fitzmyer 2008:571), not as the "rest" so as to make a third group raised from the dead.
52. Paul does not explain here what happens to the dead prior to any of these events; that subject is reserved for 2 Cor 5:1–8 (see Oropeza 2016:304–29).
53. See Heil 2005:212–13.

Solidarity in Belief of the Resurrection: Fifth Supporting Proof (15:1–58)

        D "the last . . . " (15:26)

      C^1 "for . . . all . . . under his feet" (15:27a)

    B^1 "when . . . all/every" (15:27b)

  A^1 "when . . . " (15:28)

With D as the centerpiece, **the last enemy abolished is death**. This structural form emphasizes a connection between the end and victory over the ultimate enemy of death. Among the many beliefs about the afterlife in Paul's world, it was normally believed that death could not be reversed.[54] Through reliance on the power of God via Christ's resurrection, however, it will finally be defeated. The perpetual curse of the Adamic creation will come to an end as the new creation in Christ is fully realized.

The divine necessity of having Christ reign and God placing **all enemies under** Christ's **feet** finds it ground through a conceptual blend of Ps 8:6–7 and 110[109]:1.[55] The blend is a familiar one for emergent Christians (Eph 1:20–22; 1 Pet 3:21–22; Heb 2:5–8), which may suggest that Paul did not originate the link but received it in a fixed form.[56] In the former psalm, early disciples seem to identify Christ as the "son of man" when interpreting "you [God] put all things under his [son of man's] feet" (Ps 8:4; cf. Dan 7:9–14).[57] Perhaps this term also informs Paul that Christ is the eschatological representative of humans and thus the last Adam (15:21–22, 45). The word "feet" from Ps 8:6 was then linked with 110[109]:1 to interpret that if all things are under the son of man's feet, then so are his enemies: "The Lord [God] said to my Lord [Christ, the Son of Man], 'Sit on my right hand until I make your enemies the footstool of your feet'" (cf. Mark 12:35–37). God grants Christ authority to defeat all powers opposed to his name and judge among the nations (Ps 110[109]:2–3, 5–6).

When God has sovereignly placed everything under Christ, death included, Christ will then deliver the entire dominion of this world to his Father, and the Son will **be subjected to the one** (God the Father) **who put in subjection everything to him** (the Son). This notion is consistent with what Paul writes elsewhere about the future standing of God and his kingly representative—every knee shall bow and every tongue will confess Jesus as

---

54. E.g., Herodotus *Hist.* 3.62.3–5; Plato *Cratylus* 403B; Pindar *Pyth.* 3.1–60; Aeschylus *Eum.* 647–48; Sophocles *Elect.*, 137–39; Pliny the Elder *Nat.* 7.55.190; Virgil *Georg.* 4.453–525; Ovid *Met.* 10.1–11.84.

55. The linking of catchwords between these psalms provides another example of *gezerah shavah* (cf. 10:1–11).

56. Cf. Boer 1988:117–18. Paul does not identify Jesus as "son of man" elsewhere.

57. They probably knew this from oral memories of Jesus's self-designation.

Solidarity in Belief of the Resurrection: Fifth Supporting Proof (15:1–58)

Lord *to the glory of God the Father* (Phil 2:9–11; cf. Gal 1:3–5; Rom 16:27).[58] This enthronement exhibits a king who has routed all foes and now willingly gives gifts to the deity he represents that enabled his victory. In this case Christ *gives back* all that originally belonged to God but was lost apparently through Adam. Paul's imagined triumph subverts the power of Roman ideology not only by replacing Caesar with Jesus and Jupiter with God, but also by portraying the entire creation under God's rule with His Son as viceroy who forever was, is, and remains the mediating creator of all things (8:4–6; cf. Col 1:15–18; 3:11; Eph 1:22–23). The subjection is so **that God may be all in all** (cf. Rom 9:5; 11:36).[59] The curse of sin and death, and principalities and powers, human and demonic, and all things that were separate from the Creator are reversed and now subjected to and in perfect alignment with the will, purpose, and sovereignty of God.[60] Cosmic harmony is fully restored as God rules unchallenged over all things and the divine presence dwells among all things.

EXHORTATIONS AND SUPPORTING ARGUMENTS RELATED TO RESURRECTION (15:29–34)

The following verses raise four questions aimed at persuading against resurrection denial. For Paul this denial encourages unethical behavior, and so he includes some moral imperatives in this section. The first and second questions relate to baptism: **what will those be doing who are baptized for the dead? If the dead are not raised at all, why are they baptized for them?** Among the numerous speculations about the meaning of baptism for the dead, two options stand out in my view.[61] The first is that "for" (ὑπέρ) suggests vicarious baptism "in place of" another person who has already died.[62] The believer is baptized again in proxy of an unbaptized dead person, so that the unbaptized person might be saved and it go well with him or

---

58. Richardson 1994:114–15; Ciampa/Rosner 2010:778.

59. The final "all" (πᾶσιν) is a comprehensive neuter suggesting "both persons and things" (Robertson/Plummer 1925:358). The totality should be understood salvifically rather than metaphysically (Barrett 1968:361).

60. The opposing forces, then, must either be converted, bound, or destroyed.

61. For surveys of interpretation, see White 2012; Hull 2005:7–47; Wolff 1996:392–96. Hull presents another alternative—Paul refers to those being baptized on account of their faith in Christ being raised from the dead and that "the dead in Christ are destined for resurrection" (235). Such a group, as Cameron/Miller 2011:284 note, tends to promote a Pauline baptismal faction when Paul opposes such factions (1:10–13).

62. E.g., Sharp 2014:36–66; DeMaris 1995:661–82. Compare Judas Maccabeus's supplication and a sin offering for his soldiers that already died; the assumption is that they will rise again (2 Macc 12:39–45).

Solidarity in Belief of the Resurrection: Fifth Supporting Proof (15:1–58)

her after death. If this is the correct interpretation, neither Paul nor other apostles teach it.[63] Paul identifies its practitioners as "they," pointing to another group distinct from his colleagues and himself. Certain Corinthians apparently practice this, and Paul assumes the deniers, if they do not do it themselves, at least accept the legitimacy of others practicing it. He himself seems ambivalent to it, neither confirming nor denying that proxy baptism is efficacious for the dead. He only mentions this practice for the sake of argument. Since baptism signifies the bodily enactment of dying and rising again (Rom 6:4), and certain Corinthians take initiative to perform this enactment in place of the dead, it follows that they should believe in bodily resurrection and the hope of one day being reunited with those for whom they were baptized.

A second perspective interprets "for" as causal with the meaning of baptism "on account of" the dead. This imagines unbaptized individuals, perhaps at emergent Christian funerals, deciding to get baptized in order to be reunited after death with their deceased loved ones who were baptized believers.[64] Despite any mixed motives for doing so, they get baptized "on account of" or because of the influence of these dead believers. With either view, it is assumed that these Corinthians believe through baptism that one's new life and washing away of sins is inclusive of one's body. Likewise, they believe in life after death, which then precludes their acceptance of views that do not, such as Epicurean philosophy.

Paul's third and fourth questions address persecutions that he and other apostles experience (15:30, 32a).[65] The third question addresses the constant nature of this hardship: **And why are we in danger every hour? . . . I face death daily**. The hyperbolic "every hour" highlights the repetitive nature of his hardships (cf. Rom 8:36; 2 Cor 4:10). His dying daily, which he confirms by oath, involves more than mere bodily jeopardies but also his own determination to die to himself and offer his body as a self-sacrifice to fulfill his calling as a missionary in the face of opposition.[66] An oral tradition originating from Jesus perhaps stands behind this idea—disciples must take up their crosses when following Jesus, implying a constant denial of self (Matt 10:38; 16:24; Mark 8:34; Luke 9:23).[67] Paul elicits pathos aiming to

---

63. Early church fathers will consider its practitioners to be aberrant or heretical: e.g., Marcionites, Cerenthians (cf. Tertullian *Marc.* 5.10; Epiphanius *Pan.* 28.6; further, Garland 2003:717).

64. E.g., Reaume 1995; Thiselton 2000:1248–49.

65. "We" in these verses excludes the Corinthians; they were not being persecuted.

66. See Edwards 1885:425–26.

67. Luke's version adds "daily." Ps 44[43]:22–23 also comes close to this.

Solidarity in Belief of the Resurrection: Fifth Supporting Proof (15:1–58)

provoke his auditors to feel sympathy for him. He constantly faces missionary hardships so that Gentiles like them might be saved.

The fourth question centers on his current opposition from where he writes this letter: **If . . . I fought with wild beasts in Ephesus, what benefit is it to me?** (cf. 16:8–9; 2 Cor 1:8–11). It is unlikely that Paul would survive an ordeal of being literally sentenced *ad bestias*. If he is a Roman citizen he would be exempt from arena battles with beasts (Justinian *Digest*, 28.1.8.4; cf. Acts 22:25–29).[68] His words **from a human standpoint** probably means that what he communicates here should be understood in a popular or figurative way (cf. 9:8; Gal 3:15; Rom 3:5; 6:19).[69] Paul probably faces human opposition that may reflect a conflict with the devotees of the goddess Artemis (Diana), who was commonly associated and depicted with animals and known as the "mistress of wild beasts" (Homer *Il.* 21.468–470).[70] If so, he presents here "an allusive instance of anti-Artemis rhetoric."[71] Luke seems to corroborate this interpretation by claiming that Paul faced opposition in Ephesus from followers of this goddess (Acts 19:21–41).

As surely as errant belief leads to errant behavior, Paul expresses the inevitable outcome of denying the resurrection:[72] **If the dead are not raised, "Let us eat and drink, for tomorrow we die!"** A well-known example of moral abandonment in the face of death takes place in Athens during the great pestilence associated with the Peloponnesian War (Thucycides *Hist.* 2. 52.3–53.4). But Paul more likely derives his words from Isa 22:13.[73] Jerusalem is on the brink of being invaded by Assyrians, and instead of showing signs of remorse or praying for the Lord's help, inhabitants decide to have an indulgent party instead, knowing their doom is near. This immoral behavior related to feasting plays a sarcastic note in which Paul intimates Corinthian behavior when causing weak members to stumble on account of their consumption of idol foods, and being inconsiderate to poor members because of their overindulgences and getting drunk at the Lord's Supper (8:1–13; 11:17–34). Their conduct at these meals reflects depraved individuals who shun accountability to God and act as though this life is all there is.

---

68. Lietzmann/Kümmel 1949:83.
69. Winter 2001:102; Keener 2005:128–29.
70. See Hooker 2013:37–46; Frayer-Griggs 2013a:459–77.
71. Frayer-Griggs 2013a:477.
72. See Garland 2003:678.
73. See other parallels in Wis 2.1–9; 1 *En.* 102.6–9; Strabo *Geogr.* 4.5.9; Athenaeus *Deipn.* 10.430C; Plutarch *Suav. viv.* 1098C; Malherbe 1968:76–79.

Solidarity in Belief of the Resurrection: Fifth Supporting Proof (15:1–58)

Lest they misinterpret his irony as encouraging the very thing he condemns, Paul directs some pointed imperatives their way evoking pathos; they should feel ashamed of their behavior. First, he charges them, **do not be deceived**! As Winter points out, they should not think that "their future was not spiritually affected by their present actions."[74] The maxim, **bad companions corrupt good habits**, best known to us from Menander (*Thais* frag. 187[218]; cf. Plutarch *Lib. ed.* 12D; Philo, *Det.* 38), contextually denounces prostitution, which happens to be a problem relevant for the Corinthians.[75] Corrupt influences may come from the outside, such as from their sexual liaisons (6:9–20), and also from insiders who live immorally but claim to be believers (5:9–11). It behooves congregation members, then, to be alert to bad influences and take the appropriate steps necessary to ensure sufficient fellowship with those who really know God, while at the same time remaining a positive influence to outsiders.[76] Second, he charges them that, instead of getting drunk and indulging in destructive vices reminiscent of their pre-converted status, they must **get sober and stop sinning**! Their present unethical conduct demonstrates that **some have no knowledge of God**, an ironic twist that especially deflates the strong members who boast of just the opposite (8:1–3). In the present context, not knowing God may be associated with lack of recognition that God knows everything including their sinful behavior to which they will be held accountable on judgment day (4:5). It also reflects their lack of dependency on God's sovereignty and power to create new things, such as raising the dead (cf. Rom 4:17b).[77]

THE NATURE OF BODILY RESURRECTION (15:35–49)

Having advanced his exhortations Paul now explains the nature of the resurrection starting with two questions: **But one will say, "How are the dead raised and with what kind of body do they come?"** The first question may either reflect an actual Corinthian question or Paul's own rhetorical question to direct the discussion in a didactic way. The second question may simply explicate the first. There seems to be implied skepticism, as though Paul were challenged by an interlocutor in a diatribe.[78] Our apostle responds in the vocative: **You foolish fellow!**[79] He answers these questions employing

74. Winter 2001:98.
75. Ibid. 99–100.
76. See Ciampa/Rosner 2010:793–94.
77. So Thiselton 2000:1256–57.
78. See Aune 2003:128; Asher 2000:67–79; Keener 2005:130.
79. With this rebuke Paul views his auditors more as students than opponents (see

Solidarity in Belief of the Resurrection: Fifth Supporting Proof (15:1–58)

analogies from agriculture, biology, and astronomy as he uses anaphora with the repetitive "another" (15:36–41), four antithetical statements (42–46), comparisons and antitheses (47–51), more anaphora along with asyndeton (the omission of conjunctions: 15:52), and paronomasia (similar sounding words: 15:53–54; cf. vv. 42–43). The structural order in 15:35–58 parallels 15:12–34 (see above).

He first associates the body and resurrection with planting seeds: **what you sow does not come alive unless it dies. And what you sow is not the body that it will become, but you sow a bare kernel** (15:36b–37).[80] He returns here to the metaphor of firstfruits at the Feast of Weeks (15:20–23). Having already associated agrarian imagery with Christ and the believers' resurrection, he now expands on it, this time focusing not on the fully grown grain but on its radical transformation from a mere seed to the finished product. To this imagery he seems to blend in an allusion from the creation story in which plants yielding their seed are created on the third day (Gen 1:11–12). But now he is more interested in the new creation and thus relates seeds to human bodies, more precisely dead bodies that are buried, which in Christ will be raised again. Both John 12:24 and 1 Clement 24.5 likewise associate seed burial with the resurrection. This analogy may be something widely taught by early Christ followers.

Our apostle also mentions that the kernel without its husk is nude, which may resonate a faint echo recalling human bodies returning naked to the dust of death, thus departing from this world in the same bodily state they entered it (Job 1:21; Eccl 5:15). This nudity may also presuppose the Genesis creation. Adam and Eve were not ashamed of their original nakedness (Gen 2:25; cf. 3:7–11). According to certain traditions, Adam's original body was clothed with righteousness and divine glory (*Vita Adam* 12.1; 13.2–3; 14.2).[81] This glory or radiance that reflects God's presence was stripped from his body when he sinned (*Apoc. Mos.* 20–21; 39.2), but there is anticipation for a future body of the righteous that will again be clothed with it (1 *En.* 62.15–16).[82] Along these interpretative lines, Adam saw that he was "naked," which perhaps meant that he was stripped of divine glory,

---

Asher 2000:77–79).

80. The comparison should not be pressed, however. In farming the seed does not technically "die" when covered with earth but remains hidden in the ground invisible to the human eye before its spouts. Likewise, the grain that arises to "life" from the seed does not live forever but eventually dies, unlike those who are raised from the dead.

81. See further references in Kim 2004:39–42, 52–57; Pate 1991:60; 1993:69–77, 88–89.

82. Kim 2004:56.

Solidarity in Belief of the Resurrection: Fifth Supporting Proof (15:1–58)

and he would now be subject to death and decay (Gen 3:17–19).[83] The garments of "skins" that God made for Adam and Eve (Gen 3:21), though sometimes understood as animal skins, is sometimes interpreted as the original couple being clothed with mortal human flesh (*Gen. Rab.* 20:12; Job 10:11; cf. Ezek 37:6–8).[84] An idea similar to this may be presupposed by Paul's use of nudity that analogously compares a bare kernel with both the mortality and the external flesh of the human body. This same body will be transformed into an immortal one clothed with divine glory through the resurrection (15:49, 53–54).

For Paul it would seem that regardless of whether dead bodies are reduced to particles, ashes, or bones, they are given new life and transformed to possess and reflect divine glory. God, who created all things, is powerful enough to rework and restore bodies from whatever materials or lack of them remain. Even so, the seed sown in the ground looks very different than what grows from it, and so it is possible to surmise that this analogy suggests that the raised body will be different than the buried one. Perhaps more accurately, though, both continuity and discontinuity are meant contextually.[85] The perishable body of Jesus sown in burial was recognizable as the same person in the resurrected state, even though he was now glorified. As the firstfruit, so will be the harvest regarding the nature of resurrection.

Further analogies that reflect the resurrected body include Paul's mention of different types of animal and celestial bodies, both of which probably allude to their creation in Gen 1–3. The celestial/heavenly bodies refer to the stars and other lights in the sky, though it is not impossible that they might be interpreted by some to include angels from heaven.[86] Both heavenly and earthly bodies possess glory, suggesting the goodness of creation, and despite Adam's sin and subsequent death, some residual glory is maintained among humans and creatures.[87] All have variegating degrees of **glory** (i.e., beauty and radiance) endowed to them by the good pleasure of their Creator. In 15:42, **in this manner also** assumes and takes up the content of 15:36b–41 in a fourfold manner astutely described by Thiselton: "(a) the *discontinuity* between the old body which is '**sown**' (v. 37) and the new body which is **raised** (v. 42); (b) the sovereign power of God to enact far-reaching

---

83. Differently, philosophical schools might interpret nudity as the soul persisting after death stripped of the body: Plato *Gorgias* 523A–524A; Philo *Virt.* 76.

84. See Anderson 2001:124–26, 217.

85. On the terms, see Gillman 1982:332.

86. Meyer 1887:2.87, argues for angels as the heavenly bodies, marshalling Gospel traditions that connect resurrection with being like the angels (Matt 22:30; Mark 12:25; Luke 20:36).

87. See Worthington 2011:176, 185.

Solidarity in Belief of the Resurrection: Fifth Supporting Proof (15:1–58)

transformation of his own devising, however unimaginable this may be to human mortals now (v. 38); (c) the *variety* of modes of existence that lie within the sovereign capacity of God to create; and (d) the *continuity of identity* suggested by such terms as *each . . . its own* body (v. 38)."[88]

The four antithetical statements that follow attempt to clarify the distinction between the present and resurrected body (15:42–44). "It" in these verses refers to the human body in contrasting pairs (cf. 15:37), and from this we can affirm continuity between the body that dies and one that rises. Each has to do with a state, condition, or mode of existence rather than substance.[89] The first antithesis contrasts the present human body as **perishable**, buried in death, and implicating the sentence of death given to Adam after he sinned. It will be **raised imperishable**, never to die again. Second, the body is **sown in dishonor** but **raised in glory**. This dishonor probably refers to the original Adamic glory that was lost after Adam's fall (see 15:37). This state of dishonor will be over when the body radiates again at the resurrection even more than before to shine as bright as the stars of heaven (2 Cor 3:18 cf. Dan 12:3; 1 *En.* 62.15–16; 104:2–6).[90] Third, the body is **sown in weakness**, but **it is raised in power**. This weakness reflects physical limitations, deformities, disabilities, and diseases experienced in aging and frail bodies, of which Paul's body is an example (2 Cor 4:7–12; Phil 3:21). All such weaknesses will be replaced by the resurrected body that exemplifies transformation and revitalization being animated and energized by God's Spirit (1 Cor 2:1–5; 2 Cor 12:9–10; Rom 8:11).

Fourth and finally, the human body is first sown as a **soulish-animated body**, and raised a **Spirit-animated body** (15:44). God's Spirit is the active power who transforms the soulish-animated person (ψυχικός) into the Spirit-animated person (πνευματικός). The ψυχικός body is made of dust and belongs to the original creation. It is animated by the natural human life force that characterizes Adam into whom God bestowed the breath of life when he became a soul or living being (Gen 2:7).[91] Here "soul" (ψυχή) means

---

88. Thiselton 2000:1271 (boldface and italics in the original).

89. See Johnson 2003:304; Ware 2014a:831.

90. This does not mean, however, that Paul believed the resurrected body *becomes* a star; it only shines like one. See Collins 1993:394; Rabens 2013:88–90; *pace* Engberg-Pedersen 2010:42–43. Some Corinthians, though, might believe the dead become stars. On ancient sources related to celestial immortality, see, Litwa 2012:140–46.

91. The Genesis context helps interpret "soul" (ψυχή/נֶפֶשׁ) as a property of both humans and other creatures as living beings (Gen 1:20, 24; cf. Rev 16:3). What distinguishes human from beast is God's image (εἰκών/צֶלֶם), not the ψυχή (Gen 1:26; 5:1–3). It would seem that for Paul, the first Adam was created with a body composed of dust and with a human "spirit" (cf. 1 Thess 5:23; 2 Cor 7:1), but not normatively animated by the divine Spirit associated with Christ's resurrection.

Solidarity in Belief of the Resurrection: Fifth Supporting Proof (15:1–58)

for Paul the "'life-force': that is, the sense of aliveness, operating through breath and blood, energy and purpose, which is common to humankind."[92] The point is one of animation rather than composition. As the ψυχικός body does not designate a body consisting of "soul-substance," so the πνευματικός body does not designate a body formed out of "Spirit-stuff."[93] Rather, as Wright affirms, πνευματικός "describes, not what something is *composed of*, but what it is *animated by*. It is the difference between speaking of a ship made of steel or wood on the one hand and a ship driven by steam or wind on the other."[94] The πνευματικός body characterizes those who are in Christ; their existence via the Spirit overcomes the state of death characterizing the first Adam and creation, and they participate with the **last Adam** (Christ) in the new creation. In the resurrection, they experience the fulfilment of the final deposit of the Spirit (2 Cor 1:22; 5:5; cf. Rom 8:23).[95] As such, they become fully empowered by the Spirit to the extent which God had ultimately intended. It may be said that in the resurrection, the soul as the principle that animates the body is replaced by the Spirit.[96] Rather than philosophies of the spiritual or immaterial self escaping from the body at death, Paul promotes the body undergoing a qualitative transformation at the resurrection with the self intact.[97]

In 15:45 Paul claims, **so also it is written: "The first man Adam became a living being"; the last Adam** *became* **a life-giving Spirit**. Genesis

---

92. Wright 2003:350.

93. So Rabens 2013:95. Some suggest that πνεῦμα was thought to consist of lighter material "stuff" than the heavier matter of things such as flesh and bone; and the πνευματικός body is comprised of this lighter substance (e.g., Engberg-Pedersen 2009:125; Martin 1995:21–25, 128). To what extent Paul wished to equate or distinguish material properties and πνεῦμα, however, remains unclear and risks asking questions Paul was not attempting to answer. In normal grammatical use the adjectival ending of -ικος in ψυχικός and πνευματικός generally connote *likeness* or *mode of existence* or *having the characteristic of* (rather than its substance as with -ινος endings). This may suggest that the material nature of these bodies is not what is at stake (cf. Brodeur 2004:124, 130; Brown 2014:206, 216). Since the adjective πνευματικός is contrasted with ψυχικός, it "must similarly refer to the source of the body's life and activity, describing the risen body as given life by the Spirit" (Ware 2014b:488–89).

94. Wright 2003:352, who references Aristotle *Hist. Anim.* 584b.22; Vitruvius *Architecture* 10.1.1.

95. Schnabel 2006:968.

96. With Wright 2003:346.

97. Differently, Engberg-Pedersen 2009:126–28, likens this transformation to Aristotle's view of "substantive change" in which a substance becomes new substance, rather than a qualitative change in which the substance remains but alters its properties, qualities, or manner of existence. See discussion in Ware 2014a:828.

Solidarity in Belief of the Resurrection: Fifth Supporting Proof (15:1–58)

2:7 informs the first sentence,[98] and perhaps Ezek 37:1–14 informs the second. Ezekiel's vision of the valley of dry bones connects God's Spirit with giving new life to the dead, and the idea of new life coming about by the breath or spirit alludes back to God breathing life into Adam in Gen 2:7.[99] We could surmise that Paul interprets this vision to be anticipating resurrection, and since it echoes the old creation of Adam, he contrasts this creation with a new one related to resurrection. Both cases result in *bodies* being formed. With this backdrop in place, along with 15:44 and 46 that assume the respective soulish- and Spirit-animated bodies, we can adduce that both the first Adam and last Adam have bodies even though the word "body" (σῶμα) does not appear in verse 45. Paul's ellipsis assumes his audience can readily draw the contextual inference that both Adam (the living soul being) and the risen Christ (the life-giving Spirit being) have not suddenly lost their bodies in one verse! The apostle elaborates on what was already said in 15:22—to be in Adam is to participate in the soulish animated existence and die; to be in Christ is to participate with the spiritual animated existence and rise from the dead to new life. God, Christ, and the Spirit all participate in raising what is dead to new life (2 Cor 3:6; Rom 4:17; 8:11; cf. 1 Tim 6:13; John 5:21; 6:63), so much so that Paul refers to Christ and God's Spirit interchangeably not only here but also in 2 Cor 3:17 and Rom 8:9–11. As the "soul" gives the body its animation and activity in the old creation, in the resurrection, so Christ as the life-giving Spirit gives the transformed body life and activity in the new creation.[100]

More antitheses follow in 15:46–49. Adam, the soulish-animated **man from the dust** of the earth came first, and then the second man came, the Spirit-animated man, Christ who is **from heaven**. With the soulish Adam being first, Paul revisits the order of salvific and transformative events (cf. 15:20–23), which perhaps suggests that some Corinthians need to be reminded about this order. Also, Paul may be stressing distance between the present and future bodies here.[101] The first Adam represents the rest of humankind in the present state—mortals who dwell on earth and are perish-

---

98. Paul adds "first" (πρῶτος) and possibly "Adam" (Ἀδάμ), which are not found in the LXX (unless he used a tradition similar to Theodotion and Symmachus, which include the latter: Gladd 2009:299). Both words are included to aid his comparison of this man with Christ.

99. See Ciampa/Rosner 2010:820.

100. See further, Ware 2014a:832–33.

101. Hultgren 2003:355–57. Differently, Philo's heavenly man based on Gen 1:26 comes first, then the earthly man from Gen 2:7 (see comparisons in Horsley 1998:211–13; Perkins 2012:189). For a critique of the notion that Paul is reacting to either Philonic/Alexandrian or Gnostic traditions or realized eschatology, see Hultgren 2003:343–70.

able, made of dust since they originate from the man of dust. Paul's words, **just as we have worn the image of *the man* of dust,** recall Adam being created in God's image and from the dust (Gen 1:26-27; 2:7). The "image" nonetheless also points to Gen 5:1-3. Adam fathers Seth in his own image; that is, Adam's son bore the same qualities and likeness of his human father.[102] For Paul, then, *image* (εἰκών) speaks to bodily identity and affiliation with predecessors, whether with Adam and imperfection or Christ and perfection.[103] Differently, Christ, the last Adam, is a heavenly man, not because in the resurrection he has been created of some sort of heavenly substance void of any continuum with his earthly body, but because he is now associated with the realm of heaven (1 Thess 1:10; 4:16; Rom 10:6). What is heavenly characterizes the state or mode of existence Paul already mentioned in 15:42-45. The risen Christ has a body that is Spirit-energized, imperishable, and glorious, shining with radiance from being in the immediate divine presence (2 Cor 4:4, 6). Those who follow the last Adam will be transformed into the last Adam's image; i.e., into the likeness of the risen Savior who, among other things, is imperishable and glorious (Phil 3:20-21; 2 Cor 3:18; Rom 8:29). Important here is the implication that the believers' resurrection will be of the same sort as Christ's resurrection. They are "offered a possibility to imitate the resurrected Christ."[104] The final words in this section both urge and anticipate the full realization of that transformation at the second coming as though wearing radiant apparel—**let us also wear the image of the man of heaven.**[105]

Transformation and the Defeat of Death (15:50-58)

The conjunctive **now** (δέ) combined with the vocative **brothers and sisters** and **this I say . . . that** suggest a new paragraph starts at 15:50.[106] The unstated question that opens this pericope probably asks, "What happens

---

102. See e.g., Worthington 2011:192-94.

103. Cf. Lorenzen 2008:256, 272.

104. Endsjø 2009:143.

105. Ancient witnesses are divided between the future rendering, "we will also wear (φορέσομεν)" and the hortatory subjunctive, "let us also wear (φορέσωμεν)." If the greater amount of ancient witnesses and harder reading is preferable in such decisions, φορέσωμεν should clearly be the winner: e.g., p46, ℵ, A, C, D (φορέσομεν is supported by e.g., B). Paul wants to convince his auditors to accept their future resurrection; without doing so their faith might turn out to be in vain, and if that were the case, they would miss out on that transformation. Notice that Paul also ends three distinct pericopae with exhortations (15:33-34, 49, 58).

106. Cf. 1:10; 7:29; Fee 1987:797-98.

Solidarity in Belief of the Resurrection: Fifth Supporting Proof (15:1–58)

to the faithful who are alive when Christ returns? How could they be resurrected if they have never died?" Paul responds that **flesh and blood are not able to inherit the kingdom of God, neither does the perishable inherit imperishable**. Humans in their current perishable bodies are unfit for God's kingdom; their bodies must be transformed into imperishable bodies. "Flesh and blood" is idiomatic for living as "frail and sinful human beings" (Gal 1:15–16; Matt 16:17; 17:31).[107] More specifically Paul deploys the phrase in a way that conveys God's decree on Adam (Gen 3:17–19; Sir 14:17–18). It connotes the human body as perishable, belonging to the old creation in Adam. This state is juxtaposed with the imperishable risen body fit for the new creation in Christ. This body is not comprised of immaterial spirit but an immortal body animated by the Spirit.[108] Paul's mention of God's kingdom is perhaps informed by the underlying context of Isa 25, which he quotes in 15:54—the larger context places this victory over death during the Lord's future reign (Isa 24:23).[109] This section also structurally recapitulates earlier imagery related to Christ's dominion and reign over all things, including death (15:23–28).

Our apostle continues that the bodies of those who are alive will be transformed at the second coming of Christ: **we will not all sleep, but we will all be changed**. The first person plural "we" might suggest that some of his auditors and perhaps Paul himself are expected to survive until Christ returns. This perspective, however, conflicts with 6:14 and 2 Cor 4:14 which assume that "we" will die and then be raised again. Such tensions give the impression that Paul does not know whether he and his recipients will be alive or dead at Christ's return. If he is familiar with an oral tradition of Jesus's thief in the night discourse (1 Thess 5:1–11; cf. Matt 24:36–51; Mark 13:32–37), perhaps he is also familiar with the saying that no one knows when Jesus will return (Matt 24:36; Mark 13:32–33; cf. Acts 1:7).[110] This is compatible with Paul speaking in a **mystery**, something known by God and disclosed by his messengers, which assumes that normally speaking such futuristic knowledge is kept hidden. In 15:51, then, "we" may be inclusive of all of Christ's followers. Whether alive or dead at the time of the Parousia, every believer's body will be **changed**. Their identities are persevered

---

107. Johnson 2003:304. The first half of 15:50 is thus more or less explained in the second half (Wright 2003:359).

108. Though Paul does not use the language, his view may be compatible with the idea that flesh in Adam is not the same as resurrected flesh (cf. Luke 24:39).

109. See Wilk 2005:146–47.

110. His later brushes with death and imprisonment likely forced him to think even more soberly of the strong possibility that he might die before Christ returns (2 Cor 1:8–11; Phil 1:20–24).

Solidarity in Belief of the Resurrection: Fifth Supporting Proof (15:1–58)

even though transformed—Paul imagines a change of apparel (ἀλλάσσω),[111] which is virtually synonymous with the "putting on" (ἐνδύω) of the imperishable, immortal covering (15:53). The self under the garment, though fully sanctified, remains the same.[112]

The body's transformation will be instantaneous rather than a long process: **in a moment, in the twinkling of an eye, at the last trumpet**. These words resemble 1 Thess 4:15–18, but there is no mention of a catching away and gathering in the air to meet the Lord. Paul is more interested in describing the nature of bodily transformation here. The final trumpet imagines Israel's feasts again as in 15:20–23. This time the Feast of Trumpet Blasts seems foregrounded. On the first day of the seventh month it signaled that a holy gathering was to take place and the people were to rest from their labors (Lev 23:23–25). Another blast signaled the Day of Atonement ten days later, and work was to cease. This same blast marked the year of Jubilee or "ram's horn" every fifty years (Lev 25:9–13; cf. 23:27–32). In that year, as Christopher Wright affirms, "there was a proclamation of liberty to Israelites who had become enslaved for debt, and a restoration of land to families who had been compelled to sell it out of economic need in the previous fifty years. . . . It was these two components of the jubilee, freedom and restoration, that entered into the metaphoric and eschatological use of the jubilee in prophetic and later NT thought."[113] The convocation seems to have influenced later apocalyptic traditions in which a trumpet blast marked the final Jubilee and gathering of God's exilic people throughout the world to enter into a final time of rest (Isa 27:13; *Pss. Sol.* 11.1–9; Matt 24:31). Paul apparently developed these connections from Leviticus and Isa 25–27, and interpreted such an event in light of Christ's second coming in which Gentiles would be gathered with God's people to celebrate ultimate deliverance, similar to that which Jubilee describes but inclusive of death's defeat.

The outcome of this transformation is derived from Isa 25:8: **then will happen the word that is written: "Death was swallowed up into victory."** Paul's quote follows the Hebrew text closer than Septuagint. The former has God as the subject who swallows up death "forever" (לנצח), whereas the latter in better manuscripts has death as the empowered subject that swallows up nations and people, which then contrasts the Lord God who takes away every tear from every face. Neither version includes the words, "in victory" (εἰς νῖκος), which may suggest that Paul follows a tradition similar

---

111. E.g., Gen 35:2; Appian *Bell. Civ.* 5.122§504.

112. With Ware 2013b:487, we notice that the subject of the perishable and imperishable body remains the same in 15:53–54.

113. Wright 1992:3.1025.

Solidarity in Belief of the Resurrection: Fifth Supporting Proof (15:1–58)

to Theodotion or Aquila that include νῖκος.[114] Otherwise, it is possible that he reads "forever" (לנצח) not in its earlier temporal sense but in its later Aramaic sense in which the root נצח conveys the idea of conquering or being victorious.[115] All the same, Isaiah's context is suitably set in apocalyptic anticipation of divine judgement on heavenly and earthly forces (Isa 24:20–21).[116] At that time Gentile nations will worship and pay homage to the Lord in Zion, and the people who trust in the Lord are saved and protected (25:9; 26:3–4). Although dead enemies who are trampled underfoot will not rise again, "the dead will rise, and those in the tombs will be raised" (26:19; cf. 26:20–27:1). The thematic parallels from Isaiah that inform Paul seem to include the defeat of death, enemies under the feet of the righteous, images of the resurrected life, and the prophetic fulfilment of Gentiles joining God's people.

A second quote originates from Hos 13:14b: **Where, O death, is *your* victory? Where, O death, is *your* goad?**[117] Paul seems to be freely reconfiguring the text or citing a version unavailable to us.[118] The Septuagint renders for the first question, "where is your penalty (δίκη)?" The Hebrew has "where are your plagues (דְּבָרֶיךָ)?" before asking Sheol, "where is your destruction?" Paul's use of "victory" (νῖκος) seems influenced by his previous quote from Isa 25:8, which he now links with Hos 13:14. The quote's interpretation is not helped by the Hebrew context of Hos 13 because there God decides in favor of bringing death to his rebellious people with an Assyrian invasion on the horizon. This context suggests Hos 13:14a be rendered as questions: e.g., "Shall I ransom them from the power of Sheol? Shall I redeem them from death?" (NASB), to which the questions in 13:14b have God bringing on death rather than preventing it (*contra* NIV, NKJV). The Septuagint at 13:14a, however, might be read as statements rather than questions, as Hays translates it: "I will deliver them from the hand of Hades, and will redeem them from Death."[119] If Paul understood the verse this

---

114. Also, like Paul, the passive voice is used for "swallow" in Symmachus (though without νῖκος). See variants in Heil 2005:248–49.

115. Contrast the Hebrew meaning for נצח in BDB and Aramaic in CAL, *ad. loc.* (though the latter is a verb; the Aramaic noun form is נִצְחָן). Boer 1988:127, fuses the two senses by suggesting the victory is a permanent one.

116. The idea of death being swallowed up reverses the role of Sheol (Hades), which enlarges itself to swallow up the dead (Isa 5:14).

117. Unlike Hosea, Paul moves his "your" (σου) in front of the vocative "death" (θάνατε) so as to stress the possessive pronoun and make the taunt more vivid (cf. Heil 2005:250).

118. See Stanley 1992:211–15, for options.

119. Hays 1997:276.

Solidarity in Belief of the Resurrection: Fifth Supporting Proof (15:1–58)

way, it might have provided him with the leverage necessary to interpret God as a deliverer *from* death.[120] Better still, his selection of Hosea is not arbitrary but exemplifies another example of his use of midrash known as *gezerah shavah* (see 1 Cor 10:1–11). He links the hook word "death" from Isaiah with Hosea's text so that the concepts of the former are read into the latter. With this hermeneutic intact, the futuristic time, deliverance, and image of resurrection yet to be fulfilled from Isaiah's text could be read by Paul into Hosea's words so as to evoke a taunt against death rather than invite its mayhem, as Hosea's context does.

Since death is the foreboding lot of all humans (Pliny *Ep.* 5.5; Philostratus *Vit. Soph.* 1.17.504; Seneca, *Lucil.* 49:9–11; 66.42–43; 77.11–19), the prospect of dying prompted philosophers to find ways to assuage that fear, as Seneca evinces: "Death follows old age precisely as old age follows youth. He who does not wish to die cannot have wished to live. For life is granted to us with the reservation that we shall die; to this end our path leads. Therefore, how foolish it is to fear it, since men simply await that which is sure, but fear only that which is uncertain! Death has its fixed rule—equitable and unavoidable. Who can complain when he is governed by terms which include everyone?" (*Lucil.* 30.10–11). Again he writes, "Do you regard as more fortunate the fighter who is slain on the last day of the games than one who goes to his death in the middle of the festivities? Do you believe that anyone is so foolishly covetous of life that he would rather have his throat cut in the dressing-room than in the amphitheatre? ... Death visits each and all; the slayer soon follows the slain ... what does it matter for how long a time you avoid that which you cannot escape?" (93:12). The prophetic taunt that Paul interprets from Scripture inadvertently answers Seneca by signaling the final triumph over life's most unbeatable foe. Through God and the resurrection, death is utterly defeated. The rhetorical questions of "where" death's victory and goad are to be found prompt the auditors to respond, "They are nowhere to be found!"

The **goad of death is sin** is often translated as the "sting of death," but κέντρον in this sentence does not connote the mere sting of an insect (unless a scorpion is meant). More plausible here is the sharp point of a goad used as an instrument of torture (Herodotus, *His.* 3.130) or representing enslavement with a view to treating humans like beasts with goads and whips (Plato *Leg.* 777A). It may be precisely this type of enslavement that prompts Paul's mention of sin not just with death via Adam but also in relation to the Law. In other letters, enslavement is one way Paul describes being in bondage to

---

120. Perhaps he also found this interpretation reinforced by the restoration that takes place in Hos 14:4–7 (cf. Keener 2005:134).

Solidarity in Belief of the Resurrection: Fifth Supporting Proof (15:1-58)

sin, and his arguments against the works of the Law are compatible with his claim that **the power of sin is the Law** (Gal 2:4; 4:8–11; 4:21—5:1; Rom 6:6–7, 20; 8:2). For Paul, Moses's Law, though attempting to create proper boundaries around sin and bring punishment against sinners, exacerbates the problem because it makes humans more aware of sin, condemns them because of it, and cannot ultimately deliver them from it—freedom from sin comes through faith in Christ (Gal 3:19–26; Rom 7:1—8:11). Paul does not elaborate on the Law in our current text or elsewhere in this letter (but see 7:17–19; 9:20–21). We could surmise that he previously taught the Corinthians about it in similar terms as his other letters, and they agreed with him. Hence, he assumes they will agree with him on its role in relation to sin without further explanation.

Paul's thanksgiving over death in 15:57 perhaps informs his later thanksgiving in Rom 7:25, since both are mentioned in relation to sin and the Law. He praises God for granting believers **victory through Jesus Christ our Lord**, which invites us to imagine a final triumphal procession scene, this time reversing the imagery of Christ's death on the cross (1:18) and the apostles' death as captives of war (4:9–15). The procession is clearly in honor of the believers in Christ who are now conquerors over sin and death.

The concluding exhortation recalls the similar pattern of exhortations in 15:29–34 and thus completes the second formal sequence of the A, B, C, D pattern in this chapter (see above). Paul's urge for his auditors to **be steadfast** and **immovable** forms an *inclusio* with their standing and holding firm the gospel in 15:1–2.[121] They must persevere in the gospel proclaimed to them, which anticipates their own bodily resurrection. The final appeal for them to be **always abounding in the work of the Lord, knowing that your labor is not in vain in the Lord** alludes to Isa 65:23 in which God's "chosen ones" will "not labor (κοπιάω) in vain." The context speaks of consolation for God's people who anticipate the promised creation of the new heaven and new earth (65:17).[122] Perhaps Paul reconfigures this promise to mean that the believers' present service done for the Lord's sake, despite any difficulties they might face, would not be in vain but result in their glorious transformation when the new creation is fully present. A reward for one's labor seems more relevant to Paul's own labor than the Corinthians', but our apostle seems to envision a day of recompense for all the faithful in Christ throughout the world (2 Cor 5:10; Rom 2:6, 16; cf. 1 Cor 3:8–15; 4:5). At that time the people who have hoped in God will celebrate over their salvation, "because God will give us rest" (Isa 25:10 LXX).

121. See Fee 1987:808.
122. Rightly, Fitzmyer 2008:608.

Closing Matters (1 Cor 16:1–24)

The closing content of ancient letters commonly discuss business affairs, travel plans, or announcement of visitations, as in 16:1–12.[1] At the same time, Paul may be responding to a Corinthian request for Apollos and inquiries about how to administrate the collection Paul recently implemented. In rhetorical messages the *peroratio* section identifies the arrangement's conclusion and often highlights pathos and recapitulation, among other features.[2] Paul's words in 16:13–24 recapitulates some of the letter's earlier exhortation topics in nuce (16:13–14) and prompts pathos by a fearful warning (16:22). More significantly, this letter shares closing conventions in 16:13–24 in common with other ancient letters, notably Paul's own, which add final appeals, greetings, something written by Paul's own hand, a holy kiss and prayer-wish or doxology, and a final benediction (2 Cor 13:11–13; Gal 6:11–18; 1 Thess 5:23–28; 2 Thess 3:16–18; Col 4:7–18; Rom 16:16–27).[3] We do need to decide between an epistolary or rhetorical close. Anders Eriksson rightly asserts that if rhetoric is regarded "as a theory studying persuasive structures in a text, it can be used to analyze rhetorical features, not only in texts which are the result of a conscious application of that learned theory, but for all oral and written productions that have persuasive [features]."[4]

THE COLLECTION AND ANNOUNCEMENT OF VISITS (16:1–12)

Paul again introduces new topics with the words, **now concerning** (16:1, 12; cf. 7:1, 25; 8:1; 12:1). The closing business matter concerns **the collection for the saints**. We learn from 2 Cor 8:6, 10, that Paul first sent Titus to Corinth for this task.[5] He normally identifies saints as Christ's followers

---

1. See papyri examples in Arzt-Grabner et al. 2006:506–7.
2. See examples and further features in Cicero *Inv.* 1.52.98; *Rhet. Her.* 2.30.47; Aristotle *Rhet.* 3.19.1419b; Quintilian *Inst.* 6.1.2.
3. On closing conventions, see Doering 2012:422–48.
4. Eriksson 1998:282.
5. In 2 Cor 8:10 and 9:2 (c. 55/56 CE), "a year ago" roughly coincides with when he wrote 1 Corinthians, though obviously Titus introduced the collection a little earlier. See Oropeza 2016:478–79.

Closing Matters (1 Cor 16:1–24)

(1:2); here he means the poor among Christ's followers in Jerusalem (Rom 15:25–27, 31; cf. 2 Cor 8:4, 13–15; 9:1, 12; Acts 24:7).

Some possibilities for their poverty include a famine that struck Palestine, the result of being persecuted, or a long-term outcome of church members attempting to share all material goods (Acts 4:32–37; 8:1; 11:28–30; 12:1). The term for the collection, λογεία, relates to various types of business transactions and sometimes religious collections such as for a temple or god.[6] Paul uses this term for a voluntary contribution which seems to have religious and prophetic significance from his perspective. No doubt he hoped that this blessing might mend a developing riff between Judean Christ-followers devoted to Mosaic Law and Gentile converts of his circumcision-free gospel.[7] He may have likewise believed this act would fulfill prophecies about Gentiles bringing their wealth to Zion (Isa 42:6; 49:6; 60:1–19).[8] Some other motivations behind this collection may include Paul's adherence to the Jerusalem apostles' request for him to remember the poor (Gal 2:10) and his commitment to love others (Gal 5:14; Jas 2:1–17; 1 John 3:11–18). His imperative for the Corinthians to do what the Galatian churches currently do centers not on mandatory giving but instruction on *how* they are to contribute—by setting aside money every week. He repeatedly identifies the collection as an act of grace (2 Cor 8:1, 4, 6–7; 9:14), and even after they delayed this collection for a year, he stresses that their giving be done without compulsion (2 Cor 9:6–7; cf. 8:10).

Churches in Galatia, Macedonia, and Achaia assist in this giving; Corinth belongs to the latter's region (16:1; 2 Cor 8:1–5; 9:2; Rom 15:26). This collection perhaps marks the earliest unified international cause among many churches under the banner of charity. Paul instructs the congregation how to proceed: **on the first day of the week, let each one of you set aside something, storing it up as he or she may prosper**. These words suggest that either each person is to save money at home at the beginning of each week, or at that time bring this money to the congregation's designated person for storage.[9] If the former, then no evidence suggests the first of each week was "pay day" for the Corinthians and thus assigned by Paul for that reason.[10] If the latter, then the first of the Sabbath week (μίαν σαββάτου) suggests Sunday as a prominent day for church gatherings, doubtless because Jesus

---

6. See Arzt-Grabner et al. 2006:506–7, who corrects Deissmann 1965:105–7.

7. Along these lines is Nickle 1966:154–55.

8. See Oropeza 2016:513–16; Georgi 1992:100–102. For an overview of interpretations, see Downs 2008:3–26.

9. The phrase παρ' ἑαυτῷ could mean "at home" (BDAG 757) or stress each person individually (Schnabel 2006:1001).

10. Laansma 1997:680.

Closing Matters (1 Cor 16:1–24)

rose again on that day (Luke 24:1; cf. Acts 20:7; Rev 1:10; *Did.* 14.1).[11] The Corinthian church consists of both poor and non-poor members (11:22), though like the Macedonian churches, even poor members might be stirred to give (cf. 2 Cor 8:1–5). Although no standard amount is required or recommended, Paul anticipates each person giving *something* rather than nothing, and they are to give from their prosperity rather than sacrificially; they are not expected to starve so that others might eat.

Paul mentions again his second visit to Corinth (16:2b-9; cf. 4:17–20).[12] He will remain in Ephesus, from where he writes this letter, **until Pentecost**, which is in spring (16:8).[13] Then he will travel through Macedonia visiting other congregations. After a few months he plans to visit Corinth and might **spend the winter** there. Members could then assist him for his travel to **Jerusalem** and handling of the collection (cf. 2 Cor 1:16; Rom 15:25).[14] If some of their own members are approved by them for the task, he will write **letters** of recommendation for them to the Jerusalem church and any others they might visit. Paul submits his plans to **the Lord** (16:4, 7), who through circumstances and the Spirit's guidance ultimately determines whether Paul's plans will be carried out (cf. 4:19).[15] Meanwhile, he says he **will remain in Ephesus . . . for a wide and effective door has opened for me, and there are many adversaries**. This opportunity to proclaim the gospel brings about opposition from the locals (see 15:32).

Another visiting announcement concerns **Timothy** (16:10–11). Whenever Timothy arrives in Corinth, the church is to **see to it that he may be with you without fear**. Timothy's arrival **whenever** (ἐάν) seems less certain than in 4:17.[16] Apparently, as Paul and his writing team composed the letter, it was decided that Timothy should first visit some of the neighboring churches going through Macedonia before arriving in Corinth. Paul expresses less certainty about the timing of Timothy's arrival given this

---

11. On resurrection Sunday as the first day of the new creation, see Oropeza 2016:356.

12. He previously stayed there one and a half years according to Acts 18:11

13. The Corinthians (mostly Gentiles) knew of this Jewish festival (Lev 23:15; Tob 2:1), presumably because they were taught an apostolic tradition related to it (e.g., Acts 2).

14. Although Paul refuses pay for preaching (1 Cor 9), he is not opposed to *every* form of assistance from the Corinthians. He doubtless will lodge there with friends and accept travelling assistance.

15. It will turn out that God had other plans for Paul, a change that upsets the Corinthians (2 Cor 1:12—2:13; 7:4–16; Oropeza 2016:2–18).

16. The aorist tense "I sent" (ἔπεμψα) in 4:17 suggests either that Timothy already left or, if an epistolary aorist is assumed, he would be leaving with this letter (but now Stephanas's group will be carrying the letter).

route.¹⁷ It seems that Stephanas's group may be arriving earlier by ship to Corinth with this letter (16:15–18). Even though the Corinthians apparently know Timothy already (Acts 18:5), Paul commends him in the style of a letter of recommendation—he discloses the name of the one commended and his relationship with that person. Timothy is Paul's coworker whose qualifications include being faithful in services pertaining to the Lord, and his assignment is to train up the Corinthians in all of Paul's ways (16:10–11; cf. 4:17).¹⁸ Given the competitive way the Corinthians compare leaders and evaluate speaking performances, Paul, with good reason, has apprehension about how they might scrutinize and intimidate Timothy. Unless he strongly urges them to treat his protégé well, Timothy might not gain their approval.¹⁹ He sternly charges them to **let no one despise** Timothy, **but send him in peace so that he may come to me**. He expects the congregation to return Timothy safely, "facilitated by the practical support of necessary provisions and other practical needs."²⁰ To assure his safe travel, Timothy should be accompanied by whichever **brothers and sisters** the church might want to send Paul at that time.

The Corinthians make a request (or inquiry) that **Apollos** should visit them again (16:12).²¹ Some who consider Apollos their leader probably made this request, and Paul responds that he **strongly urged** Apollos **that he might come** to them along with those bringing this letter, **but he was quite unwilling to come at this time**. These words seem to betray Apollos's reluctance to visit them on hearing about their divisions over allegiances to him (cf. 1:12). He probably thinks that in their current condition a visit might be counterproductive.²² Paul's urge to Apollos reflects that he does not think Apollos had instigated this faction, and none should infer from these words that there existed tensions between the two missionaries.²³

---

17. For various travel explanations, see Barrett 1968:390–91; Fitzmyer 2008:622.

18. On the contours of letter recommendation, see further Kim 1972; Collins 1999:595, 602.

19. This might especially be the case if later characterizations of Timothy being despised as a youth has merit (1 Tim 4:12). Timothy's alleged timidity, however, which some interpret from 2 Tim 1:7 and 2:1–3, is more fiction than fact according to Hutson 1997:58–73.

20. Thiselton 2000:1331.

21. Alternatively, Garland 2003:761, thinks that Paul anticipates their displeasure when hoping for and not finding Apollos among those presently being sent. He thus attempts to defuse any suspicions they might have that he prevented Apollos from returning to them.

22. Wolff 1996:433–34 and Thiselton 2000:1332, notice that Paul mentions no greeting to the Corinthians from Apollos, when one might be expedient in 16:19.

23. Rightly, Mihaila 2009:191–93.

Closing Matters (1 Cor 16:1–24)

Apollos may visit them later on when a future **opportunity** arises; Paul leaves unmentioned that that opportunity may be contingent upon the Corinthians ending their rivalries.

Epistolary Close (16:13–24)

Paul advances some closing exhortations, a feature typically found toward the end of his letters (e.g., 2 Cor 13:11; 1 Thess 5:16-22; Phil 4:8-9; Rom 16:17). The brief imperatives in 16:13-14 are in the present tense, "calling for a continuous response."[24] The first four are agonistic, resembling exhortations common to military battles, such as when Archidamus exhorts Peloponnesian officers before their expedition against the Athenians (Thucydides, *Hist.* 2.11.9) and Ajax encourages the Argives to continue fighting the Trojans (Homer, *Il.* 15.559-65). Paul encourages the Corinthians to struggle successfully against influential forces that might undermine the gospel of their salvation. The imperative, **be alert**, will ensure that no such influences catch them off guard so that their spiritual life is jeopardized before Christ's second coming (e.g. 1:7-8; 3:13; 4:3-5; cf. 1 Thess 5:6-10). They must **stand firm in faith**, which has as its object belief in and commitment to Christ and the gospel (15:1-2, 14, 17, 58). The imperatives, **show courage** and **be strong**, are found together when General Joab encourages his brother Abishai to be valorous in battle against Israel's enemies (2 Sam 10:12 [LXX]).[25] Paul, however, seems to have in view a battle against life's hardships along with resisting temptation. Cowardice in this realm can lead to spiritual defection (cf. *Mart. Pol.* 4.1; 9.1; Rev 21:8). Paradoxically, when it comes to vice, sometimes the bravest thing to do is flee from it (6:18; 10:14). The last brief imperative recalls our apostle's words about being considerate of others and fostering unity among members: **Let everything you do be done in love** (cf. 8:1-3; 12:31—13:13).

Final appeals in this letter urge compliance with ministerial workers currently with Paul in Ephesus and soon leaving for Corinth (16:15-18). The congregation is to submit to all such workers, and in particular the **house of Stephanas**, which may include family members, slaves, or freedmen. Stephanas may be fairly wealthy as the head of a large household and with means to travel. This household, along with Crispus and Gaius, were the only converts baptized by Paul when he was in Corinth (1:14-16). As such,

---

24. Collins 1999:599.

25. The former is more literally to "act like a man" (ἀνδρίζομαι), which may be contrasted with acting childishly and cowardly (Thiselton 2000:1336). Differently, Mayordomo-Marin 2011:515-28, contrasts it with acting womanish (but see Musonius Rufus, *Lect* 4, on women having courage).

Closing Matters (1 Cor 16:1-24)

they are **the firstfruits of Achaia**—the first of his converts who have grown to the point of being able and willing to serve as ministers of the collection.[26] Perhaps the district of Achaia is mentioned instead of its capitol, Corinth, because Stephanas's group will be assisting with the collection for the entire district inclusive of other churches. They **appointed themselves** to be directly involved with assisting in the collection mentioned earlier—the idea of one's dedication **for the service to the saints** becomes a technical term associated with the collection (Rom 15:26; 2 Cor 8:4; 9:1, 12).[27] Their self-appointment, which involves labor and toil, is not motivated by vainglory or ambition to rule others, but as Barrett adduces, it is due to noticing a need and then "in a spirit not of self-assertion but of service and humility they appointed themselves. In other words, they were appointed directly by God, who pointed out to them the opportunity of service and (we may suppose) equipped them to fulfil it."[28] To **submit** to all such workers in a community that truly exemplifies love (cf. 16:14) is not concerned about abuse related to the exploitation of power and positions.[29] Incidentally, the Corinthians' submission is not gender specific; they are to comply with female workers, too, such as Prisca and Phoebe (Rom 16:1).[30]

The coming of **Stephanas and Fortunatus and Achaicus** is the cause of Paul's rejoicing. Fortunatus and Achaicus are either independent fellow believers or members of Stephanas's house.[31] Paul is **refreshed** by them because he longs to have fellowship with and nurture the Corinthians; what was lacking of their physical presence these three representatives have fulfilled.[32] But in what sense did they also refresh the Corinthians (16:18a)? Since these men are probably couriers for Paul's letter,[33] he anticipates that

---

26. Here firstfruits implies growth (Weiss 1910:386) and probably emphasizes being outstanding rather than literally being first. Edwards 1897:471, argues that the region's first converts were Athenians (Acts 17:34). It is not clear in Acts, however, that Paul baptized them.

27. Zeilinger 1997:1.266.

28. Barrett 1968:394.

29. Similarly, see Hays 1997:290.

30. Rightly, Witherington 1995:319, who adds Chloe to this list.

31. Fee 1987:831, claims that both names are common to slaves and freedmen.

32. Compare Paul's emotionally distraught temperament ("spirit") longing to find Titus, which is then refreshed after seeing him and hearing his positive report of the Corinthians (2 Cor 2:12-13; 7:5-7).

33. In less reliable manuscripts, the letter's subscript includes these names with Timothy as apparent couriers of the letter (see Metzger/United Bible Societies 1994:504). Did they also earlier bring the Corinthians' letter to Paul? Since Paul writes a recommendation for Stephanas and those with him in 16:15-18, this implies that the Corinthians might be reluctant to cooperate with them (Witherington 1995:319-20).

Closing Matters (1 Cor 16:1–24)

upon their arrival in Corinth, the congregants there will be relieved to know that these members returned to them safely and brought joy and comfort to the apostle.[34] The Corinthians are to **acknowledge such *persons* as these**. This imperative (ἐπιγινώσκετε) relates to honoring, respecting, or recognizing the merit of the persons to whom it is attributed.[35] We also have here an early glimpse of leadership being raised up among a congregation's own members.[36]

In conventional fashion Paul sends final greetings from other brothers and sisters (16:19–20). The **churches in Asia Minor** that greet them include Ephesus and perhaps Troas, Miletus, Colossae, Hierapolis, and Laodicea (2 Cor 2:12; Col 1:2; 4:13, 15–16; Acts 16:8; 20:5, 15–38).[37] **Aquila and Prisca** also greet them along with **the church that is in their house**. Some ancient manuscripts use the diminutive Priscilla ("little Prisca"), as in Acts 18:2, 18, 26, but this form may have developed from later scribes attempting to harmonize it with the more original "Prisca."[38] Prisca is the more respectful name (Rom 16:3–5; 2 Tim 4:19).[39] According to Acts 18, she and her husband Aquila had been banished from Rome by the edict of Emperor Claudius because they were Jews (see Introduction). As tentmakers, they probably owned a small shop in Corinth when they met Paul who then lodged and worked in their shop. They seem to have some financial means despite their modest trade; later they apparently return to another house of theirs in Rome (Rom 16:3–5). Paul either relays their greetings from Rome, or they also have a house in Ephesus (cf. Acts 18:24–26). To avoid complaints that he omits anyone else wanting to send them greetings, Paul includes **the brothers and sisters all greet you**.[40] Another closing convention is the charge to **greet one another with a holy kiss** (cf. 1 Thess 5:26; Rom 16:16; 1 Pet 5:14; Justin *Apol.* 1.65.2). Its holy quality removes this kiss from the realm of sensuality into the space of spiritual family members who welcome one another with it as a sign of godly affection. Whether at this

---

This makes us question whether some would have entrusted Stephanas's team with their own letter. In any case, Chloe's group seems involved in the earlier task (see 1:11).

34. See Barrett 1968:395. Alternatively, Fitzmyer 2008:626, suggests that these three were already a source of comfort to the Corinthians prior to their sending them.

35. See 1 Thess 5:12, though this verse uses οἶδα.

36. Cf. Hiigel 2003:110–11.

37. Schnabel 2006:1027.

38. See e.g., C, D, TR, vg.

39. See possible implications related to these traditions' perception of women in Kurek-Chomycz 2006:107–28.

40. Thiselton 2000:1344.

time or later, it also conveyed peace and reconciliation and may be associated with the "kiss of peace" mentioned by church fathers.[41]

Paul's greeting with his **own hand** helps validate the letter (16:21; cf. Gal 6:11; Phlm 19; Col 4:18).[42] Prior to this moment, a secretary wrote what Paul dictated. Ability to write placed the individual among a minority of ancient people with education and high social standing. And the ability to have someone else write when one could write for oneself exemplified even higher status. Paul's penmanship signals him as someone worthy of the audience's respect and attention: "Look, I can write, but I can avoid doing so. Most of you can do neither, so listen to me."[43] If his own handwriting elicits ethos, his follow-up warning elicits pathos: **If anyone does not love the Lord, let that person be accursed. Maranatha!** Loving the Lord recalls again the reconfigured *Shema* from 8:3–6 and implies covenantal love between God and God's people inclusive of loyalty and obedience (Deut 6:4–6).[44] Given this backdrop from Deuteronomy, Paul's *anathema* may also originate from this scripture, which enunciates utter destruction upon the object of God's curse (Deut 13:16, 18; 20:17).[45] If so, when coupled with the idea of Christ's second coming described by *maranatha*, what is imagined by this curse is the Lord at the end times punishing those who are disloyal to the new covenant.[46] Such warning Paul hopes would elicit fear enough to deter the Corinthians from any more factions. Curses may be an effective tool for persuading the Corinthians against misbehavior, who as a people in general seem to believe that oaths to deities could not be taken back (Pausanius *Descr.* 2.2.1).[47] Roman Corinthians appear to be quite fearful of curses as is evident by discoveries of curse epitaphs and numerous metal curse tablets (*defixiones*) found in their city.[48]

John Fotopoulos argues that Paul's conditional curse, when linked with the Aramaic *maranatha*, is evidence of mystically empowered foreign words (*voces mysticae*), which were often used in curses and understood

---

41. See Weima 1994:113.

42. Arzt-Grabner et al. 2006:521.

43. Keith 2008:56.

44. This love is more than mere emotions (Bachmann 1936:478) or friendship (Moffatt 1938:281–82) or both (Sampley 2002:1002); albeit, such ideas are not opposed to covenant love since Paul doubtless encourages personal friendship with the Lord (cf. Tilling 2012:191).

45. These verses fit better our current text than the curses in Deut 27–30, since κατάρα, not ἀνάθεμα, is used in the latter (Tilling 2012:192).

46. Similarly, Eriksson 2001:124; Konradt 2003:455.

47. On magical rituals in Corinth, see further, Stroud 2014:187–202.

48. See evidence in Fotopoulos 2014:283–91.

as potent if not translated into the vernacular of the curse's recipients. The unintelligent words inscribed on the statue of Artemis in Ephesus provides an example.[49] Since Paul writes from Ephesus, it is just possible that what prompted his use of mystical words was seeing such inscriptions. We do not know, however, that Paul's Gentile audience did *not* understand what *maranatha* means. It is always possible that he introduced the phrase and its meaning to them when staying in Corinth. His Gentile converts are, after all, familiar with foreign words such as the Hebrew *amen* and Aramaic *abba* (Rom 8:15; Gal 1:5; 4:6; Phil 4:20).

Mar means Lord, but a major question is whether Paul's word is to be understood as the perfect *maran atha* ("Our Lord has come") or the imperative *marana tha* ("Our Lord, come!").[50] Kenneth Bailey argues that for centuries Middle Eastern churches read this as a confession, and Syriac, Aramaic, and Hebrew translations render this as "Our Lord has come."[51] This, he suggests, is expressed in celebration of the Eucharist that affirms the Lord's presence at the meal—the Lord has come or "Our Lord is here."[52] Problematic with this view is that Paul's Eucharist anticipates consumption of the meal by looking forward to a *futuristic* time "until he [Christ] comes" (11:26). For Matthew Black, ambiguity and flexibility with Paul's term may have invited various uses early on, so that we find the phrase as a confession or imprecation or in Eucharistic settings (cf. *Did.* 10.6).[53] Revelation 22:20 supports the imperative meaning, "Come, Lord Jesus!" (ἔρχου κύριε Ἰησοῦ) in anticipation of Christ's return. Ultimately, a structural aspect in Paul's letter supports that the imperatival/confessional meaning of *marantha* is correct or at least should not be excluded. Paul ends this letter as he began it—with a prayer to the Lord Jesus and expectation of his coming (1:2, 7–8), though in 16:22 Paul exhibits the potential converse of his recipients being blameless at the Lord's coming. The imperative meaning for *maranatha* also supports rather pointedly that the earliest followers of Jesus, who spoke Aramaic, prayed to Jesus as Lord, associating him with the sacred name for God in the Hebrew Scriptures.[54]

The final benediction, **the grace of our Lord Jesus be with you**, with variations, ends all of Paul's undisputed letters as his virtual trademark (e.g.,

---

49. Ibid., esp. 284.

50. See options and manuscript evidence in Fitzmyer 2008:630; 1981:223–29; Schnabel 2006:1027.

51. Bailey 2011:496–97.

52. Ibid. 498.

53. Black 1973:196. Black posits two main options as "'the Lord will (soon, surely) come' at the Parousia" (cf. Phil 4:5) or 'Our Lord, come.'"

54. See Hurtado 2003:21, 110.

Closing Matters (1 Cor 16:1-24)

Rom 16:20; Gal 6:18; 1 Thess 5:28; Phil 4:23). This benediction parallels the Jewish blessing-wish, "The Lord be with you" (Luke 1:28; 2 Thess 3:16; 2 Tim 4:22), but adds the concept of grace and identifies the Lord as Jesus.[55] Paul's final blessing, **my love be with you all in Christ Jesus**, reminds them of his affectionate love as their spiritual father (cf. 4:15; 2 Cor 6:11–13; 12:14–15). The closing tag, **Amen**, can express various things including praise or a response of confirmation.[56] The Hebrew word can be translated "so be it" or "truly" in Septuagint Greek (Ps 106[105]:48; Num 5:22; Deut 27:15; Jer 28:6[35:6]).[57] This expression typically closes other benedictions and doxologies of Paul (Rom 1:25; 9:5; 11:36; 16:27; Gal 1:5; 6:18; Phil 4:20).[58] The expression, though, is not uniquely his; other early Christian authors use it, too (Heb 13:21; 1 Pet 5:11; Jude 25; Rev 1:6). Its importance in these communities probably stems back to Jesus's use of the expression, "Amen, I say to you" (Matt 5:18; John 1:51; cf. Luke 4:25). Amen!

---

55. Zeller 2010:548.
56. Among the oldest manuscripts, only B omits "amen"; we retain it.
57. Chilton 1992:1.184.
58. Ibid. 1.185.

Bibliography

Adams, Edward, and David G. Horrell, eds. 2004. *Christianity in Corinth: The Quest for the Pauline Church*. Louisville: Westminster John Knox.
Adams, Sean. 2008. "Crucifixion in the Ancient World: A Response to L. L. Welborn." In *Paul's World*, edited by Stanley E. Porter, 111–30. PS 4. Leiden: Brill.
Aernie, Jeffrey W. 2012. *Is Paul Also Among the Prophets?* LNTS 467. London: T. & T. Clark.
Aguilar Chiu, José Enrique. 2007. *1 Cor 12–14: Literary Structure and Theology*. AnBib 166. Rome: Editrice Pontificio Istituto Biblico.
Ahn, Yongnan Jeon. 2013. *Interpretation of Tongues and Prophecy in 1 Corinthians 12–14*. JPTSS 41. Blandford Forum, UK: Deo Publishing.
Allo, P. E.-B. 1956. *Saint Paul: Première Épitre aux Corinthiens*. Paris: Librairie Lecoffre, J. Galda et Cie.
Anderson, Gary A. 2001. *The Genesis of Perfection: Adam and Eve in Jewish and Christian Imagination*. Louisville: Westminster John Knox.
Anderson, R. D. 1998. *Ancient Rhetorical Theory and Paul*. Rev. ed. Kampen: Kok Pharos.
———. 2013. "Progymnasmatic Love." In *Christian Origins and Greco-Roman Culture: Social and Literary Contexts for the New Testament*, edited by Stanley E. Porter and Andrew W. Pitts, 551–60. TENTS 9. Leiden: Brill.
Arzt-Grabner, Peter. 2010. "Paul's Letter Thanksgiving." In *Paul and the Ancient Letter Form*, edited by Stanley E. Porter and Sean A. Adams, 129–58. PS 6. Boston: Brill.
Arzt-Grabner, Peter, et al. 2006. (with Ruth Elisabeth Kritzer, Amphilochios Papathomas, and Franz Winter). *1. Korinther*. Papyrologische Kommentare zum Neuen Testament 2. Göttingen: Vandenhoeck & Ruprecht.
Ascough, Richard S. 2012a. "Meals, Memories, and Methods: (Re-)Constructing the Origins of Christianity." In *Translating Religion*, edited by Mary Doak and Anita Houck, 21–35. College Theological Society Annual 58. Maryknoll, NY: Orbis.
Ascough, Richard S., Philip A. Harland, and John S. Kloppenborg. 2012b. *Associations in the Greco-Roman World*. Baylor: Baylor University Press.
Asher, Jeffrey R. 2000. *Polarity and Change in 1 Corinthians 15: A Study of Metaphysics, Rhetoric, and Resurrection*. Hermeneutische Untersuchungen Zur Theologie 42. Tübingen: Mohr-Siebeck.
Aune, David E. 1983. *Prophecy in Early Christianity and the Ancient Mediterranean World*. Grand Rapids: Eerdmans.
———. 2003. *The Westminster Dictionary of New Testament and Early Christian Literature and Rhetoric*. Louisville: Westminster John Knox.
Aus, Roger David. 2005. *Imagery of Triumph and Rebellion in 2 Corinthians 2:14–17 and Elsewhere in the Epistle*. Studies in Judaism. Lanham: University Press of America.
Bachmann, Philipp. 1936. *Der erste Brief des Paulus an die Korinther*. KNT 7. Leipzig: A. Deichert.

Bibliography

Bailey, Kenneth E. 2011. *Paul through Mediterranean Eyes: Cultural Studies in 1 Corinthians*. Downers Grove, IL: InterVarsity.

Balch, David L. 1983. "1 Cor 7:32–35 and Stoic Debates About Marriage, Anxiety, and Distraction," *JBL* 102: 429–39.

———. 2015. "The Church Setting in a Garden (1 Cor 14:30; Rom 16:23; Mark 6:39–40; 8:6; John 6:3, 10; Acts 1:15; 2:1–2)." In *Contested Ethnicities and Image: Studies in Acts and Art*, 311–43. WUNT 345. Tübingen: Mohr-Siebeck.

Bandstra, A. J. 1971. "Interpretation in 1 Corinthians 10:1–11." *CTJ* 6:5–21.

Barclay, John M. G. 1991. "Paul, Philemon and the Dilemma of Christian Slave-Ownership." *NTS* 37:161–86.

———. 2004. "Poverty in Pauline Studies: A Response to Steven Friesen." *JSNT* 63:363–66.

———. 2008. "Grace and the Transformation of Agency in Christ." In *Redefining First Century Jewish and Christian Identities: Essays in Honor of Ed Parish Sanders*, edited by Fabian E. Udoh, 372–89. Notre Dame Christianity & Judaism Antiquity 16. Notre Dame: University of Notre Dame Press.

———. 2015. "Crucifixion as Wisdom: Exploring the Ideology of a Disreputable Social Movement." In *The Wisdom and Foolishness of God: First Corinthians 1–2 in Theological Exploration*, edited by Christophe Chalamet and Hans-Christoph Askani, 1–20. Minneapolis: Fortress.

Barker, K. L. 1999. *Micah, Nahum, Habakkuk, Zephaniah*. NAC 20. Nashville: Broadman & Holman.

Barnes, Nathan J. 2009. "Women in Philosophy and the Agon Motif of 1 Corinthians 9." *PRSt* 36:49–60.

———. 2014. *Reading 1 Corinthians with Philosophically Educated Women*. Eugene, OR: Pickwick.

Baron, Lori, and B. J. Oropeza. 2016. "Midrash." In *Exploring Intertextuality: Diverse Strategies for New Testament Interpretation of Texts*, edited by B. J. Oropeza and Steve Moyise, 63–80. Eugene, OR: Cascade.

Barram, Michael. 2011. "Pauline Mission as Salvific Intentionality." In *Paul as Missionary: Identity, Activity, Theology, and Practice*, edited by Trevor J. Burke and Brian S. Rosner, 234–46. LNTS 420. London: Bloomsbury Collections.

Barrett, C. K. 1968. *The First Epistle to the Corinthians*. BNTC. Grand Rapids: Baker Academic.

———. 1982. "Cephas in Corinth." In *Essays on Paul*, 28–39. London: SPCK.

Bartchy, S. Scott. 1973. *ΜΑΛΛΟΝ ΧΡΗΣΑΙ: First-Century Slavery and the Interpretation of 1 Corinthians 7:21*. SBLDS 11. Missoula, MT: SBL.

Barton, Stephen C. 1986. "Paul's Sense of Place: An Anthropological Approach to Community Formation in Corinth." *NTS* 32:225–46.

———. 1998. "'Glorify God in Your Body' (1 Corinthians 6:20): Thinking Theologically about Sexuality." In *Religion and Sexuality*, edited by M. A. Hayes, W. Porter, and D. Tombs, 366–79. Studies in Theology and Sexuality 2. Sheffield: Sheffield Academic Press.

Bassler, J. M. 1982. "1 Cor. 12:3—Curse and Confession in Context." *JBL* 101:415–18.

Baum, Armin Daniel. 2014. "Paul's Conflicting Statements on Female Public Speaking (1 Cor 11:5) and Silence (1 Cor 14:34–35): A New Suggestion." *TynBul* 65:247–74.

Beard, Mary. 2007. *The Roman Triumph*. Cambridge: Harvard University Press.

Bibliography

BeDuhn, Jason David. 1999. "'Because of the Angels': Unveiling Paul's Anthropology in 1 Corinthians 11." *JBL* 118:295–320.

Belleville, Linda L. 2003. "Κεφαλή and the Thorny Issue of Head Covering in 1 Corinthians 11:2–16." In *Paul and the Corinthians: Studies on a Community in Conflict: Festschrift in Honour of Margaret M. Thrall*, edited by Trevor Burke and J. Keith Elliott, 215–31. NovTSup 109. Boston: Brill.

Berger, Klaus. 1978. "Zur Diskussion über die Herkunft von 1 Kor. II.9." *NTS* 24:270–83.

Betz, Hans Dieter. 1986. "The Problem of Rhetoric and Theology According to the Apostle Paul." In *L'Apôtre Paul: Personnalité, Style et Conception du Ministère*, edited by A. Vanhoye, 16–48. BETL 73. Leuven: Leuven University Press/ Uitgeverij Peeters.

Bird, Michael F. 2009. *Introducing Paul: The Man, His Mission, and Message*. Downers Grove, IL: InterVarsity Academic.

———. 2016. *An Anomalous Jew: Paul among Jews, Greeks, and Romans*. Grand Rapids: Eerdmans.

Bitner, Bradley J. 2015a. "Coinage and Colonial Identity: Corinthian Numismatics and the Corinthian Correspondence." In *The First Urban Churches 1: Methodological Foundations*, edited by James R. Harrison and L. L. Welborn, 151–87. WGRWSup 7. Atlanta: SBL.

———. 2015b. *Paul's Political Strategy in 1 Corinthians 1–4: Constitution and Covenant*. SNTSMS 163. Cambridge: Cambridge University Press.

Black, Matthew. 1973. "The Maranatha Invocation and Jude 14, 15 (1 Enoch 1:9)." In *Christ and Spirit in the NT: Studies in Honour of C. F. D. Moule*, edited by Barnabas Lindars and Stephen S. Smalley, 189–96. Cambridge: Cambridge University Press.

Blattenberger, David. 1997. *Rethinking 1 Corinthians 11:2–16 through Archaeological and Moral-Rhetorical Analysis*. SBEC 36. Lewiston: Edwin Mellen.

Boer, Martinus C. de. 1988. *The Defeat of Death: Apocalyptic Eschatology in 1 Corinthians 15 and Romans 5*. JSNTSS 22. Sheffield: JSOT.

Bonner, Campbell. 1950. "A Reminiscence of Paul on a Coin Amulet." *HTR* 43:165–68.

Bookidis, Nancy. 2005. "Religion in Corinth: 164 B.C.E. to 100 C. E." In *URRC*, 141–64.

Borgen, Peder. 1995. "'Yes, No, How Far?' The Participation of Jews and Christians in Pagan Cults." In *Paul in His Hellenistic Context*, edited by Troels Engberg-Pedersen, 30–59. Minneapolis: Fortress.

Boring, Eugene. 1991. *The Continuing Voice of Jesus: Christian Prophecy and the Gospel Tradition*. Louisville: Westminster John Knox.

Boswell, John. 1980. *Christianity, Social Tolerance, and Homosexuality*. Chicago: University of Chicago Press.

Bowersock, G. W. 1969. *Greek Sophists in the Roman Empire*. Oxford: Clarendon.

Bowie, E. L. 1982. "The Importance of the Sophists." *Yale Classical Studies* 27:29–59.

Bradley, Keith R. 1991. *Discovering the Roman Family: Studies in Roman Social History*. Oxford: Oxford University Press.

Brändl, Martin. 2006. *Der Agon bei Paulus: Herkunft und Profil paulinischer Agonmetaphorik*. WUNT 2/222. Tübingen: Mohr-Siebeck.

Braxton, Brad Ronnell. 2000. *The Tyranny of Resolution: I Corinthians 7:17–24*. SBLDS 181. Atlanta: Scholars Press.

Bray, Gerald. 1999. *1–2 Corinthians*. ACCS. New Testament VII. Downers Grove, IL: InterVarsity.

Bibliography

Brenk, Frederick E. 2012. "Most Beautiful and Divine: Graeco-Romans (especially Plutarch) and Paul on Love and Marriage." In *Greco-Roman Culture and the New Testament*, edited by David A. Aune and Frederick E. Brenk, 87–11. NovTSup 143. Leiden: Brill.

Briones, David E. 2013. *Paul's Financial Policy: A Socio-Theological Approach*. LNTS 494. London: Bloomsbury.

Brodeur, Scott. 2004. *The Holy Spirit's Agency in the Resurrection of the Dead: An Exegetico-Theological Study of 1 Corinthians 15,44b–49 and Romans 8,9–13*. TGST 14. Rome: Editrice Pontificia Universita Gregoriana.

Broneer, Oscar. 1962. "The Apostle Paul and the Isthmian Games." *BA* 25: 2–31.

Brookins, Timothy A. 2014. "The Supposed Election of Officers in 1 Cor 11.19: A Response to Richard Last." *NTS* 60:423–32.

Brooten, Bernadette J. 1996. *Love between Women: Early Christian Responses to Female Homoeroticism*. The Chicago Series on Sexuality, History, and Society. Chicago: University of Chicago Press.

Brown, Paul J. 2014. *Bodily Resurrection and Ethics in 1 Cor 15: Connecting Faith and Morality in the Context of Greco-Roman Mythology*. WUNT 2/360. Tübingen: Mohr-Siebeck.

Bruce, F. F. 1971. *1 and 2 Corinthians*. NCBC. London: Marshall, Morgan, & Scott.

Bryan, Christopher. 2011. *The Resurrection of the Messiah*. Oxford: Oxford University Press.

Bryan, Steve. 2008. "Christianizing Spiritual Manifestations: Worldview and Spiritual Gifts in 1 Corinthians 12–14." *Africa Journal of Evangelical Theology* 27:93–107.

Bullinger, E. W. 1898. *Figures of Speech Used in the Bible*. London: Eyre & Spottiswoode.

Burke, Trevor J. 2003. "Paul's Role as 'Father' to His Corinthian 'Children' in Socio-Historical Context (1 Corinthians 4:14–21)." In *Paul and the Corinthians: Studies on a Community in Conflict. Essays in Honour of Margaret Thrall*, edited by Trevor J. Burke and J. Keith Elliott, 96–113. NovTSup 109. Leiden: Brill.

Butarbutar, Robinson. 2007. *Paul and Conflict Resolution: An Exegetical Study of Paul's Apostolic Paradigm in 1 Corinthians 9*. Paternoster Biblical Monographs. Milton Keynes: Paternoster.

Byron, John. 2004. "Paul and the Background of Slavery: The *Status Quaestionis* in New Testament Scholarship." *CBR* 3:116–39.

———. 2008. "Slaves and Freed Persons: Self-Made Success and Social Climbing in the Corinthian Congregation." *Jian Dao* 29:91–107.

Callow, Kathleen. 1992. "Patterns of Thematic Development in 1 Corinthians 5:1–13." In *Linguistics and New Testament Interpretation: Essays on Discourse Analysis*, edited by David Alan Black, Katharine Barnwell, and Stephen Levinsohn, 194–206. Nashville: Broadman.

Calvin, John. 1996. *1 Corinthians*. Reprint, Grand Rapids: Eerdmans.

Cameron, Ron, and Merrill P. Miller. 2011. *Redescribing Paul and the Corinthians*. ECL 5. Leiden: Brill.

Campbell, Constantine R. 2012. *Paul and Union with Christ: An Exegetical and Theological Study*. Grand Rapids: Zondervan.

Campbell, R. A. 1991. "Does Paul Acquiesce in Divisions at the Lord's Supper?" *NovT* 33:61–70.

Capes, David B. 1992. *Old Testament Yahweh Texts in Paul's Christology*. WUNT 2/47. Tübingen: Mohr-Siebeck.

Caragounis, Chrys C. 1996. "'Fornication' and 'Concession'? Interpreting 1 Cor 7,1-7." In *CorBETL*, 543-96.
———. 2006. "What did Paul Mean? The Debate on 1 Cor 7,1-7." *ETL* 82:189-99.
Carter, Christopher L. 2010. *The Great Sermon Tradition as a Fiscal Framework in 1 Corinthians: Towards a Pauline Theology of Material Possessions*. LNTS 403. London: T. & T. Clark.
Castelli, Elizabeth A. 1991. *Imitating Paul: A Discourse of Power*. LCBI. Louisville: Westminster John Knox.
Charette, Blaine. 2005. "Tongues as of Fire: Judgment as a Function of Glossolalia in Luke's Thought." *JPT* 13:173-86.
Chester, Stephen J. 2003. *Conversion at Corinth: Perspectives on Conversion in Paul's Theology and the Corinthian Church*. London: T. & T. Clark.
———. 2005. "Divine Madness? Speaking in Tongues in 1 Corinthians 14.23." *JSNT* 21:417-46.
Cheung, Alex T. 1999. *Idol Food in Corinth: Jewish Background and Pauline Legacy*. JSNTSS 176. Sheffield: Sheffield Academic.
Chilton, Bruce. 1992. "Amen." In *ABD* 1.184-86.
Choi, Sung Bok. 2007. *Geist und christliche Existenz: Das Glossolalieverständnis des Paulus im Ersten Korintherbrief (1 Kor 14)*. WMANT 115. Neukirchen-Vluyn: Neukirchener.
Chow, John K. 1992. *Patronage and Power: A Study of Social Networks in Corinth*. JSNTSS 75. Sheffield: Sheffield Academic Press.
Ciampa, Roy E. 2009. "Revisiting the Euphemism in 1 Corinthians 7.1." *JSNT* 31:325-38.
———. 2013. "Prophecy in Corinth and Paul's Use of Isaiah's Prophecy in 1 Corinthians 14:21-25." Paper presented at the SBL conference. Scripture in 1 Corinthians. Baltimore.
Ciampa, Roy E., and Brian S. Rosner. 2010. *The First Letter to the Corinthians*. PNTC. Grand Rapids: Eerdmans.
Clarke, Andrew D. 1993. *Secular and Christian Leadership in Corinth: A Socio-Historical and Exegetical Study of 1 Corinthians 1-6*. AGJU 18. Leiden: Brill.
Clivaz, Claire, and Sara Schulthess. 2015. "On the Source and Rewriting of 1 Corinthians 2.9 in Christian, Jewish and Islamic Traditions." *NTS* 61:183-200.
Collier, Gary D. 1994. "'That We Might Not Crave Evil': The Structure and Argument of 1 Cor. 10:1-13." *JSNT* 55:55-75.
Collins, Adela Yarbro. 1980. "The Function of Excommunication in Paul." *HTR* 73:251-63.
Collins, John J. 1994. *Daniel*. Hermenia. Philadelphia: Fortress.
Collins, Raymond F. 1996. "Reflections on 1 Corinthians as a Hellenistic Letter." In *CorBETL*, 39-61.
———. 1999. *First Corinthians*. SP 7. Collegeville, MN: Michael Glazier/Liturgical.
Concannon, Cavan W. 2014. "'Not for an Olive Wreath, but Our Lives': Gladiators, Athletes, and Early Christian Bodies." *JBL* 133:193-214.
Conzelmann, Hans. 1975. *1 Corinthians: A Commentary on the First Epistle to the Corinthians*. Hermeneia. Philadelphia: Fortress.
Cook, John Granger. 2008. "1 Cor 9,5: The Women of the Apostles." *Bib* 89:352-68.
———. 2011. "Crucifixion and Burial." *NTS* 57.2:193-213.

Bibliography

———. 2014. *Crucifixion in the Mediterranean World.* WUNT 327. Tübingen: Mohr-Siebeck.

Cope, Lamar. 1990. "First Corinthians 8–10: Continuity or Contradiction?" *ATRSupp* 11:114–23.

Coppins, Wayne. 2010. "Doing Justice to the Two Perspectives of 1 Corinthians 15:1-11." *Neot* 44.2:282–91.

———. 2011. "Paul's Juxtaposition of Freedom and Positive Servitude in Cor 9:19 and its Reception by Martin Luther and Gerhard Ebeling." *Lutherjarbuch* 78: 277–98.

Countryman, L. William. 1988. *Dirt, Greed and Sex: Sexual Ethics in the New Testament and their Implications for Today.* Philadelphia: Fortress.

Court, John M. 1982. "Paul and the Apocalyptic Pattern." In *Paul and Paulinism: Essays in Honour of C. K. Barrett*, edited by Stephen J. Wilson and Morna D. Hooker, 57–66. London: SPCK.

Coutsoumpos, Panayotis. 2005. *Paul and the Lord's Supper: A Socio-Historical Investigation.* SIBL 84. New York: Peter Lang.

———. 2008. "Paul, the Cults in Corinth, and the Corinthian Correspondence." In *Paul's World*, edited by Stanley E. Porter, 171–81. Leiden: Brill.

Cribiore, Raffaella. 1996. *Writing, Teachers, and Students in Graeco-Roman Egypt.* American Studies in Papyriology 36. Atlanta: Scholars Press.

Crocker, Cornelia Cyss. 2004. *Reading 1 Corinthians in the Twenty-First Century.* London: T. & T. Clark.

Crüsemann, Marlene. 2000. "Irredeemably Hostile to Women: Anti-Jewish Elements in the Exegesis of the Dispute about Women's Right To Speak (1 Cor. 14.34–35)." *JSNT* 79:19–36.

Dahl, Nils A. 1967. "Paul and the Church at Corinth according to 1 Corinthians 1:10—4:21." In *Christian History and Interpretation: Studies Presented to John Knox*, edited by William R. Farmer, C. F. D. Moule, and R. R. Niebuhr, 313–35. Cambridge: Cambridge University Press.

Davidson, Richard M. 1981. *Typology in Scripture: A Study of Hermeneutical τύπός Structures.* Andrews University Seminary Doctoral Dissertation Series 2. Berrien Springs: Andrews University Press.

Davis, James A. 1984. *Wisdom and Spirit: An Investigation of 1 Corinthians 1.18—3.20 Against the Background of Jewish Sapiential Traditions in the Greco-Roman Period.* Lanham: University Press of America.

Dawes, Gregory W. 1998. *The Body in Question: Metaphor and Meaning in the Interpretation of Ephesians 5:21–33.* BIS 30. Leiden: Brill.

Dawson, Kathy Barrett. 2012. "The Incestuous Man of 1 Cor 5, LXX Banishment Texts, and Eating with Sinners." Paper presented at the annual SBL conference, Atlanta.

De Vos, Craig Steven. 1998. "Stepmothers, Concubines and the Case of *Porneia* in 1 Corinthians 5." *NTS* 44:104–14.

Deissmann, Adolf. 1965. *Light from the Ancient East.* 4th ed. Grand Rapids: Baker.

Delobel, J. 2002. "The Corinthiaans' (Un-)belief in the Resurrection." In *Resurrection in the New Testament: Festschrift J. Lambrecht*, edited by Reimund Bieringer, Veronica Koperski, and Bianca Lataire, 343–55. Leuven: Peeters.

DeMaris, R. E. 1995. "Corinthian Religion and Baptism for the Dead." *JBL* 114: 661–82.

Deming, William. 1995. *Paul on Marriage and Celibacy: The Hellenistic Background of 1 Corinthians 7.* New York: Cambridge University Press.

———. 1996. "The Unity of 1 Corinthians 5–6." *JBL* 115:289–312.

Derrett, J. Duncan M. 1979. "'Handing Over to Satan': An Explanation of 1 Cor. 5:1–7." *RIDA* 3:11–30.
deSilva, David A. 2000. *Honor, Patronage, Kinship and Purity: Unlocking New Testament Culture*. Downers Grove, IL: InterVarsity.
DiMattei, Steven. 2008. "Biblical Narratives." In *As It is Written: Studying Paul's Use of Scripture*, edited by Stanley E. Porter and Christopher D. Stanley, 59–96. Atlanta: SBL.
Dingeldein, Laura B. 2013. "'ὅτι πνευματικῶς ἀνακρίνεται': Examining Translations of 1 Corinthians 2:14." *NovT* 55:31–44.
Dodson, Joseph R. 2012. "Paul and Seneca on the Cross: The Metaphor of Crucifixion in Galatians and *De Vita Beata*." Conference paper presented at the Society of Biblical Literature conference. Intertextuality in the New Testament, Chicago.
Doering, Lutz. 2012. *Ancient Jewish Letters and the Beginnings of Christian Epistolography*. WUNT 298. Tübingen: Mohr-Siebeck.
Downs, David J. 2008. *The Offering of the Gentiles: Paul's Collection for Jerusalem in Its Chronological, Cultural, and Cultic Contexts*. WUNT 2.248. Tübingen: Mohr Siebeck.
Dunn, James D. G. 1970. *Baptism in the Holy Spirit*. Study in Bible Theology 2/15. London: SCM.
———. 1975. *Jesus and the Spirit*. Philadelphia: Westminster.
———. 1998. *Theology of Paul the Apostle*. Grand Rapids: Eerdmans.
———. 1999. "Jesus: Teacher of Wisdom or Wisdom Incarnate." In *Where Shall Wisdom be Found: Wisdom in the Bible, the Church and the Contemporary World*, edited by Stephen C. Barton, 75–92. Edinburgh: T. & T. Clark.
Dutch, Robert S. 2005. *The Educated Elite in 1 Corinthians: Education and Community Conflict in Graeco-Roman Context*. LNTS 271. London: T. & T. Clark.
Ebojo, Edgar Battad. 2009. "How Persuasive is 'Persuasive Words of Human Wisdom?' The Shortest Reading in 1 Cor 2.4." *BT* 60:10–21.
Edsall, Benjamin. 2013. "When Cicero and St. Paul Agree: Intra-Group Litigation Among the *Luperci* and the Corinthian Believer." *JTS* 64:25–36.
Edwards, Thomas Charles. 1897. *A Commentary on the First Epistle to the Corinthians*. 3rd ed. London: Hodder and Stoughton.
Ehrensperger, Kathy. 2009. *Paul and the Dynamics of Power: Communication and Interaction in the Early Christ-Movement*. LNTS 325. London: Bloomsbury.
Ellington, Dustin W. 2011. "Imitating Paul's Relationship to the Gospel: 1 Corinthians 8.1–11.1." *JSNT* 33:303–15.
Ellingworth, Paul, and Howard A. Hatton. 1993. *A Handbook on Paul's First Letter to the Corinthians*. New York: United Bible Societies.
Elliott, Neil. 1997. "The Anti-Imperial Message of the Cross." In *Paul and Empire: Religion and Power in Roman Imperial Society*, edited by Richard A. Horsley, 167–83. Harrisburg: Trinity.
Elliott, Neil, and Mark Reasoner. 2011. *Documents and Images for the Study of Paul*. Minneapolis: Fortress.
Ellis, J. Edward. 2007. *Paul and Ancient Views of Sexual Desire: Paul's Sexual Ethics in 1 Thessalonians 4, 1 Corinthians 7, and Romans 1*. LNTS 354. London: T. & T. Clark.
Endsjø, Dag Øistein. 2008. "Immortal Bodies, before Christ: Bodily Continuity in Ancient Greece and 1 Corinthians." *JSNT* 30:417–36.

Bibliography

———. 2009. *Greek Resurrection Beliefs and the Success of Christianity*. Palgrave: Macmillan.
Engberg-Pedersen, Troels. 2009. "Complete and Incomplete Transformation in Paul—a Philosophical Reading of Paul on Body and Spirit." In *Metamorphoses: Resurrection, Body and Transformative Practices in Early Christianity*, edited by Turid Karlsen Seim and Jorunn Økland, 123–46. Berlin: de Gruyter.
———. 2010. *Cosmology and Self in the Apostle Paul: The Material Spirit*. Oxford: Oxford University Press.
———. 2013. "Paul and Universalism." In *Paul and the Philosophers*, edited by Ward Blanton and Hent De Vries, 87–104, 157–61. New York: Fordham University.
Engels, Donald. 1990. *Roman Corinth: An Alternative Model for the Classical City*. Chicago: University of Chicago.
Enns, Peter E. 1996. "The 'Moveable Well' in 1 Cor 10:4: An Extrabiblical Tradition in an Apostolic Text." *BBR* 6:23–38.
Eriksson, Anders. 1998. *Traditions as Rhetorical Proof: Pauline Argumentation in 1 Corinthians*. CBNTS 29. Stockholm: Almqvist & Wiksell.
———. 2001. "Fear of Eternal Damnation: *Pathos* Appeal in 1 Corinthians 15 and 16." In *Paul and Pathos*, edited by Thomas Olbricht and Jerry Sumney, 115–26. Atlanta: SBL.
Evans, Craig A. 2014. "Getting the Burial Traditions and Evidences Right." In *How God became Jesus*, edited by Michael F. Bird et al., 71–93. Grand Rapids: Zondervan.
Fee, Gordon D. 1987. *The First Epistle to the Corinthians*. NICNT. Grand Rapids: Eerdmans.
———. 1996. *Paul, the Spirit and the People of God*. Peabody, MA: Hendrickson.
———. 2003. "1 Corinthians 7:1–7 Revisited." In *Paul and the Corinthians: Studies on a Community in Conflict. Essays in Honour of Margaret Thrall*, edited by Trevor J. Burke and J. Keith Elliott, 197–213. NovTSup 109. Leiden: Brill.
Ferguson, Everett. 2014. "Of Veils and Virgins Greek, Roman, Jewish, and Early Christian Practice." *ResQ* 56:223–43.
Feuillet, A. 1973. "La dignité et le rôle de la femme d'après quelques textes pauliniens: comparison avec l'ancient Testament," *NTS* 21:157–91.
Finney, Mark T. 2005. "Christ Crucified and the Inversion of Roman Imperial Ideology in 1 Corinthians." *BTB* 35:20–33.
———. 2010. "Honour, Head-Coverings and Headship: 1 Corinthians 11.2–16 in its Social Context." *JSNT* 33:31–58.
———. 2012. *Honour and Conflict in the Ancient World: 1 Corinthians in its Greco-Roman Social Setting*. LNTS 460. London: T. & T. Clark.
Fiore, Benjamin. 1985. "'Covert Allusion' in 1 Corinthians 1–4." *CBQ* 47:85–102.
———. 1990. "Passion in Paul and Plutarch: 1 Corinthians 5–6 and the Polemic against Epicureans." In *Greeks, Romans, and Christians: Essays in Honor of Abraham J. Malherbe*, edited by David L. Balch, Everett Ferguson, and Wayne A. Meeks, 135–43. Minneapolis: Fortress.
———. 2003. "Paul, Exemplification, and Imitation." In *PGRW*, 228–57.
Fishbane, Michael. 1986. "Through the Looking Glass: Reflections on Ezek. 43:3, Num. 12:8, and 1 Cor. 13:8." *HAR* 10:63–75.
Fisk, Bruce. 1989. "Eating Meat Offered to Idols: Corinthian Behavior and Pauline Response in 1 Corinthians 8–10 (A Response to Gordon Fee)." *TrinJ* 10:49–70.
———. 2000. *First Corinthians*. Interpretation Bible Studies. Louisville: Geneva.

Bibliography

Fitzgerald, John T. 1988. *Cracks in an Earthen Vessel: An Examination of the Catalogues of Hardships in the Corinthian Correspondence.* SBLDS 99. Atlanta: Scholars Press.
Fitzmyer, Joseph A. 1981. *To Advance the Gospel: Biblical Studies.* New York: Crossroad.
———. 2008. *First Corinthians.* AYB 32. New Haven: Yale University Press.
Focant, Camille. 1996. "1 Corinthiens 13: Analyse Rhétorique et Analyse de Structures." In *CorBETL,* 199-245.
Forbes, Christopher. 1995/1997. *Prophecy and Inspired Speech in Early Christianity and its Hellenistic Environment.* Peabody, MA: Hendrickson.
Ford, J. Massyngberde. 1993. "Bookshelf on Prostitution." *BTB* 23.3:128-34.
Forkman, Göran. 1972. *The Limits of the Religious Community: Expulsion from within the Qumran Sect, within Rabbinic Judaism, and within Primitive Christianity.* Lund: CWK Gleerup.
Fotopoulos, John. 2003. *Food Offered to Idols in Roman Corinth: A Social-Rhetorical Reconsideration of I Corinthians 8:1-11.* WUNT 2/151. Tübingen: Mohr-Siebeck.
———. 2014. "Paul's Curse of Corinthians: Restraining Rivals with Fear and Voces Mysticae (1 Cor 16:22)." *NovT* 56:275-309.
Frayer-Griggs, Daniel. 2013a. "The Beasts at Ephesus and the Cult of Artemis." *HTR* 106:459-77.
———. 2013b. "Neither Proof Text nor Proverb: The Instrumental Sense of διά and the Soteriological Function of Fire in 1 Corinthians 3.15." *NTS* 59:517-34.
Frestadius, Simo. 2011. "The Spirit and Wisdom in 1 Corinthians 2:1-13." *Journal of Biblical and Pneumatological Research* 3:52-70.
Friesen, Steven J. 1999. *Theology of the First Letter to the Corinthians.* New Testament Theology. Cambridge: Cambridge University Press.
———. 2004. "Poverty in Pauline Studies: Beyond the So-Called New Consensus." *JSNT* 26:323-61.
———. 2005. "Prospects for a Demography of the Pauline Mission." In *URRC,* 351-70.
———. 2010. "Erastus." In *CTXT,* 321-56.
Furnish, Victor P. 1968. *Theology and Ethics in Paul.* Nashville: Abingdon.
Gäckle, Volker. 2005. *Die starken und die Schwachen in Korinth und in Rom: Zu Herkunft unde Funktion der Antitheses in 1 Kor 8,1—11,1 und Röm 14,1—15,13.* WUNT 2/200. Tübingen: Mohr-Siebeck.
Gagnon, Robert A. J. 2001. *The Bible and Homosexual Practice: Texts and Hermeneutics.* Nashville: Abingdon.
Galloway, Lincoln E. 2004. "Preaching Freedom to the Corinthians." *Homiletic* 29:15-23.
Gardner, Paul Douglas. 1994. *The Gifts of God and the Authentication of a Christian: An Exegetical Study of 1 Corinthians 8-11:1.* Lanham: University Press of America.
Garland, David E. 2003. *1 Corinthians.* BECNT. Grand Rapids: Baker.
Garnsey, Peter. 1970. *Social Status and Legal Privilege in the Roman Empire.* Oxford: Oxford University Press.
Gaventa, Beverly Roberts. 1996. "Mother's Milk and Ministry in 1 Corinthians 3." In *Theology and Ethics in Paul and His Interpreters: Essays in Honor of Victor Paul Furnish,* edited by Eugene H. Lovering and Jerry L. Sumney, 101-13. Nashville: Abingdon.
———. 2005. "God Handed Them Over: Reading Romans 1:18-32 Apocalyptically." *ABR* 53:42-53.

Bibliography

Gebhard, Elizabeth R. 2005. "Rites for Melikertes-Palaimon in the Early Roman Corinthia." In *URRC*, 165–204.

Gebhard, Elizabeth R., and M. W. Dickie. 2003. "The View From the Isthmus, ca. 200 to 44 B.C." In *Corinth, the Centenary 1896–1996: Results of Excavations Conducted by the American School of Classical Studies at Athens*, edited by Charles K. Williams and Nancy Bookidis, 261–78. Vol. 20. Princeton: American School of Classical Studies at Athens.

Georgi, Dieter. 1992. *Remembering the Poor: The History of Paul's Collection for Jerusalem*. Nashville: Abingdon.

Gerhardsson, Birger. 2003. "Evidence for Christ's Resurrection According to Paul." In *Neotestamentica et Philonica: Studies in Honor of Peder Borgen*, edited by David E. Aune, Torrey Seland, and J. Henning Ulrichsen, 75-91. NovTSup 106. Boston: Brill.

Giblin, C. H. 1975. "Three Monotheistic Texts in Paul." *CBQ* 37: 527–47.

Gill, D. W. J. 1990. "The Importance of Roman Portraiture for Head-Coverings in 1 Corinthians 11.2–16." *TynBul* 41:245–60.

Gillespie, Thomas W. 1994. *The First Theologians: A Study in Early Christian Prophecy*. Grand Rapids: Eerdmans.

Gillihan, Yonder Moynihan. 2002. "Jewish Laws on Illicit Marriage, the Defilement of Offspring, and the Holiness of the Temple: A New Halakic Interpretation of 1 Corinthians 7:14." *JBL* 121:711–44.

Gillman, John. 1982. "Transformation in 1 Cor 15,50–53." *ETL* 58:309–33.

Gioia, Dana. 1995. "Introduction." In vol. 2 of *Seneca: The Tragedies*, edited by David R. Slavitt, vii–xliv. Baltimore: Johns Hopkins University Press.

Glad, Clarence E. 2003. "Paul and Adaptability." In *PGRW*, 17–41.

Gladd, Benjamin. 2009. "The Last Adam as the 'Life-Giving Spirit' Revisited: A Possible Old Testament Background on One of Paul's Most Perplexing Phrases." *WTJ* 7:297–309.

Gladstone, Robert J. 1999. "Sign Language in the Assembly: How Are Tongues a Sign to the Unbeliever in 1 Cor 14:20–25?" *AJPS* 2:185–92.

Glancy, Jennifer. 1998. "Obstacles to Slaves' Participation in the Corinthian Church." *JBL* 117:481–501.

———. 2015. "The Sexual Use of Slaves: A Response to Kyle Harper on Jewish and Christian *Porneia*." *JBL* 134:215–29.

———. 2006. *Slavery in Early Christianity*. Minneapolis: Fortress.

Godet, Frédéric L. 1893. *Commentary on St. Paul's First Epistle to the Corinthians*. 2 vols. Edinburgh: T. & T. Clark.

Goldingay, John. 2014. *Isaiah 56–66*. ICC. London: T. & T. Clark.

Goldstein, Jonathan A. 1968. *The Letters of Demosthenes*. New York: Columbia University Press.

Gooch, Peter D. 1993. *Dangerous Food: 1 Corinthians 8–10 in Its Context*. Studies in Christianity and Judaism 5. Waterloo: Wilfrid Laurier University Press.

Goodacre, Mark. 2011. "Does περιβόλαιον Mean 'Testicle' in 1 Corinthians 11:15?" *JBL* 130:391–96.

Goodrich, John K. 2012. *Paul as an Administrator of God in 1 Corinthians*. SNTSMS 152. Cambridge: Cambridge University Press.

Gordon, J. Dorcas. 1997. *Sister or Wife? 1 Corinthians 7 and Cultural Anthropology*. JSNTSS 149. Sheffield: Sheffield Academic Press.

Goulder, Michael. 2002. *Paul and the Competing Mission in Corinth*. LPS. Peabody, MA: Hendrickson.
Gräbe, Petrus J. 2008. *The Power of God in Paul's Letters*. 2nd ed. WUNT 2/123. Tübingen: Mohr-Siebeck.
Grant, Robert M. 2001. *Paul in the Roman World: The Conflict in Corinth*. Louisville: Westminster John Knox.
Greenbury, James. 2008. "1 Corinthians 14:34–35: Evaluation of Prophecy Revisited." *JETS* 51:721–31.
Grindheim, Sigurd. 2002. "Wisdom for the Perfect: Paul's Challenge to the Corinthian Church (1 Corinthians 2:6–16)." *JBL* 121:689–709.
Grudem, Wayne. 1985. "Does Kephalē ('Head') Mean 'Source' or 'Authority Over' in Greek Literature: A Survey of 2,336 Examples." *TrinJ* 6:38–59.
———. 1988. *The Gift of Prophecy in the New Testament and Today*. Eastbourne: Kingsway.
———. 1990. "The Meaning of Kephalē ('head'): A Response to Recent Studies." *TrinJ* 11:3–72.
Gundry Volf, Judith M. 1990. *Paul and Perseverance: Staying In and Falling Away*. Louisville: Westminster John Knox.
———. 1997. "Gender and Creation in 1 Corinthians 11.2-16: A Study in Paul's Theological Method." In *Evangelium, Schriftauslegung, Kirche*, edited by J. Adna, Scott J. Hafemann, and O. Hofius, 151–71. Göttingen: Vandenhoeck & Ruprecht.
Gupta, Nijay K. 2010. "Which 'Body' Is a Temple (1 Corinthians 6:19)? Paul Beyond the Individual/Communal Divide." *CBQ* 72:518–36.
Hafemann, Scott. 2000. "Roman Triumph." In *DNTB*, 1004–8.
Hägerland, Tobias. 2008. "Rituals of (Ex-)Communication and Identity: 1 Cor 5 and 4Q266 11; 4Q270 7." In *Identity Formation in the New Testament*, edited by Bengt Holmberg and Mikael Winninge, 43–60. WUNT 227. Tübingen: Mohr-Siebeck.
Hamilton, Edith. 1969. *Mythology: Timeless Tales of Gods and Heroes*. 3rd ed. New York: Meridian.
Hanges, James C. 1998. "1 Corinthians 4:4 and the Possibility of Written Bylaws in the Corinthian Church." *JBL* 117: 275–98.
Harper, Kyle. 2012. "*Porneia*: The Making of a Christian Sexual Norm." *JBL* 131:363–83.
Harrill, J. Albert. 1998. *The Manumission of Slaves in Early Christianity*. 2nd ed. Hermeneutische Unter Zur Theologie 32. Tübingen: Mohr-Siebeck.
———. 2003. "Paul and Slavery." In *PGRW*, 575–607.
Harrison, James R. 2003. *Paul's Language of Grace in its Graeco-Roman Context*. WUNT 2/172. Tübingen: Mohr-Siebeck.
———. 2008. "Paul and the Athletic Ideal in Antiquity." In *Paul's World*, edited by Stanley E. Porter, 81–109. PS 4. Leiden: Brill.
Harrisville, Roy A. 1987. *1 Corinthians*. ACNT. Augsburg: Minneapolis.
Hartman, Lars. 1974. "Some Remarks on 1 Cor 2:1–5." *SEÅ* 39:109–20.
Hays, Christine. 2002. *Gentile Impurities and Jewish Identities: Intermarriage and Conversion from the Bible to the Talmud*. Oxford: Oxford University Press.
Hays, Richard B. 1996. *The Moral Vision of the New Testament: A Contemporary Introduction to New Testament Ethics*. San Francisco: HarperSanFrancisco.
———. 1997. *First Corinthians*. Interpretation. Louisville: Westminster John Knox.
Heil, John Paul. 2005. *The Rhetorical Role of Scripture in 1 Corinthians*. SBLMS 15. Atlanta: SBL.

Bibliography

Hengel, Martin. 1977. *Crucifixion: In the Ancient World and the Folly of the Message of the Cross*. Philadelphia: Fortress.

———. 1997. *Paul Between Damascus and Antioch: The Unknown Years*. London: SCM.

———. 2001. "Das Begräbnis Jesu bei Paulus und die leibliche Auferstehung aus dem Grabe." In *Auferstehung - Resurrection*. Edited by Friedrich Avemarie and Herman Lichtenberger, 119-83. Durham-Tübingen Research Symposium. WUNT 135. Tübingen: Mohr Siebeck.

Hense, Otto, ed. 1905. *C. Musonii Rufi reliquiae*. Leipzig: B. G. Teubrier.

Héring, Jean. 1949. *La première Épître de saint Paul aux Corinthiens*. Neuchatel/Paris: Delachaux et Niestlé.

Herms, Ronald. 2006. "'Being Saved without Honor': A Conceptual Link between 1 Corinthians 3 and 1 Enoch 50?" *JSNT* 29:187-210.

Hiigel, John L. 2003. *Leadership in 1 Corinthians: A Case Study in Paul's Ecclesiology*. SBEC 57. Lewiston, NY: Edwin Mellen.

Hiu, Elim. 2010. *Regulations Concerning Tongues and Prophecy in 1 Corinthians 14:26-40: Relevance beyond the Corinthian Church*. LNTS 406. London: T. & T. Clark.

Hock, Ronald F. 1978. "Paul's Tentmaking and the Problem of His Social Class." *JBL* 97/4:555-64.

———. 2003. "Paul and Greco-Roman Education." In *PRGW*, 198-227.

———. 2008. "The Problem of Paul's Social Class: Further Reflections." In *Paul's World*, edited by Stanley E. Porter, 7-18. PS 4. Leiden: Brill.

Hodge, Caroline Johnson. 2010. "Married to an Unbeliever: Household, Hierarchies, and Holiness in 1 Cor 7:12-16." *HTR* 103: 1-25.

Hodgson, Robert. 1983. "Paul the Apostle and First Century Tribulation Lists." *ZNW* 74:59-80.

Hofius, Otfried. 1993. "The Lord's Supper and the Lord's Supper Tradition: Reflection on 1 Corinthians 11:23b-25." In *One Loaf, One Cup: Ecumenical Studies of 1 Cor 11 and Other Eucharistic Texts*, edited by Otto Knoch and Ben Meyer, 75-115. Macon: Mercer University Press.

———. 2004. "The Fourth Servant Song in the New Testament Letters." In *The Suffering Servant: Isaiah 53 in Jewish and Christian Sources*, edited by Bern Janowski and Peter Stuhlmacher, 163-88. Grand Rapids: Eerdmans.

Hogeterp, Albert L. 2006. A. *Paul and God's Temple: A Historical Interpretation of Cultic Imagery in the Corinthian Correspondence*. Bible Tools and Studies 2. Leuven/Dudley: Peeters.

Hollander, Harm W. 2009. "The Idea of Fellowship in 1 Corinthians 10.14-22." *NTS* 55:456-70.

———. 2010. "Seeing God 'In a Riddle' or 'Face to Face': An Analysis of 1 Corinthians 13.12." *JSNT* 32:395-403.

Hollander, Harm W., and Gijsbert E. Van der Hout. 1996. "The Apostle Paul Calling Himself an Abortion: 1 Cor. 15:8 within the Context of 1 Cor. 15:8-10." *NovT* 38:224-36.

Hollemann, Joost. 1996. *Resurrection and Parousia: A Traditio-Historical Study of Paul's Eschatology in 1 Corinthians 15*. Leiden: Brill.

Hooker, Morna D. 1964. "Authority on Her Head: An Examination of 1 Cor. 11:10." *NTS* 10:410-16

———. 1966. "Hard Sayings: 1 Corinthians 3:2." *Theology* 69:19-22.

———. 1996. "A Partner in the Gospel: Paul's Understanding of Ministry." In *Theology and Ethics in Paul and His Interpreters: Essays in Honor of Victor Paul Furnish*, edited by E. H. Lovering and Jerry L. Sumney, 83–100. Nashville: Abingdon.
———. 2013. "Artemis of Ephesus." *JTS* 64:37–46.
Horne, Charles M. 1965. "The Power of Paul's Preaching," *JETS* 8:111–16.
Horrell, David G. 1996. *The Social Ethos of the Corinthian Correspondence*. Edinburgh: T. & T. Clark.
———. 1997. "Theological Principle or Christological Praxis? Pauline Ethics in 1 Corinthians 8.1–11.1." *JSNT* 67:83–114.
———. 2004. "Domestic Space and Christian Meetings at Corinth: Imagining New Contexts and the Buildings East of the Theatre." *NTS* 50:349–69.
———. 2005. *Solidarity and Difference: A Contemporary Reading of Paul's Ethics*. London: T. & T. Clark.
———. 2007. "Idol-Food, Idolatry and Ethics in Paul." In *Idolatry: False Worship in the Bible: Early Judaism and Christianity*, edited by Stephen Barton, 120–40. London: T. & T. Clark.
Horsley, Richard A. 1997. "1 Corinthians: A Case Study of Paul's Assembly as an Alternative Society." In *Paul and Empire: Religion and Power in Roman Imperial Society*, 242–52. Harrisburg: Trinity International.
———. 1998. *1 Corinthians*. ANTC. Nashville: Abingdon.
———. 2008. *Wisdom and Spiritual Transcendence at Corinth: Studies in First Corinthians*. Eugene, OR: Cascade.
Hoskins, Paul M. 2001. "The Use of Biblical and Extrabiblical Parallels in the Interpretation of First Corinthians 6:2–3." *CBQ* 63:287–97.
Hovenden, Gerald. 2002. *Speaking in Tongues: The New Testament Evidence in Context*. JPTSS 22. Sheffield: Sheffield Academic.
Hübner, Hans. 1997. *Vetum Testamentum in Novo. Band 2. Corpus Paulinum*. Göttingen: Vandenhoeck & Ruprecth.
Hull, Michael F. 2005. *Baptism on Account of the Dead (1 Cor 15:29): An Act of Faith in the Resurrection*. AcBib 22. Leiden: Brill.
Hullinger, Jerry M. 2004. "The Historical Background of Paul's Athletic Allusions." *BSac* 161:343–59.
Hultgren, Stephen. 2003. "The Origin of Paul's Doctrine of the Two Adams in 1 Corinthians 15.45–49." *JSNT* 25:343–70.
Hurd, John C. 1965. *The Origin of 1 Corinthians*. London: SPCK.
Hurtado, Larry. 2003. *One Lord Jesus: Devotion to Jesus in Earliest Christianity*. Grand Rapids: Eerdmans.
Hutson, C. R. 1997. "Was Timothy Timid? On the Rhetoric of Fearlessness (1 Corinthians 16:10–11) and Cowardice (2 Timothy 1:7)." *BR* 42:58–73.
Huttunen, Niko. 2009. *Paul and Epictetus on Law: A Comparison*. LNTS 405. New York: T. & T. Clark.
Hvalvik, Reidar. 2005. "All Those Who in Every Place Call on the Name of Our Lord Jesus Christ: The Unity of the Pauline Churches." In *The Formation of the Early Church*, edited by Jostein Ådna, 123–43. WUNT 183. Tübingen: Mohr-Siebeck.
Hwang, Jerry. 2011. "Turning the Tables on Idol Feasts: Paul's Use of Exodus 32:6 in 1 Corinthians 10:7." *JETS* 54.3:573–87.
Hyland, Francis Edward. 1928. *Excommunication: Its Nature, Historical Development and Effects*. Washington, DC: Catholic University of America.

Bibliography

Inkelaar, Harm-Jan. 2011. *Conflict Over Wisdom: The Theme of 1 Corinthians 1–4 Rooted in Scripture.* CBET 63. Leuven: Peeters.

Instone-Brewer, David. 1992. "1 Corinthians 9:9–11: A Literal Interpretation of 'Do Not Muzzle the Ox.'" *NTS* 38:554–65.

———. 2002. *Divorce and Remarriage in the Bible: The Social and Literary Context.* Grand Rapids: Eerdmans.

Isaksson, Abel. 1965. *Marriage and Ministry in the New Temple.* ASNU 24. Lund: C. W. K. Gleerup.

Jacon, Christophe. 2006. *La sagesse du discours: Analyse rhétorique et épistolaire de 1 Corinthiens.* Actes et recherches. Genève: Labor et Fides.

James, Sarah A. 2014. "The Last of the Corinthians? Society and Settlement from 146 to 44 BCE." In *CTST*, 17–36.

Janzen, Marshall. 2013. "Orderly Participation or Silenced Women? Clashing Views on Descent Worship in 1 Corinthians 14." *Direction* 42:55–70.

Jeremias, Joachim. 1966. *The Eucharistic Words of Jesus.* London: SCM.

Jewett, Robert. 1971. *Paul's Anthropological Terms: A Study of Their Use in Conflict Settings.* Arbeiten zur Geschichte des antiken Judentums und des Urchristentums 10. Leiden: Brill.

Johanson, B. C. 1979. "Tongues: A Sign for Unbelievers?" *NTS* 25:180–203.

Johnson, Alan F. 2009. "A Review of the Scholarly Debate on the Meaning of 'Head' (κεφαλή) in Paul's Writings." *ATJ* 41:35–57.

Johnson, Andrew. 2003. "Turning the World Upside Down in 1 Corinthians 15: Apocalyptic Epistemology, the Resurrection Body and the New Creation." *EvQ* 75:291–309.

Judge, E. A. 1968. "Paul's Boasting in Relation to Contemporary Profession Practice." *ABR* 16:37–50.

Kammler, Hans-Christian. 2003. *Kreuz und Weisheit: Eine exegetische Untersuchung zu 1 Kor 1,10–3,4.* WUNT 159. Tübingen: Mohr-Siebeck.

Keener, Craig S. 2005. *1–2 Corinthians.* NCBC. Cambridge: Cambridge University Press.

———. 2011. *Miracles: The Credibility of the New Testament Accounts.* 2 vols. Grand Rapids: Baker Academic.

———. 2012–15. *Acts: An Exegetical Commentary.* Vols. 1–4. Grand Rapids: Baker.

———. 2016. *The Mind of the Spirit: Paul's Approach to Transformed Thinking.* Grand Rapids: Baker Academic.

Keith, Chris. 2008. "'In My Own Hand': Grapho-Literacy and the Apostle Paul." *Biblica* 89:38–59.

Kennedy, George A. 1984. *New Testament Interpretation through Rhetorical Criticism.* Chapel Hill: University of North Carolina Press.

———, trans. 2003. *Progymnasmata: Greek Textbooks of Prose Composition and Rhetoric.* Writings from the Greco-Roman World 10. Atlanta: Society of Biblical Literature.

Kent, J. H. 1966. *The Inscriptions 1926–1960. Corinth.* Vol. 8.3. ASCSA. Princeton: Princeton University Press.

Ker, Donald P. 2000. "Paul and Apollos." *JSNT* 77:75–97.

Kim, Chan-Hie. 1972. *Form and Structure of the Familiar Greek Letter of Recommendation.* Missoula: Scholars Press.

Bibliography

Kim, Jung Hoon. 2004. *The Significance of Clothing Imagery in the Pauline Corpus.* LNTS 268. London: T. & T. Clark.

Kim, Yung Suk. 2008. *Christ's Body in Corinth.* Minneapolis: Fortress.

———. 2013. "Reclaiming Christ's Body (*Soma Christou*): Embodiment of God's Gospel in Paul's Letters." *Int* 67:20–29.

Kirchhoff, Renate. 1994. *Die Sünde gegen den eigenen Leib: Studien zu porēn und porpseia in 1 Kor 6,12-20 und dem sozio-kulturellen Kontext der paulinischen Adressaten.* Studien zur Umwelt des Neuen Testaments 18. Gottingen: Vandenhoeck & Ruprecht.

Kirk, Alexander N. 2012. "Building With the Corinthians: Human Persons as the Building Materials of 1 Corinthians 3.12 and the 'Work' of 3.13–15." *NTS* 58:549–70.

———. 2015. *The Departure of an Apostle: Paul's Death Anticipated and Remembered.* WUNT 2/406. Tübingen: Mohr Siebeck.

Klauck, Hans-Josef. 1982. *Herrenmahl und Hellenistischer Kult,* Münster: Aschendorff.

———. 1984. *1. Korintherbrief.* 7. Lieferung. Wurzburg: Echter.

Klein, George L. 1989. "Hos 3:1–3—Background to 1 Cor 6:19b–20." *CTR* 3/2:373–75.

Klein, William W. 1986. "Noisy Gong or Acoustic Vase: A Note on 1 Corinthians 13.1." *NTS* 32:286–89.

Koet, B. J. 1996. "The OT Background to 1 Cor. 10:7–8." In *CorBETL*, 612–13.

Konradt, Matthias. 2003. *Gericht und Gemeinde: Eine Studie zur Bedeutung und Funktion von Gerichtsaussagen im Rahmen der paulinischen Ekklesiologie und Ethik im 1 Thess und 1 Kor.* BZNW 117. Berlin: de Gruyter.

Koperski, Veronica. 1996. "Knowledge of Christ and Knowledge of God in the Corinthian Correspondence." In *The Corinthian Correspondence,* edited by Reimund Bieringer, 377–96. Leuven: Leuven University Press.

Kreitzer, Larry J. 1993. "Resurrection." In *DPL,* 805–12.

Krentz, Edgar. 2005. "Logos or Sophia: The Pauline Use of the Ancient Dispute between Rhetoric and Philosophy." In *Early Christianity and Classical Culture: Comparative Studies in Honor of Abraham J. Malherbe,* edited by John T. Fitzgerald, 275–90. NovTSup 110. Leiden: Brill.

Kroeger, Catherine C. 2002. "1 Corinthians." In *The IVP Women's Bible Commentary,* edited by Catherine C. Kroeger and Mary J. Evans, 648–64. Downers Grove, IL: InterVarsity.

Kroeger, Catherine C., and Richard Kroeger. 1978. "An Inquiry into Evidence of Maenadism in the Corinthian Congregation." *SBLSP* 2:331–38.

Kuck, David W. 1992. *Judgment and Community Conflict: Paul's Use of Apocalyptic Judgment Language in 1 Corinthians 3:5—4:5* NovTSup 66. Leiden: Brill.

Kurek-Chomycz, Dominika A. 2006. "Is There an 'Anti-Priscan' Tendency in the Manuscripts? Some Textual Problems with Prisca and Aquila." *JBL* 125:107–28.

Kyle, Donald G. 1998. *Spectacles of Death in Ancient Rome.* London: Routledge.

Laansma, Jon C. 1997. "Lord's Day." In *The Dictionary of the Later New Testament and Its Development,* edited by Ralph P. Martin and Peter H. Davids, 679–86. Downers Grove, IL: InterVarsity.

Lakey, Michael J. 2010. *Image and Glory of God: 1 Corinthians 11:2–16 as a Case Study in Bible, Gender and Hermeneutics.* LNTS 418. London: T. & T. Clark/Bloomsbury.

Lalleman, Hetty. 2011. "Paul's Self-Understanding in the Light of Jeremiah: A Case Study into the Use of the Old Testament in the New Testament." In *A God of*

Bibliography

Faithfulness: Essays in Honour of J. Gordon McConville on His 60th Birthday, edited by Jamie A. Grant, Alison Lo, and Gordon J. Wenham, 96–111. Library of the Hebrew Bible/Old Testament Studies 538. London: T. & T. Clark.

Lambrecht, Jan. 1996. "Paul as Example: A Study of 1 Corinthians 4.6–21." In *Ekklesiology des Neuen Testaments: Für Karl Kertelge*, edited by Rainer Kampling and Thomas Söding, 316–35. Freiburg: Herder.

———. 2007. "Review of *Paulus und die Gesinnung Christi*, by C. W. Strüder." *Biblica* 88:438–40.

———. 2009. "Paul's Reasoning in 1 Corinthians 6,12–20." *ETL* 85:479–86.

———. 2013. "1 Corinthians 2:14: A Response to Laura B. Dingeldein." *NovT* 55:367–70.

Lampe, Peter. 1994. "The Eucharist: Identifying with Christ on the Cross." *Int* 48:36–49.

———. 2002. "Paul's Concept of a Spiritual Body." In *Resurrection: Theological and Scientific Assessments*, edited by Ted Peters, Robert John Russell, and Michael Welker, 103–14. Grand Rapids: Eerdmans.

Lanci, John R. 1997. *A New Temple for Corinth: Rhetorical and Archaeological Approaches to Pauline Imagery*. Studies in Biblical Literature 1. New York: Peter Lang.

Lang, Friedrich. 1994. *Die Briefe an die Korinther*. NTD 7. Göttingen: Vandenhoeck & Ruprecht.

Lapide, Pinchas. 1983. *The Resurrection Jesus: A Jewish Perspective*. Minneapolis: Augsburg-Fortress.

Last, Richard. 2013. "The Election of Officers in the Corinthian Christ-Group." *NTS* 59:365–81.

Lee, Michelle V. 2006. *Paul, the Stoics, and the Body of Christ*. SNTSMS 137. Cambridge: Cambridge University Press.

Lee-Barnewall, Michelle. 2013. "Turning Κεφαλή on its Head: The Rhetoric of Reversal in Ephesians 5:21–33." In *Christian Origins and Greco-Roman Culture: Social and Literary Contexts for the New Testament*, edited by Stanley E. Porter and Andrew W. Pitts, 599–614. TENTS 9. Leiden: Brill.

Legarreta-Castillo, Felipe de Jesús. 2014. *The Figure of Adam in Romans 5 and 1 Corinthians 15: The New Creation and Its Ethical and Social Reconfiguration*. Emerging Scholars. Minneapolis: Fortress.

Lehmann, Karl. 1968. *Auferweckt am dritten Tagnach der Schrift: Früheste Christologie, Bekenntnisbildung und Schriftauslegung im Lichte von 1 Kor. 15,3–5*. QD 38. Ereiburg: Herder.

Lestang, François. 2015. "Un autre ror que César? Implications politiques de l'évangile paulinien." *Théophilyon* XX-1:11–26.

Lewis, Scott M. 1998. *So That God May Be All in All: The Apocalyptic Message of 1 Corinthians 15,12–34*. TGST 42. Rome: Editrice Pontificia Universita Gregoriania.

Liefeld, W. L. 1986. "Women, Submission and Ministry in 1 Corinthians." In *Women, Authority, and the Bible*, edited by A. Mickelsen, 134–54. Downers Grove, IL: InterVarsity.

Lietzmann, Hans, and Werner Kümmel. 1949. *An die Korinther I-II*. HNT 9. Tübingen: Mohr-Siebeck.

Lieu, Judith M. 1985. "Grace to You and Peace: The Apostolic Greeting." *BJRL* 68: 161–78.

Lim, Kar Yong. 2009. *"The Sufferings of Christ Are Abundant in Us": A Narrative Dynamics Investigation of Paul's Sufferings in 2 Corinthians*. LNTS 399. London: T. & T. Clark.

Lim, Timothy H. 1987. "Not in Persuasive Words of Wisdom, but in the Demonstration of the Spirit and Power." *NovT* 29:137–49.

Lindemann, Andreas. 2000. *Der Erste Korintherbrief.* HNT 9/1. Tübingen: Mohr-Siebeck.

Litfin, Duane. 1994. *St. Paul's Theology of Proclamation: 1 Corinthians 1–4 and Greco-Roman Rhetoric*. SNTSMS 79. Cambridge: Cambridge University Press.

Litwa, M. David. 2012. *We Are Being Transformed: Deification in Paul's Soteriology.* BZNW 187. Berlin: De Gruyter.

Liu, Yulin. 2013. *Temple Purity in 1–2 Corinthians*. WUNT 2/343. Tübingen: Mohr-Siebeck.

Loader, William. 2012. *The New Testament on Sexuality*. Grand Rapids: Eerdmans.

———. 2013. *Making Sense of Sex: Attitudes Towards Sexuality in Early Jewish and Christian Literature*. Grand Rapids: Eerdmans.

Long, David P. 2014. "Eucharistic Ecclesiology and Excommunication: A Critical Investigation of the Meaning and Praxis of Exclusion from the Sacrament of the Eucharist." *Ecclesiology* 10:205–28.

Long, Fredrick J. 2007. "Christ's Gifted Bride: Gendered Members in Ministry in Acts and Paul in the Greco-Roman Milieu." In *Women, Ministry, and the Gospel: Exploring New Paradigms*, edited by Mark Husbands and Timothy Larsen, 98–123. Downers Grove, IL: InterVarsity.

———. 2013. "Paul's Prophesying Isa 28:11 in Context: The Signs of Unbelievers and Believers in 1 Cor 14." In *Kingdom Rhetoric: New Testament Exploration in Honor of Ben Witherington III*, edited by T. Michael W. Halcomb, 133–69. Eugene, OR: Wipf & Stock.

Long, George, ed. n.d. *Arrian's Discourses of Epictetus*. Perseus Digital Library/Logos Software. http://www.perseus.tufts.edu/hopper/.

Lopez, Rene A. 2011. "A Study of Pauline Passages with Vice Lists." *BSac* 168:301–16.

Lorenzen, Stefanie. 2008. *Das paulinische Eikon-Konzept*. WUNT 2/250. Tübingen: Mohr-Siebeck.

Lüdemann, Gerd, and William Lane Craig., et al. 2000. *Jesus' Resurrection: Fact or Fiction? A Debate Between William Lane Craig and Gerd Lüdemann*, edited by Paul Copan and Ronald K. Tacelli. Downers Grove, IL: InterVarsity.

Luzarraga, J. 1973. *Las tradiciones de la nube en la biblia y en el judaismo primitivo.* AnBib 54. Rome: Biblical Institute.

Macdonald, Margaret Y., and Leif E. Vaage. 2011. "Unclean but Holy Children: Paul's Everyday Quandary in 1 Corinthians 7:14c." *CBQ* 73:526–46.

MacGregor, Kirk R. 2006. "1 Corintians 15:3b–6a, 7 and the Bodily Resurrection of Jesus." *JETS* 49:225–34.

Mackie, Scott D. 2013. "The Two Tablets of the Law and Paul's Ethical Methodology in 1 Corinthians 6:12–20 and 10:23–11:1." *CBQ* 75:315–34.

Maier, Harry O. 2013. *Picturing Paul in Empire: Imperial Image, Text and Persuasion in Colossians, Ephesians and the Pastoral Epistles*. London: Bloomsbury.

Malcolm, Matthew R. 2013a. *Paul and the Rhetoric of Reversal in 1 Corinthian: The Impact of Paul's Gospel on His Macro-Rhetoric*. SNTSMS 155. Cambridge: Cambridge University Press.

Bibliography

———. 2013b. *The World of 1 Corinthians: An Exegetical Source Book of Literary and Visual Backgrounds.* Eugene, OR: Cascade.

Malherbe, Abraham J. 1968. "The Beasts of Ephesus." *JBL* 81:71–80.

———. 1980. "Μὴ γένοιτο in the Diatribe and Paul." *HTR* 73:231–40.

Malina, Bruce J. 2001. *The New Testament World: Insights from Cultural Anthropology.* 3rd ed. Louisville: Westminster John Knox.

Malone, Andrew S. 2009. "Burn or Boast? Keeping the 1 Corinthians 13,3 Debate in Balance." *Bib* 90:401–6.

March, J. R. 1996. "Bellerophon." In *OCD*, 237–38.

Marchal, Joseph A. 2011. "The Usefulness of an Onesimus: The Sexual Use of Slaves and Paul's Letter to Philemon." *JBL* 130:749–70.

Marshall, I. Howard. 1975. *Kept By the Power of God: A Study of Perseverance and Falling Away.* Minneapolis: Bethany.

———. 1993. *Last Supper, Lord's Supper.* Carlisle: Paternoster.

———. 2004. *Pastoral Epistles.* ICC. London: T. & T. Clark.

Marshall, Peter. 1987. *Enmity in Corinth: Social Conventions in Paul's Relations with the Corinthians.* WUNT 2/23. Tübingen: Mohr-Siebeck.

Martin, Dale B. 1990. *Slavery as Salvation: The Metaphor of Slavery in Pauline Christianity.* New Haven: Yale University Press.

———. 1995. *The Corinthian Body.* New Haven: Yale University Press.

———. 2001. "Review Essay: Justin J. Meggitt, *Paul, Poverty and Survival.*" *JSNT* 84:51–64.

———. 2006. *Sex and the Single Savior: Gender and Sexuality in Biblical Interpretation.* Louisville: Westminster John Knox.

Martin, Troy W. 2004. "Paul's Argument from Nature for the Veil in 1 Corinthians 11:13–15: A Testicle Instead of a Head Covering." *JBL* 123:75–84.

———. 2013. "Περιβόλαιον as 'Testicle' in 1 Corinthians 11:15: A Response to Mark Goodacre." *JBL* 132:453–65.

Massey, Preston T. 2007. "The Meaning of κατακαλύπτω and κατὰ κεφαλῆς ἔχων in 1 Corinthians 11.2–16." *NTS*:502–23.

———. 2011. "Long Hair as a Glory and as a Covering: Removing an Ambiguity from 1 Cor 11:15." *NovT*:52–72.

———. 2013. "Gender Versus Marital Concerns: Does 1 Corinthians 11:2-16 Address the Issues of Male/Female or Husband/Wife?" *TynBul* 64:239–56.

Mattingly, David J. 2006. "Trophies, Military." In *CDCC*, 911–12.

May, Alistair Scott. 2004. *"The Body for the Lord": Sex and Identity in 1 Corinthians 5–7.* JSNTSS 278. London: T. & T. Clark.

Mayordomo-Marin, Moisés. 2011. "'Act Like Men!' Paul's Exhortation in Different Historical Contexts (1 Cor. 16:13)." *Cross Currents* 61:515–28.

McDonough, Sean M. 2005. "Competent to Judge: The Old Testament Connection between 1 Corinthians 5 and 6." *JTS* 56:99–102.

McGowan, Andrew. 2015. "The Myth of the 'Lord's Supper': Paul's Eucharistic Meal Terminology and Its Ancient Reception." *CBQ* 77: 503–21.

McNamara, Derek. 2010. "Shame the Incestuous Man: 1 Corinthians 5." *Neot* 44:307–26.

McRae, Rachel M. 2011. "Eating with Honor: The Corinthian Lord's Supper in Light of Voluntary Association Meal Practices." *JBL* 130:165–81.

McRay, J. R. 2000. "Corinth." In *DNTB*, 227–31.

Meeks, Wayne A. 1982. "'And Rose Up to Play': Midrash and Paraenesis in 1 Corinthians 10:1–22." *JSNT* 16:64–78.
Meggitt, Justin J. 1996. "The Social Status of Erastus (Rom. 16:23)." *NovT* 38:218–23.
———. 1998. *Paul, Poverty, and Survival*. SNTW. London: T. & T. Clark.
———. 2001. "Response to Martin and Theissen." *JSNT* 84:85–94.
Meritt, Benjamin D. 1931. *Greek Inscriptions, 1896-1927*. Corinth 8.1, ASCSA. Cambridge: Harvard University Press.
Merklein, Helmut. 1984. "Die Einheitlichkeit der ersten Korintherbriefes." *ZNW* 75:153–83.
———. 1992–2000. *Der erste Brief an die Korinther*. ÖKTNT 7/1–3. Würzburg: Echter.
Metzger, Bruce M., and United Bible Societies. 1994. *A Textual Commentary on the Greek New Testament*. 2nd rev. ed. London: United Bible Societies.
Metzner, Rainer. 2000. "Paulus under der Wettkampf: Die Rolle des Sports in Leben und Verkündigung des Apostels (1 Kor 9.24–7; Phil 3.12–16)." *NTS* 46:565–83.
Meyer, Ben F. 1993. "The Expiation Motif in the Eucharistic Words: A Key to the Historical Jesus?" In *One Loaf, One Cup*, edited by Ben. F. Meyer, 11–33. Macon: Mercer University Press.
Meyer, H. A. W. 1877. *Critical and Exegetical Handbook to the Epistles to the Corinthians*. 2 vols. Edinburgh: T. & T. Clark.
Mgaya, Gerson L. 2009. "The 1 Corinthians 12:3 Ritual of Curse: Who Was Being Cursed?" *African Theological Journal* 32:79–89.
Mihaila, Corin. 2009. *The Paul-Apollos Relationship and Paul's Stance Toward Greco-Roman Rhetoric: An Exegetical and Socio-historical Study of 1 Corinthians 1–4*. LNTS 402. London: T. & T. Clark.
Miller, J. Edward. 2003. "Some Observations on the Text-Critical Function of the Umlauts in Vaticanus, with Special Attention to 1 Corinthians 14:34–35." *JSNT* 26:217–36.
Millis, Benjamin W. 2010. "The Social and Ethnic Origins of the Colonists in Early Roman Corinth." In *CTXT*, 13–36.
———. 2013. "The Local Magistrates and Elite of Roman Corinth." In *CTST*, 38–53.
Mitchell, Andrew C. 1993. "Rich and Poor in the Courts of Corinth: Litigiousness and Status in 1 Corinthians 6:1–11." *NTS* 39:562–86.
Mitchell, Margaret M. 1991. *Paul and the Rhetoric of Reconciliation*. Louisville: Westminster John Knox.
———. 2001. "Pauline Accommodation and 'Condescension' (συγκατάβασις): 1 Cor 9:19–23 and the History of Influence." In *Paul Beyond the Judaism/Hellenism Divide*, edited by Troels Engberg-Pedersen, 197–214, 298–309. Louisville: Westminster John Knox.
Mitchell, Matthew W. 2003. "Reexamining the Aborted Apostle: An Exploration of Paul's Self-Description in 1 Corinthians 15.8." *JSNT* 25:469–85.
Mody, Rohintan Keki. 2007. "'The Case of the Missing Thousand': Paul's Use of the Old Testament in 1 Corinthians 10:8—A New Proposal." *Churchman* 121:61–79.
———. 2009. "The Relationship between Powers of Evil and Idols in 1 Corinthians 8:4–5 and 10:18–22 in the Context of the Pauline Corpus and Early Judaism." *TynBul* 60:295–98.
Moffatt, James. 1938. *The First Epistle of Paul to the Corinthians*. MNTC. New York: Harper Brothers.
Montague, George T. 2011. *First Corinthians*. CCSS. Grand Rapids: Baker.

Bibliography

Morgan, Teresa. 1998. *Literature Education in the Hellenistic and Roman Worlds.* Cambridge Classical Studies. Cambridge: Cambridge University Press.

Moses, Robert E. 2013. "Physical and/or Spiritual Exclusion? Ecclesial Discipline in 1 Corinthians 5." *NTS* 59:172–91.

Moule, C. F. D. 1966. "St. Paul and Dualism: The Pauline Conception of Resurrection." *NTS* 12:106–23.

Mount, Christopher. 2005. "1 Corinthians 11:3–16: Spirit Possession and Authority in a Non-Pauline Interpolation." *JBL* 124:313–40.

Muirhead, J., ed. 1880. *The Institutes of Gaius and Rules of Ulpian.* Edinburgh: T. & T. Clark.

Mulroy. David. 2012. *75 Classical Myths: Condensed from Their Primary Sources.* San Diego: Cognella.

Murphy-O'Connor, Jerome. 1978. "Corinthian Slogans in 1 Cor. 6:12–20." *CBQ* 40:391–96.

———. 1983. *St. Paul's Corinth: Texts and Archaeology.* Good News Studies 6. Wilmington, DE: Michael Glazier.

———. 1984. "The Corinth that Saint Paul Saw." *BA* 47:147–59.

———. 1993. "Co-Authorship in the Corinthian Correspondence." *RB* 100:562–79.

———. 1996. *Paul: A Critical Life.* Oxford: Oxford University Press.

———. 2009. *Keys to First Corinthians: Revisiting the Major Issues.* Oxford: Oxford University Press.

Myrick, Anthony A. 1996. "'Father' Imagery in 2 Corinthians 1-9 and Jewish Paternal Tradition." *TynBul* 47:163–71.

Nagel, Peter. 2013. "1 Corinthians 14:21—Paul's Reflection on γλωσσα." *Journal of Early Christian History* 3:33–49.

Nanos, Mark D. 2012. "Paul's Relationship to Torah in Light of His Strategy 'To Become Everything to Everyone' (1 Corinthians 9.19–23)." In *Paul and Judaism: Crosscurrents in Pauline Exegesis and the Study of Jewish-Christian Relations*, edited by Reimund Bieringer and Didier Pollefeyt, 106–40. LNTS 463. Bloomsbury: T. & T. Clark.

Nash, Robert Scott. 2009. *1 Corinthians.* Smyth & Helwys Bible Commentary. Macon: Smyth & Helwys.

Nasrallah, Laura Sallah. 2013. "'You Were Bought With a Price': Freedpersons and Things in 1 Corinthians." In *CTXT*, 54–73.

Naylor, Peter. *A Study Commentary on 1 Corinthians.* EPSC. Durham: Evangelical, 2004.

Neirynck, Frans. 1996. "The Sayings of Jesus in 1 Corinthians." In *The Corinthian Correspondence*, edited by Reimund Bieringer, 141–76. BETL 125. Leuven: Peeters.

Newton, Derek. 1998. *Deity and Diet: The Dilemma of Sacrificial Food at Corinth.* Sheffield: Sheffield Academic.

Newton, Michael. 1985. *The Concept of Purity in Qumran and Paul.* Cambridge: Cambridge University Press.

Neyrey, Jerome H. 1990. *Paul, In Other Words: A Cultural Reading of His Letters.* Louisville: Westminster John Knox.

Nguyen, V. Henry T. 2007. "The Identification of Paul's Spectacle of Death Metaphor in 1 Corinthians 4.9." *NTS* 53:489–501.

———. 2008a. *Christian Identity in Corinth: A Comparative Study of 2 Corinthians, Epictetus and Valerius Maximus.* WUNT 2/243. Tübingen: Mohr-Siebeck.

———. 2008b. "God's Execution of His Condemned Apostles: Paul's Imagery of the Roman Arena in Cor 4." *ZNW* 99:33–48.
Niccum, Curt. 1997. "The Voice of the Manuscripts on the Silence of Women: The External Evidence for 1 Cor 14:34–35," *NTS* 43:242–55.
Nickelsburg, George W. E. 1986. "An Ἔκτρωμα, though Appointed from the Womb: Paul's Apostolic Self-Description in 1 Corinthians 15 And Galatians 1." *HTR* 79:198–205.
———. 2006. *Resurrection, Immortality, and Eternal Life in Intertestamental Judaism and Early Christianity*. Expanded ed. HTS 56. Cambridge: Harvard University Press.
Nickle, Keith F. 1966. *The Collection: A Study in Paul's Strategy*. SBT 48. Naperville, IL: Allenson.
Nunn, H. P. V. 1912. *A Short Syntax of New Testament Greek*. Cambridge: Cambridge University Press.
Nygren, Anders. 1936. *Agapē and Eros*. London: SPCK.
Oberholtzer, Thomas Kem. 1988. "The Warning Passages in Hebrews Part 3 (of 5 parts): The Thorn-Infested Ground in Hebrews 6:4–12." *BSac* 145:319–28.
Økland, Jorunn. 2004. *Women in their Place: Paul and the Corinthian Discourse of Gender and Sanctuary Space*. London: T. & T. Clark.
Oropeza, B. J. 1996. *A Time to Laugh: The Holy Laughter Phenomenon Examined*. Peabody, MA: Hendrickson.
———. 1998a. "Laying to Rest the Midrash: Paul's Message of Meat Sacrificed to Idols in Light of Deuteronomic Tradition." *Biblica* 79:57–68.
———. 1998b. "Situational Immorality? Paul's 'Vice Lists' at Corinth." *ExpTim* 110:9-10.
———. 2002a. "Echoes of Isaiah in the Rhetoric of Paul: New Exodus, Wisdom, and the Humility of the Cross in Utopian-Apocalyptic Expectations." In *The Intertexture of Apocalyptic Discourse in the New Testament*, edited by Duane F. Watson, 87–112. SBL Symposium Series 14. Atlanta: Scholars Press.
———. 2002b. "The Toronto Blessing and the Future of Revivalism." In *Religion as Entertainment*, edited by C. K. Robertson, 137–50. New York: Peter Lang.
———. 2004. "Wine and the Lord's Supper in the Gospels, Paul, and Today." In *Religion and Alcohol: Sobering Thoughts*, edited by C. K. Robertson, 45–78. New York: Peter Lang.
———. 2006. "What is Sex? Christians and Erotic Boundaries." In *Religion and Sexuality: Conflicts and Controversies*, edited by C. K. Robertson, 27–63. New York: Peter Lang.
———. 2007. *Paul and Apostasy: Eschatology, Perseverance, and Falling Away in the Corinthian Congregation*. WUNT 2/115. Reprint, Eugene, OR: Wipf & Stock.
———. 2009. "Running in Vain, but Not As an Athlete (Gal. 2:2): The Impact of Habakkuk 2:2–4 on Paul's Apostolic Commission." In *Jesus and Paul: Global Perspectives in Honor of James D. G. Dunn. A Festschrift for his 70th Birthday*, edited by B. J. Oropeza, Douglas C. Mohrmann, and C. K. Robertson, 139–50. LNTS 414. London: T. & T. Clark.
———. 2010. "Judas' Death and Final Destiny in the Gospels and Earliest Christian Writings." *Neot* 44.2:342–61.

Bibliography

———. 2011. *In the Footsteps of Judas and Other Defectors: The Gospels, Acts, and Johannine Letters*. Apostasy in the New Testament Communities, vol. 1. Eugene, OR: Cascade.

———. 2012a. *Jews, Gentiles, and the Opponents of Paul: The Pauline Letters*. Apostasy in the New Testament Communities, vol. 2. Eugene, OR: Cascade.

———. 2012b. *Churches under Siege of Persecution and Assimilation: The General Epistles and Revelation*. Apostasy in the New Testament Communities, vol. 3. Eugene, OR: Cascade.

———. 2016. *Exploring Second Corinthians: Death and Life, Hardship and Rivalry*. Sociorhetorical Exploration Commentary. RRA 3. Atlanta: Society of Biblical Literature.

———. 8/2016. "Saved with a Loss of Reward Only? Another Look at 1 Corinthians 3:10–17." https://azusa.academia.edu/BjOropeza.

———. 11/2016. "Clashes with Death, Immortality, and Being in Adam and in Christ: Corinthian Diversity of Beliefs About the Resurrection, and Paul's Response (1 Cor 15)." Paper presented at the annual SBL conference (Nov. 19, 2016). https://azusa.academia.edu/BjOropeza.

———. 1/2017. "When Will the Cessation of Speaking in Tongues and Revelatory Gifts Take Place? A Reply to Updated Interpretations of 1 Cor 13:8–10." https://azusa.academia.edu/BjOropeza.

Orr, William F., and J. A. Walther. 1976. *1 Corinthians*. AB. Garden City, NY: Doubleday.

Osiek, Carolyn. 2003. "Female Slaves, *Porneia*, and the Limits of Obedience." In *Early Christian Families in Context: An Interdisciplinary Dialogue*, edited by David L. Balch and Carolyn Osiek, 255–74 Grand Rapids: Eerdmans.

Ossom-Batsa, George. 2011. "Responsible Community Behaviour or Exclusion: Interpreting 1 Cor 5:1–13 from a Communicative Perspective." *Neot* 45:293–310.

Oster, Richard E. 1988. "When Men Wore Veils to Worship: The Historical Context of 1 Corinthians 11.4." *NTS* 34:481–505.

———. 1992. "Use, Misuse, and Neglect of Archaeological Evidence in Some Modern Works on 1 Corinthians." *ZNW* 83:52–73.

———. 1995. *1 Corinthians*. College Press NIV Commentary. Joplin, MO: College Press.

Paige, Terence. 1991. "1 Corinthians 12:2: A Pagan *Pompe*"? *JSNT* 44: 57–65.

———. 2004. "Stoicism, ἐλευθερία, and Community at Corinth." In *Christianity in Corinth: The Quest for the Pauline Church*, edited by Edward Adams and David G. Horrell, 207–18. Louisville: Westminster John Knox.

Papathomas, Amphilochios. 1997. "Das agonistische Motiv 1 Kor 9.24ff. im Spiegel zeitgenössischer dokumentarischer Quellen." *NTS* 43:223–41.

Park, Joseph S. 2000. *Conceptions of Afterlife in Jewish Inscriptions: With Special Reference to Pauline Literature*. WUNT 2/141. Tübingen: Mohr-Siebeck.

Parler, Branson. 2016. "Hair Length and Human Sexuality: The Underlying Moral Logic of Paul's Appeal to Nature in 1 Corinthians 11:14." *CTJ* 51:112–36.

Paschke, Boris A. 2007. "Ambiguity in Paul's References to Greco-Roman Sexual Ethics." *ETL* 83:169–92.

Pascuzzi, Maria. 1997. *Ethics, Ecclesiology and Church Discipline: A Rhetorical Analysis of 1 Corinthians 5* TGST 32. Roma: Editrice Pontifica Univerita Gregoriana.

———. 2009. "Baptism-based Allegiance and the Divisions in Corinth: A Reexamination of 1 Corinthians 1:13–17." *CBQ* 79:813–29.

Bibliography

Pate, C. Marvin. 1991. *Adam Christology as the Exegetical and Theological Substructure of 2 Corinthians 4:7-5:21*. Lanham: University Press of America.

———. 1993. *The Glory of Adam and the Afflictions of the Righteous: Pauline Suffering in Context*. New York: Mellen Biblical Press.

Pausanias. 1918. *Pausanias Description of Greece with an English Translation by W.H.S. Jones, Litt.D., and H.A. Ormerod, M.A., in 4 Volumes*. Cambridge: Harvard University Press.

Payne, Philip B. 2009. *Man and Woman: One in Christ*. Grand Rapids: Zondervan.

Peppard, Michael. 2014. "Brother against Brother: *Controversiae* about Inheritance Disputes and 1 Corinthians 6:1–11." *JBL* 133:179–92.

Peppiatt, Lucy. 2015. *Women and Worship at Corinth: Paul's Rhetorical Arguments in 1 Corinthians*. Eugene, OR: Wipf and Stock.

Perkins, Pheme. 2012. *First Corinthians*. Paideia. Grand Rapids: Baker.

Perriman, A. C. 1994. "The Head of the Woman: The Meaning of Kephalē in 1 Cor 11:3." *JTS* 45:602–22.

Perrot, Charles. 1983. "Les Examples du désert (1 Cor 10:6–11)." *NTS* 29:437–52.

Petersen, Anders Klostergaard. 2013. "Finding a Basis for Interpreting New Testament Ethos from a Greco-Roman Philosophical Perspective." In *Early Christian Ethics in Interaction with Jewish and Greco-Roman Contexts*, edited by Jan Willem van Henten and Joseph Verheyden, 53–81. Studies in Theology and Religion 17. Leiden: Brill.

Petrovich, Christopher G. 2015. "First Corinthians 11:2–16, Calvin, and Reformed Praxis." *WTJ* 77:111–33.

Pfitzner, Victor C. 1967. *Paul and the Agon Motif: Traditional Athletic Imagery in the Pauline Literature*. NovTSup 16. Brill: Leiden.

Phua, Richard Liong-Seng. 2005. *Idolatry and Authority: A Study of 1 Corinthians 8.1-11.1 in the Light of the Jewish Diaspora*. LNTS 299. London: T. & T. Clark.

Pickett, Raymond. 1997. *The Cross in Corinth: The Social Significance of the Death of Jesus*. JSNTSS 143. Sheffield: Sheffield Academic.

Planck, Max A. 1987. *Paul and the Irony of Affliction*. Semeia Studies. Atlanta: Scholars Press.

Pliny the Younger. 1963. *The Letters of Pliny the Younger*. Translated by Betty Radice. Baltimore: Penguin.

Pogoloff, Stephen M. 1992. *Logos and Sophia: The Rhetorical Situation of 1 Corinthians*. SBLDiss 134. Atlanta: Scholars Press.

Poirier, John C. 2010. *The Tongues of Angels: The Concept of Angelic Languages in Classical Jewish and Christian Texts*. WUNT 2/287. Tübingen: Mohr Siebeck.

Poplutz, Uta. 2004. *Athlet des Evangeliums. Eine motive schichtliche Studie zur Wettkampfmetaphorik bei Paulus*. Herders Biblische Studien 43. Herder: Freiburg im Breisgau.

Popovic, Anton. 2014. "The Christian Faith as Struggle and as Renunciation According to the First Letter to the Corinthians." *Antonianum* 89:9–42.

Portier-Young, Anathea. 2005. "On Tongues and Cymbals." *BTB* 35:99–105.

Proctor, John. 1993. "Fire in God's House: Influence of Malachi 3 in the NT." *JETS* 36:9–14.

Prothro, James B. 2014. "Who is 'of Christ'? A Grammatical and Theological Reconsideration of 1 Cor 1.12. *NTS* 60:250–65.

Pucci, Michael S. 2000. "Arenas." In *DNTB*, 111–14.

Bibliography

Quintilian. 1922. *Institutio Oratoria*. Edited by H. E. Butler. Cambridge: Harvard University Press.

Rabens, Volker. 2013. *The Holy Spirit and Ethics in Paul*. Rev. ed. WUNT 2/283. Tübingen: Mohr-Siebeck.

Ramasaran, Rolin A. 2003. "Paul and Maxims." In *PGRW*, 429–56.

Ramelli, Ilaria L. 2011. "Spiritual Weakness, Illness, and Death in 1 Corinthians 11:30." *JBL* 130:145–63.

Reaume, J. D. 1995. "Another Look at 1 Corinthians 15.29: 'Baptism for the Dead.'" *BSac* 152:457–75.

Reed, Jeffrey T. 1996. "Are Paul's Thanksgivings 'Epistolary'?" *JSNT* 61:87–99.

Regele, Michael B. 2014. *Science, Scripture, and Same-Sex Love*. Nashville: Abingdon.

Reitzenstein, Richard. 1978. *Hellenistic Mystery Religions*. Pittsburgh Theological Monograph Series 15. Reprint, Eugene, OR: Wipf & Stock.

Rengstorf, Karl Heinrich. 1964. "ὑπηρέτης, ὑπηρετέω." In *TDNT*, 8:530–45.

Richards, E. Randolph. 2004. *Paul and First-Century Letter Writing: Secretaries, Composition and Collection*. Downers Grove, IL: InterVarsity.

Richardson, Neil G. 1994. *Paul's Language about God*. JSNTSS 99. Sheffield: Sheffield Academic.

Richardson, Peter, and Paul W. Gooch. 1978. "Accommodation Ethics." *TynBul* 29:89–142.

Riddlebarger, Kim. 2013. *First Corinthians*. Lectio Contiua. Powder Springs, GA: Tolle Lege.

Robeck, C. Mel. 1988. "Prophecy, Gift of." In *Dictionary of Pentecostal and Charismatic Movements*, edited by Stanley M. Burgess and Gary B. McGee, 728–40. Grand Rapids: Zondervan.

Roberts, Erin. 2014. "Reconsidering Harmartia as 'Sin' in 1 Corinthians." *Method and Theory in the Study of Religion* 26:340–64.

Robertson, Archibald, and Alfred Plummer. 1925. *The First Epistle of St. Paul to The Corinthians*. ICC. New York: Scribner's.

Robertson, C. K. 2001. *Conflict in Corinth: Redefining the System*. SIBL 42. New York: Peter Lang.

———. 2007. "Courtroom Dramas: A Pauline Alternative for Conflict Management." *ATR* 89:589–610.

Robertson, O. P. 1990. *The Books of Nahum, Habakkuk, Zephaniah*. NICOT. Grand Rapids: Eerdmans.

Robinson, Betsy A. 2005. "Fountains and the Formation of Cultural Identity at Roman Corinth." In *URRC*, 111–40.

Röhser, Gunter. 2012. "Vorstellungen von der Präsenz Christi im Ritual nach 1Kor 11,17–34." In *Mahl und religiöse Identität im frühen Christentum/Meals and Religious Identity in Early Christianity*, edited by Matthias Klinghardt and Hal Taussig, 131–58. Texte und Arbeiten zum neutestamentlichen Zeitalter 56. Tubingen: Francke.

Rosner, Brian S. 1994. *Paul, Scripture, and Ethics: A Study of 1 Corinthians 5–7*. AGJU 22. Leiden: Brill.

———. 2014. "Paul and the Law in 1 Corinthians." Paper presented at the SBL annual conference, San Diego.

Ross, J. M. 1992. "Floating Words: Their Significance for Textual Criticism." *NTS* 38:153–56.

Rudolph, David. 2011. *A Jew to the Jews: Jewish Contours of Pauline Flexibility in 1 Corinthians 9:19–23*. WUNT 2/304. Tübingen: Mohr-Siebeck.
Russell, D. A. 1983. *Greek Declamation*. Cambridge: Cambridge University Press.
Ruthven, Jon. 1990. "On the Cessation of the Charismata: The Protestant Polemic of Benjamin B. Warfield." *Pneuma* 12:14–31.
Salmon, J. B. 1996. "Corinth." In *OCD*, 390–91.
———. 2006. "Corinth." In *CDCC*, 235–37.
Samarin, William J. 1969. "Glossolalia as Learned Behaviour." *Canadian Journal of Theology* 15:60–64.
Sampley, J. Paul. 2002. *The First Letter to the Corinthians*. In *The New Interpreter's Bible*, edited by Leander E. Keck, 10.771–1003. Nashville: Abingdon.
Sandelin, Karl-Gustav. 2003. "Drawing the Line: Paul on Idol Food and Idolatry in 1 Cor 8:1–11:1." In *Neotestamentica et Philonica: Studies in Honor of Peder Borgen*, edited by David E. Aune, Torrey Seland, and Jarl Henning Ulrichsen, 108–25. Leiden: Brill.
Sanders, Boykin. 1981. "Imitating Paul: 1 Cor. 4:16." *HTR* 74:353–63.
Sanders, Guy D. R. 2005. "Urban Corinth: An Introduction." In *URRC*, 11–24.
———. 2014. "Landlords and Tenants: Share Croppers and Subsistence Farming in Corinthian Historical Context." In *CTXT*, 103–25.
Sanders, Jack T. 1962. "The Transition from Opening Epistolary Thanksgiving to Body in the Letters of the Pauline Corpus." *JBL* 81:348–62.
Sandnes, Karl Olav. 2002. *Belly and the Body in the Pauline Epistles*. STNSMS 120. Cambridge: Cambridge University Press.
———. 2013. "A Missionary Strategy in 1 Corinthians 9:19–23?" In *Paul as Missionary: Identity, Activity, Theology and Practice*, edited by Trevor J. Burke and Brian S. Rosner, 128–41. LNTS 420 London: T. & T. Clark.
Savage, Timothy B. 2004. *Power through Weakness: Paul's Understanding of the Christian Ministry in 2 Corinthians*. SNTSMS 86. Cambridge: Cambridge University Press.
Saw, Insawn. 1995. *Paul's Rhetoric in I Corinthians 15: An Analysis Utilizing the Theories of Classical Rhetoric*. Lewiston, NY: Edwin Mellen.
Schmithals, Walter. 1971. *Gnosticism in Corinth: An Investigation of the Letters to the Corinthians*. Nashville: Abingdon.
Schnabel, Eckhard J. 2006. *Der erste Brief des Paulus an die Korinther*. HTA. Brockhaus/Giessen: Brunnen Verlag.
———. 2013. "A Jew to the Jews" (Review). *TrinJ* 34:109–11.
Schnelle, Udo. 1998. *The History and Theology of the New Testament Writings*. Translated by M. Eugene Boring. Minneapolis: Fortress.
Schottroff, Luise. 2012. "1 Corinthians: How Freedom Comes to Be." In *Feminist Biblical Interpretation: A Compendium of Critical Commentary on the Books of the Bible and Related Literature*, edited by Luise Schottroff and Marie-Theres Wacker, 718–42. Grand Rapids: Eerdmans.
Schrage, Wolfgang. 1974. "Leid, Kreuz und Eschaton. Die Peristasen Kataloge als Merkmale paulinischer Theologia Crucis und Eschatologie." *EvTh* 34:141–75.
———. 1991, 1994, 1999, 2001. *Der erste Brief an die Korinther*. EKKNT 7/1–4. Neukirchen-Vluyn: Benziger/Neukirchener Verlag.
Schubert, Paul. 1939. *Form and Function of the Pauline Thanksgivings*. BZNW 20. Berlin: Töpelmann Verlag.

Bibliography

Schüssler Fiorenza, Elizabeth. 1983. *In Memory of Her: A Feminist Theological Reconstruction of Christian Origins*. New York: Crossroad and London: SCM.

Schwiebert, Jonathan. 2008. "Table Fellowship and the Translation of 1 Corinthians 5:11." *JBL* 127:159–64.

Scott, James W. 2010. "The Time When Revelatory Gifts Cease (1 Cor 13:8–12)." *WTJ* 72:267–89.

Sechrest, Love L. 2009. *A Former Jew Paul and the Dialectics of Race*. LNTS 410. London: T. & T. Clark.

Selby, Gary S. 1997. "Paul, the Seer: The Rhetorical Persona in the 1 Corinthians 2.1–16." In *The Rhetorical Analysis of Scripture: Essays from the 1995 London Conference*, edited by Stanley E. Porter and Thomas H. Olbricht, 351–73 Sheffield: Sheffield Academic.

Sellin, Gerhard. 1986. *Der Streit um die Auferstehung der Toten: Eine religionsgeschichtliche und exegetische Untersuchung von 1 Korinther 15*. FRLANT. Göttingen: Vandenhoeck & Ruprecht.

Seneca. 1969. *Letters from a Stoic. Epistulae Morales ad Lucilium*. Translated by Robin Campbell. London: Penguin.

———. 2014. *Delphi Complete Works of Seneca the Younger (Illustrated)*. Delphi Ancient Classics 27. Translated by Richard Mott Gummere. Kindle Edition.

Shanor, Jay. 1988. "Paul as Master Builder: Construction Terms in 1 Corinthians." *NTS* 34:461–71.

Sharp, Daniel B. 2014. "Vicarious Baptism for the Dead: 1 Corinthians 15:29." *Studies in the Bible and Antiquity* 6:36–66.

Shaw, Ed. 2015. *The Plausibility Problem: The Church and Same Sex Attraction*. Leicester: IVP.

Shen, M. Li-Tak. 2010. *Canaan to Corinth: Paul's Doctrine of God and the Issue of Food Offered to Idols in 1 Corinthians 8:1—11:1*. Studies in Biblical Literature 83. New York: Peter Lang.

Sigountos, James G. 1994. "The Genre of 1 Corinthians 13." *NTS* 40:246–60.

Simon, Marcel. 1967. *Jewish Sects at the Time of Jesus*. Philadelphia: Fortress.

Skroggs, Robin. 1983. *The New Testament and Homosexuality*. Philadelphia: Fortress.

Smit, Joop F. M. 1991. "The Genre of 1 Cor 13 in the Light of Classical Rhetoric." *NovT* 33:193–216.

———. 1993. "Argument and Genre of 1 Corinthians 12–14." In *Rhetoric and the New Testament: Essays from the 1992 Heidelberg Conference*, edited by Stanley E. Porter and Thomas H. Olbricht, 211–30. JSNTSS 90. Sheffield: Sheffield Academic.

———. 1994. "Tongues and Prophecy: Deciphering 1 Cor 14,22." *Biblica* 75.2:175–90.

———. 2000a. *"About the Idol Offerings': Rhetoric, Social Context and Theology of Paul's Discourse in First Corinthians 8:1—11:1."* Leuven: Peeters.

———. 2000b. "'You Shall Not Muzzle a Threshing Ox': Paul's Use of the Law of Moses in 1 Cor 9,8–12." *Estudios Biblicos* 58:239–63.

———. 2002. "'What Is Apollos? What Is Paul?' In Search for the Coherence of First Corinthians 1:10—4:21." *NovT* 44:231–51.

Smit, Peter-Ben. 2013. "Ritual Failure, Ritual Negotiation, and Paul's Argument in 1 Corinthians 11:17–34." *Journal for the Study of Paul and His Letters* 3:165–93.

Smith, Barry D. 2010. "The Problem With the Observance of the Lord's Supper in the Corinthian Church." *BBR* 20.4:517–44.

Bibliography

Smith, David Raymond. 2008a. *"Hand This Man Over to Satan": Curse, Exclusion and Salvation in 1 Corinthians 5.* LNTS 386. London: T. & T. Clark.

Smith, Dennis E. 2003. *From Symposium to Eucharist: The Banquet in the Early Christian World.* Minneapolis: Fortress.

Smith, J. E. 2008b. "The Roots of a 'Libertine' Slogan in 1 Corinthians 6:18." *JTS* 59:63–95.

Snodgrass, Mary Ellen. 1988. *Roman Classics.* Lincoln: Cliff Notes.

Soards, Marion L. 1999. *1 Corinthians.* NIBC. Peabody, MA: Henrickson.

Sourvinou-Inwood, Christiane. 1996. "Sisyphus." In *OCD,* 1414.

South, James T. 1992. *Disciplinary Practices in Pauline Texts.* Lewiston: Edwin Mellen.

Spicq, C. 1963. *Agapē in the New Testament.* 3 vols. London: Herder.

Spittler, Russell P. 1988. "Glossolalia." In *Dictionary of Pentecostal and Charismatic Movements,* edited by Stanley M. Burgess and Gary B. McGee, 335–41. Grand Rapids: Zondervan.

Spurgeon, Andrew B. 2011. "Pauline Commands and Women in 1 Corinthians 14." *BSac* 168:317–33.

Stamps, Dennis L. 2002. "The Christological Premise in Pauline Theological Rhetoric: 1 Corinthians 1.4–2.5 as an Example." In *Rhetorical Criticism and the Bible,* edited by Stanley E. Porter and Dennis L. Stamps, 441–57. JSNTSS 195. Sheffield: Sheffield Academic.

Stanley, Christopher D. 1992. *Paul and the Language of Scripture: Citation Technique in the Pauline Epistles and Contemporary Literature.* SNTSMS 74. Cambridge: Cambridge University Press.

———. 2004. *Arguing with Scripture: The Rhetoric of Quotations in the Letters of Paul.* London: T. & T. Clark.

———. 2016. "Rhetoric of Quotation." In *Exploring Intertextuality: Diverse Strategies for New Testament Interpretation of Texts,* edited by B. J. Oropeza and Steve Moyise, 42–62. Eugene, OR: Cascade.

Starling, David. 2014. "'We Do Not Want You to Be Unaware': Disclosure, Concealment and Suffering in 2 Cor 1–7." *NTS* 60:266–79.

Stein, Hans Joachim. 2008. *Frühchristliche Mahlfeiern: Ihre Gestalt und Bedeutung nach der neutestamentlichen Briefliteratur und der Johannesoffenbarung.* WUNT 2/255. Tübingen: Mohr-Siebeck.

Steyn, Gert J. 1996. "Reflections on ΤΟ ΟΝΟΜΑ ΤΟΥ ΚΥΡΙΟΥ in 1 Corinthians." In *CorBETL,* 479–90.

Still, E. Coye. 2002. "The Meaning and Uses of Εἰδωλόθυτον in First Century Non-Pauline Literature and 1 Cor 8:1–11:1: Toward Resolution Of The Debate." *TrinJ* 23:225–34.

Stowers, Stanley K. 1990. "Paul on the Use and Abuse of Reason." In *Greeks, Romans, and Christians: Essays in Honor of Abraham J. Malherbe,* edited by D. L. Balch, Everett Ferguson, and Wayne A. Meeks, 253–86. Minneapolis: Fortress.

———. 2008. "What is 'Pauline Participation in Christ'?" In *Redefining First Century Jewish and Christian Identities: Essays in Honor of Ed Parish Sanders,* edited by Fabian E. Udoh, 352–71. Notre Dame: University of Notre Dame Press.

Strobel, August. 1989. *Der erste Brief an die Korinther.* Zürcher Bibelkommentare 6. Zürich: Theologischer.

Stroud, Ronald S. 2014. "Religion and Magic in Roman Corinth." In *CTST,* 187–202.

Bibliography

Strüder, Christof W. 2003. "Preferences Not Parties: The Background of 1 Cor 1,12." *ETL* 79:431–55.

———. 2005. *Paulus und die Gesinnung Christi: Identität und Entscheidungsfindung aus der Mitte von 1 Kor 1–4.* BETL 190. Leuven: Peeters/Leuven University Press.

Stuckenbruck, Loren T. 2001. "Why Should Women Cover Their Heads Because of Angels? (1 Corinthians 11:10)." *SCJ* 4:205–34.

Stumpff, Albrecht. 1964. "ζῆλος, ζηλόω, ζηλωτής, παραζηλόω." In *TDNT*, 2.877–88.

Sumney, Jerry L. 1999. *"Servants of Satan," "False Brothers" and Other Opponents of Paul.* JSNTSS 188. Sheffield: Sheffield Academic.

———. 2000. "The Place of 1 Corinthians 9:24–27 in Paul's Argument." *JBL* 119:329–33.

Sweeney, Marvin A. 2003. *Zephaniah: A Commentary.* Hermenia. Minneapolis: Fortress.

Talbert, Charles E. 1987. *Reading Corinthians.* New York: Crossroad.

Tariq, Tahmina. 2013. "Let Modesty Be Her Raiment: The Classical Context of Ancient-Christian Veiling." *Implicit Religion* 16:493–506.

Taussig, Hal. 2009. *In the Beginning was the Meal: Social Experimentation and Early Christian Identity.* Minneapolis: Fortress.

Theissen, Gerd. 1982. *The Social Setting of Pauline Christianity: Essays on Corinth.* Minneapolis: Fortress.

———. 1983. *Psychological Aspects of Pauline Theology.* Philadelphia: Fortress.

———. 2001. "The Social Structure of Pauline Communities: Some Critical Remarks on J. J. Meggitt, *Paul, Poverty and Survival.*" *JSNT* 84:65–84.

———. 2003. "Social Conflicts in the Corinthian Community: Further Remarks on J. J. Meggitt, *Paul, Poverty and Survival.*" *JSNT* 25:371–91.

Thiessen, Jacob. 2012. "Firstfruits and the Day of Christ's Resurrection: An Examination of the Relationship between the 'Third Day' in 1 Cor 15:4 and the 'Firstfruit' in 1 Cor 15:20." *Neot* 46:379–93.

Thiselton, Anthony C. 1978. "Realized Eschatology at Corinth." *NTS* 24: 510–26.

———. 1979. "The Interpretation of Tongues: A New Suggestion in the Light of Greek Usage in Philo and Josephus." *JTS* 30:15–36.

———. 2000. *The First Epistle to the Corinthians.* NIGTC. Grand Rapids: Eerdmans.

Thomas, Christine M. 2005. "Placing the Dead: Funerary Practice and Social Stratification in the Early Roman Period at Corinth and Ephesos." In *URRC*, 281–303.

Thompson, Cynthia L. June 1988. "Hairstyles, Headcoverings, and St. Paul: Portraits from Roman Corinth." *BA* 51.2:99–115.

Thucydides. 1881. *History of the Peloponnesian War.* Edited by Benjamin Jowett. Vol. 1. Medford, MA: Clarendon.

Thurén, Lauri. 2001. "By Means of Hyperbole (1 Cor 12:31b)." In *Paul and Pathos*, edited by Thomas H. Olbricht and Jerry L. Sumney, 97–113. SBLSS 16. Atlanta: SBL.

Tibbs, Clint. 2006. *Religious Experience of the Pneuma: Communication with the Spirit in 1 Cor 12 and 14.* WUNT 2/230. Tubingen: Mohr-Siebeck.

Tilling, Chris. 2012. *Paul's Divine Christology.* WUNT 323. Tübingen: Mohr-Siebeck.

Tolmie, D. Francois. 2011. "Angels as Arguments? The Rhetorical Function of References to Angles in the Main Letters of Paul. " *Hervormde Teologiese Studies* 67:1–8.

Trebilco, Paul. 2012. *Self-Designations and Group Identity in the New Testament*. Cambridge: Cambridge University Press.

Treggiari, Susan. 1991a. "Divorce Roman Style: How Easy and How Frequent Was it?" In *Marriage, Divorce, and Children in Ancient Rome*, edited by Beryl Rawon, 31–46. Oxford: Oxford University Press.

———. 1991b. *Roman Marriages: Iusti Coniuges From the Time of Cicero To the Time of Ulpian*. Oxford: Oxford University Press.

Tucker, J. Brian. 2011a. *Remain in Your Calling: Paul and the Continuation of Social Identities in 1 Corinthians*. Eugene, OR: Pickwick.

———. 2011b. *You Belong to Christ: Paul and the Formation of Social Identity in 1 Corinthians 1–4*. Eugene, OR: Pickwick.

Tuckett, Chistopher M. 1996. "The Corinthians Who Say 'There is no Resurrection of the Dead' (1 Cor 15.12)." In *CorBETL*, 247–75.

———. 2002. "Paul, Scripture, and Ethics." In *New Testament Writes and the Old Testament: An Introduction*, edited by John M. Court, 71–97. London: SPCK.

Turner, Max. 2006. "Early Christian Experience and Theology of 'Tongues': A New Testament Perspective." In *Speaking in Tongues: Multi-Disciplinary Perspectives*, edited by Mark J. Cartledge, 1–33. Milton Keynes, UK: Paternoster.

Tyler, Ronald L. 1998. "First Corinthians 4:6 and Hellenistic Pedagogy." *CBQ* 60:97–103.

Valentine, Katy E. 2013. "1 Corinthians 7 in Light of Ancient Rhetoric of Self-Control." *RevExp* 110:577–90.

Van der Horst, Pieter W. 1998. "Conflicting Images of Women in Ancient Judaism." In *Hellenism—Judaism—Christianity: Essays on Their Interaction*, 73–92. 2nd ed. CBET 8. Leuven: Peeters.

van Kooten, George H. 2008. *Paul's Anthropology in Context: The Image of God, Assimilation to God, and Tripartite Man in Ancient Judaism, Ancient Philosophy and Early Christianity*. WUNT 232. Tübingen: Mohr-Siebeck.

Van Voorst, Robert E. 2010. "Why Is There No Thanksgiving Period in Galatians? An Assessment of an Exegetical Commonplace." *JBL* 129.1:153–72.

Vander Broek, Lyle. 1994. "Discipline and Community: Another Look at 1 Corinthians 5." *Reformed Review* 48:5–13.

Verbruggen, Jan. 2006. "Of Muzzles and Oxen: Deuteronomy 25:4 and 1 Corinthians 9:9." *JETS* 49:699–711.

Versnel, H. S. 1970. *Triumphus: An Inquiry Into the Origin, Development and Meaning of the Roman Triumph*. Leiden: Brill.

Via, Dan O., and Robert A. J. Gagnon. 2003. *Homosexuality and the Bible: Two Views*. Minneapolis: Fortress.

Vollenweider, Samuel. 1989. *Freiheit als neue Schöpfung: Eine Untersuchung zur Eleutheria bei Paulus und in seiner Umwelt*. FRLANT 147. Göttingen: Vandenhoeck & Ruprecht.

Von Thaden, Robert H. 2012. *Sex, Christ, and Embodied Cognition: Paul's Wisdom for Corinth*. ESEC. Blandford Forum, UK: Deo.

Vos, Johan S. 1995. "Der μετασχηματίζμος in 1 Kor 4.6." *ZNW* 86:154–72.

———. 1996. "Die Argumentation des Paulus in 1 Kor 1,10—3,4." In *Corinthian Correspondence*, edited by Reimund Bieringer, 87–119. Louvain: Peeters/Leuven University Press.

Bibliography

Vriezen, T. C. 1962. "Essentials of the Theology of Isaiah." In *Israel's Prophetic Heritage: Essays in Honor of James Muilenburg*, edited by Bernard W. Anderson and Walter Harrelson, 128–35. New York: Harper.

Waaler, Erik. 2008. *The Shema and the First Commandment in 1 Corinthians: An Intertextual Approach to Paul's Re-reading of Deuteronomy*. WUNT 2/253. Tübingen: Mohr-Siebeck.

Walbank, Mary E. Hoskins. 1996. "Evident for the Imperial Cult in Julio Claudian Corinth." In *Subject and Ruler: The Cult of the Ruling Power in Classical Antiquity*, edited by Alastair Small, 201–14. JRASup 17. Ann Arbor: Journal of Roman Archaeology.

———. 2003. "Aspects of Corinthian Coinage in the Late 1st and Early 2nd Centuries A. C." In *Corinth, the Centenary: Results of Excavations Conducted by the American School of Classical Studies at Athens*, edited by Charles K. Williams and Nancy Bookidis, 337–49. Vol. 20. Princeton: American School of Classical Studies at Athens.

———. 2005. "Unquiet Graves: Burial Practices of the Roman Corinthians." In *URRC*, 249–80.

Wallace, Daniel B. 1996. *Greek Grammar Beyond Basics: An Exegetical Syntax of the New Testament*. Grand Rapids, Zondervan.

Walters, James C. 2005. "Civic Identity in Roman Corinth and Its Impact on Early Christians." In *URRC*, 397–417.

———. 2010. "Paul and the Politics of Meals in Roman Corinth." In *CTXT*, 243–64.

Wanamaker, Charles A. 2006. "A Socio-Rhetorical Analysis of 1 Cor 4:14—5:13." In *The New Testament Interpreted: Essays in Honour of Bernard C. Lategan*, edited by Cilliers Breytenbach, Johan C. Thom, and Jeremy Punt, 339–64. NovTSup 124. Leiden: Brill.

Ware, James. 2014a. "Paul's Understanding of the Resurrection in 1 Corinthians 15:36-54." *JBL* 133:809–35.

———. 2014b. "The Resurrection of Jesus in the Pre-Pauline Formula of 1 Cor 15.3–5." *NTS* 60: 475–98.

Waters, Guy. 2006. *The End of Deuteronomy in the Epistles of Paul*. WUNT 2/221. Tübingen: Mohr-Siebeck.

———. 2013. "Curse Redux? 1 Cor 5:13, Deuteronomy, and Identity Formation in Corinth." Paper presented at the SBL annual conference, Baltimore.

Watson, Duane F. 1989. "1 Corinthians 10:23—11:1 in the Light of Greco-Roman Rhetoric: The Role of Rhetorical Questions." *JBL* 108:301–18.

———. 2000a."Education: Jewish and Greco-Roman." In *DNTB*, 308–313.

———. 2004. *The Rhetoric of the New Testament: A Bibliographic Survey*. Blandford Forum, UK: Deo.

Watson, Francis. 2000b. *Agape, Eros, Gender: Towards a Pauline Sexual Ethic*. Cambridge: Cambridge University Press.

Watson, Nigel. 1992. *The First Epistle to the Corinthians*. Epworth Commentaries. London: Epworth.

Webb, William J. 2004. "Balancing Paul's Original-Creation and Pro-Creation Arguments: 1 Corinthians 11:11–12 in Light of Modern Embryology." *WTJ* 66:275–89.

Wedderburn, A. J. M. 1981. "The Problem of the Denial of the Resurrection in I Corinthians XV." *NovT* 23:229–41.

Bibliography

Wegener, Mark I. 2004. "The Rhetorical Strategy of 1 Corinthians 15." *CurTM* 31:438–55.
Weima, Jeffrey A. D. 1994. *Neglected Endings: The Significance of the Pauline Letter Closings*. Sheffield: JSOT.
Weiss, Johannes. 1910. *Der erste Korintherbrief*. Göttingen: Vandenhoeck & Ruprecht.
Welborn, L. L. 1987a. "A Conciliatory Principle in 1 Cor. 4:6." *NovT* 29:320–46.
———. 1987b. "On the Discord in Corinth: First Corinthians 1–4 and Ancient Politics." *JBL* 106:85–111.
———. 2005. *Paul the Fool of Christ: A Study of 1 Corinthians 1–4 in the Comic-Philosophic Tradition*. London: T. & T. Clark.
———. 2011. *An End to Enmity: Paul and the "Wrongdoer" of Second Corinthians*. BZNW 185. Göttingen: de Gruyter.
———. 2013. "The Corinthian Correspondence." In *All Things to All Cultures: Paul among Jews, Greeks, and Romans*, edited by Mark Harding and Alanna Nobbs, 205–42. Grand Rapids: Eerdmans.
Wendland, Heinz-Dietrich. 1946. *Die Briefe and die Korinther*. Göttingen: VandenHoeck & Ruprecht.
West, A. B. 1931. *Latin Inscriptions, 1896–1926*. Corinth 8/2. Cambridge, MA: ASCSA.
Whiston, W. 1987. *The Works of Josephus: Complete and Unabridged*. Peabody, MA: Hendrickson.
White, Joel R. 2012. "Recent Challenges to the *communis opinio* on 1 Corinthians 15.29." *CBR* 10:379–95.
———. 2015. "'He Was Raised On the Third Day According to the Scriptures' (1 Corinthians 15:4): A Typological Interpretation Based on the Cultic." *TynBul* 66:103–19.
Wickkiser, Bronwen L. 2010. "Asklepios in Greek and Roman Corinth." In *CTXT*, 37–66.
Wilckens, Ulrich. 1979. "Zu 1 Kor. 2, 1–16." In *Theologia Crucis—Signum Crucis: Festschrift Erich Dinkler*, 501–37. Tübingen: Mohr-Siebeck.
Wilk, Florian. 2005. "Isaiah in 1 and 2 Corinthians." In *Isaiah in the New Testament*, edited by Steve Moyise and Maarten J. J. Menken, 133–58. London: T. & T. Clark.
Williams, Charles K. 1986. "Corinth and the Cult of Aphrodite." In *Corinthiaca. Festschrift for D. A. Amyx*, edited by M. A. Del Chiaro, 12–24. Columbia: University of Missouri Press.
Williams, H. H. Drake. 2001. *The Wisdom of the Wise: The Presence and Function of Scripture within 1 Corinthians 1:18—3:23*. AGJU 49. Leiden: Brill.
Willis, Wendell L. 1985. *Idol Meat in Corinth: The Pauline Argument in 1 Corinthians 8 and 10*. SBLDS 68. Chico, CA: Scholars.
———. 2007. "1 Corinthians 8–10: A Retrospective after Twenty-Five Years." *ResQ* 49:103–12.
Wilson, Andrew. 2013. "Apostle Apollos?" *JETS* 56:325–35.
Winter, Bruce W. 2001. *After Paul Left Corinth: The Influence of Secular Ethics and Social Change*. Grand Rapids: Eerdmans.
———. 2002. *Philo and Paul among the Sophists*. 2nd ed. Grand Rapids: Eerdmans.
———. 2003. *Roman Wives, Roman Widows: The Appearance of New Women in the Pauline Communities*. Grand Rapids: Eerdmans.
———. 2015. *Divine Honours for the Caesars: The First Christians' Responses*. Grand Rapids: Eerdmans.

Bibliography

Wire, Antoinette C. 1990. *The Corinthian Women Prophets: A Reconstruction through Paul's Rhetoric*. Minneapolis: Fortress.
Wischmeyer, Oda. 1981. *Der höchste Weg. Das 13 Kapitel des 1 Kor*. Studien zum Neuen Testament 13. Gütersloh: Mohn.
Witherington, Ben, III. 1988. *Women in the Earliest Churches*, SNTSMS 59. Cambridge: Cambridge University Press.
———. 1995. *Conflict and Community in Corinth: A Socio-Rhetorical Commentary on 1 and 2 Corinthians*. Grand Rapids: Eerdmans.
———. 1998. *The Acts of the Apostles: A Socio-Rhetorical Commentary*. Carlisle: Paternoster.
———. 2006. *Letters and Homilies for Hellenized Christians*. Vol. 1. Nottingham: Apollos.
Wolff, Christiaan. 1996. *Der erste Brief des Paulus an die Korinther*. THKNT 7/2. Leipzig: Evangelische.
Works, Carla Swafford. 2014. *The Church in the Wilderness: Paul's Use of Exodus Traditions in 1 Corinthians*. WUNT 2/379. Tübingen: Mohr-Siebeck.
Worthington, Jonathan D. 2011. *Creation in Paul and Philo: The Beginning and Before*. WUNT 2/317. Tübingen: Mohr-Siebeck.
Woyke, Johannes. 2005. *Götter, Götzen, Götterbilder: Aspecte einer paulinischen "Theologie der Religionen."* BZNW 132. Berlin: de Gruyter.
Wright, Christopher J. H. 1992. "Jubilee, Year of." In *ABD*, 3.1025–30.
Wright, N. T. 1991. "One God, One Lord, One People: Incarnational Christology for a Church in a Pagan Environment." *Ex Auditu* 7:45–58.
———. 2003. *The Resurrection of the Son of God*. Christian Origins and the Question of God 3. Minneapolis: Fortress.
Wright, Wilmer Cave, trans. 1998. *Philostratus: Lives of the Sophists; Eunapius: Lives of Philosophers*. Reprint ed. LCL. Cambridge: Harvard University Press.
Yeo, Khiok-Khng. 1995. *Rhetorical Interaction in 1 Corinthians 8 and 10: A Formal Analysis with Preliminary Suggestions for a Chinese Cross-Cultural Hermeneutic*. Leiden: Brill.
Yinger, Kent L. 1999. *Paul, Judaism, and Judgment According to Deeds*. SNTSMS 105. Cambridge: Cambridge University Press.
Young, Norman H. 1987. "*Paidagogos*: The Social Setting of a Pauline Metaphor." *NovT* 29:150–76.
Zeilinger, Franz. 1997. *Krieg und Friede in Korinth: Kommentar zum 2. Korintherbrief des Apostels Paulus*. Vol. 1. Vienna: Bohlau.
Zeller, Dieter. 2010. *Der erste Brief an die Korinther*. Kritisich-exegetischer Kommentar über das Neue Testament. Göttingen: Vandenhoeck & Ruprecht.
Zerhusen, Robert. 1997. "The Problem of Tongues in 1 Corinthians 14: A Reexamination." *Biblical Theology Journal* 27:139–52.

Author Index

Adams, Edward, 3, 4, 19
Adams, Sean, 27, 59
Aernie, Jeffrey, 119, 181, 182, 184, 185
Aguilar, Chiu, Jose Enrique, 170
Ahn, Yognan Jeon, 164, 165
Allo, P., 67, 68, 86, 101, 104, 106, 112
Anderson, Gary, 214
Anderson, R. D., 172
Artz-Grabner, Peter, 13, 17, 18, 24, 46, 51, 56, 89, 102, 104, 105, 107, 112, 131, 149, 160, 174, 176, 188, 207, 224, 225, 231
Ascough, Richard, 153
Asher, Jeffrey, 212, 213
Aune, David E., 212
Aus, Roger David, 24

Bachmann, Philipp, 231
Bailey, Kenneth, 71, 72, 78, 82, 118, 190, 232
Balch, David, 103, 153
Bandstra, A. J., 128
Barclay, John, 8, 25, 27, 28, 29, 100, 202
Barker, K. L., 191
Barnes, Nathan, 123, 187
Baron, Lori, 126, 127, 128
Barram, Michael, 137
Barrett, C. K., 20, 22, 45, 115, 131, 135, 152, 189, 209, 227, 229, 230
Bartchy, S. Scott, 100
Barton, Stephen, 62, 87
Baum, Armin Daniel, 188
Beard, Mary, 24, 34, 149
BeDuhn, Jason David, 147
Belleville, Linda, xi, 144
Berger, Klaus, 39, 143
Betz, Hans, Dieter, 13
Bird, Michael, xi, 121
Bitner, Bradley, 5, 45, 54, 56

Black, Matthew, 232
Blattenberger, David, 143
Boer, Martinus de, 206, 208, 221
Bookidis, Nancy, 4, 108, 112
Borgen, Peder, 111, 133
Boswell, John, 79
Bowersock, G.W., 35
Bowie, E.L., 35
Bradley, Keith, 42
Brändl, Martin, 123
Braxton, Brad Ronnell, 97, 100, 237
Bray, Gerald, 39
Brenk, Frederick, 92
Broines, David, 120
Brodeur, Scott, 216
Broneer, Oscar, 125
Brookins, Timothy, 151
Brooten, Bernadette, 79, 80
Brown, Paul, xiii, xvi, 196, 200, 202, 203, 205, 206, 216
Bruce, F. F. 43, 190
Bryan, Christopher, 165
Bullinger, E.W. 46, 51, 53, 158
Burke, Trevor, 62
Butarbutar, Robinson, 119
Byron, John, 99, 100

Callow, Kathleen, 67
Calvin, John, xiv, 110
Cameron, Ron, 145, 209
Campbell, Constantine, 206
Campbell, R. A., 152
Capes, David, 41
Caragounis, Chrys, 90
Carter, Christopher, 75, 102, 123
Castelli, Elizabeth, 137
Charette, Blaine, 185
Chester, Stephen, 21, 183
Cheung, Alex, 107, 109, 138

Author Index

Chilton, Bruce, 233
Chow, John, 66
Ciampa, Roy, 13, 14, 26, 27, 44, 72, 74, 76, 85, 88, 89, 91, 94, 96, 99, 116, 117, 121, 124, 131, 134, 144, 146, 147, 156, 172–75, 178, 180, 185, 186, 188, 209, 212, 217, 239
Clarke, Andrew, 19, 66
Clivaz, Claire, 39
Collier, Gary, 129
Collins, Adela Yarbro, 66
Collins, John J., 215
Collins, Raymond F., 17, 35, 66.101, 115, 116, 119, 160, 165, 170, 178, 179, 194, 227, 228
Concannon, Cavan W., 60, 125
Conzelmann, Hans, 2, 63, 70, 100, 136, 161, 170, 180
Cook, John Granger, 27, 115, 116
Cope, Lamar, 138
Coppins, Wayne, 120, 198
Countryman, L. William, 79
Court, John M., 130
Coutsoumpos, Panayotis, 4, 108, 152
Cribiore, Raffaella, 56
Crocker, Cornelia, 9, 90
Crüsemann, Marlene, 193

Dahl, Nils, 51
Davidson, Richard, 128
Dawes, Gregory, 110
Dawson, Kathy Barrett, 66
De Vos, Craig Steven, 22, 40
Deissmann, Adolf, 4, 49, 67, 225
DeMaris, R. E., 209
Deming, William, 66, 89, 98, 103
Derrett, J. Duncan M., 68
deSilva, David, 159
DiMattei, Steven, 128
Dingeldein, Laura, 41
Dodson, Joseph, 27
Doering, Lutz, 13, 224
Downs, David, 225
Dunn, James D. G., 166, 168, 178, 184, 187
Dutch, Robert, 9, 25, 36, 42, 44, 57, 63, 124, 125

Ebojo, Egar Battad, 30
Edsall, Benjamin, 77, 143, 150
Edwards, Thomas, Charles, 38, 115, 210, 229
Ehrensperger, Kathy, 137
Ellington, Dustin W., 126
Ellingworth, Paul, 41, 119
Elliott, Neil, 27, 37, 63
Ellis, J. Edwards, 92
Endsjø, Dag Øistein, 203, 218
Engberg-Pedersen, Troels, 120, 121, 215, 216
Engels, Donald, 3, 7
Enns, Peter, 128
Eriksson, Anders, 113, 132, 161, 196, 197, 199, 201, 204, 224, 231

Fee, Gordon D., 4, 13, 18, 21, 31, 40, 41, 42, 63, 90, 94, 96, 97, 98, 99, 119, 131, 138, 141, 146, 147, 151, 161, 164, 165, 176, 180, 187, 218, 223, 229
Ferguson, Everett, 143
Feuillet, A., 146
Finney, Mark T., 55, 143, 144
Fiore, Benjamin, 54, 62
Fishbane, Michael, 175
Fisk, Bruce, 87, 138, 174
Fitzgerald, John T., 56, 57, 131
Fitzmyer, Joseph A., 1, 3, 7, 12, 20, 23, 27, 39, 40, 51, 69, 72, 77, 82, 93, 105, 109, 130, 135, 147, 154, 179, 191, 202, 207, 223, 227, 230, 232
Focant, Camille, 169
Forbes, Christopher, 159, 164, 168, 171, 179, 184, 187
Ford, J. Massyngberde, 82
Forkman, Göran, 67
Fotopoulos, John, 67, 82, 107, 108, 112, 113, 133, 135, 152, 231
Frayer-Griggs, Daniel, 46, 47, 48, 211
Frestadius, Simo, 40
Friesen, Steven J., 8, 52, 153
Furnish, Victor P., 52

Gäckle, Volker, 132
Gagnon, Robert A., 79, 80

Author Index

Galloway, Lincoln E., 120
Gardner, Paul Douglas, 108, 115, 134
Garland, David E., 17, 29, 43, 45, 71, 83,
    85, 89, 91, 95, 97, 100, 106, 110,
    111, 115, 119, 120, 123, 136,
    142, 146, 147, 152, 156, 159,
    160, 164, 165, 169, 177, 179,
    180, 183, 188, 191, 201, 206,
    210, 211, 227
Garnsey, Peter, 75
Gaventa, Beverly Roberts, 42
Gebhard, Elizabeth, 3, 5
Georgi, Dieter, 225
Gerhardsson, Birger, 198, 200
Giblin, C.H., 110
Gill, D.W., 96, 143, 178, 181, 214
Gillespie, Thomas W., 178, 181
Gillihan, Yonder Moynihan, 96
Gillman, John, 214
Glad, Clarence E., 120
Gladd, Benjamin, 217
Gladstone, Robert J., 184
Glancy, Jennifer, 100, 101
Godet, Frederic, 76, 163
Gooch, Paul W., 120
Gooch, Peter, 107, 112, 120
Goodacre, Mark, 150
Goodrich, John, 8, 52, 118, 119, 120
Gordon, J. Dorcas, 95
Goulder, Michael, 20
Gräbe, Petrus J., 32
Grant, Robert M., 91
Greenbury, James, 189
Griendheim, Sigurd, 36
Grudem, Wayne, 171
Gundry, Judith M., 70, 146
Gupta, Nijay K., 86

Hafemann, Scott, 59
Hägerland, Tobias, 72
Hamilton, Edith, 2, 5
Hanges, James C., 55, 56
Harper, Kyle, 101
Harrill, J. Albert, 99, 100
Harrison, James R., 3, 123, 125, 159
Harrisville, Roy, 64
Hays, Christine, 96

Hays, Richard B., 13, 21, 42, 44, 64, 70,
    73, 80, 116, 135, 137, 151, 169,
    172, 183, 184, 221, 229
Heil, John Paul, 74, 85, 116, 117, 148,
    184, 207, 221
Hengel, Martin, 1, 27, 19
Héring, Jean, 130
Herms, Ronald, 48
Hiigel, John L., 230
Hiu, Elim, 164, 178, 184, 187, 188, 191,
    192
Hock, Ronald F., 56, 116
Hodge, Caroline Johnson, 95
Hodgson, Robert, 60
Hofius, Otfried, 152, 155, 158, 198, 199
Hogeterp, Albert L., 46, 48
Hollander, Harm W., 174
Hooker, Morna D., 42, 123, 147, 211
Horrell, David, G., 3, 4, 8, 19, 75, 100,
    121, 133, 138, 153
Horsley, Richard A., 13, 36, 83, 151, 160,
    165, 175, 217
Hoskins, Paul M., 76
Hübner, Hans, 119
Hull, Michael F., 209
Hovenden, Gerald, 178
Hullinger, Jerry M., 124, 125
Hultgren, Stephen, 217
Hurd, John C., 19
Hurtado, Larry, 232
Hutson, C. R., 227
Huttunen, Niko, 100, 103
Hvalvik, Reidar, 13
Hwang, Jerry, 129

Inkelaar, Harm-Jan, 16, 28, 29, 41, 45,
    50
Instone-Brewer, David, 94, 117

Jacon, Christophe, 9
James, Sarah, xiv, 3
Janzen, Marshall, 188
Jeremias, Joachim, 154, 197
Johanson, B.C. 183, 184
Johnson, Alan F., 142
Johnson, Andrew, 215, 219

269

Author Index

Kammler, Hans-Christian, 22
Keener, Craig S., 1, 4, 7, 22, 37, 49, 94, 152, 157, 178, 189, 201, 211, 212, 222
Keith, Chris, 231
Kennedy, George, 9, 11, 16, 33, 34, 36
Kent, J. H., 3, 8
Ker, Donald P., 45
Kim, Chan-Hie, 227
Kim, Jung Hoon, 213
Kim, Yung Suk, 165
Kirchhoff, Renate, 82
Kirk, Alexander, 46
Klauck, Hans-Josef, 67, 153
Klein, George L., 88
Klein, William W., 171
Konradt, Mattias, 49, 53, 66, 68, 75, 112, 157, 231
Koperski, Veronica, 109
Kritzer, Ruth Elisabeth, *See,* Arzt-Grabner
Kroeger, Catherine, 145
Kuck, David, 48
Kümmel, Werner, 105, 198, 211
Kurek-Chomycz, Dominika, 230
Kyle, Donald, 60, 61

Laansma, Jon, 225
Lakey, Michael, 141
Lambrecht, Jan, 41, 42, 60
Lampe, Peter, 152, 158
Lanci, John, 2, 48
Lang, Friedrich, 44, 175
Last, Richard, 151
Lee, Michelle, 165, 167
Lee-Barnewall, Michelle, 142, 143
Legarreta-Castillo, Felipe de Jesus, 206
Lehmann, Karl, 199
Lestang, Francois, 37
Liefeld, W.L., 191
Lietzmann, Hans, 105, 198, 211
Lieu, Judith, 13
Lim, Kar, Yong, 29
Lindemann, Andreas, 32, 51, 120, 174
Litfin, Duane, 22, 30, 53
Litwa, M. David, 215
Liu, Yulin, 48, 49, 84, 165
Loader, William, 78, 80, 91, 94, 101, 105

Long, David, 73
Long, Fredrick J., 184, 190
Lopez, Rene, 78
Lorenzen, Stefanie, 218
Luzarraga, J., 127

Macdonald, Margaret, 95
MacGregor, Kirk, 198
Mackie, Scott D., 87
Maier, Harry, 25
Malcolm, Matthew R., 18, 25, 65, 104, 156, 175
Malherbe, Abraham, 84, 211
Malina, Bruce J., 43
Malone, Andrew S., 172
March, J. R., 5
Marchal, Joseph, 92
Marshall, I. Howard, 154, 157, 192, 193
Marshall, Peter, 54, 59, 122
Martin, Dale B., 8, 32, 39, 79, 84, 87, 92, 100, 144, 145, 164, 165, 167, 179, 216
Martin, Troy, 150
Massey, Preston T., 143, 145, 150, 188, 189
Mattingly, David J., 25
May, Alistair Scott, 70, 89, 103
Mayordomo-Marin, Moises, 228
McDonough, Sean M., 74
McGowan, Andrew, 152
McNamara, Derek, 66
McRae, Rachel M., 152
McRay, J. R., 7, 8
Meeks, Wayne A., 8, 129
Meggitt, Justin J., 8, 153
Meritt, Benjamin D., 4
Merklein, Helmut, 19, 69, 85, 100
Metzger, Bruce M., 31, 43, 133, 229
Metzner, Rainer, 123, 125
Meyer, Ben F., 155, 198
Meyer, H. A. W., 26, 40, 166, 202, 214
Mgaya, Gerson L., 160
Mihaila, Corin, 8, 22, 33, 44, 46, 54, 227
Miller, J. Edward, 145, 188, 209
Millis, Benjamin W., 3
Mitchell, Andrew C., 75

Author Index

Mitchell, Margaret M., 9, 16, 17, 19, 23, 57, 70, 75, 82, 88, 89, 114, 117, 120, 124, 151, 165, 170
Mody, Rohintan,Keki, 129, 133
Moffatt, James, 231
Montague, George, 48, 116, 172
Morgan, Teresa, 57
Moses, Robert, 68
Mount, Christopher, 141, 161
Mulroy, David, 6, 19,
Murphy-O'Conner, Jerome, 1, 2, 7, 83, 86, 96, 108, 153, 156
Myrick, Anthony, 63

Nagel, Peter, 182
Nanos, Mark, 120
Nash, Robert, Scott, 21, 196,
Nasrallah, Laura Sallah, 87
Neirynck, Frans, 61, 93
Newton, Derek, 108, 112, 113, 133, 138
Newton, Michael, 71
Neyrey, Jerome, 67
Nguyen, V, Henry T., 9, 60, 61
Niccum, Curt, 188
Nickle, Keith, 225
Nygren, Anders, 172

Oberholtzer, Thomas K., 47
Oropeza, B. J., 9, 12, 15, 20, 25, 33, 34, 45, 47, 59, 65, 67, 68, 69, 78, 92, 97, 98, 104, 106, 113, 120, 123, 126, 127, 128, 129, 131, 138, 154, 155, 157, 160, 174, 176, 187, 192, 193, 197, 202, 203, 207, 224, 225, 226
Orr, William, 190
Ossom-Batsa, George, 73
Oster, Richard,E., 143, 144, 188

Paige, Terence, 27, 59, 83, 160
Papathomas, Amphilochios, 123, 125, *see,also,* Arzt-Grabner
Parler, Branson, 149
Paschke, Boris, A., 66
Pascuzzi, Maria, 21, 68
Pate, C. Marvin, 213
Payne, Philip B., 187, 192
Peppard, Michael, 77

Peppiatt, Lucy, 148
Perkins, Pheme, 24, 31, 75, 105, 153, 156, 217
Perriman, A. C., 141, 142
Perrot, Charles, 130
Petersen, Anders Klostergaard, 42
Petrovich, Christopher, G., 143
Pfitzner, Victor, C., 123
Phua, Richard Liong-Seng, 107, 130, 134
Pickett, Raymond, 32
Planck, Max A., 59
Plummer, Alfred, 68, 84, 157, 209
Pogoloff, Stephen M., 20, 22, 26, 30, 35, 36, 37, 59
Poirier, John C., 170
Poplutz, Uta, 123, 124
Popovic, Anton, 124, 125
Portier-Young, Anathea, 171
Prothro, James, B., 20
Pucci, Michael S., 50

Rabens, Volker, 166, 215, 216
Ramasaran, Rolin A., 97
Ramelli, Ilaria, 157
Reasoner, Mark, 27, 63
Reaume, J. D., 210
Regele, Michael B., 79
Rengstorf, Karl Heinrich, 51
Richards, E. Randolph, 11, 18, 138
Richardson, Neil G., 209
Richardson, Peter, 120
Riddlebarger, Kim, 32, 179.
Robertson, Archibald, 68, 84, 157, 209
Robertson, C. K., 76, 77
Robertson, O. P., 191
Robinson, Betsy, A., 5, 6
Rosner, Brian S., 13, 14, 26–27, 44, 70, 72, 74, 76, 85, 88, 89, 91, 94, 96, 98, 99, 116, 117, 121, 124, 131, 134, 144, 146, 147, 156, 171–75, 178, 180, 186, 188, 209, 212, 217
Ross, J. M., 188
Rudolph, David, 121
Russell, D. A., 31

Salmon, J. B., 2
Samarin, William J., 177

Author Index

Sampley, J. Paul, 169, 231
Sandelin, Karl-Gustav, 113
Sanders, Guy D. R., 8, 144
Sanders, Jack T., 14
Sandnes, Karl Olav, 83, 120, 121
Saw, Insawn, 196
Schnabel, Eckhard J., 1, 2, 9, 17, 27, 32, 33, 44, 58, 85, 96, 108, 121, 129, 144, 157, 160, 166, 171, 174, 177, 180, 186, 198, 200, 201, 205, 216, 225, 230, 232
Schnelle, Udo, 1, 9
Schottroff, Luise, 18, 21, 27, 115, 146, 187
Schrage, Wolfgang, 12, 42, 45, 51, 63, 87, 96, 102, 128, 133, 147, 166, 171, 185, 187, 202
Schüssler Fiorenza, Elizabeth, 145
Schwiebert, Jonathan, 71
Sechrest, Love L., 121
Selby, Gary S., 31
Sellin, Gerhard, 202
Shanor, Jay, 45
Sharp, Daniel B., 209
Shaw, Ed, 81
Shen, M. Li-Tak, 109
Sigountos, James G., 170
Simon, Marcel, 189
Skroggs, Robin, 79
Smit, Joop F. M., 24, 45, 117, 138, 169, 183, 184
Smit, Peter-Ben, 156, 158
Smith, Barry D., 153, 154
Smith, David Raymond, 67
Smith, Dennis, E., 152, 154
Smith, J. E., 86
Soards, Marion L., 80, 189
Sourvinou-Inwood, Christiane, 4
Spicq, C., 172
Spurgeon, Andrew, B., 189
Stamps, Dennis, L., 14
Stanley, Christopher, D., 25, 50, 117, 181, 183, 221
Starling, David, 127, 159
Stein, Hans, Joachim, 156
Steyn, Gert, J., 17
Still, E. Coye, 108
Stowers, Stanley K., 84, 111

Strobel, August, 123
Stroud, Ronald S., 160, 231
Strüder, Christof W., 19, 42
Stuckenbruck, Loren T., 147
Stumpff, Albrecht, 43
Sumney, Jerry L., 19, 123
Sweeney, Marvin A., 191

Talbert, Charles E., 183
Taussig, Hal, 152
Theissen, Gerd, 8, 158, 165
Thiessen, Jacob, 200, 207
Thiselton, Anthony C., 8, 11, 12, 14, 18, 43, 49, 55, 59, 70–71, 76, 98, 100, 103, 110, 114, 116, 124, 136, 141, 144, 145, 146, 154, 160, 162, 163, 164, 165, 168, 169, 172, 177, 179, 186, 187, 189, 194, 197, 203, 204, 206, 210, 212, 214, 215, 227, 228, 230
Thomas, Christine M., 203
Thompson, Cynthia L., 143, 144
Thurén, Lauri, 169
Tibbs, Clint, 161, 162, 163, 179, 187
Tilling, Chris, 12, 109, 132, 231
Tolmie, D. Francois, 147
Trebilco, Paul, 17
Treggiari, Susan, 94, 104, 105
Tucker, J. Brian, 15, 98, 103, 115
Tuckett, Chistopher, M., 202
Turner, Max, 164, 171
Tyler, Ronald L., 55, 56

Vaage, Leif E., 95
Valentine, Katy E., 89
Van der Horst, Pieter W., 193
Van Kooten, George H., 146
Van Voorst, Robert, E., 13
Vander Broek, Lyle, 73
Verbruggen, Jan, 116
Versnel, H. S., 24, 59
Via, Dan O., 80
Vollenweider, Samuel, 120
Von Thaden, Robert, H., 90
Vos, Johan S., 22, 40
Vriezen, T. C., 182

Waaler, Erik, 109, 110

Author Index

Walbank, Mary E. Hoskins, 4, 203
Wallace, Daniel B., 40, 170, 173
Walters, James, C., 3, 4, 60, 158
Walther, J. A., 190
Wanamaker, Charles, A., 63
Ware, James, 199, 215, 216, 217, 220
Waters, Guy, 74, 134
Watson, Duane F., 62, 114, 136
Watson, Francis, 150
Watson, Nigel, 45
Wedderburn, A. J. M., 202
Wegener, Mark I., 196
Weima, Jeffrey A. D., 231
Weiss, Johannes, 11, 32, 57, 61, 113, 131, 206, 229
Welborn, L. L., 9, 18, 20, 27, 29, 36, 43, 54, 55, 56, 59, 75
Wendland, Heinz-Dietrich, 48
West, A. B., 4
White, Joel R., 200, 209
Wickkiser, Bronwen L., 167
Wilk, Florian, 25, 26, 181, 185, 219
Williams, Charles, K., 2
Williams, H. H. Drake, 26, 27, 33, 39, 44, 45, 47
Willis, Wendell L., 107, 128
Wilson, Andrew, 59

Winter, Bruce W., 9, 15, 18, 20, 29, 31, 32, 33, 35, 36, 43–44, 59, 62, 66, 75, 76, 77, 82, 83, 102, 104, 109, 133, 144, 145, 147–48, 151, 153, 158, 160, 211, 212
Winter, Franz, *See* Arzt-Grabner
Wire, Antoinette C., 146, 187–88, 193
Wischmeyer, Oda, 169, 173
Witherington, Ben, 3, 16, 62, 114, 149, 176, 189, 191, 192, 201, 229
Wolff, Christiaan, 163, 171, 209, 227
Works, Carla Swafford, 69, 134, 154
Worthington, Jonathan D., 214, 218
Woyke, Johannes, 132
Wright, Christopher, J. H., 220
Wright, N. T., 201, 205, 216, 219
Wright, Wilmer, C., 34, 58

Yeo, Khiok-Khng, 138
Yinger, Kent L., 47, 48, 49
Young, Norman, H., 63

Zeilinger, Franz, 229
Zeller, Dieter, 12, 57, 76, 102, 109, 110, 123, 160, 166, 171, 202, 233
Zerhusen, Robert, 179

Subject Index

a fortiori, *see qal waḥomer*
Adam, 24, 40, 90, 143, 146–48, 192–93, 196–97, 205–6, 208–9, 213–19, 222
afterlife, *see* death
allusion/echo, 25, 27, 29, 33–34, 44–45, 54, 90, 108, 119, 129, 133–34, 146, 155, 171, 175, 184, 191, 213–14, 217, 223, *see* quotation
allegiances, 9, 16–17, 19–20, 23, 43, 50–51, 70, 161, 227
analogy, 39, 118, 124n87, 132, 178, 213–14
anaphora, *see* rhetorical style
angel(s), 68, 75–76, 130, 133, 147f, 164, 170–71, 178–80, 214
antithesis, *see* rhetorical style
apocalyptic, 12n7, 23, 36, 38, 45, 47, 51, 53, 68, 76, 102–3, 123, 130, 142, 200, 205–6, 220–21, *see* eschatology
Apollos, 9, 19–20, 23–24, 33, 44–46, 51–55, 58, 59n181, 158n95, 224, 227–28
apostasy, 28n29, 47, 110, 112–13, 126, 129–31, 138, 154n74, 160
apostleship, 11, 20, 32, 115–17, 168–69
archaeology, inscriptions, *see* Corinth
arena, 59–60, 211
arrogance, 5, 11, 13, 20, 42, 50, 53–55, 58f, 63, 66, 69, 172, 194
associations, 4n19, 148, 152, 153n67
authority, *see* rights

baptism, 12, 21, 67, 78, 95, 127, 161, 165–66, 180, 209–10, 228, 229n36
 baptism for the dead, 209–10
 Spirit-Baptism, 165–66
Barnabas, 116–17, 201

benefaction, patronage, 14, 20n23, 60, 66, 100, 125, 127, 136, 159
benefit (divine, salvific), 14, 29–30, 39, 41, 51, 58, 100, 117, 119n60, 122, 126–27, 172, 184f
boasting, 3, 4, 9, 23, 28–30, 35, 42, 44–45, 48–51, 54, 57–59, 66, 69, 77, 118–20, 159, 163, 167, 169, 172, 202, 212
body (human), *see* flesh
body of Christ (church), 15–16, 67, 71, 72, 84, 100, 114, 132, 140, 156, 158–59, 161–62, 165–67, 170

celibacy, 81, 89–92, 94, 101, 105, *see* Virgin(ity)
chiasm, 23, 65, 82, 88, 97, 114, 118, 126, 140f, 147, 158f, 167, 174, 207
Chloe, 8, 16, 18, 65, 88, 229n30, 230n33
Christology, 12–14, 41–42, 108–9, 141–42, 160–61, 169, 207–8, *see* body of Christ, cross, Lord's supper, Maranatha, resurrection, Trinitarian
church, 12, *see* body of Christ
circumcision, un-, 20, 66n66, 97–98, 121, 166, 225
citation, *see* quotation
collection (the), 224–26, 229
command(ments), 78, 83, 86, 87, 89–91, 93, 98–99, 100, 119, 122, 132, 134, 154, 171n159, 176, 185f, 188, 194
conversion, 11, 14, 17, 21, 28, 30, 40, 70n31, 78, 79, 92, 97, 100, 105, 115, 127, 160–61, 166
Corinth (city), 1–8, 31–33, 52, 82, 108, 135, 144, 153, 179, 231
covert allusion, 45, 54n161

275

Subject Index

cross, crucifixion, 9, 11, 15f, 21–28, 30–32, 35, 37f, 40, 42, 45, 48, 50, 51, 56, 60–62, 68–69, 84, 100, 114, 121, 154–56, 169, 198, 200, 207, 210, 223
curse, accursed, 27, 61, 67, 130, *160*, 163, 190n263, 206, 208–9, 231–32
cynics, 51, 103

death, *see also* cross, resurrection
    afterlife, 4–6, 9, 14, 39n84, 51, 163, 203
    cremation, 203
    defeat of death, 143, 196–99, 205–23
    views of, 202–3
deliberative (rhetoric), 9, 16, 17n4, 51, 114, 136, 140, 170, 176, 196, 203n36
delivery (speech), 22, 33–35
demon(s)(-ic), 96, 107, 109, 133–35, 137, 164, 209
diatribe, 82, 84, 98, 114, 212
Dionysian, 145n26
discord/divisions, 9, 15–16, 18–22, 43–44, 47, 51, 53, 62, 75, 88, 108, 144, 151–52, 158, 165, 227
divorce, 89, 92–94, 106, 142
domestic, 65, 88, 94, 101, 153
drunkenness, 70–71, 78, 82, 87, 97, *154*, 178, *182*, 211–12

echo, *see* allusion
education, *see* pedagogy
elitism, 3, 9, 15, 25–26, 29, 34, 36–37, 40, 42, 44, 57–58, 60, 75, 83, 92, 144, 148, 152, 165, 167, 203
ellipsis, 53, 122, 184, 217
eloquence, 9, 19–20, 22–24, 26, 29–31, 34–35, 43, 77, 162, 170n156
encomium, *see* rhetoric
Epicurean, 27, 210
epideictic (rhetoric), 151, 169
eranos, 152
Erastus, 8, 52
eschatology, 29, 47–49, 59, 76, 143, 174, 184, 206–8, 217n101, 220, *see* apocalyptic

ethics, 12, 42, 87, 94, 98, 110, 127, 138, 140, 165, 178, 196–97, 209, 212
ethos, 93, 101n174, 114, 180, 194, 231
extra-natural, 39–40, 163–64, 178, 179n205, *see* miracle

factions, *see* discord, allegiances
faith, *15*, 21, 27, 29n34, 32, 46, 49, 56, 61, 62, 72, 73, 75, 78, 95, 99, 101, 111–13, 122, 125, 138, 148, 155, 160, *163*, *171*, 173, *175*, 185, 193, 204–7, 209n61, 218n105, 223, 228
faithful(ness)/unfaithful, 14–15, 38, 51, 52–53, 68, 81, 93, 100, 111, 131, 134, 143, 145, 147, 155, 166, *175*, 219, 223, 227, *see* obedience
family, 4, 6, 7, 17–18, 42, 53, 62, 73–76, 85, 88, 97–98, 109n9, 111, 127, 142, 145, 176, 226, 228, 230
flesh, 28, 42–42, 61, 67–68, 82, 85, 102, 117, 132, 175, 199, 214, 216n93, *219*
foolishness, 23–28, 40, 50, 59–60, 212, 222
forensic (rhetoric), 114, *196*, 200, 203n36, *see* judicial
fornication, 15, 64–67, 70, 74, 78, 80–92, 101, 129, 132, *see* immorality

gezerah shavah, 127n105, 208n55, 222
gender distinction/equality, 140–51, 166n134, 188, 190–91, 229
gentiles, 1, 8, 13, 23, 26–27, 38–39, 49, 66, 76, 80, 98, 117, 121–22, 133n136, 159, 161, 183–85, 211, 220–21, 225–26
gifts (spiritual), 9, 14–15, 40, 42, 44, 46, 55, 58, 92, 140, 158–80, 185–86, *190*, 194, 209
gladiator(s), 60, 125n97
glory, 29, *38*, 87, 125, 134, 137, 146–47, 149–50, 175, 201, 209, 213–15, 218, 223
glossolalia, *see* tongues (speaking in)
God, *see shema*, Trinitarian

Subject Index

grace, favor, *13–14*, 34, 45, 112, 126, 128, 130, *202*, 225, 232–33, *see* benefit
Greeks, *see* gentiles, Hellenism

hardships, 2, 11, 25, 47n126, 53, 60–62, 77, 122, 125, 131, 155, 157, 163, 167–68, 173, 177, 198, 202, *206*, 210–11, 228
head coverings, 140–51
Hellenism/Greeks, 1–8, 13, 18, 22, 27, 34, 37, 61, 66, 71, 122, 132n133, 137, 166, 174, 178n201
heroes (mythological), 4–6, 203
Holy Spirit, *see* baptism, gifts, tongues, wisdom
homoeroticism, *see* same-sex
honor/dishonor, 3, 5–6, 28–29, 31, 34, 43, 48, 53–54, *62*, 81, 86–88, 100–101, 104n187, 122, 125, 136–38, 140f, 143–47, 149–50, 152–53, 156, 159, *167*, 187, 191–92, 215, 223, 230, *see* shame
hook words, 50, 222, *see* gezerah shavah
household, 18, 21, 62, 65, 75, 88, 91, 94–86, 101, 105, 109n9, 145n24, 166, 228, *see* family, domestic
hyperbole, *see* rhetorical style

idol foods/idolatry, 9, 15, 70–72, 78, 93–97, 107–15, 121f, 124, 126, 129–39, 144, 159–60, 164, 211
imitation, 9, 17, 23, 51, 53, 56, 60, 62–63, 110, 114, 117, 121, 137–38, 176, 218
immorality, 2, 7, 15, 49, 53, 72, 102n179, 122, 211–12, *see* fornication, ethics
immortality, *see* death
incest, 6, 65–68, 70, 74, 79–80, 89
intertextuality, *see* allusion, parallels, quotation
irony, *see* rhetorical style

James (brother of the Lord), 116, 121, 198, 200–201
Jesus sayings/tradition, 20, 37, 41, 78, 93, 102, 108, 115, 119, 142, 152, 154–55, 176, 194, 197–98, 201, 219
Jew(ish), 4, 7–8, 14, 21, 23, 25, 27, 47n130, 90n121, 98, 101, 104, 107n3, 108, 112, *121*, 135n150, 137, 143n13, 161, 166, 170, 175, 184, 189n257, 200, 226n13, 230
  blessing 14n21, 233
  food laws, 112, 115n41, 121, 135n150
  sources, traditions, 13, 26, 28, 49, 61, 76, 78–79, 86, 92n132, 93n134, 94n138, 97, 123nn82–83, 128, 146n29, 174, 186, 188, 193, 199, 205
Jewish literary devices/features, *see* chiasm, gezerah shavah, midrash, qal wahomer
Judas (Iscariot), 154n74, 200
judicial (rhetoric), 203n36, *see* forensic
judgment (divine, church), 7, 14–15, 25–26, 29–30, 45, 47–53, 65–67, 72, 74–76, 112–13, 119, 124, 126–28, *130*, 134, 151, 156–57, 168, 182–83, 185, 194, 207, 212, *see* litigation, punishment
justification, 30, 78, *see* righteous(ness)

knowledge, *13*, 15, 33, 41–42, 48, 58, 107–8, 110, 112–13, 127, 131, 134, 162–63, 169–75, 178, 212, 219

Law (Mosiac), 66n3, 79, 98–99, 112, 115n41, 116, 117n51, 121–22, 135n150, 155, 181, 188, 190, 198, 222–23, 225
litigations, 65, 174–77
logos (rhetorical proof), 35, 82, 114, 203
love, 2, 6, 38–39, 43, 63, 73, 77, 81, 87, 91–92, 99, 104, 107–8, 110,112, 124, 135, 137–39, 140, 146, 160, 169–76, 194, 210, 225, 228–29, 231, 233
Lord's supper, 151–58
macellum, 8, 135

277

Subject Index

marriage, re-, unmarried, 6, 66, 78, 80–81, 85, 88–98, 101–6, 116n44, 144, see celibacy, divorce
maranatha, 231–32
metaphor, 25, 38, 42–46, 48, 52–54, 63, 69, 71, *84*, 87, 97, *100*, 105, 115, 123–26, 141–42, 165, 171, 201, 213, 220
midrash, 127, 222
mingling (with unbelievers), 70–74, 122
miracle(s, discourse), *32*, 63, 163, 185, see extra-natural
morals, see ethics, immorality, virtues
myth(ology), 1, 4–6, 18, 143, 147, 172, 203n34
mystery (-religions), 21, 31, 38, 145n26, 219

narratio, 16
new creation, 24, 39, 43, 51, 81, 90, 109–10, 121, 140, 143, 148, 190n263, 193, 206, 208, 213, 216–17, 219, 223
New Exodus, 38

obedience, 98, 125, 137, 231, see faithful(ness)
opponents (Paul's), 72, 98n157, 158n95, 212n79

parallels, 39, 61, 64, 67n12, 68, 86, 87, 93n134, 132, 154n77, 156, 166n134, 211n73, 221, 233
participation in Christ, see body of Christ
passover, 65, 68–69, 132 n,134, 154–55, 206
pathos, 16, 17, 42, 45, 53, 60, 65, 74–75, 114, 119, 126, 151, 152, 197, 202, 210f, 212, 224, 231
patron/client, see benefaction
Paul
  apostleship, 11, 19–20, 32, 115, 194
  calling/ministry, 11–12, 14, 114–23
  Damascus experience, 1, 113–14, 120, 201–2
pedagogy, 3, 36–37, 40, 56–57, 62, 97, 190, 192–93, 231

perseverance, 14, 47, *131*, 173, 219f, 223
peroratio, 224
Peter (Cephas), 19–20, 45n115, 50–51, 116–17, 121, 163, 185, 191, 196, *200*
poor, 7–8, 28, 57, 60, 76, 99, 116, 118, 122, 153–54, 156, 158, 172, 211, 225–26,
prayer, 14n21, 61, 67, 73, 91, 96, 111, 125, 140–41, 143–44, 147–48, 163, 169, 177, 179–80, 186, 190, 194, 211, 224, 232
prerepresentation, 128, 130, 193
priest(ly), 37, 45, 143, 148, 182
Prisca, 7, 8, 116, 193, 229, *230*
probatio, see proofs
proofs (rhetorical), 10, 16, 23n1, 32n54, 35f, 36n67, 39, 53, 65, 107, 114, 140, 196–97, 200n20, 202–3
prophecy, prophetic, 5–6. 12–14. 20, 23, 27, 29, 31n46, 32, 36, 61, 61, 67, 103, 115, *119*, 123n84, 127, 140–45, 152, 153, 159, 159–64, 166, 168–95, 197–98, 200, 205, 220–22, 225
prostitution, 2, 65, 78–79, 82, 84–87, 89, 93, 212
prothesis/propositio, 10, 16
punishment (divine), 4, 14, 47, 49, 66–68, 72, 126, 128, 134, 223, 231, see judgment

qal wahomer, 75, 117
questions (rhetorical), 6, 16, *21*, 23, 25–26, 39, 41–42, 44–45, 48 53, 57, 58, 59, 65. 70, 74–75, 77, 82, 84, 95, 98, 101–2, 132–36, 141, 151, 154, 158–60, *167*, 169, 176, 178, 180, 187, 194, 196, 202, 209–12, 216n93, 221–22
quotation (scripture), 25, 36, 38–39, 41, *50*, 55–58, 70, 74n46, 82, 85, 87, 114, 116–17, 123, 129, 176, 181, 184, 198n9, 201n22, 219–21

reconciliation, 56, 73, 93, 95, 110, 231
redemption, 30, 68–69, 84, 87–88, 100, 132, 154n24, 155, 221

278

Subject Index

resurrection, 9, 14, 25, 27, 30, 32, 38, 51, 84, 110, 125, 155, 165n128, 168, 196–223

rhetoric
- arrangement, *see* prothesis, narratio, etc.
- artificial/inartificial proof, 197, 200n20, 203
- encomium, 169–70, 173
- enthymeme, 204

rhetorical elements/misc., *see* deliberative, delivery, eloquence, epideictic, ethos, forensic, Jewish literary devices, judiciary, logos, pathos, proofs, sophists, *synkrisis*

rhetorical style/devices (literary)
- anabasis, 53
- anaphora, 16, 23, 30, 82, 102, 158, 170, 213
- antithesis, 23–24, 26, 30, 39–40, 53, 75, 103, 108, 160, 170, 213, 215, 217
- aphorisms, 53, 63
- asyndeton, 45, 53, 158, 170, 213
- epanalepsis, 53
- hyperbole, 53, 66, 119, 169n147, 170n156, 176, 180
- irony, 16, 20, 21, 23, 28, 35, 48, 53, 59–60, 62n202, 65–66, 75, 77, 116, 127, 134, 152–53, 212
- paronomasia, 151, 213
- polysyndeton, 53, 75, 102
- *reductio ad absurdum*, 70, 146
- sarcasm, 53, 77, 106, 152, 211
- sorites, 204, 205

rich/wealthy, 1, 7, 9n49, 13, 29, 31, 34, 36, 52, 58–60, 75, 89, 148, 153–54, 225, 228

righteous(ness), 29–30, 47, 61, 76–78, 83, 110, 156, 164, 213, 221

rights, 91, 112, 114–20, 123, 126, 133, 137, 139, 147

Romans/Roman Empire, 2–9, 15, 22, 24f, 28, 32, 34, 37, 52, 59–60, 66, 75, 90n121, 92, 93n134, 100, 104–5, 143–45, 148–49, 153, 158n94, 179, 202, 209, 211, 231

Caesar, 3–4, 7, 12, 24, 27, 37, 62, 66n4, 105, 109n9, 133n138, 143–44, 160–61, 207, 209, 230
ideology, 3, 37, 209, *see* elitism
imperial cult, 4, 109, 133n138, 135
Rome, 2–3, 7, 24–25, 100n170, 203, 207, 230

salvation, 12, 14–15, 24, 28n29, 31, 38, 42, 47, 52, 67–68, 110, 120, 122–25, 127, 130, 197, 205, 223, 228, *see* justification
same-sex, 78–81
Satan, 24, 37, 40, 67–68, 74, 87, 90–91, 96, 109, 133, 155, 193, *see* demons
sex, *see* fornication, gender, immorality, marriage, prostitution, same-sex
shame, 25, 27, 29, 35, 42, 53, 61, 65–66, 75, 77, 85, 134, 140–41, 144, 146, 152, 154, 156, 159, 191–92, 202, 212–13, *see* honor/dishonor
sin, 24, 30, 61, 68–69, 71–72, 81–82, 86–87, 100, 111–13, 125, 130, 155, 163, 198, 204–6, 209–10, 212–15, 219, 222–23, *see* vice
singing in the spirit, 180, 186
shema/one God, 94–95, 108–10, 136, 231
slave(ry), enslavement, 2, 8n43, 18, 27–28, 37, 44, 52, 60, 79, 84, 86–89, 91–92, 94, 97–101, 120, 122, 136, 153, 155, 160, 166, 205, 220, 222, 228, 229n31
slogan (corinthian), 19n21, 83, 89, 188n249
sophists, 7, 9n49, 13, 18, 22, 26, 29–31, 33–36, 43–44, 54, 59, 62, 118, 149, 179
solidarity, 5, 9–10, 16–17, 21, 23, 42, 50, 65, 75–77, 84–85, 107, 110, 113–14, 126, 132, 140, 150, 158, 165, 167–68, 170, 176, 195, 196, 206, 228

279

Subject Index

s/spirit
 human, 36, 66–68, 104, 164, 165, 177, 179–80, 187, 215
 Holy/God's, 10, 12, 20, 26, 32–33, 36–43, 48–49, 63–64, 67–68, 78, 80–86, 95–97, 106, 122, 127, 135, 158, 160–66, 168–69, 175n183, 177–78, 186–94, 207, 215–19, 226
 other, 95, 133, 160–64, 179, 229
 spirit of the world, 37–40
stoic(s),-ism, 27, 34, 50, 59, 83, 85–87, 103, 124, 131, 165
strong (members), the, 29, 107–114, 121, 124, 136, 130–38, 164, 212, *see* weak
suffering, *see* hardships
symposium, 82, 83, 129, 152, 176
synkrisis, 176

thanksgiving, 11, 13–14, 152, 182, 223
Timothy, 7, 63, 106n198, 121, 162, 192, 226–27, 229n33
tongues (speaking in), 14, 140, 159, 161, 164–66, 169–86, 189–90, *194*
transformation, 1, 14, 22, 23, 28, 32, 40, 63, 78, 80–81, 84, 90, 97, 114, 155, 160, 198, 202–3, 213–20, 223
triclinium, 153n67
Trinitarian, proto-, 161, 217
triumphal procession, 24–25, 38, 59, 160n103, *207*, 209, 223
tropaion, 24–25

unity, *see* solidarity

veil(ed), 140–51
virgin(ity), 88, 92, 101–5
vice(s), 15, 19n18, 43, 47, 54, 69–74, 77–79, 81–82, 84, 86–87, 113, 123, 126, 131–32, 154n71, *157*, 212, 228, *see* drunk, fornication, idol foods/idolatry, sin
hubris, 54, 59
list, 43, 70–71, 78, 82, 113, 126
virtue(s), 29, 35, 43, 52, 86, 92, 124, 169–75, 186–87

wealth, *see* rich
weak(ness), 11, 20, 23–24, 27–28, 30–33, 37, 42–43, 50, 60, 62, 96, 101, 107–114, 117, 121–22, 126, 130, 135–36, 138, 156, 158n94, 172, 198, 202, 211, 215, *see* idol foods, strong
widows/widowers, 6, 28, 88, 91–92, 101, 105–6
wilderness, 38, 124, 126–30, 133, 155
wisdom, xi, 9, 10, 22–43, 50–56, 59, 77, 83, 88, 101, 103, 107, 176, 181
 philosophical, 22, 27, 33, 34, 36, 62, 83
 speech(eloquence)/clever/human/ worldly, 22–37, 40, 42, 49, 50, 59, 60, 77, 82, 164, 170n156
 spiritual, 9, 16, 20, 23–24, 30, 135–43, 56
 spiritual gift/word of wisdom, 162–63, 164n120, 169, 171, 178n200
 traditions/discourse, 14n18, 23, 29, 32, 50, 51, 63, 76, 86, 88
women, 2, 18, 37, 66, 85–86, 89–93, 101n172, 105–6, 115, 123, 129, 140–50, 187–93, 300n20, 228n25, 230n39
 Eve, 85, 90, *146*, 148, 190n263, 192–93, 213–14
 prophesying, 140–41, 144–45, 147–48, 185–93
 speakers, 185–93
works/deeds (human/of the law), 7, 14, 46, 49, 79, 85, 87, 98, 223

280

Biblical and Ancient Literature Index

OLD TESTAMENT

Genesis

1	46
1–3	190, 214
1:11–12	213
1:20	215
1:24	215
1:26–27	146, 215, 217–18
1:31	148
2	146
2–3	192
2:7	40, 142, 146, 215–18
2:18	90
2:18–23	146
2:21–23	142
2:24	85
2:25	213
3	206
3:7–11	213
3:16	190
3:17–19	214, 219
3:21	214
4	43
5:1–3	146, 215, 218
17:3	185
17:9–14	98
26:8	129
32:4	147
35:2	220
37	43
39:7–13	86

Exodus

3–4	119
4:22	128
6:6–9	87
7–9	64, 154
12	68
12:12–23	130
12:14	155
12:16	12
13:9	155
13:21–22	127
14:21–24	127
16:1—17:7	127
17:2	129
17:5–6	128
17:7	129
18:12	132
20:3–5	134
24	129
24:8–11	155
25:3–7	46
12:3–20	69
21:10–11	91, 94
22:26	150
23:33	112
24:1–11	132
29:11–23	132
32	129
32:6	129
32:28	129
33:11	175
34:12	112
34:22	207
35:31–33	46

Leviticus

1–5	198
3:12—4:24	132
6:2–5	75
11:44–45	12

Biblical and Ancient Literature Index

Leviticus (continued)

12:3	98
14:16	128
14:29–33	128
16	198f
18:6–30	80
18:7–8	65
18:22	79
19:1–8	12
19:15–18	76
19:18	108
20:7–11	128
20:13	79
23:1–16	199
23:1–22	206
23:15	226
23:16–25	207
23:27–32	220
25:9–13	220

Numbers

5.11–31	145
5:22	233
11	129
11:4–9	129
11:16–30	127
11:34	129
12:1–15	191
12:6–8	175
12:8	146, 175
12:12	201f
16:1–50	130
16:11	130
16:22	185
16:41	130
18:8–19	118
20:1–13	127
20:15	127
21:4–9	129
21:16–18	127
25	85
25.1	82
25:1–18	129
25:2	129
25:9	129
25:10–17	134
26:62	129

28:26ff	207
28:22	69

Deuteronomy

1:11	128
1:16–17	76
4:37–38	28
5:7–9	134
6:4–5	108–09
6:4–6	231
6:16	129
7:6–7	28
7:9	14
10:17	109
12:5–18	132
13:1–5	70
13:6	74
13:16	231
13:18	231
14:23–26	132
16:1–8	69
16:3	155
16:9–10	207
16:18–20	76
17:2–7	70, 74f
17:6–7	67, 74
17:8–13	75
18:1–8	118–19
18:15–22	164
19:15	67
19:16–19	70, 74
20:17	231
21:21	74
21:22–23	27
22:12	150
22:13–21	101
22:18–22	70
22:21–24	74
22:30	65, 70, 74
23:1	65, 74
24:7	70
24:13–14	116
24:27	74
25:4	116
27–30	231
27:15	233

Biblical and Ancient Literature Index

27:19	76
27:20	65
28:30	90
32	129, 131
32:4	14, 131
32:10	175
32:12	108
32:17	133
32:19–21	134
32:21	108
32:30	134
32:31	108
32:36–39	134
32:39	108

Joshua

23:13	112

Judges

2:3	112
3:19	191
4–5	193
13–16	149
21:21	129

1 Samuel

2:10	29
10:5	178
18	43

2 Samuel

6:6–7	49
7:12	83
7:14	63
10:12	228
16:11	83

Ezra

9:1–2	93

Nehemiah

9:9–34	127

Job

1:21	213
5	50
5:11–15	50
9:32	134
10:11	214
29:21	191
34:11	49

Psalms

2	38
2:1–2	37
8:4	208
8:4–6	76
8:6–7	208
15	78
16	199
16:8–11	199
17[16]:15	146
24:1	134, 135
24:8	134
24:10	134
33[32]:10	25
44[43]:22	210
78[77]:49	130
78[77]:18–19	129
78:3–5	127
78:13–14	127
85[84]:12	59
94[93]:1–3	50, 57
94[93]:8–9	50
94[93]:11	50, 57
101:5	71
106[105]	129
106:28	134
106[105]:36	112
106[105]:28–31	129
106[105]:32–33	127
106:36–37	133

Biblical and Ancient Literature Index

Psalms (continued)

106[105]:48	233
110[109]	208
110[109]:1	208
110[109]:2–3	208
110[109]:5–6	208
118:22	45
132[131]:11	83
139:1–12	53
150:3–5	186

Proverbs

3:11–12	63
5:1–11	86
5:15–18	92
6:10	39
6:29	89
7:4–27	86
8:22–31	38
15:11	53
21:8	61
22:15	63
22:21	14
24:23	76
26:27	49

Ecclesiastes

5:15	213
6:10	134

Song of Solomon (Canticles)

2:16	91
6:3	91

Isaiah

1:3	182
3:3	45
5:8–22	119
5:13	182
5:14	221
6:1–10	115
6:5	119
6:8–10	182
11:1–2	162
11:10	162
13:6–9	14
13:16	90
19:3	25
19:11–14	25
19:12	25
19:16	31
22:13	211
24:20–21	221
24:23	219
25	219
25–27	220
25:8	220–21
25:9	221
25:10	223
26:3–4	221
26:19	199, 221
26:20—27:1	221
27:1	25
27:13	220
28	182–83
28:5	182
28:7–12	181–82
28:10	182
28:11–12	181–82, 185
28:12–13	182
28:16	27, 45, 182
29:1–12	25
29:9–14	39
29:10	166
29:14	25
29:16–23	29
29:18–19	25
30:1–7	25
30:3	29
30:5	29
30:9–11	39
31:1	25
32:6–20	38
33:17–22	39
33:18	25–26
40	38
40:3	38
40:5	38, 39, 175
40:6–8	38
40:9	197
40:10	48
40:12–15	41

40:13	41	8:9	29
40:18–21	108	9:12	29
41:4	108	9:22–24	28–30, 57
42:1	38	10:3–11	108
42:1–10	119	10:7	29
42:6	225	15:10	119
42:18–20	39	16:1–4	103
43:2–17	38	17:5	29
43:10	108	17:11	29
44:3	38	20:7–10	119
44:25	26	23:10	29
45:7	148	28:6[35:6]	233
45:9	134	31:31–33	155
45:14	184, 185	32:19	49
48:20–21	38	32:38–40	155
49:6	225		
52:7	197	*Ezekiel*	
52:10	39		
52:13—53:12	155, 198	7:12	103
52:15	39	16:38	134
53:5	155, 198	20:18	70
53:9–11	199	23:25	134
53:12	155	32:56	166
54:5	85	37:1–14	199, 217
54:13	40	37:6–8	214
58:4–7	38	45:21–25	69
59:4	38	45:22	69
59:15	38		
59:21	38	*Daniel*	
60:1–19	225		
61:1–2	197	1–2	162
61:1–3	198	2	130
61:1–4	38	2:47	184
63:7–14	127	2:22	53
64:3[4]	39	2:28	31
65:17	39, 223	7:9–15	53
65:23	223	7	130
66:15–19	47	7:9–14	207–08
66:18–19	38, 39	7:12–14	76
66:22	47	7:15	31
66:24	47	7:21	12
		7:22	76
Jeremiah		7:27	76
		8	130
1:4–10	115, 119	10:7–9	31
1:10	46	12:1–3	199
5:26–29	29	12:2	205
8:8–11	29	12:3	215

Biblical and Ancient Literature Index

Hosea

3:1–3	88
4:12	78
6:2	199
7:8	70
7:13	119
13	221
13:14	221f
14:4–7	222

Joel

2:1	14
2:16	12, 103
2:28–32	12, 166, 184, 190
2:31	14
3:1–5[LXX]	12, 166, 184, 190

Amos

3:7–8	119
5:8	148
5:18	14
6:1	119

Jonah

1:17[2:1]	199

Obadiah

15	14

Habakkuk

2:4	128
2:20	191

Zephaniah

1:7	191
1:18	47

Zechariah

2:13	191
4:6–10	33
8:23	184

Malachi

1:6	146
1:7	133
1:11	13
1:12	133
3:2–3	47
3:18–19	47

APOCRYPHA

Tobit

2:1	226
3:8	90
3:14–15	101
4:12–13	92, 93
5:19	61
6:16–22	91

Judith

7:4	128
8:14	39
9:11–14	28

Wisdom

2.1–9	211
3:1–8	76
4:2	123
4:16	76
9:1–18	48
9:6	37
9:17	37
10:10–12	123
14:11	112
14:22–31	78
18:20–25	130

Biblical and Ancient Literature Index

Sirach

1:1–10	38
1:10	39
3:8–11	62
4:15	76
4:28	123
14:17–18	219
17:25	112
19:1–4	87
21:18	14
23:8	78
26:10–12	101
27:25–27	49
30:1–2	63
34:16	112
41:17	82
41:17–22	86
42:9–14	104

Baruch

3:26–27	28

Bel and the Dragon

31	59

Pseudepigrapha

1 En.

6–7	147
15	76
14.14	31
22:13	199
41.8	76
50.1·5	48
62.8	12
62.15–16	213, 215
91.9–11	47
93	130
95.3	76
100.7	49
102.6·9	211
104.2–6	215

1 Maccabees

1:14–15	98

2 Maccabees

1:1	13
1:10–11	13
7:4–5	172
7:10–11	199
7:14	199
11:11	128
12:39–45	209

1 Esdras

4:33–41	169

3 Maccabees

5:26	158

4 Maccabees

5:2	112

2 Bar.

10.13–14	103
48.39	47
81.4	31

3 Bar.

8.5	19

4 Ezra

16.18	103
16.33–34	103
16.40–50	103

Biblical and Ancient Literature Index

Apoc. Elij.

2.31	103

Apoc. Mos.

20–21	213
39.2	213

Apoc. Zeph.

8.3–4	171

Jos. Asen.

10:12–13	112
21:13–14	112

Jub.

30.7–17	85
32.19	76
49:7–23	155

Let. Arist.

152	79

Pss. Sol.

11.1–9	220

Ps.-Philo

L.A.B.

10.7	128
26.13	39
64.7	48

Ps.-Phocylides

Sent.

3	79
8	62
192	79
219	170

Sib. Or.

2.95	112
2.279–81	101
2.327–29	103

T. Abr.

13.6	76
19.7	130

T. Benj.

4:1	137
10.6–9	199
10.10	76

T. Jac.

7.19–20	78

T. Job

37.6	39
48.3	180
48–50	164, 171

T. Jos.

3.8	82

T. Jud.

25.4	205

T. Lev.

9.9–10	92, 93
10.2	130

T. Mos.

8.3	98
8.8	91

T. Naph.

3.4–5	79

T. Reub.

3–6	78
4.6–11	86
5.5–6	147
6.1–4	91

T. Sol.

26	93

T. Zeb.

10.3	47

Vita Adam

12.1	213
13.2–3	213
14.2	213

New Testament

Matthew

1:18–19	105
3:12	47
5:18	233
5:20	78
5:31	93
5:40	77
6:25–28	103
7:12	99
7:14–21	164
7:21–23	78, 194
8:11–12	78
8:23–27	163
9:9–13	72
10:10	119
10:19–20	41
10:27	53
10:28	113
10:33	194
10:35–36	152
10:38–42	29, 210
11:1	119
11:19	72
12:38–40	199
12:42	76
12:46–50	116
13:22	103
13:41–42	78
13:54–55	116
16:4	199
16:16–18	45
16:17–18	20, 219
16:24	210
17:20	171
17:31	219
18:6–9	113
18:15–17	68–69
18:15–20	72
19:3–12	93
19:5	85
19:9	93
19:28	76
22:30	90, 214
22:33–37	99
23:11–12	142
24:7	103
24:10	112
24:31	220
24:36	219
24:36–51	219
24:38	105
25:11–12	194
25:14–15	120
25:34–46	78
25:40	113
25:45	113
26–27	37
26:15	154
26:17–28	69, 154
28:10	200

Biblical and Ancient Literature Index

Mark

2:3–5	157
2:6–8	163
2:15–17	72
3:14–15	163
4:17	112
4:19	103
4:33	177
4:35–41	163
5:35–43	164
6:3	116
6:35–44	163
8:11	26
8:34	210
8:35	113
8:38	29
9:33–35	168
9:34–35	142
9:42–49	113
9:48	47
10:2–12	93
10:28–30	172
10:42–45	142
12:25	214
11:20–24	163, 171
12:25	90, 105
12:28–34	99, 108
12:35–37	208
13:8	103
13:15	71
13:32–33	219
13:32–37	219
14:10	154
14–15	37
14:12–25	69, 154
15:29–32	26
16:7	200
16:17	170, 178

Luke

1:28	233
2:36–38	193
4:25	233
5:30–32	72
6:27–28	61
7:21–22	163
8:19–21	116
9:1	133
9:1–2	163
9:26	29
9:23	210
9:29	201
9:52	147
10:7–8	115, 119
10:25–28	99
11:14–21	133
12:11–12	41
12:32–33	172
15:1–2	72
16:18	93
17:2	112, 113
17:26–37	103
18:11	78
18:22	172
19:10	72
20:34–35	90
20:36	214
21:11	103
21:12–15	41
22–23	37
22:3–4	37, 154
22:17–23	69, 154
22:22	119
22:29–30	76
24:1	226
24:25–27	198
24:34	200
24:39	219
24:39–42	201
24:44	116
24:44–46	198

John

1:29	69
1:42	163
1:47–50	67, 163
1:51	233
2:12	116
3:3–5	78
4:17–18	90
5:21	217
6:27	184

Biblical and Ancient Literature Index

6:30	26	7:54—8:3	1
6:63	217	8:1	225
7:3–5	116	9:1–30	1, 115, 201
9:2	157	9:14	12
10:10	78	9:17	201
10:34	181	9:27	201
12:24	213	10:36–41	199
12:44	184	10:44—11:18	166
13:26–27	37	10:48	12
14:27	71	11:23–30	1
14:30	37	11:27–28	164, 168
16:1	112	11:28–30	225
18:5	154	12:1	225
18:13–14	37	12:2	145
18:39	150	12:5–16	163
20:17	120	12:17	191
20:2–10	200	13:1–3	168
21:1–19	200	13:1—15:25	1
		13:6–11	64
Acts		13:11	163
		13:14	121
1–2	20, 168	13:34–37	199
1:7	219	13:39	116
1:13–29	200	13:42–48	121
1:14	116	14:1	121
2	185, 226	15:1–20	66
2:1	207	15:9	58
2:1–13	170, 178	15:19–29	80
2:1–22	190	15:22–29	99
2:13	182	15:29	136
2:5–13	164, 185	16:1–3	121
2:14–36	185	16:8	230
2:17	193	16:16–18	133, 163
2:17–22	12, 141	17:18	59
2:21	160	17:31–32	27, 32, 199
2:24–32	199	17:34	59, 229
2:33	207	18:1–8	98
2:37–41	185	18:1–20	1, 7, 30, 32, 44, 62, 116, 230
2:38	12, 67, 160	18:2	8, 116, 230
2:42–46	152	18:3	61, 116
4:25–28	37, 38	18:4	4
4:27	37	18:5	227
4:32–37	225	18:6	8
5:1–11	163	18:7–8	7–8, 21
5:3–10	68	18:9–13	32
5:42	145	18:11	226
7:2	38	18:12–17	148

291

Biblical and Ancient Literature Index

Acts (continued)

18:17	11
18:18	230
18:24–26	230
18:24—19:1	19
18:26	116, 193, 230
18:27—19:1	9
19:1	44
19:11–12	133
19:12	31
19:21–41	211
19:22	52
19:35	25
20:5	230
20:7	226
20:7–11	152
20:15–38	230
21:8–9	193
21:40	191
21:10–12	164, 168
22:2–21	1, 11
22:6–11	201
22:16	12, 78, 160
22:25–29	211
23:18	188
24:7	225
26:4–23	1
26:11	160
26:12–18	201
26:14–15	113
26:16	201

Romans

1:7	13
1:18	173
1:25	233
1:26–27	79, 80
1:29	19
2:6	49, 223
2:16	47, 49, 53, 76, 222
2:24	77
3:5	211
3:19	81
3:20	98
3:24	30, 78
3:24–25	87, 155, 198
3:26	78
3:27	122
4:1	132
4:11	115
4:17	212, 217
4:22–24	117
4:25	198, 205
5:1–5	175
5:8	137
5:9	47, 87, 198
5:12	205
5:12–20	24, 206
5:18–21	110
6:1–2	148
6:3	127
6:4	210
6:6–7	100, 223
6:12–13	71
6:15–23	110
6:19	211
6:20	223
6:23	205
7:1—8:11	223
7:2	94
7:4	85
7:13	169
7:25	223
8:1–16	78
8:2	122, 223
8:4	97
8:9	40, 160, 165
8:9–11	217
8:10–11	207
8:11	86, 165, 215, 217
8:14	160
8:15	2
8:16	39
8:18	38
8:23	23, 25, 30, 86, 206, 215
8:23–25	176
8:24	164
8:26–27	164, 177, 178
8:27	53, 161
8:28–30	38
8:29	206, 218
8:35	60
8:36	210

Biblical and Ancient Literature Index

8:38	133, 163, 207	16:17	228
9:1–4	121	16:17–20	120
9:3–4	132	16:20	109, 207, 233
9:5	209, 233	16:21–23	8
9:32–33	45, 27, 29, 182	16:22	11
10:6	218	16:23	7, 8, 21, 52, 153
10:9–13	12, 78, 160, 205	16:27	209, 233
10:11	29		
11:1	121		
11:17–26	127	*1 Corinthians*	
11:22	131	1:1–3	8, 11–13
11:33–34	39	1:4–9	13–15
11:34	41	1:10	10, 16–18
11:36	209, 233	1:10–17	16–22
12:1	17, 172	1:10—4:21	16
12:4–8	162, 166	1:11	8, 10, 18–19
12:6	159	1:12	19–21
12:8	168, 172	1:13–17	8, 21–22
12:12	172	1:17—2:12	9
13:7–10	81, 99	1:18	23–25
13:9	55	1:18–31	23–30
13:13	19, 43	1:18—4:21	23
14:1	158	1:19–21	25–26
14:10	53, 101	1:22–25	26–282
14:12	49	1:26–31	8, 28–30
14:13	112	2:1–5	30–35
14:14	112, 124	2:6–8	35–39
14:15	113, 130	2:9–16	39–42
14:17	63	3:1–4	42–44
14:21	89, 101	3:5–9	44–45
15:1	107	3:10–15	45–48
15:1–6	158	3:16–17	48–49
15:3	117	3:18–23	49–51
15:7	158	4:1–5	8, 51–53
15:4	117, 138, 178	4:6	54–58
15:12	162	4:6–21	53–64
15:15	55	4:7–8	58–59
15:18–19	32, 133	4:9–10	59–60
15:20	21	4:11–13	60–61
15:25–27	27, 225–26	4:14–17	61–63
15:26	225, 229	4:16	9, 61–63
15:31	225	4:18–21	63–64
16:1	8, 193, 229	5:1–8	10, 65–70
16:3–5	116, 230	5:1—7:40	2, 65–106
16:7	116, 193	5:9–13	70–74
16:8	145	6:1–8	74–77
16:16	230	6:9–11	77–81
16:16–24	224		

Biblical and Ancient Literature Index

1 Corinthians (continued)

6:12–20	82–88
6:12–13	83–84
6:14–20	84–88
7:1–2	88–90
7:1–9	10, 88–92
7:1–40	88–106
7:3–9	90–92
7:10–16	93–96
7:17–24	97–101
7:25–40	101–6
8:1–2	9, 10, 107–8
8:1—11:1	107–39
8:3–6	4, 108–10
8:7	8, 110–12
8:8–13	9, 112–14
9–11	183
9:1–2	114–15
9:1–18	114–20
9:3–8	115–16
9:9–10	116–17
9:11–18	117–20
9:19–23	120–23
9:24–27	123–26
10:1–13	126–31
10:1–4	126–28
10:5–11	2, 128–30
10:12–13	130–31
10:14–22	132–34
10:14–18	132
10:19–22	133–34
10:23–29a	8, 134–36
10:23—11:1	9, 134–39
10:29b—11:1	9, 136–39
11:2—14:40	140–95
11:2–16	140–51
11:2	141
11:3	141–43
11:4–9	143–47
11:10	147–48
11:11–16	148–51
11:17–34	8, 151–58
11:17–22	151–54
11:23–26	154–56
11:27–34	156–58
12:1–31	158–69
12:1	10, 159
12:2–3	159–61
12:4–7	161–62
12:8–10	162–65
12:11	161–62
12:12–13	165–66
12:14–27	8, 166–68
12:28–31	168–69
13:1–13	169–76
13:1–3	169–72
13:4–7	172–73
13:8–13	173–76
14:1–40	176–95
14:1–5	176–78
14:6–19	178–81
14:20–25	181–85
14:26–40	9, 185–86
14:26–33	186–87
14:34–35	187–94
14:36–40	194–95
15:1–58	6, 196–223
15:1–11	197–202
15:3–4	197–200
15:5–11	200–202
15:12	9, 10, 202–4
15:12–19	202–6
15:12–28	202–9
15:20–28	206–9
15:29–34	209–12
15:32	1, 211
15:35–49	212–18
15:35–41	212–15
15:42–45	215–17
15:46–49	217–18
15:50–53	218–20
15:54–58	220–23
16:1–4	8, 10, 224–26
16:1–24	224–33
16:2b-11	226–27
16:12	10, 227–28
16:13–24	228–33
16:13–20	8, 228–31
16:21–23	231–33

2 Corinthians

1:1	11
1:3–7	168

1:8	169	7:4–16	226
1:8–11	211, 219	7:5–7	229
1:12—2:13	226	7:12	55
1:14	48, 53	8:1	225
1:16	226	8:1–5	8, 225, 226
1:22	86, 115, 161, 207, 216	8:4	225, 229
		8:6–7	224, 225
2:4	55	8:10	224, 225
2:9	55	8:13–15	225
2:12–13	229, 230	9:1	225, 229
2:14–16	24, 206	9:2	224, 225
2:15	47, 130	9:5	78
3	20, 80	9:6–7	225
3:2–3	115	9:12	225, 229
3:3	43	9:14	225
3:3–6	155	10:8	46
3:3–16	98	10:10	31, 33
3:6	217	10:13–16	115
3:17	217	11:2–3	85, 105
3:18	175, 215, 218	11:6	31, 33, 163
4:4	40, 68, 109, 218	11:7–11	120
4:6	175, 218	11:9	118
4:7–12	60, 215	11:10	119, 173
4:9	61	11:22–33	60, 172, 202
4:10	86, 210	11:23–25	61
4:11	68	11:23–27	125
4:14	175, 219	11:27	60, 116
5:1–8	207	11:29	112–13
5:5	207, 216	11:32–33	1
5:6–8	39, 68	12:1–9	201
5:7	175	12:2–3	39
5:10	7, 14, 47, 49, 52, 76, 207, 223	12:3–4	170
		12:7	133
5:17	24, 90, 109, 121, 193, 206	12:9–10	202, 215
		12:12	32, 133
5:18–19	110	12:13–16	118
5:19	30	12:14–15	233
5:19–20	123	12:19	46
5:21	30, 198	12:20	19, 43, 54
6:2	24	12:21	2, 89
6:4–5	61	13:1–2	64, 67
6:4–10	60	13:5	156
6:6–8	61	13:10	46
6:11–13	233.	13:11	228
6:14	106	13:11–13	224
6:16	113	13:13[14]	161
7:1	12, 104, 215		

Biblical and Ancient Literature Index

Galatians

1:1	11
1:3	13, 232
1:3–5	209
1:4	24, 68
1:5	233
1:6–9	164
1:10	120
1:11—2:15	1
1:11–12	115
1:12–16	201
1:13–14	121, 169
1:15	128
1:15—2:1	198
1:15—2:10	11
1:15–16	21, 119, 219
1:17–20	201
1:19	116
1:20	55
2:1–15	20
2–3	80
2:3–5	121
2:4	223
2:5	173
2:7–9	117
2:9	201
2:10	225
2:16	78, 98
2:20	166
2:21	197
3:1	31
3:4	197
3:5	32
3:6–9	127
3:9	184
3:10–25	98
3:13	27, 160
3:15	211
3:19–26	117, 223
3:24–25	62
3:27	166
3:27–29	21, 127, 166
3:28	91, 100, 101, 121, 145, 148, 166, 193
4	101
4:3	160
4:8–9	160
4:8–11	223
4:6	86, 232
4:7	101
4:8–9	109
4:11	47, 197
4:18	89
4:21—5:1	223
4:23	132
5:1–4	121, 131
5:6	98
5:13–16	122
5:14	55, 81, 99, 225
5:16–25	43, 97
5:18	160
5:19–21	43, 78, 131, 157
5:20	19
5:21	78
5:22–23	78, 92, 161, 175
6:2	99, 122
6:10	81
6:11	231
6:11–18	224
6:15	90, 98
6:16	121
6:18	233

Ephesians

1:7	87
1:14	207
1:17	38
1:19–20	207
1:20–22	208
1:22–23	209
2:1–3	159
2:1–5	201
2:2	68
2:11–12	159
2:13	87
2:19–22	46
4:11–13	36, 162
4:17–19	159
4:25	188
5:5	78
5:18–21	190
5:19	180
5:21–23	85

6:1-2	62	4:10	116
6:12	109, 207	4:13	230
		4:15	145
		4:15-16	230
Philippians		4:18	231
1:2	13		
1:7	120	*1 Thessalonians*	
1:20-24	68, 219		
2:5-11	121	1:3-8	175
2:9-11	209	1:5	32
2:16	47-48, 53	1:10	207, 218
2:16-17	172	2:1	47
3:4-6	1	2:5	120
3:4-9	121	2:9	116, 118
3:11-14	123	2:12	178
3:14	125	2:13	32
3:20	54	2:18	68
3:20-21	206, 218	2:19-20	48, 53
3:21	86, 215	3:5	47
4:5	232	3:13	14, 53
4:8-9	228	4:1-3	12, 97
4:10-19	120	4:6	101
4:12	60	4:9	89
4:20	232, 233	4:9-12	77
4:23	233	4:10	17
		4:13-15	105, 205
		4:13-17	207
Colossians		4:15-18	220
1:2	230	4:16	218
1:15-18	109, 209	5:1	89
1:16	207	5:1-8	207
1:20	87, 155	5:1-11	219
1:22	14	5:6-10	228
1:22-23	15	5:8	175
1:28	36	5:9	110
2:5	67	5:9-10	137
2:6	160	5:12	230
2:15	109	5:14	17, 178
2:20	109	5:14-15	172
3:5	78	5:16-22	228
3:11	121, 209	5:19-21	164
3:16	180	5:23	14, 30, 104, 215
3:17	166	5:23-28	224
3:25	49	5:26	230
4:7-18	224	5:28	233

Biblical and Ancient Literature Index

2 Thessalonians

1:6–10	207
1:8	47
2:3–4	109
2:8	109, 207
2:10	130
2:13	207
3:8	118
3:14–15	70, 72
3:16	233
3:16–18	224

1 Timothy

1:3–7	192
1:10	79
1:13	160
1:19–20	68
2:9–15	192–94
2:12	192
2:13–14	192
4:1	164
4:1–3	193
4:12	227
5:5–16	192
5:13–15	193
5:14	106
5:17–18	119
5:18	116
5:23	162
6:13	217

2 Timothy

1:7	227
2:1–3	227
4:6	172
4:19	230
4:20	52, 162
4:22	233

Titus

	13
1:11	192
2:1	36

Philemon

2	145
10	101
16	101
18–19	75
19	231
21	55

Hebrews

2:5–8	208
4:11	131
4:12–13	53
5:12–14	42
9:14	155
10:38	128
11	163
11:28	68
12:5	71
12:5–11	157
12:27–29	47
13:21	233
13:22	178

James

1:17	59
1:18	207
2:1–17	225
3:13–16	43
5:14–15	157, 163

1 Peter

1:18–19	69
2:4–8	46
2:13	155
3:1	95
3:18–22	199, 208
4:10–11	162
4:15	78
5:4	75
5:11	233
5:14	230

2 Peter

2:4	76
2:12	49
3:7	47

1 John

1:7	155
2:28	29
3:2	175
3:11–18	225
4:1	164
4:6	164

2 John

12	188

Jude

6	76
7	79

10	49
20	177
25	233

Revelation

1:5	155
1:6	233
1:10	226
2:14	136
2:20	193
2:21–23	157
2:26–27	76
6:8	103
14:4	102, 207
16:3	215
18:8	103
18:23	103
20:4	76
21:8	78, 228
22:4	175
22:15	78
22:20	232

DEAD SEA SCROLLS

1QpHab

5.4	76
7.4–8	31

1QM

3.5	12

1QS

4.9–14	78
6.10–13	191
6.24	72
7.25	72
8.5–8	46
8.16–18	72

1QSb

1.5	12

4QNah[4Q169]

3+4 i 4–9	27

4Q257

5.7–13	78

4Q266

11.14–15	72

11QTemple[11Q19]

64.6–13	27

CD

[A]4.15–20	91
[A]8.1–9	78

Rabbinic Writings

Gen. Rab.

20:12	214

Lev. Rab.

1:14	175

m. Abod. Zar.

2:3	135

m. Git.

9:3	94

m. Hul.

1:1	135

m. Ketubim

5:6	91

m. Pesaḥim

10:1–7	154
10:7	132

m. Qidd.

2:1–3.12	96

m. Sanh.

7:4B	67

m. Yebamot

14.1	93

t. Meg.

4:11	193

Tg. Ps.-Jonathan Hab.

	199

Greco-Roman Writings, Josephus, Philo

Aeschines

Fals. leg.

21–22	31
34–35	31

Aeschylus

Eumen.

647–48	

Alciphron

Ep.

3.24[iii.60]	7

Anaximenes

(see Rhet. Alex.)

Aphthonius

Prog.

8[38.25R-40.27R]	170

Apollodorus

Libr.

1.9.3	4
1.9.27	6

Apollonius

Argonautica 6

Appian

Bell. civ.
5.122.504   220

Bell. Mith.
17.116–17   59

Bell. Pun.
9.66   59

Hist.
8.136   7

Apuleius

Metam.
4.13   60
28   145

Aristides (Aelius)

Or.
1.330   27
24.42   170
33.19   35
51.29–34   31

Aristophanes

Ach.
1085–94   152

Frag.
354   2

Thesm.
837–38   152

Aristotle

Ath. Pol.
53.2   200

Gen. an.
747a.5–20   149

Hist. Anim.
584b.22   216

N.E.
6.7.2   27
8.11   100
8.12.2   62
8.12.15   62

Oec.
3.A-C[1–135]   188

Pol.
1.1–7   100
7.14.12   89

Rhet.
1.1.11   32
1.1.14   30
1.1.14—2.2   32
1.5.4   29
1.5.5   9
1.6.14   32
1.9.36–41   176
1.10.3–6   78
1.15   197
1.15.1–33   36
1.2.2–8   36, 204
2.2.5–6   59

Rhet. (continued)

3.1[1403b]	33
3.13.1–2	16, 23
3.14.1	11
3.19[1419b]	224

ATHENAEUS

Deipn.

8.365AB	152
10.430C	211
13.573C-574	82

AULUS GELLIUS

Noct. att.

4.4	102

CICERO

De or.

1.xxvi.120	31
1.xxvii.123	31
2.lii.209	43

Fam.

9.25.3	76

Fin.

3.22.75	51

Inv.

1.1	22
1.19.27–30	16
1.52.98	224

Leg.

2.57	203

Leg. man.

5	3

Off.

1.32.114	156
1.[45.]160	62
3.6.26	114
3.6.28	77

Part. or.

23.23.79	22

Rab. perd.

5.16	27

Verr.

5.169–70	27

CASSIUS DIO

Hist. rom.

21[9.31]	2
60.6.6	7
67.8.2	60

CRATES

Ep.

7	78
15	86

DEMETRIUS

Eloc.

227	67

Demosthenes

Ep.

1.10	17

Or.

19.314	54
59.97	54
59.122	92

Dio Chrysostom

Or.

3.10	83
3.104–7	165
6.21	54
7.133–34	82
8.9	7, 35, 43, 76
8.11–19	125
11.22	164
14.13–17	83
30.19	54
32.10	35
32.29	176
33.16	167
34.48	75
37.36	1
39.3	176
40.29	104
40.34	117
47.1	22
47.22	31
58.5	54
62.3	83
64.3	146

Diodorus Siculus

Bib. hist.

4.71.1–4	203
5.21.5	46
20.63.1	122
20.65.1	46
32.27.1	3
34/35.5.5	30

Diogenes (Ps.-)

Ep.

47	103

Diogenes Laertius

Vit. [phil.]

3.92	62
7.121	83
7.122	59
6.2.54	103
6.37	51

Dionysius Halicarnassus

Ant. rom.

3.71.5	143, 150
12.16.3–4	143

Epictetus

Diatr

1.16.9–14	149
2.1.23	83
2.8.11–14	85–86
2.10.25	86
2.16.10	54
2.16.26–37	42
2.17.19–22	6
3.1	35
3.1.1–45	149
3.10.18	86
3.13.4–5	203
3.15.2–12	124
3.22.23	147
3.22.49	59
3.22.69–72	103
3.22.82	51
3.22.95	51

Biblical and Ancient Literature Index

Ench.

15	98

Eunapius

Vit.

466	30
470	30
475	30

Euripides

Bell.

	5

Med.

	6

Suppl.

40–41	188

Galen

De Usu Partium

1.445.14–17	142

Herodotus

Hist.

2.57	179
3.62.3–5	208
3.80	59
4.77.1	27

Hesiod

Theog.

188–206	2

Hippocrates

Generation

1–2	149

Nat. puer.

9	149

Homer

Il.

2.729–33	203
6.151–54	4
6.152–202	5
15.559–65	228
21.468–70	211

Od.

1.226–27	152
6.182–84	88
11	203

Horace

Ep.

1,1.41	86

Isocrates

Antidosis

199–200	36
253–57	34

Dem.

4.11	62, 75

Ep.

1.5	17

Or.

4.11	75
4.171	75
5.13.114	17

Soph.

13.3–5	35
13.17–18	62
14	35

Josephus

Ant.

1.63–64	89
2.311–13	69
4.49	51
4.126–58	85
4.219	200
5.7	82
7.321	151
7.351	158
8.108–114	48
12.241	98
15.259	93
20.100	147

Ag. Ap.

2.25.199	79, 91
2.25.273	79

Bell.

1.4.6[97]	27
6.2.4	49
6.46–47	203
6.418	60
7.5.4–6	24
7.23–24	60
7.37–40	60
7.131	59

Justinian

Digest

28.1.8.4	211

Livy

Hist. rom.

2.32.12–33	165
34.1.5	188
45.38–40	24

Longinus

Subl.

44.1	30

Lucian

Dial.d

20	19

Fug.

27	146

Hermot.

16	59

Lex.

6–13	152

Marcus Aurelius

Med.

2.1	165
6.32	86
7.13	165

Maximus of Tyre

Diss.

20.2	170

Biblical and Ancient Literature Index

MENANDER

Thais

187[218]	212

MUSONIUS RUFUS

Lect.

4	228
8	59
10	77
12	87, 91, 101
13A	91

OVID

Fasti

3.544–49	92
3.740–42	171

Her.

21.195–96	104

Met.

10.1—11.84	208

Tristia

5.10.37	179

P. AMH.

2.21	57

P. HARR.

1.59	57

P. MICH.

8.473.29	13

P. MUR.

19	93, 94

P. OXY.

3.469	57
42.3004	57

PAUSANIUS

Descr.

1.14.7	2
2.1.1	4
2.1.2	2
2.1.3	5
2.1–5	108
2.2.1	110, 231
2.3.6–11	6
2.5.1	4
2.16.5–6	203
2.27.4	203
7.7.1–16	2

PHILO

Abr.

135–37	79
216	117
245–46	91

Congr.

18–19	42

Contempl.

3.32–33	189

Det.

32–49	36
33–35	34, 59
34	44, 118
38	212
65–68	36
132–33	36

Gig.

18.6	151

Her.

246	18

Jos.

4.20	77
34[210]	152
254	57

Leg. (All.)

2.34	68
3.78	159
8.839E–840C	124
8.840A	89

Legat.

53	62
69.225	54
86.154	54
281	4

Migr. Abr.

116	63

Mos.

1.178	71
1.302	129
2.162	129

Mut.

10	18

Post.

80	59
119	75
150	35

Prob.

26	123

QG

3.20–21	91

Sacr.

32	78

Somn.

1.147	120
1.232–33	120
2.2.9	124

Spec.(Leg.)

2.29	44
2.50	79
2.231–32	63
3.12.72	102
3.37–38	149
3.37–42	79
3.51–56	145
4.34	75

Virt.

76	214
182	78

PHILOSTRATUS

Gymn.

52	124

Vit. soph.

1.489	34, 149
1.490	62
1.491	34
1.498	30
1.[17.]504	222
1.519–20	34, 171

Vit. soph. (continued)

1.537	34
2.564	34
2.570	34
2.571–72	31
2.576	35
2.579–80	35
2.586–88	35, 62
2.609	58
2.611	4
2.615	118

Pindar

Ol.

13.63–92	5

Pyth.

3.1–60	208

Plato

Crat.

403B	208
403E	36

Leg.

777a	222

Crat(ylus).

403B	208

Pliny the Elder

Nat.

7.45	28
7.53[52]	203
7.55[54]	203
7.55.190	208

Pliny the Younger

Ep.

1.10	34
1.20	162
2.6	154
5.5	222
7.17	31
10.96	160

Euth(yd).

287D	188

Gorg. 22, 33

509C	77
523A–524A	214

Leg.

[6.]777A	222
8.839E–840C	124
8.840A	89

Phaedr.

245C–249D	203
269E	36

Prot(ag).

313C–D	35
326D	56
335A	35

Rep.

[3.]404D	2
5.473C–D	59
[7.]516A	150
10.613D	48

Symp.

197C-E	170

Biblical and Ancient Literature Index

PLUTARCH

Aem.

32.3–34.4	24, 59

Amat.

21[767F]	2

Cic.

887b	54

Conj. praec.

9–10[139C]	91
16[140B]	92
142C-E	188

De esu

2.2[997B-C]	82

De Iside et Osiride

353b	250n47

De Laude

12[543E-F]	22

Fragmata

85	104

Frat. amor.

2.1[478D-479B]	17
485A	31–32
485D	31–32

Garr.

503E-504A	188

Is. Os.

76[383A-B]	174

Lib. ed.

120	212

Mor. (see also respective titles)

1.2B-C	44
943C-D	48

Phil.

21	7

Praec. ger. rei publ.

13.1[806F-807A]	122

Quaest. rom.

267C	143

Rect. rat. aud.

39C	191
42F-43C	192
48A-B	192

Reg. imp. apophth.

178D	104

Rom.

27.3–28	203

Solon

20.3	91

Stoic abs.

1058B-C	59, 83

Biblical and Ancient Literature Index

Suave viv.

1098C	211

Tu san.

4[123E–F]	82

Polybius

Hist.

5.104.1	18
23.11.2–3	170

Ps.-Plato

Alcibiades

2.145E	54

Ps.-Plutarch

Vit.

845d	33–34

Quintilian

Inst.

1.1.27	56
2.1.1–2	36
2.4.8–9	44
2.4.22	78
2.8.1–8	36
2.15.3–4	32
4.2.1–3	16
4.2.31	16
5.1	197
5.10.7	32
6.1.2	224
11.3.4–103	34
12.2.6	22
12.5.1–5	34

Rhet. Alex.

1433a.25–29	192

Rhet. Her

1.2.3	33
1.3.4	23
2.30.47	224
3.4.8	23
3.19–27	34

Seneca

Ben.

1.10.2–5	78
2.18.1	58
3.37.1–3	62
4.6.3	58
6.3.1–4	58
7.2.5	24

Clem.

1.3.5	142

Ep. (Lucil.)

11	31–32
19.10	71
30.10–11	222
40.1–4	67
47.1	100
47.10–13	100
47.17	100
48.4	135
49.9–11	222
56.1–4	179
66.42–43	222
77.11–19	222
78.16	124
80.3	124
83.9–27	154
90.9–10	46
93.12	222
94.51	56
95.52	165

Tranq.

3.1	124

Biblical and Ancient Literature Index

4.3–4	98

Vit. Beat.

19.3	27

SEXTUS EMPIRICUS

Prof.

1.261–62	203

SOPHOCLES

Elect.

137–39	208

Oed. Rex	6, 66

STASINUS

Cypria	19

STRABO

Geogr.

4.5.9	211
8.6.19	1
8.6.20a	1
8.6.20c	2
8.6.23d	1
23a	2

SUETONIUS

Calig.

24.1	66
53.2	43

Claud.

18.2	102
21	60

25.4	7
39.2	66

Julius

1.1	105

SVF

1.53.1–2 [216]	131

TACITUS

Ann.

12.43.1	102
15.37	80

Germ.

19	146

THEMISTIUS

Or.

23.288–89	35

THEON

Prog.

2[66]	86
2.70–71	62
3[5]97	110
10[9]112–15	176

THUCYDIDES

Hist.

1.13.2–5	1
1.132.1–3	54
2.11.9	228
2.52.3—2.53.4	211
3.38.2–7	34

Biblical and Ancient Literature Index

Virgil

Aen.

3.403–9	143
4.96–102	92
4.642–705	92
6	203

Eclog.

10.86	173

Georg.

4.453–525	208

Vitruvius Pollio

Architecture

10.1.1	216

Xenophon

Mem.

1.2.3	62
1.2.25	54
2.3.18	165

Early Christian Writings

1 Clement

3.1—6.4	43
24.5	213
34.8	39
35.5	19

Didache

6.3	136
10.6	232
14.1	226

Epiphanius

Pan. 28.6	210

Eusebius

H. E.

5.24.16	69

Gregory the Great

Dial.

4.39	48

Ignatius

Smyr.

1.1–2	199

Thrall.

9	199

Irenaeus

Her.

3.4	71

Jerome

Vir. Inl.

2	201

John Chrysostom

Hom. 1 Cor.

29:5	163

Justin Martyr

Apol.

1.21.1	199
1.65.2	230

Origen

Philocalia

9.2	181

Protoevangelium of James

9.1–2	116

Tertullian

Ad Mart.

3	60

Marc.

5.10	210

Virg.

1.12	145

www.ingramcontent.com/pod-product-compliance
Lightning Source LLC
Chambersburg PA
CBHW030433300426
44112CB00009B/980